# Empires of the Mind

'The empires of the future woul[...] ...es of the mind' declared Churchill in 1943, envisaging universal empires living in peaceful harmony. Robert Gildea exposes instead the brutal realities of decolonisation and neo-colonialism which have shaped the postwar world. Even after the rush of French and British decolonisation in the 1960s the strings of economic and military power too often remained in the hands of the former colonial powers. The more empire appears to have declined and fallen, the more a fantasy of empire has been conjured up as a model for projecting power onto the world stage and legitimised colonialist intervention in Afghanistan, Iraq and Syria. This aggression, along with the imposition of colonial hierarchies in metropolitan society, has excluded, alienated and even radicalised immigrant populations. Meanwhile nostalgia for empire has bedevilled relations with Europe and played a large part in explaining Brexit.

**Robert Gildea** is Professor of Modern History at the University of Oxford. He has written extensively on French and European history in the nineteenth and twentieth centuries. Among the many awards his publications have garnered, *Fighters in the Shadows: A New History of the French Resistance* was longlisted for the Samuel Johnson prize and *Marianne in Chains: In Search of the German Occupation* won the Wolfson History Prize.

# Empires of the Mind

The Colonial Past and the Politics of the Present

Robert Gildea
*University of Oxford*

CAMBRIDGE
UNIVERSITY PRESS

# CAMBRIDGE
## UNIVERSITY PRESS

University Printing House, Cambridge CB2 8BS, United Kingdom

One Liberty Plaza, 20th Floor, New York, NY 10006, USA

477 Williamstown Road, Port Melbourne, VIC 3207, Australia

314–321, 3rd Floor, Plot 3, Splendor Forum, Jasola District Centre, New Delhi – 110025, India

79 Anson Road, #06–04/06, Singapore 079906

Cambridge University Press is part of the University of Cambridge.

It furthers the University's mission by disseminating knowledge in the pursuit of education, learning, and research at the highest international levels of excellence.

www.cambridge.org
Information on this title: www.cambridge.org/9781107159587
DOI: 10.1017/9781316671702

First published 2019
Paperback edition first published 2021
Reprinted 2021

Printed in the United Kingdom by TJ Books Limited, Padstow Cornwall

A catalogue record for this publication is available from the British Library.

Library of Congress Cataloging-in-Publication Data
NAMES: Gildea, Robert, author.
TITLE: Empires of the mind : the colonial past and the politics of the present / Robert Gildea, University of Oxford.
DESCRIPTION: Cambridge, United Kingdom ; New York, NY, USA : Cambridge University Press, [2019] | Includes bibliographical references and index.
IDENTIFIERS: LCCN 201804277 | ISBN 9781107159587 –
SUBJECTS: LCSH: Imperialism – History. | Imperialism – Social aspects. | Postcolonialism – History. | Postcolonialism – Social aspects. | International organization. | World politics 21st century.
CLASSIFICATION: LCC JC359 .G465 2019 | DDC 325/.32–dc23
LC record available at https://lccn.loc.gov/2018042770

ISBN 978-1-107-15958-7 Hardback
ISBN 978-1-316-61233-0 Paperback

# CONTENTS

# FIGURES

# INTRODUCTION

In February 2016, during the run-up to the British referendum on Europe, former Mayor of London Boris Johnson boasted, 'We used to run the biggest empire the world has ever seen', 'Are we really unable to do trade deals?'[1] A year later, in February 2017, French presidential candidate Emmanuel Macron visited Algiers and declared his country's colonialism 'a crime against humanity, a real barbarity. It is a past that we must confront squarely and apologise to those we have harmed.'[2]

These two comments encapsulate a tension at the heart of thinking about empire. On the one hand it stands for prosperity and greatness on a vast geographical scale. It invites comparison with other empires, above all the Roman Empire. And it suggests that even if the British Empire is a thing of the past, its heirs claim entitlement still to act as a major force in international affairs. On the other, particularly when empire is called 'colonialism', a quite different narrative is conjured up. It is pilloried as a 'crime against humanity', a project that accumulated wealth and power by war, plunder, expropriation, torture and massacre. Empire was thus both a fantasy of glory and a chronicle of anguish. Taken together, however, the two comments suggest that the terms 'empire' and 'colonialism' have multiple resonances today. They refer to things that happened in the past but they also express ways in which the contemporary world has been constructed in terms of power, violence, money, inequality and exclusion.

Speaking before 6,000 uniformed Harvard graduates on 6 September 1943, on the occasion of his being awarded an honorary degree in laws, Winston Churchill spoke of a world council that would bring together both the nations which were emerging victorious from the Second World War and those which had been subjected to oppression. 'The empires of the future', he declared, 'would be the empires of the mind'.[3] What he meant by this was that future empires would not be armed titans at war with each other, but rather universal empires living in peace and harmony. The concept of 'empires of the mind' is nevertheless a fluid one and has been taken as the title of this book in order to explore how empire has been imagined, mythologised and contested.

Empire was never a single thing. It was protean, taking many forms. It was improvised before it was ever thought of as a whole. It drove forward but was resisted and driven back. When it failed in one form or in one domain it did not withdraw but was reinvented, reconstructed in a different way. Such was the anguish of loss and the drive for power and prosperity that the lessons of defeat were rarely learned. Instead, there was a tendency to repeat what had gone before, in terms of practices or institutions, and thus to run the risk that defeat would follow once again.

Though empires were protean, they generally took one of three forms: empires of trade, colonies of settlement and territorial empires. Myths of empire held that intrepid sailors and bold investors forged new trade routes, that pioneering colonists cleared virgin territories and made them fertile, and that enlightened administrators followed them to ensure the benign rule of the mother country. The purpose of these myths was to make colonisation palatable to peoples at home concerned about the costs and risks of war, but they concealed the realities of empire. The most profitable trade in the eighteenth century was the slave trade, providing slave labour for the plantations of the Caribbean and American colonies. Trade was generally imposed on reluctant non-European empires or their vassals by force, sending in the gunboats where necessary and imposing 'unequal treaties' which enshrined the privileges of the Europeans. Colonial settlement did not take place in virgin lands but entailed the displacement, often the massacre of indigenous populations, and subjection of the rest to segregation and exceptional laws. Imperial rule over large territories was authoritarian. While the colonies of white settlement – from Canada to South Africa and Australia, and the French and European settlers of Algeria – acquired substantial powers of self-government, and imperial rule was always happy to work with local princes and tribal rulers, the vast majority of indigenous peoples were systematically excluded from the prospect of exercising power and, if they laid claim to it, were brutally suppressed.

The phase of empire that lasted until the end of the nineteenth century has often been called 'informal empire' or 'free trade imperialism' based on 'gentlemanly capitalism'. The 'race for empire' between the great powers in the later nineteenth century obliged them to strengthen their grip on their possessions as they moved from 'informal empire', based on alliances with local rulers, to the 'formal empire' of direct rule. Imperial rivalry was also a major factor in the outbreak of war in 1914, when European empires of Britain, France, Belgium, Germany, Italy and Russia were arguably at their height. Imperial powers claimed to be fighting for freedom and civilisation and colonised peoples, who were drafted by the hundreds of thousands into their armies, soon claimed the same from their colonial masters. They also appealed to new forms of legitimacy endorsed by the United States and the League of Nations that all nations were equal and had claims to self-government. After 1918 territories taken from the former Ottoman Empire in the Middle East or from the German Empire in Africa were divided up between the victorious powers as mandates, theoretically on a path to self-government. Few lessons, however, were learned by the imperial powers. Concessions made to colonial peoples were minimal and often withdrawn, and when those peoples resisted, in the mandates of Syria and Iraq just as much as in the colonies, they were forcibly put down.

In the Second World War Germany tried to rebuild its lost colonial empire on the Continent, while imperial Japan all but destroyed the British and French Empires in the East. The United Nations set up in 1945 endorsed a programme of decolonisation by which self-government was finally accorded to the colonies. Financially crippled by the cost of war, and facing resistance and revolt in their colonies, Britain and France were obliged to let some of their possessions go. The trauma of losing some colonies, however, only increased the desire to hold on to those that remained, if necessary by the maximum use of force and fraud. The French fought a brutal war between 1956 and 1962 to hold on to French Algeria, while the British perpetrated atrocities in a bid to retain Kenya.

Even after the rush of decolonisation in the 1960s the strings of economic and military power often remained in the hands of the former empires. This became known as neo-colonialism. It was practised by the

French south of the Sahara in what became known as *Françafrique* and by the British in Southern Africa. The 1982 Falklands War and French military intervention in New Caledonia in 1988 were perfect examples of neo-colonialism. South Africa left the Commonwealth in 1960 but British financial investments remained secure, defended by the apartheid regime. This opened the way to a form of empire which might be called global financial imperialism. Military power was hidden while the world's richest countries used the financial levers of the World Bank and International Monetary Fund to require indebted countries to concede what was effectively indirect rule and to open themselves up to exploitation by multinational companies.

After Iran became an Islamic republic in 1979 and the Soviet Union invaded Afghanistan in 1980 imperialism reinvented itself once again. Initially the West supported Afghan *mujahideen* fighting the Soviets, but this only served to attract, train and spread networks of Islamic fighters opposed to Western imperialism. In the face of new global threats from Islamic powers and Islamism, a new edition of neo-imperialism, led this time by the United States, justified colonialist intervention in Afghanistan, Iraq and Syria, which had formerly been parts of the British or French empires, and where the British and French had brutally intervened in the 1920s. The consequence, however, was the 'blowback' of Islamist jihad, forming an Islamic state on the rubble of Iraq and Syria and inspiring Islamist attacks on the continent of Europe.

Empires existed not only 'out there', in the Americas or Caribbean, Africa, Asia or the Antipodes, but also 'back here', in the metropolis. After the Second World War large numbers of Britons went to live in the former colonies of settlement, while subjects of the British or French Empires, many of whom had fought in the imperial armies during the war, were invited to live and work in Britain or France, in order to rebuild economies shattered by that war. Those who arrived on the *Empire Windrush* from the former slave colonies of the Caribbean, from an India violently partitioned or from French colonies where they were denied citizenship and subject to an arbitrary penal code came with dreams of a better life. Jamaican singer Louise Bennett described this wittily as a process of 'colonisation in reverse', by which the former colonisers were themselves colonised.

For most British or French people of the metropolis, however, this 'colonisation in reverse' was no joke. The loss of empire 'out there' seemed to coincide with the arrival of former colonial peoples, threatening their jobs, their communities, their 'way of life'. The response in the metropolis was to reimpose colonial hierarchies, colonial segregation and colonial laws of exception. Black and Arab populations were confined to ghettos in inner-cities of suburbs, denied access to education and jobs, and subjected to the arbitrary powers of the police. Parties such as the National Front in France and the UK Independence Party set the political agenda by arguing that the country was being overrun by immigrants who could not be assimilated. The perceived threat of immigration from the colonies stimulated redefinitions of British or French national identity which explicitly or implicitly excluded immigrant populations. The possibility that Britain or France might become multicultural nations in which all ethnic communities were respected was flirted with, then rejected. Histories were written which posited the continuous existence of homogeneous white nations who dominated colonial peoples. 'British values' were asserted which immigrant populations were deemed not to understand or to share. In France citizenship was open to individuals who accepted the values of the Republic, above all its *laïcité* or secularism. Muslim veils were banned from public spaces such as schools and town halls. Attempts by minorities to hold on to their religious or ethnic identities were rejected as a 'communitarianism' which undermined the universal Republic which all citizens were required to embrace.

Ambitions and fantasies about empire in the global and metropolitan spheres had an important impact on a third sphere too: Europe. After two world wars, which have sometimes been seen as European civil wars, moves were made to construct a European Common Market and a European Union. Not all European countries were equally enamoured of the idea. The driving forces of the European project were West Germany and France, which were variously recovering from defeat, foreign occupation and division. Britain, which had not been defeated, occupied or divided, took a very different view of Europe. It imagined that it had 'stood alone' against Hitler after the fall of France in 1940, relying on the solidarity of its Empire and Commonwealth before being rescued by the United States (little or nothing was said about Soviet Russia). It was reluctant to join a Europe that endangered both its ties with the Commonwealth and its 'special relationship' with the United States. Britain was therefore absent from the first phase of European construction. In the 1960s, when it changed its mind, it was told twice by France that it could not join because it was too caught up with its Commonwealth and the United States. France, by contrast, saw the European project as a way of building Europe as an acceptable version of the Napoleonic Empire, the core of which had been the Low Countries, western Germany and northern Italy. It kept Britain out as it had under Napoleon's Continental System, while having no compunction about holding onto its own *Françafrique*.

When Britain finally did join the European Community in 1973, the success felt like a defeat. It had swapped a world empire for membership of a European empire that was controlled by France and then, after reunification in 1990, by Germany. One felt like a bad rerun of the Napoleonic Wars, the other like a repeat of the Second World War that this time ended in defeat. France too was concerned about the hegemony of Germany but decided that the best way to manage her was to tie her in to an ever more federal Europe. Used to telling colonial subordinates what to do, and sending in the gunboats if they did not comply, Britain had little experience of negotiating with equals. Neither did she like the idea of an ever more federal Europe and set her sights on retaining or recovering as much sovereignty as possible. In the new century, as wars in Iraq, Libya and Syria drove new waves of refugees towards Europe, the European Union's single market and doctrine of the free movement of people stirred up in Britain a toxic brew of hostility to European federalism and panic about new waves of foreign immigration.

Increasingly, it became clear that British and French imperial power was more illusion than reality. These old countries no longer wielded serious influence over the rest of the globe. For a long time the United States had been the hegemonic power, Russia returned to the international fray after imploding in the 1990s and formerly colonised or semi-colonised powers such as India or China now became global players. Besides, neither Britain nor France had the means to sustain adequate armed forces. This did not prevent them from reinventing empire one more time. Indeed, the more empire appeared to have declined and fallen, and the more national identity was threatened, the more a fantasy of empire was conjured up as the answer to all ills. It provided the model for projecting power onto the world stage and for imposing control on immigrant populations, whether they were seeking entry into the metropolis or were already there. In Britain's case it offered an alternative to European partnership, now dubbed vassalage, in a global dimension which was variously called 'global

Britain', 'Empire 2.0' or 'the Anglosphere', a version of the Commonwealth that included the Dominions and the United States but silently excluded the Caribbean 'Windrush generation' and African members of the Commonwealth. France, meanwhile, while denouncing colonialism as a 'crime against humanity', retained Françafrique and mobilised French-speaking countries of Francophonie as a response to the Commonwealth.

Intractable questions of empire were for a long time squeezed out of public consciousness. This was partly because of the anguish of the loss of empire for the imperialists and the pain it involved for the colonised. Myths were spun about the orderly 'transfer of power' from the imperial capital to national elites. Documents relating to the brutality of decolonisation were hidden or destroyed. Whereas empire at its height had been celebrated by pageantry and stories of the civilising mission, neo-colonialist operations against freedom fighters were often carried on under the radar, and murder covered up. During the Falklands War reporting restrictions were in place and the public message was that this was a miniature rerun of the Second World War.

As empire passed away, moreover, it was reimagined nostalgically as a world in which everything and everyone was in his or her place, according to their class or rank or gender, and of course according to their race. In Britain, the Indian Raj was the main subject of this fantasy. In 1974, BBC Radio 4 broadcast *Plain Tales from the Raj*, written by Charles Allen, who was born to officials of the Raj in 1940, moved back to England with his family in 1947 but rediscovered India doing Voluntary Service Overseas in 1966–7. *Autobiography of a Princess* in 1975 and *Heat and Dust* in 1983 were among the elegiac films recovering the lost world of the Raj by Bombay-born producer Ismail Merchant and American director James Ivory from screenplays or novels by Ruth Prawer Jhabvala. In France the cult of empire affected the general population less but 'nostalgérie' was powerfully nurtured by French settlers who had been forced to leave Algeria in 1962. Alexandre Arcady's 1979 *Le Coup de Sirocco* dealt with their plight, while a group of former settlers rebuilt their ideal Algerian community in the provençal village of Carnoux, near Marseille. Their narrative was that French Algeria was a great deal better than the 'gâchis' or mess into which that country had fallen after their departure.[4]

Lack of interest in empire was also explained by the fact that until the 1970s histories of empire were written by academics who were outside the mainstream of national history-writing, yet national histories dealt rarely with empire. In France, the history of Algeria was the monopoly of two men, Charles-André Julien, whose family had emigrated to Algeria in 1906, and his pupil Charles-Robert Ageron, who taught there between 1947 and 1957. The two volumes of their history of Algeria, divided chronologically at 1870, were published in 1964 and 1979.[5] Neither Algeria nor any other French colonies had a place in the first part of Pierre Nora's compendium on French collective memory, *Les Lieux de Mémoire*, published in 1984–92, apart from one essay by Ageron on the colonial exhibition of 1931.[6]

In 1944 Caribbean historian Eric Williams, who experienced racism in 1930s Oxford, demonstrated that the British industrial revolution and consequent world power had been founded on the slave plantations. By contrast leading British economic historian Peter Mathias, while stressing the importance of a 'commercial revolution' kick-starting the industrial revolution, had only two references to the slave trade and none to plantations in his 1969 *First Industrial Nation*.[7] Cambridge historians Ronald Robinson and John Gallagher, who had both served in the Empire during the war, published *Africa and the Victorians* in 1967, as a contribution not to the history of Africa so much as to 'the general theory of imperialism'. Moreover their study bought into a myth that explained empire-building by virtue of the fact that 'the Victorians regarded themselves as the leaders of civilisation, as pioneers of industry and progress'.[8]

The most dismissive judgement on the irrelevance of African history was nevertheless made by Hugh Trevor-Roper, Regius Professor of History at Oxford. Lecturing on the BBC in 1963 he declared:

> Perhaps, in the future, there will be some African history to teach. But at present there is none: there is only the history of the Europeans in Africa. The rest is darkness, like the history of pre-European, pre-Columbian America. And darkness is not a subject for history [. . .] History, I believe, is essentially a form of movement, and purposive movement too. It is not a mere phantasmagoria of changing shapes and costumes, of battles and conquests [. . .] the unrewarding gyrations of barbarous tribes in picturesque but irrelevant corners of the globe.[9]

In recent years, however, things have changed dramatically. The story of empire has much more grip on public consciousness and is indeed a subject of passionate public debate. A number of reasons may be suggested. First, since 9/11, the War on Terror launched by the United States and Great Britain against al-Qaeda in Afghanistan and Iraq was seen by many as a New Imperialism. It provoked a spate of books and articles about empire, whether that empire was British or American, and how positive an influence it was in the world.[10] Second, the threat of global Islamism manifest in terrorist attacks in Iraq, Libya, Syria and Europe and the waves of largely Muslim refugees driven out by the war sharpened debates about national identity. Multicultural options were cast aside in favour of monocultural ones, talking up the importance of 'British values' and French republican secularism. This in turn triggered debate about who was British or French, and the ambivalent place of people from the former colonies in metropolitan society.[11] Third, the debate on the European Union questioned the ability of countries within the EU to defend their borders against immigration and their sovereignty against growing federalism. This stimulated new thinking about empire and what versions of it might offer salvation in a crisis-ridden world.

Writing about empire has also changed dramatically over the last thirty years. The emergence of global history has decentred British and European historians and made historians of empire mainstream. Chris Bayly demonstrated that global history was not simply 'world' or 'extra-European' history but interconnected history. He made connections, for example, between the Taiping rebellion in China, the Indian revolt of 1857, the European revolutions of 1848 and the American Civil War.[12] Global history created the challenge of studying colonial and metropolitan history through the same lens. This methodological agenda was reset in 1997 by American historians Frederick Cooper and Ann Laura Stoler in their seminal article, 'Between Metropole and Colony: Rethinking a Research Agenda'.[13] This has subsequently been taken up by historians such Catherine Hall, who urged 'challenging the binary' between metropole and empire, Bill Schwarz, who explored 'connections between the imperial past and metropolitan present', and Todd Shepard, who advised researchers to 'treat metropole and colony as part of the same analytic field'.[14]

In a related development, colonial history has been subverted by postcolonial history. Instead of writing the history of empire and the colonies outwards from the imperial metropolis, privileging the perspectives of the imperialists, postcolonial history is written from non-European, non-Western perspectives and privileges the experiences of those who have been at the receiving end of colonialism, down to the present day. A breakthrough in this field was the 1988 article, 'Can the Subaltern Speak?' by Columbia Professor Gayatri Chakravorty Spivak. This dismissed the colonialist conceit that the abolition of *sati* was 'white men saving brown women from brown men' and demonstrated that *sati*-suicide was espoused by women fighting for Indian independence.[15] A seminal collection *The Empire Writes Back* (1989) challenged the way the English canon had marginalised non-Western literatures in English, which must be explored and made part of the canon.[16] Postcolonial approaches were championed by historians such as Joya Chatterji, who wrote about the partition of India and the migrations and diaspora it provoked from the perspective of the Indian populations themselves.[17] David Anderson and Caroline Elkins exposed the atrocities committed by the British in their colonies, notably Kenya.[18] Elkins' book was attacked by Andrew Roberts as a 'blood libel against the British people', but as Richard Drayton, Rhodes Professor of Imperial History at King's College London, pointed out, 'An imperial history that does not think and speak for those on the underside of global processes will be inaccurate, if not delusional, about the reality of empire, and complicit with future forms of tyranny, inequality and structural violence.'[19]

In France, where colonial history in the academy remained fairly traditional, postcolonial history was developed outside the academy by historians who set up a research group called ACHAC (Colonisation, Immigration, Postcolonialism). Founded in 1989 and headed by Pascal Blanchard, it explored ways in which colonised Africans were represented in colonialist iconography.[20] In 2005 it popularised the concept of the 'colonial fracture' whereby contemporary attitudes and memories are seen to be divided by the experience of colonialism. While the so-called *Français de souche* identify with the colonisers, having one set of attitudes and memories, the children of the colonised now living in France have quite another.[21] One of the contributors, Achille Mbembe, born in Cameroon in 1957 when the French were brutally imposing their neo-colonial rule, and the author of *Postcolony*, pointed out that the French were still a long way off adopting postcolonial approaches:

Why does France persist in not thinking in a critical way about the postcolonial, about its presence in the world and the presence of the world in its bosom, before, during and after the colonial Empire? [...] As in the colonial period the model of integration is that of assimilation, agreeing to a rule of indifferentiation which refuses to allow a special status to groups on the basis that they belong to different communities. Postcolonial studies come up against a political, cultural and intellectual narcissism of which one could say that what is unthought derives from a racialising ethnonationalism.[22]

In the last thirty years, equally, there has also been a great deal of writing about the legacies and memories of empire. Writing in the aftermath of the Iraq War, Derek Gregory argued that 'many of us (I include myself) continue to think and act in ways that are dyed in the colours of colonial power'.[23] Paul Gilroy pointed out at the same time that Britain seemed less confident and more troubled by its colonial past, while immigrants served as 'the unwilling bearers of the imperial and colonial past'.[24] John Darwin highlighted a viewpoint according to which 'Britain was constituted by empire', its brutalities and inequalities traceable back to its imperial past.[25] Historians have examined how the legacies of empire are found in the former imperial or colonising country and include institutions, social structures, imaginations and mindsets.[26] On the French side, Benjamin Stora has devoted a lifetime to exploring ways in which the memory of the Algerian War was first suppressed and then burst into public consciousness around 2000, and how it structures the attitudes of both former settlers and the former colonists.[27] Non-French historians have contributed significantly to an ongoing debate about France's complicated relationship with its colonial past.[28]

The return of empire to public consciousness has not been easy. Indeed, as historians have demonstrated, the memory of empire is divided by the conflicts of empire themselves. Memory wars around empire have raged in France and in Britain. They do not, however, remain simply as memory. They structure public debate and politics in its widest sense.

In France, a law of 2005 required the nation to honour those who had died fighting to preserve the French Empire in North Africa and schools to teach the benefits of that colonial mission. The law, however, provoked sharp criticism and the formation of a group called

Les Indigènes de la République (the Natives of the Republic) who denounced the reproduction of colonial hierarchies and injustices in contemporary French society.[29] In Britain there was much public commemoration in 2007 of the bicentenary of the abolition of slave trade act as an act of national humanitarianism. Researchers led by Catherine Hall have nevertheless pointed out that much of the wealth of the British ruling class in the eighteenth and nineteenth centuries was drawn from profits of the West Indian slave plantations and that those compensated when slavery was abolished in British colonies after 1833 were not the slaves but the slave owners.[30] Debates were generated about Britain's slave-owning past, especially in cities like Bristol and Oxford, much of whose wealth derived from the slave trade and plantations.

In 2015 a campaign was mounted in South Africa for the statue of Cecil Rhodes at the University of Cape Town to be removed. Although he had been a builder of empire and a philanthropist of education, he was increasingly seen as a colonial adventurer and racist defender of white supremacy. The statue in Cape Town was taken down and a similar campaign was mounted in Oxford in 2016 to remove a statue erected above the High Street by Oriel College, where Rhodes had studied.[31] While students marched and held meetings, arguments were made by the college, university and press that 'history can't be rewritten'.[32] Rhodes was a man of his time and that was that. The counter-argument was that Rhodes was criticised even by his contemporaries and that the framework of analysis was now postcolonial. Just as statues of Napoleon, Stalin and Saddam Hussein came down when regimes changed, so the statue of Rhodes might be removed when those who had suffered the depredations of empire and their heirs gained a voice to demand the symbolic righting of wrongs.

This study began with the 2013 Wiles Lectures at Queen's University Belfast on 'Remembering and Repetition in France: Defeat, Colonialism and Resistance since 1940'.[33] These addressed two questions. First, how it was that those who liberated France from her colonial base in Algeria in 1944 were back ten years later, torturing suspected rebels who were trying to drive out the French in the Algerian War of 1954–62. How could so little have been learned from thinking about liberation and so many mistakes made? And second, how far were France's current troubles with its immigrant population, many of whom were of North African and Muslim origin, in some ways a replaying of the Algerian War? The lectures were given after the riots in France's *banlieues* in 2005 but before the *Charlie Hebdo* and Bataclan attacks in 2015, which confirmed the urgency of tracing links between France's behaviour as a neo-colonial power in Syria and the jihadist attacks in Paris.

It soon became clear that the study could not be limited to French colonialism. In order to establish the exceptionalism or otherwise of the French case, it was decided to undertake a comparative study of the experiences of another colonial power, Great Britain. The approach is both comparative and entangled, because at multiple points, from the Seven Years War and Napoleon's invasion of Egypt in 1798 and from Fashoda in 1898 to Syria in 2015, French and British foreign and colonial involvements clashed with each other. A comparative approach permits a reconsideration of the influential interpretation that while French decolonisation was violent and painful, because of the Algerian War, Britain's was a peaceful and relatively painless 'transfer of power' to national elites. It also permits an analysis of the countries' divergent attitudes to Europe. While France sought to dominate it under Napoleon, Britain preferred to maintain a balance of power between European rivals. These divergences have had an impact on their contemporary thinking.

The most important challenge of the study is to investigate what 'empires of the mind' meant to the French and British: how they fantasised about empire, came to terms with its loss and thought through the consequences of their colonial history. 'The history of the UK, France and the USA since 1945', asserted historian David Andress, 'is marked indelibly by a sense of entitlement to greatness'. He explained this by a 'cultural dementia' of societies which 'strips them of their anchorage in the past' and induces them to abandon 'the wisdom of maturity for senescent daydreams of recovered youth'.[34] This is a powerful analysis, although it is not clear that dementia is the best way of explaining dreams of empire. More persuasive might be an argument that the pain of the loss of empire has resulted in attempts to conjure up new fantasies of empire which in turn reinforce colonial divisions in contemporary society.

Helpful in this respect is Freud's 1914 essay on 'Remembering, Repeating and Working-Through'.[35] He argued that if a memory of a traumatic experience is denied or repressed, a repetition or acting out of the same experiences might follow. This might operate at the level of the individual and group as well as that of the nation. Marcel Bigeard had fought with the Resistance in France but was taken prisoner in Vietnam after the defeat of Dien Bien Phu in 1954. After the defeat in Vietnam the French military was damned if it was going to be defeated in Algeria, where rebellion broke out that same year. This was felt especially keenly at the level of military comrades. In Algeria, Bigeard recalled, 'Every evening we sat around under the light of a few paraffin lamps, talking about Dien Bien Phu and our dead comrades, how we felt at the time. We also spoke of the present war and how we needed to win it very quickly.'[36] In the event the war took six years. The French military used 'Nazi methods' of torture in order to defeat the rebels. The war was lost in Algeria but conflicts continued on French soil, between those who identified with the French Empire and Algerian immigrants who had fought for liberation. The social exclusion of youth of Algerian origin and their espousal of Islam led to a reopening of the Algerian War in the terrorist attacks of 2005. This may be seen as an example of the unthinking repetition of gestures of which Freud spoke. The alternative would be a working through of the memory of painful experiences of empire in an attempt to lay some of its demons to rest.

# 1 EMPIRES CONSTRUCTED AND CONTESTED

In the beginning, European empires were improvised. They were constructed from three strands: networks of trade, colonial settlements and land-based military empires. For a long time these existed independently or overlapped in different parts of the globe. They were often parasitic on existing non-European empires such as the Mughal, the Ottoman and the Chinese. Empires were reinvented in response to new challenges such as international competition between the great powers or resistance by indigenous peoples under their control. They were restructured, their disparate provinces brought together and under centralised administration. Non-European empires were cast aside and territorial European empires took their place. Myths were developed to legitimate empires: they were presented as forces for good – bringing wealth, or order, or civilisation. In the end, however, they were based on violence and maintained by force. The extension of trade required force of arms to underpin it. Colonial settlements brought the expropriation of people from their ancestral homelands. Territorial rule enshrined the power and prestige of the European elites at the expense of non-Europeans. Revolt and rebellion by indigenous peoples who often used European ideologies of liberty and equality against their masters were ruthlessly suppressed. By 1914 empires were defended not only by the armies and taxes they raised locally but by doctrines of white supremacy and the civilising mission.

## Trade, Settlement and Power

For a long time the British and French Empires were not huge continental territories but networks of trade. In his *Wealth of Nations* of 1776 Adam Smith described Britain as a 'great mercantile republic', an interpretation that has been endorsed by historian John Darwin.[1] This concept was developed by Gallagher and Robinson's concept of 'free trade imperialism' and by Cain and Hopkins as a 'gentlemanly capitalism' which combined trade with financial backing, much of which derived from the landed interest.[2] In practice, however, trading networks were scarcely free trading or gentlemanly. The production of colonial goods for import was based on enslavement of African peoples and the slave trade. Merchant fleets were armed and indulged in 'armed trading' that could scarcely be distinguished from piracy.[3] Chartered companies exercised sovereign powers and raised armies. 'Small wars' were launched to break down obstacles to free trade and money was lent to the rulers of defeated powers which, if defaulted upon, might lead to a direct imperial takeover.

The Caribbean plantation economy was based on slavery and the slave trade. Jamaica was acquired by the British in 1655 and imported 470,000 slaves between 1703 and 1778; high mortality meant that in 1788 the slave population on the island was less than 40 per cent of what it should have been. The slave trade and import and re-export of colonial produce such as sugar made the fortunes of Bristol and Bordeaux in the seventeenth centuries, and of Liverpool and Nantes in the eighteenth. It also sustained the landed elites who invested in the trade and owned plantations. In 1789 Jamaica yielded profits of 4 per cent but the French colony of Saint-Domingue yielded 12 per cent. Wars were repeatedly fought in the eighteenth century between Britain, France and Spain for control of the slave trade, the sugar islands and their vast profits.

The French Revolution with its doctrines of liberty and equality wrought havoc in the Caribbean. It destabilised relations between the 40,000 Europeans, 28,000 mulattos and free blacks and 450,000 black slaves on Saint-Domingue. The gospel of equal rights provoked a revolt of 100,000 slaves in August 1791, burning plantations and massacring the planters, and former slave Toussaint Louverture took command of a slave army. French armies were unable to restore order and the Republic indeed abolished slavery in 1794. By that time the terrified planters had invited the British to intervene to defend their position, but yellow fever killed off 15,000 of the 25,000 soldiers by 1798, when they had to withdraw. In 1802 Napoleon Bonaparte decided to reimpose slavery and French order, sending in 34,000 battle-hardened soldiers and sailors, but they were also overcome by disease and slave resistance. Although Toussaint Louverture was captured and froze to death in the French Alps, the Republic of Haiti was proclaimed in 1804 after the first successful anti-colonial revolt.[4]

This was not the usual pattern of events. Military superiority usually ensured the supremacy of European traders. In the eighteenth century trade with India was a monopoly of the East India Company and the Compagnie française des Indes. They established settlements or *comptoirs* as hubs of trade and negotiated trading terms with the princely vassals of the Mughal emperor. However, they were not only traders; they were empowered by royal charters to exercise political power to appoint governors and governors-general and to raise armies. The conquest of territory meant more men and more revenue for the company. Military men and governors such as Joseph-François Dupleix, down to 1754, and Robert Clive from 1756, bribed some princes with protection money, the better to take control, and eliminated those who challenged them by force. Clive defeated the Nawab or governor of Bengal at Plassey in 1757, cleared out the French from Bengal and was himself made governor of Bengal, Bihar and Orissa by the Mughal emperor in 1765. As what became known as a nabob, he made a vast fortune plundering India, which led to an investigation by the House of Commons, and is partly blamed for the Bengal famine of 1779–83.[5] Meanwhile the army of the East India Company, composed of Europeans and Indian sepoys, now became a serious colonial force, growing from 25,000 in 1768 to 40,000 in 1784 and 65,000 in 1814.[6]

One reason behind this growth of military power was the challenge of France to Britain's influence in the Ottoman Empire and to its trade routes to India. This led to a generation of warfare between the two empires. An armada under Napoleon Bonaparte landed in Alexandria on 1 July 1798, defeated the Mameluk slave army of the Ottomans at the Battle of the Pyramids on 21 July and entered Cairo in triumph. Napoleon's fleet was destroyed by Nelson at Aboukir Bay but he fought his way north into Syria, laying siege to Acre before pulling back and returning to France to seize power. In India, the British under Governor-General Richard Wellesley and his brothers Arthur and

Henry responded by crushing princes loyal to the French, such as Tipu, Sultan of Mysore, in 1799, and the Maratha confederacy at the Battle of Assaye in 1803.[7] Britain also benefited from wars against France's satellites or allies – the Dutch, the Spanish and the Irish. Britain took Cape colony from the Dutch in 1795 and again in 1806 and attacked Java in the Dutch East Indies in 1811. Britain exploited France's occupation of Spain in 1808, which provoked independence movements in Spain's Latin American colonies and gave Britain the opportunity to force trade and investment links onto the emerging countries. Buenos Aires was attacked in 1806 and Montevideo in 1807. Meanwhile, when the French Republic supported the Irish rebellion of 1798, Britain imposed full control over Ireland by the 1800 Act of Union.

After the destruction of his fleet at Trafalgar, Napoleon concentrated on building a European land empire. Britain was excluded from trading with it by Napoleon's Continental System, while Britain in turn imposed a blockade on Napoleonic Europe. In 1807, meanwhile, Britain abolished the slave trade, but in order not to be at a disadvantage forced France and Spain to abolish their own slave trades, if necessary by boarding their ships and bombing slave ports on Africa's west coast. Increasingly after 1815 Britain moved towards free trade, symbolised by the foundation of the port of Singapore by Sir Stamford Raffles, former lieutenant-governor of Java, in 1819. Free trade, however, required powers such as the Ottoman Empire to abolish customs and monopolies that hindered that trade. When in 1831 the Ottoman Empire faced a revolt of its governor in Egypt, Muhammed Ali Pasha, who invaded Syria and threatened Constantinople, the sultan turned to Britain for help and was obliged to accept a free trade treaty in 1838. The Crimean War of 1854–6 against Russia then obliged Constantinople to accept loans from Britain, funnelled through the Imperial Ottoman Bank, which further increased British control of her economy.[8] This was later characterised as 'informal empire', trade and investment without direct administration.

The French likewise sought to exploit the difficulties of the Ottoman Empire, whose vassals wielded power across North Africa. After the defeat of Napoleon's continental empire in 1814–15 the French monarchy began to rebuild its empire outside Europe. After the Dey of Algiers threw French traders out of the ports of Bône and La Calle (El Kala), a French force of 30,000 sailed from Toulon and seized control of Algiers on 5 July 1830. Algeria was proclaimed a military colony under a governor-general in 1834 but the French took fifteen years to defeat an alliance of Arab tribes under the brilliant leadership of young Islamic scholar and warlord Abd al-Qadir, who founded a fledgling Islamic state.[9] No serious progress was made against him until the return of General Thomas-Robert Bugeaud as governor-general in 1841 with an Army of Africa of French and Algerian auxiliaries that built up to 100,000. A veteran of the Peninsula War against Spanish guerrillas, he ordered razzias or punitive expeditions against the rebels, destroying crops and villages, stealing herds, raping or kidnapping women. Another tool of terror was the *enfumade*. In June 1845 he smoked at least 700 tribespeople to death in the caves of Dahra where they had taken refuge. Two months later one of his colonels, Saint-Arnaud, reported that in another cave 'I hermetically closed all the exits and made a vast cemetery. The earth will cover the bodies of these fanatics for ever [...] Only I know that underneath there are five hundred brigands who will not slit Frenchmen's throats any more.' About 825,000 Algerians died in the period 1830–75, to which should be added 800,000 who died in the famine of 1867–8.[10]

The French also tried to reassert their position more peacefully in Egypt. Ferdinand de Lesseps had been consul in Egypt in the 1830s and befriended Saïd, the son of Mohammed Ali. When Saïd became ruler of Egypt in 1854 de Lesseps persuaded him agree to the building of a canal across the Isthmus of Suez both to develop trade and to restore France's fortunes in the Orient. The British were hostile but were locked into an alliance with France fighting the Crimean War. A Suez Canal company was formed in 1858 and sold shares to 21,000 people, opening in 1869.[11] Meanwhile in 1852, Major Louis Faidherbe, who had served in Algeria, landed at Gorée in Senegal, on behalf of the merchants of Bordeaux who were interested in developing the palm oil trade. In 1854 he was made governor of Senegal and took on the Moorish empire of El Habj Omar. As a good pupil of Bugeaud and Saint-Arnaud, he did not hesitate to torch rebel villages. 'We burned Ouadar, N'Tougent and Ker Seyni Diop in turn, without seeing the enemy who withdrew as we approached', he told the minister in Paris in March 1858. 'Then we had to destroy Ker M'Biram a N'Diaye, two kilometres to our left, one of the most hostile villages in the whole region.'[12]

Africa and the Middle East were the focus of much trading and colonial endeavour, but India was a fulcrum of empire and looked to impose trade on China to increase its revenues. This was not easy. When

Figure 1.1 Armed trade: episode of the Second Opium War in China. Drawing by Gustave Doré (1832–1883), illustration from *Le Musée Français*, no. 41, May 1858. Getty Images / DEA / BIBLIOTECA AMBROSIANA / De Agostini / 931218102

Lord Macartney, a former governor of Madras, led an embassy to the emperor's court in 1793, and refused to kowtow, he was told bluntly, 'We have never valued ingenious articles, nor do we have the slightest need of your country's manufactures.'[13] Trade with China was permitted only through the strictly controlled port of Canton. This became intolerable when the East India Company lost its monopoly of Chinese trade in 1833. New companies such as Jardine, Matheson & Co were desperate to open up the Chinese market and found one product the Chinese were interested in: Indian-grown opium. After 40,000 chests were exported to China in 1838, the Chinese emperor ordered the opium trade to be stopped. Stocks were confiscated and British traders were imprisoned.

The British did not bother to negotiate. They sent in gunboats and the so-called Opium War of 1839–42 forced China to open her trade, allow British subjects to reside in five ports including Canton and Shanghai, and surrender Hong Kong to Queen Victoria in perpetuity (Figure 1.1). In 1858 the British took advantage of the challenge of the Taping rebellion to the emperor by forcing the doors of free trade on their terms even wider, and when the emperor resisted, marched on Peking and burned down his summer palace.[14] The French joined in the fighting to demand their own trading stations. When this was refused they attacked and besieged Saigon in 1860–1 and obliged the emperor of Annam, a vassal of the Chinese emperor, to cede his southern provinces, which became the French colony in Cochin-China. 'We must create a real empire in the Far East', declared the French minister of the navy and colonies in 1863.[15]

Trade was one of the great engines of empire; another was colonial settlement. This was rather uneven, because empires like that of China did not welcome foreigners, and colonies in West Africa were very inhospitable. In temperate regions, however, settlement provided economic opportunities for populations from the home country and a means to project national solidarity into a wider sphere. The territory coveted by the settlers was not virgin; it was occupied by indigenous peoples. This did not deter the settlers who took up arms and the soldiers of the regular army who backed them. Settlement involved the expropriation of those who were already there, their removal from the land and very often their elimination.[16]

Australia was originally a penal colony, the destination of 825 ships with 163,000 British convicts, men and women mostly punished for theft, between 1788 and 1868. However, Edward Gibbon Wakefield, languishing in Newgate prison in 1827–30 for abducting an heiress, met convicts and realised that the sale of land in Australia could finance voluntary emigration so that 'colonies would be an extension, though distant, of Britain itself'.[17] Migrants numbering 44,000 in the 1830s and 84,000 in the 1840s – artisans facing hardship in the depression after the Napoleonic Wars, paupers condemned to the workhouse, or victims of the Irish famine – had their passage assisted by the British authorities. In the 1850s gold was discovered in the state of Victoria and the European population of Australia increased from 438,000 to 1,168,000 in a decade.[18] The land, of course, was occupied by aboriginal populations, but these were simply cleared away and destroyed. A 'Black Line' was drawn in 1830 and an operation by British troops, convicts and settlers swept Tasmania and corralled the aborigines on Flinders Island and Oyster Bay. There the last Tasmanian aborigine, a 64-year-old woman called Truganini, died in 1876.[19]

Algeria was also originally populated by paupers and convicts. Assisted passages were offered after 1838 to struggling artisans and labourers needed to build roads, rather than to farmers.[20] Unemployed workers were detailed to building projects in 'national workshops' under the Second Republic in 1848. When these were closed as a security risk a popular uprising known as the June Days broke out. This was brutally put down and 4,000 prisoners were sent to Algeria along with 12,000 other former inmates of the national workshops. To these were added the thousands of opponents of Louis-Napoleon Bonaparte's coup d'état of 1851 who were deported. The defeat of Abd al-Qadir enabled the French government in Algeria to establish 200 villages for settlers, whose number multiplied from 131,000 to 189,000 between 1851 and 1857. Progress was slow and the threats to French power from the British Empire and Prussia, which defeated Austria in 1866, were great. In 1868 France's answer to Edward Gibbon Wakefield, the liberal journalist Lucien-Anatole Prévost-Paradol, wrote that 'Algeria should not be a *comptoir*, like India, or a training ground for our army [. . .] It is a French land which should be populated as soon as possible by French people [. . .] eighty or a hundred million French people, strongly rooted on both sides of the Mediterranean, will preserve the name, the language and the legitimate reputation of France'.[21] Ninety years later the French would pay dearly for this ambition.

In Australia and Algeria, the colonising British and French were confronted by indigenous peoples. In Cape colony, which was essentially a British naval base, a small British settlement had to contend with a powerful community of Dutch settlers and their African and Asian slaves as well as indigenous African peoples. In 1834 the British antagonised the Dutch settlers by abolishing slavery, and 12–14,000 Dutch set off into the African interior on what became known as the Great Trek (Figure 1.2). This brought them into conflict with African chiefdoms, driving the Ndebele north and defeating the Zulus at the Battle of Blood River in 1838 before they settled in Natal. Meanwhile the British organised their own razzias east from the Cape, forcibly removing the Xhosa and killing their cattle, so that 40,000 died of starvation and 30,000 became labourers in Cape colony.[22]

In Canada, British forces had used an American Indian confederacy under Shawnee chief Tecumseh against the Americans in the War of 1812, but the Amerindians did not benefit. Between 1824 and 1844 their population in Upper (Ontario) and Lower Canada (Quebec) fell from 18,000 to 12,000. Meanwhile unemployed British migrants, those cleared as surplus tenants by Scottish and Irish landlords, or fleeing the

Figure 1.2  The myth of white settlement: the Great Trek of the Boers into the African interior. 'The bullock-waggons wound slowly over the billowy plains' (c.1908) from H. E. Marshall, *Our Empire Story* (1920).
Getty Images / Hulton Fine Art Collection / 533389780

Irish famine, came in greater numbers. They generally moved into Upper Canada, which was industrial as well as agricultural, and whose population multiplied by twenty between 1806 and 1861. A gold strike on the Fraser River in British Columbia in 1857 led to an invasion of 25,000 gold seekers, land grabs and wars with local Amerindian tribes.[23] The British were keen for Canada to flourish economically and to maintain its security against the United States. They negotiated a free trade treaty between Canada and the United States in 1854 and British banks promoted a railway between Quebec and Halifax, Nova Scotia. Meanwhile in 1860 they abandoned responsibility for protecting the Amerindians to the Canadian authorities, effectively giving them carte blanche to eliminate the tribespeople.[24]

Questions of trade and settlement ultimately involved questions of power. Empires were developed to build the strategic might of the metropolitan power and they needed to be secure. This posed questions of governance. Were colonies to be governed from the metropolis, more or less despotically, or afforded a certain degree of self-government?

In this respect, Canada was at one end of the spectrum. The size of British investments and the importance of security persuaded the British government to bring the Canadian provinces into a confederation, and for this to enjoy a broad degree of self-government under the Crown, in return for funding its own defence. This was accorded by dominion status in 1867.[25]

At the other end of the spectrum was India. Pressures on the East India Company and its army steadily increased as external threats through Afghanistan from Persia and Russia intensified. Burma was annexed after a war in 1824–6 and Sind and the Punjab were annexed after the Afghan War of 1839–42. In 1857 the Bengal army mutinied against what it considered tyrannical and immoral British rule and has been seen as a first jihad against their hegemony.[26] The following year Britain decided finally to depose the Mughal emperor and impose direct rule from London, through a Secretary of State for India. The governor-general became viceroy, the army was henceforth recruited not in unreliable Bengal but mostly in the Punjab, which had remained loyal in 1857, and an Indian civil service was created, drawn from the best British public schools. The princes who continued to rule outside the Raj were integrated as feudal lords, bedecked with new honours. To convey the majesty of the new British Raj, Queen Victoria was proclaimed Empress of India in 1876, the capital was moved from the busy port of Calcutta to the old imperial city of Delhi, and the princes rallied to the viceroy in a highly staged ceremony there of 84,000 people on 1 January 1877. The décor and uniforms were designed by Lockwood Kipling, director of the art school at Bombay; his 12-year-old son Rudyard was at boarding school in England. The mercantile republic was now eclipsed by imperial hubris.[27]

Algeria was like a hybrid between India and Canada. The indigenous population was subject to military despotism while the European settler population increasingly called the shots. Napoleon III visited Algeria in 1860 and declared that 'our African possession is not an ordinary colony but an Arab kingdom'. Rumours spread that he wanted to make Abd el Kader its viceroy. This was not to be. The Algerian population in the countryside were governed after 1844 by the army's 'Arab bureaux'. A French law of 1863 permitted vast tracts of land to be confiscated from the indigenous populations, who were corralled into smaller and smaller regions and suffered a terrible famine in 1867–8. Another law of 1865 deemed Algerian

Muslims to be French subjects, but not citizens, on the grounds that their religious practices, such as polygamy, made it impossible for them to acknowledge the French Civil Code. In 1870 the Empire was defeated by Prussia and a massive Algerian rebellion broke out. It was brutally put down, its leaders were executed or sent to New Caledonia, and even wider tracts of land were confiscated as punishment. French citizens from Alsace-Lorraine, now annexed by united Germany, were encouraged to settle in Algeria, although only 1,200 families arrived. Meanwhile the Algerian Jewish community of 34,000, which had been petitioning for naturalisation since 1860, was collectively granted citizenship by the Republic in October 1870. This brought the European population to 245,000 in 1872, but divided them even more sharply from the millions of Algerian Muslims.[28]

## Scrambles, White Supremacy and the Civilising Mission

The colonial expansion experienced before 1880 has often been described as 'informal empire'. Trade and settlement took place for the most part without direct administration of large tracts of territory. Clearly this changed in India after 1857 and in Algeria after 1870. Usually, until then, the European powers supported imperial regimes such as the Mughal, Ottoman or the Chinese Empires or nominally vassal regimes such as that of the khedive of Egypt or emperor of Annam while extracting the maximum economic benefit. After 1880 this precarious equilibrium came under threat as a result of two factors. First, non-European governments broke down under a crisis of debt owed to the European powers and faced internal opposition which may loosely be described as nationalist to that humiliating dependency. Second, the domination of Britain and to a lesser extent France on the international scene was challenged by new imperial powers, notably Germany, Russia and Japan, eager for a place in the sun. This led to what Jules Ferry, the architect of French colonialism in the 1880s, called 'a massive steeplechase on the road to the unknown'.[29] The outcome were 'scrambles' for vast tracts of Africa and China and colonial powers increasingly assuming the direct responsibility of 'formal empire' in their new territories. More elaborate administrative structures were developed which were dominated by European official and settler elites, legitimated by consciously developed myths of white supremacy and the civilising mission.

Egypt was virtually owned by Britain and France, in terms of both government bonds and shares in the Suez Canal, and in 1876 they established dual control over Egyptian finances. In 1879 they deposed one khedive, who would not pay up, and replaced him by another, who was putty in their hands. Nationalist army officers under Colonel Ahmed Urabi revolted against this humiliation in 1881 and demanded a national parliament and government. This threatened Anglo-French investments and influence and indeed the route to India. Intervention to establish full control was unavoidable. At this point, however, the French dropped out. They were consolidating their hold on Tunisia, where they had substantial investments and dictated terms to the bey. They used the excuse of a raid into Algeria by Tunisian Krumir tribesmen to intervene militarily and force a protectorate on the bey. The French parliament had stumped up for this but one adventure was enough. Thus when riots broke out in Alexandria in June 1882 and sixty Europeans were killed, the British fleet bombarded the port, British forces defeated the Egyptians at the Battle of Tel El Kebir on 13 September and entered Cairo alone.[30] It felt like revenge for Napoleon's coup of 1798.

The dramatic shift from informal to formal empire triggered the 'scramble for Africa'. The French realised too late that they had been humiliated as a great power and sought to recoup by pressing their advantage in West Africa. Major Joseph Galliéni returned to France to great acclaim in 1881 after five years as governor-general of Senegal, having concluded a treaty with Sultan Ahmadou, the son of El Hadj Omar, which conceded France a protectorate from the source of the Niger to Timbuktu.[31] Meanwhile Captain Pierre Savorgnan de Brazza returned with a treaty he had concluded with the Congolese king Makoko, giving France a protectorate over vast areas of the Congo. The ambition was that this would open the way to Lake Chad and the Nile. The treaty was enthusiastically ratified by the French parliament on 22 November 1882, to make up for the Egyptian débâcle. King Leopold II of Belgium was provoked to assert his interests in the Congo through a company called the International Association of the Congo.[32]

The British responded with a trio of chartered companies, updated versions of the East India Company headed by latter-day buccaneers, to drive forward into Africa. They enjoyed powers to deal with local rulers and with international competitors. Former soldier

George Goldie headed the Royal Niger Company, chartered in 1886, which consolidated British control in Lower Nigeria, subdued the Asante in the Gold Coast, and took hold of Upper Nigeria in 1895 to cut off the French threat. William Mackinnon, a Scot who had developed steam lines through the Suez Canal to Aden, Zanzibar and India, chartered an Imperial British East India Company in 1888 to drive from Zanzibar to Lake Victoria, securing what became Kenya and Uganda. Finally, Cecil Rhodes, a vicar's son from Hertfordshire who had built up a diamond mining empire in Kimberley, just north of the Cape, formed a British South Africa Company in 1889 with the financier Alfred Beit. Their aim was to develop gold mining interests in the Transvaal, where gold had been found in 1886, and other mining interests in Mashonaland, later part of Southern Rhodesia. A wilder ambition was to drive a route bearing British trade, settlers and power from the Cape to Cairo.[33]

These ambitions led to a direct clash with the French. In 1896 the French sent Galliéni to annex Madagascar, where Queen Ranavalona II and her Merina aristocracy had headed a rebellion against them. The queen was exiled, her chief ministers executed, and Galliéni set about pacifying the island.[34] The same year a mission led by Captain Marchand left Marseille to drive west from Senegal to the Upper Nile in order to stake out a Central African French empire. A mere eight French officers and a hundred *Tirailleurs Sénégalais* made contact with the Mahdists of the Sudan who were challenging the British. Marchand arrived at Fashoda on 29 August 1898 and declared himself acting high commissioner on the Upper Nile and Bahr el-Ghazal. Unfortunately, Kitchener had an army of 20,000; he defeated the Mahdists at Omdurman on 2 September and arrived at Fashoda on 19 September to oust Marchand. The British government ordered the Mediterranean and Channel fleets to sail and the French government climbed down, recalling Marchand on 3 November 1898.[35] Meanwhile two more French captains, Paul Voulet and Julien Chanoine, set out from Dakar with another unit of *Tirailleurs Sénégalais* in order to take control of a borderland between the Niger River and Lake Chad which was drawn by an Anglo-French agreement of June 1898. This resulted not in humiliation but atrocity. Heirs of Bugeaud and Faidherbe, they took the view that their domination of African kingdoms could be established only by force, and they left a trail of burned villages, pillage, enslavement and massacres. On 14 July 1899

**Figure 1.3** A romanticised image of colonialism in Africa: the French attack on Kana, Dahomey, Africa, 1892. Artist Henri Meyer, *Le Petit Journal*, 19 November 1892. Getty Images / Art Media / Hulton Archive / 463929521

a colonel sent out from France to arrest them was shot by Voulet, who with Chanoine set up their own short-lived African kingdom in the heart of darkness.[36] In the same region, at the same time, the fantasies and anguish of empire were being enacted (Figure 1.3).

The 'scramble for Africa' was echoed by a 'scramble for China', where the Qing emperor's position was becoming increasingly fragile. The French tried to consolidate their influence over his vassal, the emperor of Annam, with a view to extending their influence in Tonkin, which controlled the Red River route into Southern China. Jules Ferry dangled before parliament the bone that China was a market of '400 million consumers'.[37] In 1883 a war party gained control in Peking, but the French fleet used torpedoes to sink the Chinese fleet further up the coast at Fuzhou in August 1884. Under

the Treaty of Tientsin in 1885 the emperor conceded a French protec-
torate in Tonkin. After 1889 they modelled their rule on that of the
British in India, working with the mandarinate and setting up a French
Indochinese civil service.[38]

In the end, the hammer blow to the Chinese Empire came from
another source: Japan. Confronted by Western attempts to open it up
after the Opium Wars, Japan restored the Meiji emperor in 1867 and
urgently built a modern army, bureaucracy and education system.
It undertook a breakneck programme of industrialisation and looked
to build an empire on the Chinese mainland, starting with Korea.
In 1895 Japan comprehensively defeated China on land and sea, secured
Korea as a protectorate and extracted an indemnity of 200 million taels,
almost an entire year of income, from the Qing government.[39]
The Chinese were obliged to go cap in hand to the banks of the
European powers for credit. The British Hong Kong and Shanghai
Bank combined with the Deutsche Asiatische Bank to provide three
loans between 1895 and 1898, while French and Russian banks provided other loans. This shattered the remaining ability of China to keep
the European powers and Japan out of the country. In return for loans it
was obliged to grant spheres of interest to those powers, enabling them
to build railways and sink mines far into the interior, using the revenues
to ensure that their loans were repaid.[40] These incursions provoked
economic dislocation and national humiliation, and triggered a peasant-
led rebellion of the Boxers United in Righteousness behind the motto,
'Support the Qing, expel the foreigner!' The empress dowager declared
war on the European powers, who duly brought in a joint army of
20,000 to restore order. They imposed an indemnity of 450 million
taels, payable in gold, completely opened up China to foreign trade and
reduced the Qing dynasty to a puppet of Western interests.[41]

The scrambles for Africa and China progressed with little opposition that could not be overcome by warships and the Maxim gun.
There was one exception: South Africa. The issue there was that the
British at the Cape had steadily lost control of the Boers, who built up an
interior stronghold in the Transvaal. The British tried to annex the
Transvaal in 1877 and to bring it into a South African Confederation
on the Canadian model. They defeated the Zulus at the Battle of Rorke's
Drift in January 1877 but the Boers fought for their independence and
defeated the British at the Battle of Majuba Hill on 27 February 1881.[42]
The Transvaal regained its autonomy as the South African Republic

under the presidency of former Great Trekker Paul Kruger. It consolidated its political power by an electoral reform in 1894 that disfranchised the poor whites of British origin, denigrated as *Uitlanders* or foreigners. A petition was signed by 35,000 of them, demanding their rights, and Cecil Rhodes organised a raid by one of his company administrators, Sir Leander Starr Jameson, to make common cause with them and take power in Pretoria. The raid by a mere 500 men was easily dealt with by the Boers and Kruger received a telegram of congratulation from the German Kaiser.[43]

The Germans had established themselves in Southwest Africa in 1884, giving the Boer threat an additional twist. Lord Alfred Milner was sent as High Commissioner to South Africa in 1897 but failed to make Kruger stand down over the franchise. War broke out in 1899. The British brought in the Indian Army and drafted Africans into their ranks. They corralled thousands of Afrikaners into concentration camps in which 28,000 – mainly women and children – died. In the end, the conflict between British and Boer turned out not to be the most important thing. 'The war between the white races will run its course and pass away', wrote Boer commander Jan Smuts in January 1902, 'and the day will come when the evils and horrors of this war will appear as nothing in comparison with its after effects produced on the native mind.'[44] The Boers lost the war but won the peace, forming in 1910 a Union of South Africa of Transvaal, the Orange Free State, Natal and the Cape, which – like Canada – was accorded the status of a British dominion. The Afrikaners now drew in the ethnic British to construct a racially homongeneous state. An all-white franchise was imposed, overruling the Cape where 10 per cent of the voters were coloured (mixed race) and 5 per cent African. A Native Land Act was passed in 1913, confining African populations to 7 per cent of the country's land. African workers who migrated to work in the mines were subjected to the legal bondage of indentured labour, barrack-like male-only compounds, a pass system and a ban from pavements. Slowly an African fight-back began. A South African Native National Congress was founded in 1913, becoming the African National Congress in 1923.[45]

The Boer War was a catalyst of a powerful movement within the British settlement colonies to develop what has been called a 'Britannic nationalism'.[46] The idea had been developing for some time that there was a solidarity based on English or British nationality in those Dominions dominated by settlers from the home country and which –

often for this reason – enjoyed a good degree of self-government. This made them different from parts of the Empire like India, which had next to no white settlers. 'Greater Britain is an extension of the English nationality', said Cambridge professor J. R. Seeley in 1885. 'The English Empire is in the main and broadly may be said to be English throughout.' He contrasted this with India, where there was 'no community of blood, no community of religion. And lastly no community of interest [...] England conquered India and now keeps it by means of Indian troops, paid with Indian money'.[47]

A 'colour line' was constructed between white and non-white populations, and the superiority of one over the other was asserted. In the Dominions this was often articulated by immigration control. Australia imposed restrictions on Chinese immigrants coming to work in the gold mines from the 1850s and in 1896 the New South Wales government banned 'all persons belonging to any coloured race inhabiting the continent of Asia or the continent of Africa or any island in the Pacific Ocean or Indian Ocean'.[48] On becoming a federation in 1901 Australia passed an immigration restriction act and Australian prime minister Alfred Deaken announced in 1906 that the Empire was 'divided broadly into two parts. One occupied wholly or mainly by a white ruling race, the other principally occupied by coloured races who are ruled. Australia and New Zealand are determined to keep their place in the first class.'[49] The distinction was also dramatised by discrimination and franchise reform. The young Gandhi, who qualified as a barrister at London's Inner Temple and went to South Africa in 1893 to practise, was thrown off a train in Pretoria for sitting in a first-class carriage. The following year he complained to the Natal parliament that the Indian was 'a despised being' in South Africa. 'The man in the street hates him, curses him, spits upon him. The press cannot find a sufficiently strong word in the English dictionary to damn him with', although the most common term was 'coolie'. He also protested at the disqualification of 41,000 Indians in Natal under the new franchise law, leaving only the 43,000 whites with the vote. A vote for the 500,000 Africans there was not even considered.[50]

The situation of the black populations and the emergence of this white consciousness did not go unnoticed in the wider world. A first Pan-African Congress was held in London in July 1900, the initiative of Trinidadian lawyer Henry Sylvester Williams. Ten representatives came from the Caribbean, eleven from the United States, and only four from

Africa. W. E. B. Du Bois, the first African-American to take a doctorate from Harvard, declared that 'the problem of the twentieth century is the problem of the colour line'.[51] Ten years later he denounced 'this new religion of whiteness' which portrayed non-whites, in Kipling's words, as 'half devil and half child'. He concluded that its pretended superiority derived from claims of ownership. 'What is whiteness that one should so desire it?', he asked. 'Whiteness is the ownership of the earth, forever and ever. Amen.'[52]

In the French Empire, there was equally a dominant discourse of white superiority, but it was usually articulated in terms of the *mission civilisatrice*, the civilising mission. Jules Ferry, the republican politician who presided over France's colonial expansion in the early 1880s, defended the intervention in Tunisia in 1882 as 'the triumph of civilisation over barbarism'.[53] Four years later, explaining France's entanglement in Indo-China that had forced his resignation, he declared, 'We must proclaim openly that the superior races have a right *vis à vis* the inferior races because they have a duty towards them. They have a duty to civilise them.'[54]

The French Empire, like the British, was divided into colonies where there was considerable French settlement and those where there was very little. In fact, the only real French settler colony was Algeria, and even here there were not enough French settlers to underpin France's control of the indigenous Algerian population. Even these were outnumbered by other European communities, Spanish, Italian and Maltese. To remedy this, in 1889, France decided to naturalise the children of all European settlers in Algeria. This was the founding charter of the *pieds noirs*, distinguished from indigenous Algerians because they largely lived in towns and wore shoes, who would dominate the life of French Algeria for the next seventy years.[55]

A first step of the civilising mission was the 'fusion of races' in terms of settlers of European origin. A second step, which animated the *pieds noirs* in the 1890s, was to remove the vote from the long-established Jewish population of Algeria, the members of which had been made citizens in 1870. Despite their huffing and puffing, they failed to achieve this. A third phase, to civilise the indigenous Algerians, never happened. Only a very narrow stratum of Algerians who received a French education and were prepared to relinquish their status as Muslims became French citizens, because they were seen to be betraying the Muslim community. The vast majority was rigorously excluded from any question of citizenship on the basis that it was a conquered Arab race and of Muslim religion. After 1881 Algerian Muslims were subjected to the *Code de l'Indigénat*, a discriminatory penal code that punished offences such as refusing to do forced labour on public works or to pay taxes with internment or expropriation. This code was arbitrarily administered in the Algerian countryside by sabre-carrying administrators who behaved more like satraps. The Algerians were indeed subjected to their own system of taxation, inherited from Ottoman rule, while European settlers, who lived off those taxes, paid much lighter French taxes themselves, and were accused of 'eating the native'.[56]

Meanwhile the settler community began to flex its muscles and demand a greater measure of self-government. In 1879 the succession of military governors-general ended and civilian governors-general, responsible to the Ministry of the Interior, took their place. Even this was only a start. In 1896 the settlers in Algeria saw off Governor-General Cambon who presumed to interfere in their affairs, sacking mayors for corrupt practices and seeking to silence anti-Semitic agitation. This actually increased under the leadership of a young extremist of Italian origin, Max Régis, encouraging the looting of Jewish shops and synagogues and calling for Jews to forfeit their citizenship. In 1898 Régis was elected mayor of Algiers and four out of six Algerian deputies elected to Parliament were rampant anti-Semites, including Édouard Drumont, author of *La France juive*. Anti-Semitism served to bind the European settler community together and to assert their demands for greater self-government. In 1898 they achieved budgetary autonomy through a 'colonial parliament' of *Délégations financières*, composed of forty-eight Europeans and only twenty-one indigenous Algerians. This enabled them to formalise their tax-light regime and to perpetuate the tax-heavy regime on the Arabs.[57]

The only French colony where the civilising mission worked successfully was in Senegal, and that only in the 'four communes' along the coast, including Dakar. These had a population of French and mixed-race families and of French-educated Muslims, the so-called *évolués*. They were granted French-style municipal government in 1872 and the right to elect their own deputy to parliament in 1879. Such generosity towards French-educated Muslims did not last. In 1912 the Algerian model was imported and Muslims were deprived of citizenship. Moreover, the rights of the four communes did not extend into the interior, where the *Code de l'Indigénat* and arbitrary administrators held sway.[58] One more chance came with the formation of French West Africa in 1895. This federated Senegal, French Sudan, French Guinea, the Ivory Coast, Niger, Upper Volta, Togo and Dahomey. In 1904 governor-general Ernest Roume announced that 'we wish truly to open Africa to civilisation'. This would entail the provision of railways and schools, reducing the power of 'feudal' lords and the abolition of slavery.[59] Within a few years, however, it became clear that to reduce the power of feudal lords was immensely destabilising, and the French state was better served by working together with 'traditional' authorities, which should be preserved. In this sense, the French model of 'direct rule' was discarded in favour of the 'indirect rule' theorised by Lugard in Nigeria, where working with the Muslim chiefs of the north was held up as a shining example. The indirect model was transferred to Morocco when it became a French protectorate, provisionally in 1906, formally in 1912. Hubert Lyautey, who had served under Galliéni and spent years 'pacifying' the country, decided to work with the sultan and his traditional administration of pashas and caïds, who were both administrators and judges, under the supervision of French administrators.[60]

One of the contradictions of the civilising mission is that it excluded from power the educated elites it created. In India, British rule was increasingly challenged by Calcutta lawyers, journalists, teachers and administrators, the Parsi business community of Bombay and the Brahmin priestly caste of the former Maratha confederacy interior, who joined to form the All-India National Congress in 1885. They demanded greater self-government on the dominion model, including a voice for Indians in the legislative councils and higher posts in the Indian civil service.[61] Some concessions were made in the Councils Act of 1892, but there was a backward push against them when Lord Curzon became viceroy in 1899. Curzon was obsessed by the threat of Russian expansion into Central Asia, knocking on the doors of India. India, he argued, was 'the pivot and centre' of the Empire, and for that reason its security could not be endangered.[62] In 1905 he tried to undercut the influence of the Calcutta political class by partitioning Bengal, and advised moving the capital from the 'heated atmosphere' of Calcutta to the old Mughal capital of Delhi. This took place in 1911 when the young George V presided over a durbar that brought together the princes through which the Empire must once again rule (Figure 1.4).

Figure 1.4 The Empire in perfect order: King-Emperor George V and Queen Mary at the coronation durbar in Delhi, 12 December 1911.
Getty Images / Hulton Royals Collection / Hulton Archive / Stringer / 3307019

Two significant developments were nevertheless triggered by this 'feudal reaction'. First, the partition of Bengal favoured the formation of an All-Indian Muslim League in 1906 and opened the way for a return of Muslim power for the first time since 1857. Second, the moderates in the Congress Party were outflanked by extremists led by Bal Gangadhar Tilak, who launched a Swaraj or self-rule movement backed up by a boycott of foreign goods, taxes and military service. Violence broke out in Bengal, and Tilak was tried for sedition and imprisoned in Burma in 1908–14.[63]

By 1914 empire had been reinvented as formal rather than informal, sustaining great powers with global reach. It became more structured but arguably more oppressive. Wars for the control of Africa, India or China were undertaken by regular armies rather than the private armies of trading companies. Expropriation and massacre gave way to states founded on racial segregation and racial hierarchy. Self-government was increasingly imparted to settler colonists who could be entrusted with the interests of the British and French Empires. But it was systematically denied to the Indian educated elite and Algerian Muslims were subjects not citizens, under a discriminatory tax and legal regime. Ironically, empires became better at legitimising themselves. Britannic nationalism, the recovery of national *grandeur* after the defeat of 1870, the white man's burden and the *mission civilisatrice* were developed as smoke-screens to hide brutal realities. Power was magnificently orchestrated in colonial capitals and largesse dispensed to keep a ruling group of princes and chieftains on side. Imperial rule was nevertheless contested, and those who were keen to contest it had no better moments than the two world wars in which the great empires would now became embroiled.

# 2 EMPIRES IN CRISIS: TWO WORLD WARS

On 29 May 1924 Virginia Woolf visited the British Empire Exhibition which had been erected at the end of the Metropolitan Line at Wembley. A thunderstorm was in full spate, garishly lighting up the sky and sweeping dust around the military bands and pagodas. 'Colonies are perishing and disappearing in a spray of inconceivable beauty and terror which some malignant power illuminates. Ash and violet are the colours of its decay', she wrote. 'The Empire is perishing; the bands are playing; the Exhibition is in ruins. For that is what comes of letting in the sky.'[1]

These comments now seem uncannily prescient but at that moment few foresaw the end of empire. The interwar period was one of high imperialism for both the British and the French Empires, and there was much to celebrate. The British Empire Exhibition of 1924–5 was organised to convey its size, wealth and glory to a public that was arguably more interested in the football played in the new stadium than in George V's speech opening the Exhibition. On St George's Day the king spoke to the crowd and broadcast to the nation and to 'my dominions across the seas', exalting the Empire's material and moral power. The Exhibition featured a maharaja's palace, a Burmese pavilion and a mud-baked African walled town. There was an Empire pageant of 1,200 performers, accompanied by Elgar's Empire March, a Torchlight Tattoo of 1,000 military bandsmen, and a Boy Scout Jamboree. It was attended by over 17 million visitors in 1924 and nearly ten million in 1925. The underlying message was that Britain was bestowing civilisation on a world that remained backward but full of potential if it remained under her guidance. This message was bitterly contested by Indians and Africans who

Figure 2.1 Colonial fantasy: North African tribesmen parade on camels at the 1931 Colonial Exhibition in Paris.
Getty Images / Roger Viollet / 55756837

experienced the Empire in other ways. The Bengal lawyer Chitteranjan Das, who had just founded the Swarajaya or independence party, criticised the Exhibition as a vehicle of colonial exploitation. Ladipo Solanko, a Nigerian student at University College London, held meetings that launched a West African Student Union, espoused Pan-Africanism and called for a 'Negro Empire' in Nigeria.[2]

Four years earlier, in 1920, the French Minister of Colonies, Albert Sarraut, unveiled plans for a Colonial Exhibition that would be 'the living apotheosis of the overseas expansion of France under the Third Republic'. It finally opened in Vincennes in 1931, designed as a testimony to the French 'genius for civilisation', and was attended by eight million people (Figure 2.1). They delighted in colonies that were each represented by a pavilion, with their native art, exotic costumes and culinary delights. Equally exotic animals from Africa and Asia were on show in the zoo. The centre-piece of the Exhibition was a reproduction of the Cambodian temple of Anghor Wat, which suggested that many colonies enjoyed their own civilisation. The dominant narrative, however, was that through trade, the army and the Church, France radiated a much higher civilisation. As in

Britain, there were marginal but passionate voices of protest. Vietnamese students handed out tracts denouncing the colonial brutality of France which the previous year had brutally repressed risings in Indo-China, while the French Communist Party daily *L'Humanité* pilloried the Exhibition quite simply as 'the apotheosis of crime'.[3]

These exhibitions were mounted between the two world wars which demonstrated the fragility of the European empires. The First World War destroyed the German overseas empire, its scraps shared between Britain, France and Belgium. In the Second World War Germany, which built a new empire in Europe, and Japan, expanding in the Far East, all but finished off the French and British Empires. The resources of empire in terms of men and materials were mobilised for wars fought both in Europe and beyond. Appeal was made to the solidarity felt by colonial peoples with their metropolitan rulers. This had some purchase, but more telling was resistance to demands for *their* men and *their* money for what seemed to be someone else's war. This resistance was put down by force, and often extreme violence. Empires experienced not only an existential crisis but a crisis of legitimacy. The pageantry and propaganda rolled out to persuade millions that empire was at the service of wealth, civilisation and glory ceased to persuade so readily. Other forms of legitimacy were asserted: the self-determination of peoples and the equality of nations. These were advanced at the end of the First World War by the Bolshevik revolutionaries, the League of Nations and US President Wilson, in the Second World War by President Roosevelt and the United Nations and were taken up by the colonial peoples themselves. Two big questions remained. Would the imperial powers learn from their new challenges or would they attempt to rebuild their empires regardless? And how far would international bodies and the United States insist on their ideals of liberty and equality when confronted by the imperialist interests and prejudices of their British and French Allies?

## Mobilising Empire, 1914–17

On 31 July 1914 the Australian Labour Opposition leader Andrew Fisher promised that 'should the worst happen [...] Australians will stand beside the mother country to help and defend her to our last man and our last shilling'.[4] This was a magnificent expression of Britannic nationalism in what would later be called the

Anglosphere. The worst did happen and the self-governing Dominions contributed a million men to the battlefields. A good deal of solidarity came from the fact that many of the Dominion soldiers were British-born – 70 per cent in the case of the first contingent of Canadians – but the crucible of war that killed or wounded 65 per cent of Australian servicemen also forged a new national consciousness in the Dominions and an ambition to be treated as equals by the mother country. Increasing demands for manpower and the issue of conscription after 1916 also threatened the Empire. Irish republicans launched an Easter rising in 1916 that was closely watched by Afrikaners who had sympathies with Germany. The Military Service Act in Canada drove a wedge between British and French Canadians, who overwhelmingly refused to serve.[5] Two referendums bringing in conscription in Australia in October 1916 and December 1917 were defeated. Australian workers feared that if they were drafted overseas they would be replaced by 'sullen, dark intruders with Negroid features or turbaned coolies flooding across the land'.[6]

The French colonies provided about 600,000 indigenous soldiers for the war, of whom 70,000 were killed. General Charles Mangin, who had commanded *Tirailleurs Sénégalais* on the Fashoda expedition, believed that colonial troops would be a *Force noire* because of their 'rusticity, endurance, tenacity' and an 'incomparable power of shock'.[7] North and West African soldiers distinguished themselves at Verdun in 1916 but suffered atrocious losses at the Chemin des Dames in 1917. Armed resistance broke out in the Aurès, in the mountainous region east of Algieria, in November 1916, and was violently suppressed. Conscription quotas were imposed on villages; those which did not provide soldiers were burned to the ground and manhunts were organised in what looked like a revival of the slave trade. In 1917 Clemenceau changed the tactic and sent Blaise Diagne, the first black deputy elected to the French parliament, on a tour of the West African Federation to find recruits. He found 63,000 recruits but largely in response to official lies about the future abolition of the *Code de l'Indigénat* and access of Africans to citizenship and jobs.[8]

The position in the Middle East was especially perilous. Germany had increased its influence over the Ottoman Empire by building the Berlin to Baghdad railway, and in November 1914 encouraged Sultan Mehmet V, who was also the Caliph, to declare a jihad on the British, French and Russian Empires and to call their Muslim subjects to revolt. The British imposed a protectorate on Egypt and repelled an Ottoman force that attacked the Suez Canal in February 1915.⁹ In April 1915 they pushed back a *mujahideen* army in Mesopotamia.¹⁰ They then made a series of promises that were mutually contradictory and would leave a divided legacy. Hussein the Sharif of Mecca was promised Arab independence and proclaimed himself 'king of the Arab lands'. The 1917 Declaration of Foreign Secretary Balfour promised the Jews a national homeland although qualified this by saying that 'nothing shall be done that may prejudice the civil and religious rights of existing non-Jewish communities in Palestine'.¹¹ Meanwhile the secret Sykes-Picot agreement of May 1916 cynically divided the Ottoman Empire outside the Arabian peninsula between Britain, which would get Transjordan and Iraq, France, which would get most of Syria, and Russia, which would get Constantinople and Eastern Anatolia. After the Russian Revolution the Bolsheviks published the treaty and annulled the tsarist claims. They also dropped out of the war, exposing the Middle East to a renewed German–Ottoman offensive. The British were obliged to send in more forces from the Dominions and India as a matter of urgency, occupying Jerusalem in December 1917 and Mosul and Damascus in October 1918.

India made a massive contribution to the war effort, providing 800,000 volunteers. In 1917 the viceroy made a gift of £100,000 without consulting his legislative council, which was paid for by a 65 per cent increase in the tax burden. Opposition built up in the Home Rule League led by Tilak which brought together representatives of the Congress and the Muslim League in 1916 to demand constitutional reforms, and the Khalifat movement of Mohammed and Shaukut Ali, which expressed solidarity with the Ottoman sultan. The leaders of these movements were arrested under the 1915 Defence of India Act. The new Secretary of State for India, Edwin Montague, nevertheless decided that concessions would also have to be made to keep the Indians loyal. On 20 August 1917 he announced that India would progress towards self-government. It remained to be seen whether this promise would be kept after the war.

In the Far East the war contributed to the rise of Japan and the tribulations of China. In China a revolution in 1911 finally overthrow the Qing emperor and power passed to the Guomindang or Nationalist party of Sun Yat-sen, who declared a republic. Unfortunately it had no military base and could not resist the former Qing military supremo, Yuan Shi Kai, who seized power in 1913.[12] The outbreak of war in 1914 took European forces away from the Far East, and Japan, which had been in alliance with Britain since 1902, took the opportunity to seize the German concession of Shantung. On 18 January 1915 it also presented China with twenty-one demands, including the right to develop her interests in Manchuria and to impose advisers on the Chinese central government. This last demand was withdrawn under pressure from Britain and the United States, but it was a firm indication of Japan's ambition to impose at least an informal empire on China.[13]

## 'The Wilsonian Moment': Dreams and Realities

The intervention of the United States in the war in 1917 was a turning point. This was not only because of the size of the American Expeditionary Force, about two million strong, including 350,000 African-Americans, or because of its economic strength through war loans to its European allies. The moral and ideological force of the 'Wilsonian moment' altered the balance of legitimacy between the colonial powers and the colonised. In his inaugural address on re-election on 5 March 1917 Woodrow Wilson declared that the United States would insist both that 'governments derive all their just powers from the consent of the governed' and on 'the actual equality of nations in all matters of right and privilege'. A month later, addressing Congress, he said that America was entering the war 'for democracy, for the right of those who submit to authority to have a voice in their own affairs and for the rights and liberties of small nations'. This message was echoed from an entirely different direction by the Bolsheviks who took power in Russia in October 1917. On 29 December Leon Trotsky, commissar for foreign affairs, advised Britain and France that their propaganda claim that they were fighting for the small nations of Europe, such as Belgium and Serbia, must also be extended to Ireland, Egypt, Madagascar, India and Indo-China, since 'to refuse self-determination to the peoples of their own state and colonies would mean the defence of the most naked, the most cynical imperialism'.[14]

These messages were not lost on leaders of opposition to colonial rule in the colonies, who moved mountains to come to Paris to meet and influence the decision-makers of the Peace Conference at the end of

1918 and the beginning of 1919. Emir Khaled, the grandson of Abd al-Qadir, who qualified as a captain in the French Army but was regarded with suspicion and never given a command, wrote to Woodrow Wilson in May 1918 to complain that in Algeria, 'under a so-called republican regime, the greater part of the population is ruled by exceptional laws that would make barbarians ashamed'. Egyptian nationalists under Sa'd Zaghlul formed a 'Wafd' or delegation party, hoping to be invited to Paris, and on 25 January 1919 sent a memorandum on Egyptian National Claims to Wilson. Prince Faisal, the son of Sharif Hussein of Mecca, turned up in Paris at the end of November 1918, hoping to obtain the promised independence of Syria. Bal Gangadhar Tilak went to London and on 2 January 1919 asked Lloyd George and Wilson for interviews, enclosing a pamphlet called *Self-Determination for India*. Finally, Nguyen Tat Thanh, the son of a disgraced Indochinese mandarin who went into exile in Paris in 1911, requested an audience with Wilson to present a document entitled 'The claims of the people of Annam'. He signed it Nguyen Ai Quoc, Nguyen the Patriot.[15]

It was not long before these pious hopes of the opponents of colonialism were dashed. Wilson's high ideals were designed to take the moral high ground from the German, Austro-Hungarian and Ottoman Empires rather than to bring down the colonial system. There was no problem about confiscating the German colonial empire in Africa and dividing it between Britain, France and Belgium, but Clemenceau and Lloyd George had fought the war to defend and even extend their own empires, not to liquidate them. A law sponsored by former Governor-General Charles Jonnart on 4 February 1919 gave more Muslim Algerians the vote in local elections but did not concede what they really wanted, citizenship *dans le statut*, French citizenship while remaining Muslims.[16] In Egypt Zaghlul and other Wafd leaders were arrested on 8 March 1919, triggering a revolution in Egypt in which 800 Egyptians were killed. Balfour blamed Bolsheviks and Islamists and asked the Americans to recognise the British protectorate in Egypt, which they did.[17] In March 1920 a pan-Syrian congress of national leaders met in Damascus and proclaimed the independence of Greater Syria. This was not to the taste of the French, who duly marched into Damascus and drove Faisal out. The Government of India reform sponsored by Secretary of State Edward Montagu and Viceroy Chelmsford fell far short of the self-government promise of 1917. The franchise was widened and Indians were give representation on provincial legislative councils, not in the central government. But the fear of revolutionary opposition was met by bills drafted by Justice Rowlatt to give the Indian government a battery of arbitrary powers. In protest, Gandhi launched a *satyagraha* movement of non-violent resistance and a general strike. This was met by state violence as on 13 April 1919 General Reginald Dyer ordered Indian Army troops to open fire on a meeting at Jallianwala Bagh, a walled garden in Amritsar, killing 300 and injuring a thousand people.[18] This single event tarnished the reputation of the British in India like none other. Back in France, Nguyen Ai Quoc despaired of the whole Wilsonian project. He read Lenin's 'Theses on the National and Colonial Question', presented to the second congress of the Comintern in June 1920, which urged national and colonial liberation movements to support the revolutionary proletariat. He joined the French Communist Party when it was founded in December 1920 and in 1923 travelled to Moscow to work for the Comintern. Later he would become known as Ho Chi Minh.[19]

It was not only the aspirations of former colonised countries that were given short shrift at the Paris conference. Japan was invited as a great power, but Japanese emigrants to California and elsewhere suffered discrimination because of their race. The Japanese delegation campaigned to assert a clause on racial equality into the League of Nations covenant, but was unable to overcome ideas of white superiority nurtured by Britain and its dominions.[20] Former Japanese Prime Minster Okuma criticised 'the perverted feeling of racial superiority entertained by the whites. If things are allowed to proceed in the present way [...] the peace of the world will be endangered.'[21] Twenty years later the United States and European powers would have reason to regret their racial arrogance.

As a gesture of compensation, Japan was allowed to keep the concession of Shantung, but this grossly antagonised the Chinese who came to Paris hoping for the abrogation of eighty years of unequal treaties imposed by foreign powers. Frustrated students demonstrated in Tiananmen Square on 4 May 1919 in protest against this national humiliation and formed a student union. The May 4 movement spread to professionals, office workers and traders, who boycotted Japanese goods, while dock, railway and factory workers went on strike. Like air rushing into a vacuum, China was suddenly opened up to new ideas, including communism and feminism, which challenged the Confucian cult of rulers, masters and parents. Young people were empowered to leap over a century of isolation and backwardness and to seek the triumph of East over West.[22]

## Keeping the Lid on Empire

Empire Day continued to be celebrated across the British Empire on 24 May every year after 1902, on the birthday of the Queen-Emperor Victoria.[23] British people still emigrated to the Dominions, encouraged by the Empire Settlement Act of 1922, especially as unemployment grew between the wars. Assisted passages were given to 18,600 people emigrating to Canada and 172,000 to Australia between 1922 and 1936, fewer Irish now and mostly from the industrial regions of the North of England and Scotland.[24]

There was, nevertheless, a dynamic in the Dominions and colonies after the war to assert greater independence from the Empire and equal status with the metropolis. This tendency also had an impact on relations with non-white indigenous peoples, since greater autonomy allowed the Dominions a freer hand to be brutal. Rhodesia was billed as a 'new Australia', and achieved self-government in 1923, after responsibility was transferred from Rhodes' British South Africa Company. Scottish emigrants mixed with 'poor whites' from South Africa, a third of them Afrikaners. Threatened by the majority Ndebele and Shona populations, who had launched the Chimurenga War in 1896–7, the emigrants organised a Territorial Force Reserve after 1926 to maintain white supremacy. In Kenya, which became a colony in 1920, settlement was rather different. It was dominated by officers and gentlemen, many of whom had served in India, attracted by big game hunting and the boast of 'the colony without income tax'. They were permitted a monopoly of the 'white highlands' to grow tea, coffee and maize, but were concerned about the control of towns and trade by the Indian population. In 1923 they even threatened rebellion against the Crown to prevent the Indians being allowed freer immigration and greater representation.[25] In South Africa, the pro-Empire party of General Smuts was beaten by the National Party of General Herzog in 1924. They were divided over loyalty to the Empire, but they could agree on dealing with the African threat. Together they passed a law in 1933 disfranchising the minority of Africans who still had the vote in the Cape. Smuts regarded Africa as a 'white man's country' and argued against equality. 'The British Empire does not stand for the assimilation of its peoples into a common type but for the fullest development of its peoples along their own specific lines', he told an Oxford audience in his 1930 Rhodes lecture. He urged the preservation of tribal chiefs and their councils, and the discouragement of 'urbanised and detribalised natives' which in his view would lead only to 'Bolshevism and chaos'.[26]

These ideas of indirect rule or association, working with traditional elites, became increasingly current in French Africa also. Administrators were concerned that previously held doctrines of assimilation would only lead to the emergence of French-educated, deracinated young urban blacks who nurtured ideas of equal rights. 'We came as conquerors, we appeared as liberators, we released them from the tyrannical domination of a bloody oligarchy', Martial Merlin, governor-general of French West Africa, told colonies minister Albert Sarraut in 1921. 'But the greatest source of loyalty', he said of the chiefs, 'lies in the tranquillity we assured them'.[27] Sarraut imbibed and developed these ideas, arguing later that assimilation, defined as 'mass naturalisation', was an error. France should stick to the existing practice of giving French citizenship to only an elite of indigenous people who 'give guarantees of ability and fulfil certain conditions', such as surrendering their legal status as Muslims. The masses should stay outside the *cité française*, remaining in the *cité indigène*.[28]

In North Africa, an alliance with traditional elites was less easy. In Morocco, a powerful tribal leader, Abd el-Krim, set up a fledgling Islamic state in the mountainous Rif region of northern Morocco. He defeated the Spaniards in 1921 and launched a holy war against the French in 1924. Lyautey was unable to defeat Abd el-Krim and the latter held out until 1926.[29] Meanwhile, Algeria was ruled by settlers who refused to share power with the Muslim majority. Steadily, the Muslims organised, both as an Association of Algerian Muslim ulamas, and in the populist Étoile Nord Africaine founded in 1926 by Messali Hadj, an Algerian worker in Paris. In 1927 Messali told a Congress of Peoples of the East, meeting in Brussels, that the *Code de l'Indigénat* must be abolished and Muslims should be able to vote and be elected *dans le statut*, becoming French citizens who were also Muslims. In 1936, former Governor-General Viollette persuaded socialist Prime Minister Léon Blum to offer reforms, and was prepared to allow 30,000 more Algerian electors in the first instance, who would *not* have to renounce their status as Muslims. This was rejected as insufficient by the Étoile Nord Africaine, given the Muslim population of 5.5 million, but above

Figure 2.2  The prehistory of the Iraq War: British tanks and aircraft in Mesopotamia, 1922.
Getty Images / Hulton Archive / Stringer / 2665034

all by the settlers, who organised a mass resignation of mayors against the threat of Muslim voters. The reform was withdrawn and Messali Hadj was arrested as a threat to state security.[30]

In the Middle East, where the Ottoman Empire had once ruled, the League of Nations attempted to reconcile local demands for self-government with the interests of colonial powers through the mandate system. The justification was that the subject peoples were on the road to self-government but not yet ready for it.[31] There was nevertheless the suspicion that mandates were protectorates by a different name, offering few restraints on the colonial power. There was also the problem that the mandates of Syria, Iraq and Palestine were artificial units that could not reconcile the claims of competing ethnic and religious groups. In Syria, France decided to make a virtue of this, splitting off a Christian-majority Lebanon, an Alawite state on the north coast and a Druze state in the south. In 1925 Druze rebels joined forces with former Ottoman soldiers in Damascus, but the French replied with the sustained bombing of Damascus from the air, killing 1,500 people.[32] In Iraq, the British occupation faced a rebellion in June 1920 led by 130,000 Shiite tribesmen in the south who achieved a truce with Sunnis, by former Ottoman soldiers in Baghdad, and by Kurds in the north. The British replied with massive force (Figure 2.2), including aerial bombing, and killed over 8,000 Iraqis before having Faisal crowned a puppet king.[33] In Palestine, the Arabs rioted in 1929 and launched a revolt in 1936 against growing Jewish immigration and land grabs and demanding an independent government. Several hundred Palestinian Jews were killed but British repression killed some 5,000 Palestinian Arabs.[34]

In India, the educated classes kept up the pressure for self-government through the Congress Party. In 1928, ten years after the offer of 1918, a commission was set up to explore possible revisions. Once again, though, the British refused the Indians any power in the central government. Gandhi described this as 'an insult to the whole people' and in 1930 led a *satyagraha* march to the Gujarat coast to boil sea water for salt, which was a government monopoly. His arrest in May 1930 triggered a national campaign of civil disobedience, boycotting elections to provincial legislatures, work in government offices and schools, together with a boycott of foreign cloth which undermined Indian industry. The government clamped down, throwing 29,000 Indians into jail. A truce was made with the government in 1931, but talks failed and civil disobedience began again in 1932. The main concern for the opposition was that the campaign was essentially Hindu, with very little Muslim participation. Hyderabad-born Sayyid Abdul Ala Mawdudi, aged 24, who had taken part in the Khilifat movement, published his *Jihad in Islam* in 1927. This argued that violence was necessary in 'the Holy War for the Cause of God' against the pillaging and killing of imperialists, but his ideas did not become current until after his death in 1979.[35]

Meanwhile, in 1935, another Government of India Act was passed. This finally allowed for an all-Indian federal government in which Indian ministers would staff domestic ministries in Delhi and all ministries at the provincial level. There were, however, three main drawbacks. First, the viceroy retained a vast array of emergency powers to scrap the system if anything went wrong. Second, the princes were given inordinate influence, with the power to nominate a third of the lower chamber and two-fifths of the upper chamber. Half of them also had to agree to allow the federal government to come into being, which they did not. Third, Congress did extremely well in the 1937 provincial elections, making inroads even in Muslim provinces. Muhammed Ali Jinnah of the Muslim League decided that the best policy now was to play on the threat to Islam and to move towards a separate Muslim state. On the eve of the Second World War the divisions and frustrations in India were as bad as they had ever been.[36]

In China, after the death of Yuan Shikai in 1916 China had become a prey to feuding warlords. These were challenged by both Nationalists and communists and then by an expansionist Japan, which regarded China as her India. Nationalist leader Sun Yat-sen met a Comintern emissary in 1922 and agreed that the Soviets would support the Nationalists if they in turn worked with Chinese communists. Soviets trained Chinese revolutionaries at the Whampoa Military Academy and built up a National Revolutionary Army. Unfortunately, Sun died in 1925 and the army was entrusted to the more conservative Chiang Kai-shek. Chiang regained Shanghai in 1926 and then planned a Northern Expedition to bring the warlords under control. Before leaving on the campaign he turned on the Communist Party and trade unions in Shanghai and all but destroyed them. The Northern Expedition managed less to eliminate the warlords than to absorb them, and Chiang developed a form of nationalism that integrated Confucianism.[37]

In Indo-China, long a tributary province of the Chinese Empire but now dominated by the French, the nationalist and communist revival challenged French rule. A National Party of Vietnam (VNQDD), inspired by Sun Yat-sen, organised a mutiny in a French garrison at Yen Bay, north of Hanoi, in 1930. The execution of its leaders provoked a wave of strikes and peasant disturbances. Ho Chi Minh (Nguyen Ai Quoc), who had been active as a Comintern agent in Canton in 1924–5, returned to Indo-China in 1929 to set up an Indochinese Communist Party. This exploited peasant unrest to organise rural soviets in the Nghe Tinh region of Annam from where he came. However, the French unleashed a white terror in which 3,000 peasants were killed, the communist leadership was destroyed, and Ho was lucky to escape to Moscow.[38]

Meanwhile disaster struck the Chinese Nationalists in September 1931. The Japanese Kwantung Army, anxious to cut off the nationalist threat, seized power in Manchuria, and tried to conceal their military might by setting up a puppet state of Manchuko, under the Puyi, the Chinese boy emperor who had abdicated in 1912. When the League of Nations protested, the Japanese claimed that they were exercising a mandate over a more backward nation that was not yet fit for self-government, and were behaving no differently from the British in India. In August 1936 the Japanese military published a plan for empire in East Asia – which they called a coexistence and co-prosperity sphere – with a five-year plan to develop Manchuria and Northern China as industrial bases. War with China broke out in July 1937, and by the end of the year the Japanese had captured Shanghai and the Nationalist capital of Nanking in December 1937. The death of 30,000 Chinese soldiers and 20,000 civilian men and the rape of 20,000 women in Nanking in December 1937 announced the brutal irruption of a new imperial power.[39]

## The Defeat of the French and British Empires

Whereas the British and French Empires survived the First World War, in the Second World War they suffered significant defeats. Germany under Nazi rule strove to recreate on the Continent of Europe the colonial empire it had lost in 1918, while Japan drove forward as the dominant empire in East Asia. Each took revenge on the humiliation they had suffered at the Paris Peace Conference or in the League of Nations. Those defeats encouraged colonial subjects to assert their independence with greater force and authority against France and Britain, which frequently descended into fighting each other over their endangered possessions. Meanwhile a crisis of legitimacy was caused by the intervention of the United States in the war after it was attacked by Japan at Pearl Harbor in December 1941. The United States denied that it was asserting imperial power and refused simply to rescue the embattled empires of France and Britain. It asserted the equal right to self-government of all peoples, whether they had been subjugated by Germany or Japan, France or Great Britain. The United Nations, founded in 1945, also upheld the principles of the equality of nations and self-government. The British and French Empires resisted these ideas all the way. They took advantage of an American change of attitude to the empires of Allies in the face of threats from the Soviet Union and in the short term at least managed to reassert a fragile control over their colonial possessions.

On 28 March 1940 the French and British governments made an agreement that neither would conclude a separate peace. This was put dramatically to the test by the German offensive launched in the Ardennes on 10 May 1940. The British Expeditionary Force in France evacuated at Dunkirk between 27 May and 4 June. German armies occupied Paris on 14 June. On 16 June the British government proposed a Franco-British union with a single war cabinet and supreme command but a majority of the French government, which had fled to Bordeaux, argued that this would make France into another British dominion and the French into British subjects.[40] Instead, a new French government was formed under Marshal Philippe Pétain which sued for an armistice with Germany. Charles de Gaulle, under-secretary of state for defence, flew to Britain on 17 June and in his famous appeal of 18 June urged the French not to accept the terms of the armistice but to continue the fight. This marked the inauguration of the Free French. On the same day Churchill told the House of Commons:

> I expect that the battle of Britain is about to begin [...] Hitler knows that he will have to break us in this island or lose the war. If we can stand up to him all Europe may be free, and the life of the world may move forward into broad, sunlit uplands [...] Let us therefore brace ourselves to our duty and so bear ourselves that if the British Commonwealth and Empire lasts for a thousand years men will still say, 'This was their finest hour.'[41]

Churchill's words underline the fact that this war was a struggle for empire, and that not only Germany was looking to found a Thousand Year Reich. Colonial forces were mobilised to fight in France in May–June 1940, with 100,000 Senegalese *Tirailleurs* in regiments commanded by the likes of Major Raoul Salan, who described himself as 'a soldier of the Empire'.[42] Algeria and the protectorates of Morocco and Tunisia in French North Africa provided their own indigenous *Tirailleurs* for the Army of Africa.[43]

The big issue around the armistice was whether France would continue to fight on from her empire. Charles de Gaulle was a relatively junior general and from London contacted his superior, General Noguès, commander-in-chief of all forces in North Africa and proconsul of Sultan Mohammed of Morocco. 'General, the defence of North Africa is you or nothing', he declared on 24 June. 'Yes, it is you and it is the essential element and the centre of continued resistance.'[44] However, far from using the Empire as a springboard for resistance, Noguès obeyed the dictates of hierarchy, fell into line behind Pétain and accepted the armistice that had been concluded on 22 June 1940. French North Africa was now a province of Vichy.

This caused serious problems for the British. The French had not only violated the agreement of 28 March not to conclude a separate peace, but their military resources were at the mercy of Germany. The French naval base in North Africa was anchored at Mers el-Kébir, the port of Oran, and might fall into German hands. After the French commander refused an ultimatum to sail to waters under British control the British opened fire on the French fleet on 3 July 1940, killing 1,300 French sailors. This rekindled the enmity between France and Britain over their seapower and empires that went back to Fashoda, indeed to Trafalgar. De Gaulle, in London, was now seen by Vichy as a traitor and sentenced to death in absentia.

A battle now took place between Vichy and the Free French for control of the French Empire in Africa. The British supported the Free French but there was always a suspicion on the French side that the British were seeking to exploit French weakness to extend their own colonial reach. In a first phase de Gaulle used the support of the British in Lagos for a mission by his chosen commander, General Leclerc, who flew to Africa on 6 August 1940 and in three glorious days on 26–28 August won over the French Congo, French Cameroon and Chad in French Equatorial Africa.[45] This was the Free French's baptism of fire as a serious force. However, the Free French failed to win over French West Africa, where governor-general Boisson declared for Vichy. On 23–25 September the British supported de Gaulle in a seaborne assault on Dakar, the gateway to French West Africa, but Boisson obeyed Vichy's orders to repel the Free French attack. Shore batteries and the battleship *Richelieu*, which had escaped from the British attack on the French fleet at Dakar, prevented a landing. 'I wanted to avoid a pitched battle between Frenchmen, so I pulled out my forces in time', de Gaulle wrote to his wife in London, adding, 'the ceiling is falling on my head'.[46]

In the Far East the French Empire collapsed before another rampant empire. On 22 September 1940 Japan took advantage of the French defeat in Europe to invade Vietnam, occupying Haiphong and Hanoi. Vichy's Governor-General, Admiral Decoux, agreed to an armistice on 25 September 1940, and Japanese troops entered Saigon. Although this was officially described as a 'stationing' of the Japanese Army, and Bao Dai remained nominal emperor of Vietnam, it was no less than an occupation of French Vietnam with Decoux as a Pétain of the Far East.[47]

As the imperial powers crumbled so colonial peoples saw a chance for liberation. On 1 April 1941 nationalist army officers under Rashid-Ali seized power in the former British mandate of Iraq and appealed to the Germans for support. The Germans looked at the French mandates of Syria and Lebanon and considered them an excellent bridgehead from which to attack the British Empire. The Vichy regime was happy to go along with this. First Minister Admiral Darlan flew to Berchtesgaden to meet Hitler on 11 May, announcing that 'Today is the festival of Joan of Arc, who got rid of the English.'[48] He signed the Protocols of Paris of 27 June 1941 which offered the *Luftwaffe* the right to use airbases in Syria, use of the port of Bizerta in its protectorate of Tunisia to supply the *Afrikakorps* against the British in Egypt, and the right to use Dakar as a naval and submarine base. German planes began to arrive at Aleppo and Damascus and General Wavell scraped together a force of British soldiers together with Australians and Indians, under the command of Maitland 'Jumbo' Wilson. This defeated Vichy's Levant Army, who sued for an armistice at Acre on 12 July 1941.[49] The Free French under de Gaulle were furious at being cast aside in their own mandates and tried to regain the initiative by a ceremony of independence for Syria and Lebanon on 27 September 1941 but this was only for show. In reality the British took overall control of foreign affairs while de Gaulle appointed a high commissioner responsible for internal order.[50] Tightening their grip on the region, the British orchestrated a coup in Egypt in February 1942 to force out King Farouk's anti-British ministers – an event which had a formative impact on young officer Gamal Abdul Nasser.[51] Taking their cue, the French arrested the Lebanese president in November 1943 to prevent him from unilaterally abrogating the French mandate.

It was not that the British themselves were not in imperial crisis: they were. The Battle of Britain, fought against the *Luftwaffe* between 10 July and 31 October 1940, was held up as the victory of 'the few', but it was unable to prevent the Blitz against British cities between 7 September 1940 and 10 May 1941, which killed 40,000 civilians. A photograph of the dome of St Paul's Cathedral rising above the smoke, published in *The Daily Mail* on 31 October 1940, came to symbolise Britain 'standing alone' against Nazi Germany, but if it had stood alone, it would have crumbled.

Britain relied for its survival on soldiers and supplies from its Dominions, notably Canada and Australia, and for military hardware and economic support from the United States under the Lend-Lease agreement signed by President Roosevelt on 11 March 1941. This dependency on the

Dominions and the United States dramatically tipped the balance of power away from Great Britain. Australia felt increasingly isolated from Britain as Japanese forces advanced in East Asia and in his 1942 New Year message, premier John Curtin told Roosevelt, 'Australia looks to America, free of any pangs as to our traditional links or kinship with the United Kingdom.'[52] Churchill was desperate to bring the United States into the war but had to accept that it would be on American terms, not just to shore up the British Empire. On 9–12 August 1941 Churchill met Roosevelt on the USS *Augusta* in Placentia Bay, Newfoundland, and signed the Atlantic Charter. Drafted by Under-Secretary of State Sumner Wells and published on 14 August it committed them to common principles including the freedom of the seas, equal access to trade and raw materials and the 'abandonment of the use of force'. Most controversially, it announced that 'they respect the right of all peoples to choose the form of government under which they will live; and they wish to see sovereign rights and self-government restored to those who have been forcibly deprived of them'.[53] For Churchill, this applied to the peoples subjugated by Germany and Japan, but not to those peoples of the Empire that Britain would in its own time nurture towards independence. How to reconcile the equal rights of nations to self-government and the historic claims of colonial powers became one of the most intractable questions of the war.

The inexorable advance of Japanese forces posed this question in momentous terms for the future of the British Dominions and British India. On 7 December 1941 the Japanese bombed Pearl Harbor in Hawaii, and overran the Philippines, which the United States had conquered from the Spanish in 1898. The United States declared war on Japan, then on Germany and Italy. On 10 December British seapower in the region was crippled by the sinking of *The Prince of Wales* and *Repulse* by Japanese aircraft off the Malay coast. Churchill rushed to Washington and spent Christmas with Roosevelt, planning what to do next. Next came the Japanese attack on Singapore on 8 February 1942. Two days later Churchill sent a message to General Wavell, now commander-in-chief in India and supreme commander in the Far East. 'There must be at this stage no thought of saving the troops or sparing the population', he instructed. 'The battle must be fought to the bitter end at all costs [...] Commanders and senior officers should die with their troops. The honour of the British Empire and the British Army is at stake.'[54] All this was to no avail. Wavell was forced to retreat to Java in the Dutch East Indies. General Arthur Percivall was left to surrender the Singapore garrison of

Figure 2.3  The British Empire humiliated: the surrender of British forces to the Japanese, 15 February 1942.
Getty Images / Modadori Portfolio / 141556273

85,000 men to 30,000 Japanese troops on 15 February 1942 (Figure 2.3). In all, over 130,000 men were taken prisoner by the Japanese, more than half of them Indian. Churchill was devastated. He described the fall of Singapore as 'the worst disaster and largest capitulation in British history'.[55]

The fall of Singapore weakened relations between Britain and the Dominions, which lost faith in the mother country's ability to defend them and sought greater autonomy or a rapprochement with the United States. On 19 February 1942 the Japanese bombed the North Australian port of Darwin. Australian Premier John Curtin was quick to welcome General Douglas MacArthur, newly appointed Supreme Commander of the South Pacific Area, in March 1942. Jan Smuts, Prime Minister of the Union of South Africa, told members of the Empire Parliamentary Association at Westminster in November 1943 that Britain had 'nothing left in the till' as a result of the war and retreat. It should concede a more decentralised model of the British Empire, in which the Dominions become 'sharers and partners'. Concerned too that the Japanese tornado and the faltering myth of white supremacy might encourage black Africans to demand liberation, he proposed that Dominions like South Africa should extend that dominion over the British colonies around them in order to deal with 'the problem of race and colour'.[56] Here was a sign that greater autonomy for South Africa might lead to greater racial oppression.

Even more serious were the consequences of Japan's advance for British India. For sixty-six years the British monarch had been empress or emperor of India and the Indian elites had been denied self-government. Military defeat changed all this. The Japanese captured Rangoon in British Burma on 7 March 1942. The Burma Road, along which the British were supplying the Nationalist Chinese under Chiang Kai-shek against the Japanese, was abandoned, and Indian, Anglo-Indian and Anglo-Burmese populations of Burma were forced to flee to India. In April 1942 the Japanese bombed Calcutta and the British naval base at Colombo, Ceylon. Fearing a Japanese invasion of Bengal, the British ordered scorched-earth measures there as early as February 1942. Power stations and oil installations were demolished, rolling stock, boats and even elephants that might be used by the invaders were confiscated and rice stocks were requisitioned and stockpiled for the British Army. Together with a cyclone, tidal waves and floods in October 1942, these measures provoked a famine in Bengal in 1943 that caused over three million deaths and all but destroyed the reputation of the British as a colonial power.[57]

The day after the fall of Singapore the Prime Minister General Hideki Tojo told the Japanese parliament, 'It is a golden opportunity for India to rid herself of the ruthless despotism of Britain and participate in the construction of the Great East Asian Co-Prosperity Sphere. Japan expects that India will restore its proper status as India for the Indians.'[58] Both the Japanese and the Germans supported the formation of an Indian National Army under Subhas Chandra Bose, a nationalist who had broken with Gandhi in 1939, formed from Indian soldiers captured after the loss of Singapore. One of its officers, Captain Prem Kumar Sagel, reflected on the new balance of global power: 'The fall of Singapore finally convinced me of the degeneration of the British people and I thought that the last days of the British Empire had come.'[59]

The British government was desperate to hold on to the Indian Army, almost two million strong, to help drive back the Japanese but at the same time was forced to make concessions to the Indian Congress movement. Urgently, Churchill sent a Cabinet mission under Sir Stafford Cripps to India in March 1942 promising independence after the war and in the meantime a greater role for Indians in the government of India. This was not enough and Gandhi famously described the offer as 'a post-dated cheque on a failing bank'.[60] The Indian Congress rejected the deal on 10 April 1942 and in August launched the Quit India campaign. Gandhi, Nehru and their colleagues were thrown into prison and crowds took matters into their own hands.

The British were now terrified that the Japanese would gain control of the Indian Ocean and snap the routes that kept the Empire together. The island of Madagascar, a French colony since 1896 and which had declared for Vichy, exposed East and Southern Africa and the route by the Cape. The British sent in a force largely of South African and East African troops and took Diego Suarez on 5 May 1942. A deal was then done with the Vichy governor, much to the fury of the Free French. The island was handed over with poor grace to the Free French when their high commissioner arrived in January 1943, but the British did not leave until 1946.[61]

## 'The Age of Imperialism is Ended'

Faith in the British Empire was shaken even among the British people. The BBC dropped a programme of Kipling readings for Empire Day, 24 May 1942. As Captain David Gammans MP said, 'The old Kipling idea of Empire is dead.'[62] Although they were now fighting alongside the British against the Axis powers, the Americans did not offer the British much hope for saving their Empire. In a Memorial Day address at the Arlington Memorial Amphitheatre, on 30 May 1942, Sumner Welles declared:

> If this war is in fact a war for the liberation of peoples, it must assure the sovereign equality of peoples throughout the world as well as in the world of the Americas. Our victory must bring in its wake the liberation of all peoples. Discrimination between peoples because of their race, creed or colour must be abolished. The age of imperialism is ended.[63]

The American press was clear in its support for the Indian National Congress when it launched its Quit India campaign against the British. The editors of *Life* magazine published an open letter to the people of England on 12 October 1942. This was accompanied by pictures of huge crowds listening to the All-India Congress Committee meeting in

Bombay, on 7 August 1942, calling for total disobedience to British rule, and recording the riots that broke out after the arrest of Gandhi. The letter was explicit:

> One thing we are sure we are not fighting for is to hold the British Empire together. We don't want to put the matter so bluntly, but we don't want you to have any illusions. If your strategists are planning a war to hold the British Empire together they will sooner or later find themselves strategizing alone [...] Quit fighting the war to hold the Empire together [...] if you cling to the Empire at the expense of the United Nations you will lose the war.[64]

In the teeth of this challenge, the riposte of Churchill was equally explicit. At a press conference on Armistice Day, 11 November 1942, he asserted, 'Let me make this clear, in case there should be any mistake about it in any quarter. We mean to hold our own. I have not become the King's First Minister in order to preside over the liquidation of the British Empire.'[65]

Despite these tensions over empire, Britain and America agreed on the need to defeat the Axis. Operation Torch landed their forces in French North Africa, from Casablanca to Algiers, on 8 November 1942. This was intended as a bridgehead for the liberation of Europe from German power, but the Americans had no more thought of saving the French Empire than they had of saving the British. 'What inherent right has France to territory which she has seized, sometimes by war, as recently as the 1880s', Roosevelt had asked in August 1942, 'any more than has Japan to seize by force certain territories of China which she has now occupied? The only difference is in point in time.'[66] Equally, Roosevelt had no reason to prefer the Free French over Vichy. The Free French had antagonised the Americans by seizing from Vichy the island of Saint-Pierre-et-Miquelon, off Nova Scotia and only 500 miles off US territory, on Christmas Eve 1941. The Americans did not feel let down by France's armistice with Germany and Roosevelt's ambassador at Vichy, Admiral Leahy, got on very well with Vichy's First Minister, Admiral Darlan. De Gaulle was not told of Operation Torch and when he found out exclaimed, 'Fine. I hope that Vichy throws them back into the sea. You don't enter France like a burglar.'[67]

Vichy French forces indeed put up stubborn resistance. The Americans wanted to conclude a ceasefire as soon as possible and did this with Admiral Darlan, who was then in Algiers. The so-called 'Darlan deal' seemed to betray the much-trumpeted idealism of the United States, and Labour MP Aneurin Bevan asked, 'What kind of Europe are we thinking of? A Europe built by rats for rats?'[68] Roosevelt brushed off the pact with Vichy as a 'temporary expedient, justified solely by the stress of battle'.[69] In the event, Admiral Darlan was assassinated on Christmas Eve 1942 but Roosevelt did not then turn to de Gaulle. Rather he endorsed de Gaulle's arch-rival, General Giraud, who had sworn an oath of loyalty to Marshal Pétain. When Roosevelt met Churchill at Casablanca in January, de Gaulle was persuaded to meet Giraud and work with him. The Americans joked about the 'shotgun marriage' between Giraud the groom and de Gaulle the bride.[70] At this stage the marriage did not work out and de Gaulle flew back to London, leaving Giraud in charge in North Africa.[71]

The presence of the Americans and the discomfiture of the French Empire provided much encouragement to Algerian nationalists. Ferhat Abbas, a nationalist campaigner and local councillor in Algeria, who had fought with the French in 1940 and then returned to Sétif where he owned a pharmacy, observed that France's defeat by Germany and bail-out by the Americans had altered the balance of power between colonisers and colonised. Broadcasts from London, Washington and Moscow, he noticed, were educating Africans and Asians in the principle of the liberty and equality of all nations. In February 1943 he therefore drafted a Manifesto of the Algerian People that was endorsed by a group of fifty-six Muslim leaders. It appealed to 'those nations fighting both against Germany and for the liberation of peoples', denouncing the French colonial regime in Algeria as 'imperialistic and anachronistic [...] a modern form of slavery'. A second draft demanded an Algerian state with a constitution drafted by an Algerian assembly elected by all its inhabitants.[72] The Manifesto was submitted first to Giraud in March and then to de Gaulle who returned to Algiers on 30 May 1943 to set up the French Committee of National Liberation – in effect the French provisional government – jointly with Giraud. This was badly timed. Both the French and the Algerians were pursuing liberation, but for the French this meant restoring the unity of the French Empire, a unity that was being challenged by Algerian nationalists. Ferhat Abbas was placed under house arrest.

## Liberation or the Restoration of Empire?

In North Africa, where the provisional government of the French Republic was now based, a new French army was built up under Giraud as commander-in-chief that amalgamated de Gaulle's Free French and Vichy's Army of Africa and was essentially funded and equipped by the Americans. From it was drawn an Expeditionary Force that took part in the Allied landings in Italy in the autumn of 1943, provoking the overthrow of Mussolini, armistice with the Italians and a long battle against the Germans who now defended the peninsula. This French force was also heavily reliant on African forces: it included 100,000 men from West Africa and 176,000 from North Africa.[73] One of the soldiers fighting in Italy was 24-year-old Ahmed Ben Bella, an Algerian of peasant origin who had fought as a sergeant with the French in 1940, returned to the farm and was called up to rejoin the Algerian, then Moroccan *Tirailleurs* in 1943–4. He fought at Monte Cassino and was decorated by de Gaulle when they got to Rome, but was already thinking about how Algerian independence might have to be gained by armed struggle.[74]

The great offensive against Japan in the Pacific and Indian Oceans, commanded by General McArthur and Lord Mountbatten, got under way. The manpower of the British Empire was fully mobilised but proved increasingly reluctant simply to serve and obey. The British focus was the Burma campaign led by General Slim to defeat the Japanese and secure the British Raj. About 70,000 Indian and 120,000 African troops took part in the Burma offensive.[75] Soldiers were recruited from West and East Africa to join the fight. One of these was 17-year-old Isaac Fadoyebo, a Hausa from Nigeria educated in an Anglican missionary school, who had wished to train as a teacher. He was drafted into the Royal West African Frontier Force, swore an oath to King and Empire, and was shipped via Cape Town to Bombay, by rail to Calcutta and across the Bay of Bengal to Chittagong, arriving in August 1943.[76] However, the recruitment of colonial soldiers became increasingly problematic, as the British Empire seemed to totter and rhetoric of national liberation gained force. Soldiers of the King's African Rifles who had defeated the Italians in Ethiopia refused to board ships for the East at Massawa in February 1942, saying that they had won their war and did not want to fight 'Bwana's war', the boss's war.[77] Similarly, a battalion of black Mauritian troops who had been sent to occupy Madagascar mutinied in December 1943 rather than go to fight the Japanese in Burma.[78]

Despite these challenges, the ambition of the British and French was simply this: to restore their empires. For the Free French, France was being liberated from the springboard of the African Empire. After that the rest of the empire in the Middle East and Far East would be recovered, and with it all, the French greatness so cruelly shattered in 1940. In January 1944 de Gaulle called a conference to Brazzaville in the French Congo, effectively the capital of its empire. It brought together representatives of a Provisional Consultative Assembly that had been convened in Algiers the previous November and colonial governors in Africa. There were no representatives from Indo-China, which was under Japanese control, and only one black man, namely Félix Eboué, the governor of Chad who had come over to de Gaulle in 1940. De Gaulle told the delegates that France, 'plunged into crisis by a temporary defeat, found help and a point of departure for its liberation in its overseas territories, so that there is now a definitive link between the metropolis and the Empire'. The outcome of the conference spoke of widening citizenship but was clear about business as usual: 'the goals of the work of civilisation undertaken by France eliminate any idea of autonomy, any possibility of development outside the French imperial bloc; there can be no question even of a distant self-government in the colonies'.[79]

The restoration of grandeur was still a long way off. The goal of the Allied Supreme Command was to drive German forces back into Germany with a minimum of political complications and no political disorder in France. The US government had not excluded establishing an Allied Military Government in Occupied Territory (AMGOT), as they had in Italy. On the eve of D-Day Churchill summoned de Gaulle and told him that the French would not be taking part in the Normandy landings. When the general protested, Churchill said that these were Roosevelt's orders. He added that if he had to choose between Roosevelt and de Gaulle he would always choose Roosevelt, and if he had to choose between Europe and the wider world he would always choose the wider world.[80] These words would come back to haunt the British government fewer than twenty years later.

General Leclerc's 2nd Armoured Division did not land on the Normandy coast until 1 August, while the French B Army, amalgamating the Free French and Vichy's Army of Africa, landed in Provence as part of Operation Dragoon on 15 August. African colonial troops were so prominent that Churchill quipped that the divisions involved were 'three American and four Frog blackamoors'.[81] Whether these colonial forces could be deployed in Europe was a matter for deep discussion. General Leclerc had asked de Gaulle in August 1943 for 'white reinforcements to replace the blacks who are unsuitable for war in Europe'.[82] After the liberation of Paris in August 1944, and as the French Army pressed towards the German frontier, most colonial troops were disbanded by a process of so-called *blanchiment* or 'whitening'. The excuse given was that they would not survive the winter on the Franco-German border and that there was not enough equipment to go round; the reality was that they challenged racial hierarchies in Europe itself. Black troops were replaced by fresh troops drawn from resistance fighters of the Forces Françaises de l'Intérieure (FFIs) and corralled in camps in the south of France or Brittany, awaiting repatriation to West Africa. They were deprived of uniforms, blankets and pay and generally treated as inferiors restored to the bottom of the colonial hierarchy. Mutinies broke out, most famously at Thiaroye near Dakar, where loyal Senegalese troops on French orders opened fire on the mutineers, killing thirty-five.[83] This massacre has often been seen as a founding moment of African nationalism. 'You did not die in vain', wrote Léopold Sédar Senghor, who had fought with the *Tirailleurs* and been a POW in 1940, 'You are the witnesses of immortal Africa, you are the witnesses of tomorrow's new world.'[84]

## Dilemma in the United Nations

As the Allied forces drove into Germany in the spring of 1945, the debate about the relative merits of the equal rights of all nations and the historic claims of colonial powers was moved to an entirely different setting, the founding conference of the United Nations in San Francisco. Between April and June 1945, 282 delegates met and heard the voices of many subject peoples demanding equality and self-determination. W. E. B. Du Bois, veteran leader of the National Association for the Advancement of Coloured People (NAACP), had warned that the 'tentative plan for world government designed especially to curb aggression' might also 'preserve imperial power, and even extend and fortify it'.[85] In San Francisco he denounced 'the colonial system of government' as 'undemocratic, socially dangerous and a main cause of wars' and rallied support from countries such as Haiti, Liberia, Ethiopia and Egypt.[86] The Philippines delegation demanded a voice for the thousands of the colonised who did not have a voice and independence for colonised countries.

The colonial powers, however, had absolutely no will to open the door to worldwide self-government. The British delegate, Robert Gascoyne-Cecil, Viscount Cranborne, educated at Eton and Christ Church, Oxford, nicknamed 'Bobetty', saw no reason to depart from the time-honoured script. He argued that the world was divided into 'peoples of different races, peoples of different religions and peoples of different stages of civilization'. Colonial powers had 'a duty to train and educate the indigenous peoples to govern themselves', but as yet they were 'non self-governing peoples' with a long way to go.[87] League of Nations mandates were renamed trusteeships, but this category was designed for the colonies of the defeated Axis powers; in those areas, Great Britain, France, Belgium and the Netherlands, together with South Africa, Australia and New Zealand, were to act as trustees. The French delegate, resistance leader and Foreign Minister Georges Bidault, firmly rejected the idea that Vietnam might become a trusteeship.

The death of Roosevelt on 12 April 1945 and the succession of Harry Truman brought about a change of opinion in Washington. Truman was concerned mainly about the growth of Soviet power and saw the British and French Empires as important counterweights. This change of opinion fed through to the United Nations Charter, published on 26 June 1945. Its Chapter 11 established the principle of non-self-governing territories, but spoke of 'their progressive development towards self-government or independence as may be appropriate to the particular circumstances of each territory and its peoples' (article 76). This permitted the postponement of independence until that 'development' was assured. Meanwhile, article 80 endorsed the established claims of colonial powers: 'nothing in this Chapter shall be construed in or of itself to alter in any manner the rights whatsoever of any states or any peoples or the terms of existing international instruments to which Members of the United Nations may respectively be parties'. Self-government in the colonies was for another day.

## Empire by Force of Arms

One of the ironies of French history in 1944 and 1945 is that the rhetoric of liberation applied to the metropolis did not transfer to the Empire. This is because liberation was a means to re-establish French greatness, not an end in itself. On 25 May 1945 Gaston Monnerville, a black lawyer and deputy from French Guyana, who was perfectly assimilated into the French system, told the French Provisional Consultative Assembly, which had transferred to Paris, 'Without the Empire, France would not be a liberated country'; 'Thanks to her Empire, France is a victorious country.'[88] This tension had led to disastrous results in Algeria less than three weeks before, on 8 May 1945. As French crowds in the metropolis and Algeria celebrated the victory of democracy against Nazism, Algerian nationalists protested against the imprisonment of Messali Hadj, leader of the clandestine Algerian Popular Party (PPA), and demanded an end to colonialism. At Sétif the Algerian flag was flown. Clashes with police became riots and then an insurrection during which 103 Europeans were killed. In turn French repression killed between 6,000 and 8,000 Algerians, although the PPA claimed 30–45,000 martyrs.[89] Far from seeing this as a legitimate demand for Algerian liberation, the French authorities treated it as dangerous disorder, while the Communist Party, seeking to preserve the discourse of Resistance on the French side, denounced a fascist plot and blamed 'troublesome elements of Hitlerian inspiration'.[90] Messali Hadj wrote to the American president to say that 'the fundamental evil from which the Algerian people suffer is colonialism' and the massacre at Sétif became a founding moment for Algerian nationalism.[91]

This desperate attempt to recover or reassert empire was repeated in other regions. In the same month of May 1945 Senegalese troops were landed in Syria from the cruiser *Richelieu* and when the Syrians refused to concede French paramountcy the French shelled Damascus between 29 and 31 May 1945, killing 800 Syrians. Hypocritically, the British denounced this 'reign of terror' and intervened, driving the French back to barracks. In the Provisional Consultative Assembly Foreign Minister Georges Bidault declared that 'justice is the only issue, honour is at stake and the *patrie* is our passion'. Opposing him was Pierre Cot, a charismatic leader on the French Left. He argued that:

To refuse to deal with the Syrian, Lebanese or Arab peoples as equals, to hold on to old privileges and old ways at any price, is the politics of the past. The politics of the future, on the other hand, is that which champions the independence of peoples still subjected to colonial or semi-colonial regimes and acts as a fraternal guide on their path to liberty.[92]

On this occasion, Cot's argument carried the day, and no credits were forthcoming to keep France in Syria. The 'politics of the past', however, were far from over. De Gaulle, who had served in Syria–Lebanon in 1929–31, regretted that the opposition 'did not say a word about the work of civilisation undertaken by France in Syria and Lebanon, the efforts of our soldiers who helped to free them from the yoke of the Ottoman Empire in the First World War and helped to protect them from Hitler's domination in the second'.[93] The French had far from given up on Syria.

While scolding the French, the British took the opportunity to strengthen their position in the Middle East. 'The Middle East is a region of vital consequence for Britain and the British Empire' concluded the British Cabinet's Palestine Committee, chaired by Herbert Morrison, on 8 September 1945. 'It forms the point in the system of communication by land, sea and air which links Britain with India, Australia and the Far East; it is also the Empire's main reservoir of oil. The attitude of the Arab states to any decision is a matter of first importance. Unfortunately the future of Palestine bulks large in all Arab eyes.'[94] In their Palestine mandate the British tried to limit the influx of Jewish refugees in order to minimise provoking Palestinian Arabs. This uneasy balance was upset by the Holocaust. In 1945 David Ben Gurion toured former concentration camps and told survivors in a Bavarian hospital, 'a vibrant Jewish Palestine exists and that even if its gates are locked the Yishuv [settlement] will break them open with its strong hands'.[95] The British remained obstinate, and two Zionist resistance organisations, the Haganah and Irgun, launched attacks on British railways, oil refineries and other installations in Palestine on 31 October 1945 in a bid to force them to rethink the virtues of a Jewish Palestine.[96]

In the Far East the position of France was at a nadir. The Japanese, feeling less secure after the fall of Vichy in France, with the American recapture of the Philippines in December 1943 and facing US bombing raids as far as Saigon, decided to round up the French authorities and remaining military in Vietnam on 6 March 1945, taking direct control. French Vietnam with its 20,000 settlers was not only discredited but destroyed. In a somewhat fanciful way, de Gaulle's government issued a declaration on 25 March 1945, announcing that when France did returned to Indo-China the five countries of Tonkin, Annam, Cochin-China, Laos and Cambodia would be joined in an Indochinese federation within the French Empire under a French governor-general. On 15 June 1945 de Gaulle persuaded General Leclerc to lead an expeditionary force to recover Indo-China, but this took months to arrive.

The balance of forces was completely transformed by the atomic bomb attacks on Hiroshima and Nagasaki and the capitulation of Japan on 15 August 1945. The communist-led League for the Independence of Vietnam or Vietminh under Ho Chi Minh emerged from the shadows to seize Hanoi on 22 August and Saigon on 25 August. He invited Emperor Bao Dai to abdicate, and on 2 September 1945 proclaimed a democratic Vietnamese republic and its independence. The American Declaration of Independence of 1776 and the French Declaration of the Rights of Man of 1789 were quoted in an attempt to win the Americans over to Vietnamese claims to self-government and to expose the contradiction between French revolutionary principles and colonial practices. 'They have built more prisons than schools', Ho taunted. 'They have mercilessly slain our patriots; they have drowned our uprisings in rivers of blood.'[97]

As the Vietnamese began to attack French settlers, the French themselves were dependent on the British Army to hold the fort until the arrival of Leclerc. General Douglas Gracey of the Indian Army and a veteran of the Burma campaign arrived on 13 September 1945 with troops from India, Burma and Malaya, which had just been recaptured, to take the Japanese surrender. The tricolour was raised in Saigon and French settlers went on the rampage against the Vietnamese, while French and British soldiers looked on.[98] General Leclerc finally arrived on 5 October 1945 and began to organise French forces for a push into North Vietnam, and also into Cambodia and Laos.

In 1940–2 the European colonial empires were all but defeated. The humiliation of white supremacy and the rhetoric of resistance and liberation from Nazi power encouraged colonial peoples to seek their own liberation. They were supported in this by the United States proclaiming the 'end of empire' and the United Nations defending the equal right of all countries to self-government. The beleaguered empires, however, were reluctant to abandon the territories that were the foundation of great power status, and which had contributed to their victory over the Axis. In 1945 they were therefore blind and deaf to claims to independence of subject peoples they had once governed and were prepared to use massive force to impose their will. These violent attempts to recover empire by colonial powers, as if nothing had happened, only set up problems for the future.

# 3 THE IMPERIALISM OF DECOLONISATION

After 1945 Britain and France faced a dilemma. Exhausted after six years of war, deeply in debt to the United States and other countries, confronted by rising demands for self-government and independence in their empires, and shaken by the United Nations' declarations on the equality of all nations, they might have been forgiven for recognising that the age of imperialism was indeed over and jettisoning their colonies. The difficult challenge of decolonisation would be embarked upon. Europe, emerging from the same six years of war, tyranny and devastation, could now be seen as the arena in which former allies and former enemies could build peace and prosperity.

Many other factors, however, mitigated against such choices. The loss of some colonies did not necessarily serve as a model for losing others. On the contrary, the pain of losing some colonies intensified the desire to hold fast to what remained. Britain's loss of India, the jewel in the crown, in 1947, increased the need to develop its influence in the Middle East and eastern and southern Africa. France's loss of Indo-China in 1954 made it imperative to preserve Algeria, even at the cost of another six-year war. Threats of Arab nationalism to their strategic positions in the Middle East and North Africa and the spectre of the Munich agreement prompted France and Britain, together with the new colonial state of Israel, to intervene militarily in Suez in 1956. Other factors too favoured imperialism rather than decolonisation. The colonies were a source of foodstuffs and raw materials that could sustain the mother countries and help build their postwar economies. European settler communities, especially in Algeria and eastern and southern Africa, put intense pressure on the metropolis to defend their vested interests vis-à-vis the indigenous Algerian or African population. Lastly, in a new Cold War order dominated by the United States and the Soviet Union, empires underpinned the great power status of Britain and France and kept them as serious players on the world stage. All this had a serious impact on the European project but here France and Britain behaved very differently. While France put itself at the heart of the new Europe, Britain feared loosening its ties with the Commonwealth and remained outside the negotiations that founded the new Europe.

Returning by sea from America on 21 September 1945, John Maynard Keynes concluded that 'we cannot police half the world at our own expense when we have already gone into pawn for the other half'.[1] Britain not only owed $153 billion to the United States but $3 billion to India and Egypt for the cost of defending them. Six months later, in March 1946, Indian Congress leader Jawaharlal Nehru published an article in the New York Times Magazine announcing that 'the whole system known as colonialism must go'. There was, he said, 'a passion and hunger for freedom, equality and better living conditions which consume millions of people in Asia and Africa'.[2] West Indian journalist George Padmore and Gold Coast activist Kwame Nkrumah organised the 5th Pan-African conference in Manchester in October 1945 which defined a Gandhian strategy of non-violent socialist revolution in Africa.[3] In Tangiers, on 10 April 1947, Sultan Mohammed V of Morocco, who had hosted a meeting of Churchill, Roosevelt and French leaders de Gaulle and Giraud in Casablanca in 1943, gave a speech in which he stated, 'Morocco took an active part in the last war through its sons and all the means at its disposal, until the final victory.' As a result, he asserted, 'Morocco ardently desires to recover its full rights [...] the Arab peoples form a single nation; whether they are in Tangier or Damascus they are one.'[4]

Britain and France were obliged to rethink their relationship with their empires. Abandoning them wholesale at this stage, however, was not an option. Rationalisation was attempted: some regions were slated for progress towards independence, while others were to be held on to at all costs. Greater autonomy was conferred in a new architecture of governance, but the metropolis and settler populations retained the upper hand. Economic development was undertaken, but the aim was always to supply the metropolis with what it needed, not to provide

competition. The result in the immediate postwar years was less decolonisation than what has been called a 'second colonial occupation', 'the
imperialism of decolonisation' or, in the case of Britain, 'the fourth
British empire'.[5]

## The British Empire: Letting Go and Clinging On

The so-called white settler Dominions were still at the heart of
the British Empire/Commonwealth, although the dynamics between
them were changing. Canada, which had been known as the 'arsenal
of empire' during the Second World War, was expressing a degree of
'Dominion nationalism' and moving close to the United States in economic and defence terms. It passed its own citizenship act in 1946, to
which the British were forced to respond with a British Nationality Act
in 1948, to ensure that British citizens in Canada would remain British
subjects in the United Kingdom and elsewhere in the Commonwealth.[6]
In South Africa, Smuts' South Africa Party was swept aside in May 1948
by the Purified Nationalist Party, who saw it as their God-given mission
to take power for the Afrikaners. Relations with Britain became cooler,
and one response to this was to combine Southern and Northern
Rhodesia and Nyasaland in a Central African Federation in 1953 as
a 'Central African Australia', dynamic, stable and '100% British'.[7]

In Australia and New Zealand, by contrast, ties with the United
Kingdom strengthened after the war. In order to power their economic
growth they continued to prefer 'British stock' in preference to migrants
from southern or eastern Europe or the Third World. Australian
Immigration Minister Harold Holt planned to bring in 100,000
migrants a year from 1950 under an Assisted Passage Scheme, of
whom half would be British. By 1961 the journey had been made by
over 360,000 British migrants, known as 'Ten Pound Poms'.[8] Trade
with the Dominions was also privileged: in 1950 Britain still supplied
50 per cent of Australia's imports and 60 per cent of New Zealand's,
while these countries with South Africa and Canada provided
20 per cent of Britain's imports and the London capital market was
still central to their economies.[9] The Dominions were still very much
part of Britain's defence system. South Africa provided the naval port of
Simonstown, Australian and New Zealand forces were used to defend
Malaya and Suez, and Australia became a testing ground for the United
Kingdom's infant nuclear deterrent. Britannic nationalism and the idea

of Greater Britain was still a force. Robert Menzies, known as 'the last of the Queen's men', who returned to power in Australia in 1949 said that 'the boundaries of Great Britain are not on the Kentish Coast but at Cape York [Queensland] and Invercargill [New Zealand]'.[10]

While the white Dominions were held on to, India, the jewel in the crown, was relinquished with regret – and much bloodshed. The Cabinet mission under Sir Stafford Cripps – sent to India by Churchill in 1942 but unable to find a solution – was sent back by the newly elected Attlee government and arrived in New Delhi on 24 March 1946. Its ambition was to found a United States of India with foreign policy and defence through the Indian Army still in the hands of the British, while Hindu and Muslim states would enjoy states' rights.[11] This was not possible. The Congress Party insisted on full independence and had demonstrated its legitimacy in provincial elections held in 1945 and 1946. The British policy of divide and rule that had encouraged Muslim politics since the 1930s had another effect. Congress did poorly in Muslim-majority provinces such as Bengal, where Jinnah's Muslim League was returned to power. The Muslim League boycotted elections to the Constituent Assembly and agitated for the establishment of a separate Pakistan. The Hindu minority of Bengal feared subordination to the Muslim majority and also pressed for partition, so that they could remain part of a Hindu-majority India.[12]

Attlee decided to cut the Gordian knot. Earl Mountbatten, who had been Supreme Allied Commander in South-East Asia, was sent out as the last viceroy in March 1947 with full powers to negotiate a British withdrawal. This should not, in the words of historian John Darwin, appear to be a 'scuttle', an 'inglorious retreat' or a 'first step in the dissolution of empire' but as 'a voluntary transfer of power to a democratic government'.[13] Brigadier Enoch Powell, who served in India during the war, feared 'an outbreak of violence in India such as will dwarf 1857'. He is said to have burst into Churchill's office in 1946 and offered to reconquer the Raj if he were given ten divisions.[14] On the question of violence Powell was not far from the mark. Government was suddenly devolved to India and Pakistan and the Punjab and Bengal were partitioned. About a million people died as a result of communal violence and ethnic cleansing. Over a million Muslims fled from East to West Punjab and another million non-Muslims fled from West to East Punjab.[15] Similarly, over a million Hindus fled from East Bengal and

1.5 million Muslims fled from West Bengal. Muslims accounted for a third of the population of Calcutta in 1941 but only 14 per cent in 1951.[16] In spite of this catastrophe the British worked hard to develop the myth of the peaceful transfer of power. Mountbatten later argued that the transfer took place between men of the same background. Of Nehru he said that 'having been educated at Harrow and Trinity, and having lived so many of his formative years in England, I found communication with him particularly easy and pleasant'.[17] Moreover India, despite becoming a republic, was persuaded to remain part of the Commonwealth of Nations

The loss of India increased the need for Britain to hold on to other possessions, for both strategic and economic reasons. 'Quitting India', said historian Jack Gallagher, 'has to seen in the light of the simultaneous decision to push British penetration deeper into tropical Africa and the Middle East [...] Africa would be a surrogate for India, more docile, more malleable, more pious.'[18] The threat of the atheist Soviet Union which was pushing into the Middle East as the Cold War intensified, made it all the more important to hold on to empire as an arc that stretched from South Africa round the Indian Ocean to Australia, and the key route via Suez.

'In war, Egypt would be our key position in the Middle East', the chiefs of staff told the Cabinet in January 1947, and it was 'necessary that we should hold Palestine as a screen for the defence of Egypt'.[19] Holding on to the Palestine mandate, and preserving the ideal of a bi-national state, however, did not go according to plan. Jewish paramilitary groups waged a relentless campaign against the British presence, attacking its administrative headquarters in the King David Hotel in Jerusalem on 22 July 1946. Zionist Dr Nahum Goldmann flew to Washington in August 1946 to persuade President Truman of the justice of their cause. Not least to garner the Jewish vote at home, Truman declared his support for partition and a Jewish state on Yom Kippur, 4 October 1946.[20] Attlee was furious but the British were losing the propaganda war. Scandal was caused by the flogging of a Zionist terrorist too young to hang on 27 December 1946 and by the British refusal to allow *The Exodus*, carrying Jewish refugees from France, to disembark in Haifa in July 1947, sending them back to displaced persons camps in Germany.[21] The United Nations passed a resolution on partition on 29 November 1947. This spelled the end of Palestinians' hopes for an Arab state and attacks were launched on Jewish businesses and settlements. The Jewish military replied by destroying 286 Arab villages by August 1948 and creating 750,000 Palestinian refugees. The State of Israel was proclaimed on 14 May 1948 and was recognised three days later by the United States, but the Arab League states of Egypt, Transjordan and Syria declared war on Israel. This enabled Israelis to further occupy Arab lands, massacring 250 in the Arab towns of Lydda and Ramleh on 12 July 1948. Some 750,000 Palestinians became refugees in Lebanon, Transjordan and Egypt while the Israelis increased their grasp from 56 per cent to 78 per cent of the territory of the former mandate.[22] Arguably Israel became the most recent settler colony, turning the remaining Palestinians into colonial subjects.[23]

British authority in the Middle East lay shredded and challenges to its colonial position were being mounted in West and East Africa. One of the legacies of the Second World War was the return home of conscripted African soldiers who had witnessed the fragility and brutality of the British imperial machine. They decided to press their demands on the colonial authorities. How far these held on or let go depended partly on the strategic significance of the region and partly on the presence or otherwise of white settler populations.

On 28 February 1948 Gold Coast colonial veterans who had fought in India and Burma marched to the governor-general's castle in Accra to present their grievances. They were shot at by police and three were killed. Riots broke out, in which twenty-nine more people were killed. Leaders of the newly-formed United Gold Coast Convention (UGCC) were arrested. Its general secretary was Kwame Nkumah, who had a master's degree from the University of Pennsylvania and a flair for inspiring the Africa masses – youth, veterans, farmers, workers and women stallholders. In 1949 he broke with the UGCC to found the Convention People's Party (CPP) with the demand of immediate self-government. The British authorities hoped to deal with tribal leaders who were opposed to the CPP, and offered limited constitutional concessions, while stifling the CPP. Nkrumah organised the elections of February 1951 from his prison cell, writing instructions to his liaison agents on toilet paper.[24] African-American author Richard Wright, who visited the Gold Coast in 1953, was impressed by the crowds motivated by politics plus. 'It bordered on a religion'. They greeted Nkrumah with shouts of 'Free-dom! Free-dom!'[25] The British had to accept him as prime minister and concede a fully elected assembly, in which the CPP gained majorities in successive elections. Nkrumah formally demanded independence on 3 August 1956, and this came into force on 6 March 1957.

Very different was the situation in Kenya. Strategically it was key to the Indian Ocean, and had provided thousands of troops for the King's African Rifles to fight during the Second World War. It had a powerful settler community 35,000 strong, farming tea and coffee. Their numbers had been augmented after the war by emigrants from Britain and retirees from the Raj in India. The development of plantation in the White Highlands required expropriating the African population, transforming them into little more than serfs with tiny plots of their own land. They did forced labour service on the plantations or were driven into the cities to face unemployment and homelessness. 'Europeans only' racial segregation operated in schools, restaurants and leisure facilities. The political system was undemocratic and stacked against the Africans. In the legislative assembly the 35,000 Europeans had forty representatives, while 5, 250,000 Africans had six – all nominated – as did 100,000 Asians, while 20,000 Arabs had only two representatives.[26] In any case, real power was in the hands of the colonial governor in Nairobi and the colonial secretary in London.

An opposition movement developed through the Kenya African Union (KAU) led by Jomo Kenyatta, which petitioned the Westminster Parliament in July 1953 to address the land question. But resistance was also direct, orchestrated by a rural secret society, the Mau Mau, which launched attacks on white farms. The colonial governor declared a state of emergency on 20 October 1952. The British Army did its job as best it knew how. Don McCullin, a north Londoner sent to Kenya on National Service, reflected that 'to us the Mau Mau were monster baddie Indians. As to Great Britain's right to throw its weight around on another continent, that went without question [...] My country could do no wrong.'[27] Kenyatta and the KAU were accused of masterminding the Mau Mau; he and his close allies were arrested, put on trial and convicted. Suspects were detained without trial, curfews were imposed, public meetings and the opposition press were banned and the armed forces burned villages thought to harbour terrorists. Operation Anvil in February 1954 herded 250,000 Kenyans into camps for screening in what was later called Britain's colonial gulag.[28] According to one British officer who wrote anonymously to the British press in 1955 they were giving an 'exhibition of Nazi methods' (Figure 3.1).[29]

Figure 3.1 Colonial repression: Mau Mau suspects under police guard in Nairobi, 24 April 1954.
Getty Images / Popperfoto / 79036598

Although in Britain the Mau Mau were generally portrayed as bloodthirsty terrorists, a small anti-colonial opposition nevertheless developed. Fenner Brockway, the Calcutta-born son of missionaries who had been imprisoned as a conscientious objector in the First World War, had been invited to meet Gandhi, Nehru and Jinnah in India in 1929, and was elected Labour MP for Eton and Slough in 1950. He visited Kenya that year at the invitation of Kenyatta.[30] Returning there in 1954 under the emergency he argued with the settlers and colonial administration on behalf of the Kenyans who had no voice. He was one of the founders of the Movement for Colonial Freedom, set up in April 1954, drawing on constituency Labour parties and trade unions. Tony Benn, treasurer of the movement, likened their mission to that of Chartism.[31] One of the members, Blackburn Labour MP Barbara Castle, went on her own fact-finding tour of Kenya in November 1955, financed by Hugh Cudlipp of *The Daily*

*Mirror*. She unearthed stories of suspects being flogged to death in colonial jails and was attacked in the Commons by the Colonial Secretary Lennox Boyd. She nevertheless later commented, 'The *Mirror* had done me proud and splashed my articles under headings such as "What Price Justice? Kenya land of Fear".'[32]

However bad Kenya was, it was only a pale reflection of what was going on in South Africa. After 1948 the Purified Nationalist Party dealt with what it saw as the 'swamping' of its cities by Africans by imposing apartheid, the 'separate development' of the white, Coloured (mixed race), Indian and African races. Every child was assigned a race by birth under the 1950 Population Registration Act, and these races were kept rigidly separate by the 1949 Prohibition of Mixed Marriages and the 1950 Immorality Act. Africans were cleared out of the cities in rural reserves under separate tribal administrations. They were obliged to migrate daily to the towns to work, and allowed to travel only with passes. The Bantu Education Act of 1953 ended the policy of assimilation of Africans through mission schools and instituted what was dubbed 'education for barbarism'. Black Africans had lost the vote in 1936; Indians, who had kept their voting rights in 1946, were now disfranchised along with Coloureds.[33]

Opposition was led by the African National Congress (ANC), alongside the South African Indian Congress and (Coloured) African People's Organisation (APO). Leaders of the Communist Party, banned as the Cold War became colder in 1950, joined the ANC. A Defiance Movement violating the pass laws was launched in 1952, resulting in 8,000 arrests and riots in the Eastern Cape, where 250 Africans were shot dead on 9 November 1952.[34] That same year, 3,000 delegates of the ANC, Indian Congress, APO and underground Communist Party met in a Congress of the People outside Johannesburg to adopt a Freedom Charter that declared, 'South Africa belongs to all who live in it, black or white.' Over 150 activists, including Nelson Mandela, were arrested and put on trial for treason, on the grounds that opposing apartheid was betraying the state.[35]

Opposition to apartheid in Britain was spearheaded by priests such as Canon John Collins and Trevor Huddleston, who as a missionary had witnessed the expulsion of Africans from Sophiatown in 1955. But the British government was constrained by three factors: the dominant position of the white settler population, the value of investments in and trade with South Africa, including the sale of military aircraft and ships, and the strategic importance of the naval route round the Cape. In 1951 the Conservative Commonwealth Minister told an audience in Cape Town, 'We are both great African powers.'[36] In June 1955 the British agreed to hand over its Simonstown naval base to South Africa, on condition that the Royal Navy might still use it in time of war. The sea-lanes round South Africa were deemed crucial to the defence of both Africa and the Middle East in the face of the Soviet threat.[37] For the moment, power-political considerations trumped the evils of apartheid.

## Defending the French Union

France was the country of the rights of man that had liberated itself from Nazi domination and restored the Republic. It was under great pressure from the peoples of its empire to pass on to them the liberty and equality for which they had fought in French armies. It was inevitable that its relationship with its empire would alter. And yet many factors mitigated against significant change. Metropolitan France had been liberated from its empire. This demonstrated that the existence of empire was indispensable to France's survival. The Empire enabled France to recover its rank as a great power that had been lost with such humiliation in 1940 and to negotiate with Great Britain, the United States and the Soviet Union. Charles de Gaulle, speaking in the Algerian city of Constantine in August 1946, affirmed that 'United with its overseas territories, which she opened up to civilisation, France is a great power. Without those territories, she would risk being one no longer.'[38] Algeria, the cornerstone of its African empire, was in fact considered a part of metropolitan France, ruled directly from Paris. Moreover it was home to a million European settlers, French citizens who lorded it over nine million Muslim Arabs who were not. To cede freedom and equality to that subject population would imperil their very existence, let alone their domination.

After the liberation things initially augured well for a rethink of France's relationship with its overseas possessions. The first Constituent Assembly elected in October 1945 was dominated by communists and socialists. Of the 586 deputies, 64 were elected from the colonies, although half of them by Europeans represented in separate colleges. Aimé Césaire, elected a deputy for Martinique, announced in April 1946, 'The colonial empires are going through an infinitely serious crisis. The various peoples associated with the destiny of France have also become aware of their strength, their opportunities, and of aspirations that until now have been confused.'[39] Léopold Sédar Senghor, elected deputy in Senegal, declared that 'the most important thing about the constitution of 1946 will be its recognition of the Rights of Man and the Citizen, not only of French women but also – I was going to say above all – of the men and women from overseas'.[40] A law sponsored by Lamine Guèye, mayor of Dakar and SFIO (Section Française de l'Internationale Ouvrière) deputy for Senegal, was passed on 25 April 1946, giving citizenship to all adults from France's overseas territories, including Algeria.

The draft constitution offered opportunities of greater democracy in the colonies and the possibility of their secession. However, it was rejected by the French electorate on 5 May 1946 as too radical, and on 2 June a second Constituent Assembly was elected, in which the majority shifted to the right. This was decisive. In July 1946 the colonial lobby met in an Estates General of French Colonisation and elected veteran Mayor of Lyon and radical politician Édouard Herriot as its chair. When the French Union was again debated in the Assembly, Herriot warned that if colonies like Senegal, Madagascar and Vietnam were allowed to secede, other powers would simply take them over. Neither could equal citizenship be accorded to inhabitants of the colonies. The Muslim population of Algeria had tripled or quadrupled over a century and the upshot would be catastrophic: 'France would become the colony of its former colonies.'[41] Senghor could well shout out, 'that is racism!', but the new model of the French Union was established in October 1946, with the sovereignty of the Republic and primacy of national defence trumping autonomy and the racial hierarchy of separate electoral colleges of the European settlers and indigenous populations perverting democracy. That was the extent of the rethink.

As these debates continued, on the ground, from West to East, French soldiers and administrators were busy ensuring that colonial territories that had temporarily been lost to Vichy and the Japanese were recovered for the French Republic. The surrender of Japan offered France an opportunity to reclaim its colonies and protectorates in the Far East, but it had also made possible the creation of the Democratic Republic of Vietnam. General Leclerc, arriving late in Saigon and with limited forces, was obliged to make a deal with Ho Chi Minh on 6 March 1946. The French would recognise the Vietnamese Democratic Republic as a 'free state' within an Indochinese Federation and within the French Union on the familiar US model. A union of the protectorates of Tonkin and Annam and the colony of Cochin-China would be put to a referendum. Ho Chi Minh duly went to France to have this endorsed at a conference in Fontainebleau but the French press ranted against the 'politics of abandonment' and a new Munich and the talks broke down. In Indo-China the French double-crossed the Vietnamese: they proclaimed an independent republic of Cochin-China, stalled on the referendum and went back to war. On 20 November 1946 they bombarded the port of Haiphong, through which the Vietminh were bringing military supplies, killing 6,000 people. Ho Chi Minh sent a telegram of protest to French Communist veteran Marcel Cachin, but the French Communist Party supported the ideals of the French Union and Cachin did not mention Haiphong when, as Father of the House, he made the opening speech to the new National Assembly.[42] It was left to Claude Bourdet, a resister with Combat during the war, to express his horror privately and after the event. 'For me, and for a good part of the left-wing Resistance, the Indochinese war is what opened our eyes in 1946–47. We understood that roles had reversed. It was the same Resistance, but on the other side.'[43]

In Indo-China, as the Vietminh sustained their struggle to win independence for their republic, the French appealed to the Ex-Emperor Bao Dai for an independent Vietnam within the French Union. Everything, however, was thrown into the air by Mao Tse-tung's Communists coming to power in China in 1949. Communist China recognised Ho Chi Minh's Democratic Republic of Vietnam, and supported North Korean forces which attacked South Korea. In Vietnam the French suffered a major defeat in October 1950 at Cao Bang. General de Lattre de Tassigny, who had led the First French Army into Germany in 1945, was sent out to take control of the situation. A new phase of the Cold War now completely altered the way in which anti-colonial insurgency might be seen. De Lattre was aware that for French public opinion, the war in Indo-China was 'an exhausting and painful burden', but he was also aware that it was a test of French greatness. In addition he realised that the Cold War gave France the opportunity of reimagining the war in Vietnam not as a redundant colonial war but part of a new anti-communist mission which would attract support from the Americans. 'If we fail, we will be the "sick man" of the second half of the twentieth century', he declared in March 1951. 'Besides, because we are fighting the Communist enemy in Indo-China, the campaign in East Asia has become one of the episodes in the war between the two blocs. Tonkin is one of the frontiers of liberty.'[44]

To hold on to Vietnam was always going to be a challenge for the French. Madagascar, which had finally been repossessed by the Free French, was a strategic stepping stone on the route to Vietnam. In the elections to the first Constituent Assembly three nationalist Malgaches were elected and formed the Democratic Movement for Malgache Renewal (MDRM). Three times in the Assembly they requested that Madagascar be established as a free state within the Union, and each time they were ignored.[45] Meanwhile the MDRM was spread in Madagascar by secret societies and had 300,000 members after a year. French settlers intensified a programme to drive Malgache peasants off the land and reduce them to serfdom. Over 15,000 Malgaches had served in the French armies during the war and expected some return on their fight for liberation, but they were held in French camps while awaiting repatriation. When 8,000 of them returned in August 1946 and found that colonial exploitation was even worse, they rioted.[46] On 29 March 1947 a full-scale insurrection broke out on the island. The French High Commissioner, Pierre de Chevigné, a former Free French soldier and comrade of General Leclerc, did not hesitate to defeat the insurgents by overwhelming force and torture, using French North African forces on their way to Vietnam.[47] The three Malgache deputies were deprived of their parliamentary immunity and sent for trial with twenty-nine others in Tananarive. They were sentenced to death in July 1948, although their sentences were commuted by the president of the Republic to hard labour for life and they were imprisoned in distant parts of the French Empire.[48] Estimates of the numbers of Madagascans killed vary from official figures of 11,000 to 100–200,000, the most reliable figure being 30–40,000.[49]

The way in which French high ideals about the Union degenerated into dirty dealing and extreme violence was just as stark in North Africa. In Algeria, the Democratic Union for the Algerian Manifesto (UDMA), led by Ferhat Abbas and demanding an autonomous Algerian republic within the French Union, triumphed in elections to the first Constituent Assembly. The PPA boycotted the election but Messali Hadj was released from prison in the summer of 1946 and the PPA fought the second election through a Movement for the Triumph of

Democratic Freedoms (MTLD). But no autonomy and democracy was forthcoming. Algeria remained a part of metropolitan France, governed by the Ministry of the Interior, and while nine million Muslim males were given the vote, they were also corralled into one electoral college with sixty representatives, while a million Europeans and a thin stratum of educated Algerians elected the other sixty representatives in a separate college. As if this were not bad enough, the elections of April 1948 were rigged by the socialist governor-general in order to prevent the Muslim parties from gaining more than a few seats.[50] 'The rigging disgusted Algerians with what we dared call "democracy"', said former wartime resister Claude Bourdet. 'It explained the fact that young people and many others turned towards much harsher forms of nationalism, and ultimately to armed struggle.'[51]

While Algeria was ruled from Paris, Morocco and Tunisia were protectorates in which the local ruler remained but under the thumb of a French resident-general. In Morocco the nationalist Ishqlal party persuaded Sultan Mohammed V to take a more independent stance against the French. General Juin, born in Algeria and a veteran of the Army of Africa, returned in May 1947 to take over as resident-general. He was shocked by the change in the sultan, whom he had last seen at the Casablanca conference of 1943, but who addressed a nationalist audience in the internationalised city of Tangier on 10 April 1947 in tones that seemed pan-Arabist and Islamist.[52] Juin just about kept the lid on the pot in Morocco and when he left in 1951 asked the government to appoint another hard-line general, Augustin Guillaume. In 1953 Guillaume deposed the unruly sultan and exiled him to Madagascar, provoking massive unrest.[53]

In Tunisia, the nationalist Neo Destour party was under the control of Habib Bourguiba, exiled by the French to Cairo, where he embraced Arab nationalism. In February 1945 a nationalist Tunisian front demanded 'the internal autonomy of the Tunisian nation and democracy under a constitutional monarchy'.[54] In 1947 the French resident-general put more Tunisian ministers on the ministerial council, and a Tunisian trade union movement emerged under Farhat Hached. Fenner Brockway was invited to Neo Destour's congress in March 1951, but the French government then decided to halt progress towards reform. The resident-general who arrived in January 1952 – Jean de Hautecloque, an elder cousin of General Leclerc – immediately dismissed the Tunisian ministers, cancelled the nationalists' congress and placed Bourguiba under house arrest. Farhat Hached was murdered by the French services on 5 March 1952, provoking riots across North Africa. Brockway 'felt as though he had lost a friend' and moved closer to founding the Movement for Colonial Freedom.[55]

Meanwhile France's efforts to reassert itself as an imperial power in the Far East came to nothing. Her opponents were no longer the rebels confronted by Galliéni or Lyautey in the 1880s but a practised revolutionary army with popular support and Chinese Communist backing. French officers complained that formerly loyal black or North African soldiers were being seduced by Vietminh propaganda and vanishing into the jungle. The French occupied Dien Bien Phu in the north of the country, to build up as a strategic land and air base, in November 1953. But the Vietnamese under General Giap laid siege to the town and forced 10,000 French soldiers to surrender on 7 May 1954. They turned the concept of resistance against the French themselves. 'The great Resistance War of our people', Giap later wrote, 'has eloquently substantiated a truth of our time: if a people, however weak they may be, rise up and fight resolutely for independence and peace, they have all possibilities to defeat the most cruel aggressive army of the imperialists.'[56]

Dien Bien Phu was a catastrophic military defeat for France and a massive blow to her pride as a colonial power. For many French people it revived cruel memories of the defeat of 1940: the same humiliation of the armed forces, the same rounding up of POWs (Figure 3.2), the same exodus of civilians fleeing the enemy. Marcel Bigeard, who had been a POW in 1940, escaped and joined the Army of Africa in 1943 before joining the French Resistance and serving in Indo-China as a parachutist, found himself in a Vietminh POW camp on 18 June 1954. '18 June 1954 [...] 18 June 1940. What good was General de Gaulle's call to arms? [...] Here I am, a prisoner of those little Vietnamese who we in the army thought only fit to be nurses or drivers. Whereas these men with an extraordinary morale, starting from zero in 1945 with an ideal and a mish-mash of weapons, had only one goal: to get rid of the French.'[57] Raoul Salan, who became commander-in-chief in Indo-China after the death of de Lattre de Tassigny, remembered 'the horrible exodus of several thousand people. They held on to

Figure 3.2 The French Empire humiliated: French POWs escorted by Vietminh after the defeat of Dien Bien Phu, July 1954.
Getty Images / Bettmann / 514677668

our lorries for dear life. They tried to follow us in their carts and to get onto our boats. Had we not told them that our flag would never be lowered in this land of Indochina? Had they not believed us?'[58]

In Paris, the government held responsible for the defeat was toppled on 11 June 1954. Pierre Mendès-France, a centrist politician of Jewish origin, who had escaped from a Vichy prison to join the Free French and attended the 1944 Bretton Woods conference which laid down the roots of postwar economic recovery, was invited to form a ministry. He was persuaded that France must modernise economically, socially and militarily within the framework of a new Europe and without the burden of colonial wars. From 1950 he urged France get out of the war in Indo-China and in June 1954 repeated that France must get out of this 'bloody rut'.[59] He negotiated directly with the Vietminh in Geneva and within a month, as he promised, made peace and extracted France from Indo-China, getting rid of what he called 'the enormous material burden' and 'the heavy mortgage'.[60] Mendès-France then acted swiftly to deal with the North African protectorates. On 31 July 1954, flanked by General Juin, he made a speech at Carthage granting Tunisia internal autonomy. In Morocco, he allowed the sultan deposed by the French government in 1953 to return, and independence was conceded. He suffered attacks as a capitulator and

Jewish street-trader, selling off the Empire. Yet he reacted very differently when the Front de Libération Nationale (FLN), emboldened by the success of the Vietminh, launched insurrection in Algeria on 1 November 1954. French Algeria was a red line. Mendès-France expressed this when he declared that 'compromise is not possible when it is a question of defending the domestic peace of the nation and the unity and integrity of the Republic. The departments of Algeria are part of the Republic. They have been French for a very long time and are so irrevocably.'[61]

## Reconciling Europe and Empire

It is often imagined that the process of decolonisation and the development of European integration went hand in hand. As colonies became less important, so Europe became more so. Empire was the past, Europe the future. Things were a good deal more complicated than this. In the first instance, no contradiction was felt for a long time between the possession of colonies and European integration. On the contrary, colonial power underpinned the greatness of European powers. That said, however, fear of losing sovereignty undermined the commitment to Europe both of France, which feared losing its army, and of Britain, which feared losing its empire.

Despite subsequent attempts to claim him as a British bulldog opposed to Europe, Churchill was in fact an early advocate of European union. As leader of the opposition he launched a United Europe committee in January 1947 and told a meeting of 10,000 in the Albert Hall on 14 May 1947:

> We may be sure that the cause of United Europe, in which the mother country must be the prime mover, will in no way be contrary to the sentiments which join us all together with our Dominions in the august circle of the British crown.[62]

The following year, in September 1948 British Foreign Minister Bevin met French Premier Ramadier to talk about a Western Union that would bring together the two countries and their colonial empires in Africa to constitute an economic and military third force in the face of the United States and the USSR. This was announced to Parliament by Bevin on 22 January 1948. The plan did not progress very far. As the Cold War intensified, Britain realised that it would have to stick close to the United States, which launched the Marshall Plan and encouraged the formation of an Organisation of European Economic Cooperation (OEEC) in April 1948 as a vehicle to implement it in Europe. In May 1948 Bevin failed to turn up to the Congress of Europe at The Hague, which later gave rise to the Council of Europe. Party-political reasons were in one sense to blame, since its honorary president was none other than Churchill. More important, however, was Bevin's fear of losing the sovereignty that had been so stoutly defended in the Second World War and concern that ties with the Commonwealth would be endangered. In this he was more fearful than Churchill. At a meeting with French Foreign Minister Robert Schuman and American Secretary of State Dean Acheson on 10 May 1949, Bevin pointed out 'the danger to our common policy if, through ill-informed criticism at home and abroad, the United Kingdom electorate were forced to choose between association with the Commonwealth and with Western Europe [. . .] the United Kingdom – because of its overseas connexions – could never become an entirely European country'.[63]

At that moment Schuman was planning how to deal with the problem of German revival which, during two world wars, had been based on the coal resources of the Ruhr and, when it captured them from France, the iron ore resources of Lorraine. His solution was a supranational authority, in which France, Germany and the Benelux countries were represented, to control those pooled coal and steel resources. He announced this plan at a press conference on 9 May 1950, ahead of a visit to London. The British felt that they had not been adequately consulted and remained outside the treaty which was signed in April 1951. Meanwhile the Americans were pressing hard for Germany to be rearmed and included in the North Atlantic Treaty Organization (NATO). This time it was the French who were terrified by the spectre of the Wehrmacht returning only six years after it had left French soil. Defence Minister René Pleven proposed to evade the threat through a European Defence Community (EDC) which would rearm the Germans within a European army, without rearming Germany as a country. Britain did not express concern: it was always going to command its own armies alongside the EDC. The majority of the French, however, could not be reconciled to what looked like the dissolution of its own army. Charles de Gaulle argued that NATO would make France into an American protectorate and the EDU expose her to German militarism. 'France can only be itself when it is the front rank', he wrote at the opening of his 1954 war memoirs. 'France cannot be

France without greatness.'[64] The statements of Édouard Herriot, now 82, made a different but equally powerful appeal: 'The army is the soul of the fatherland. It is because the feelings developed by the French Revolution had such depth that they were able to give the men who fought on the Marne the courage to die in conditions we must not forget.' The EDC was voted down by the National Assembly on 30 August 1954 to shouts of 'Down with the Wehrmacht' and chants of the *Marseillaise*.[65]

The European leaders returned to the drawing board and proposed a much less threatening Common Market. Ministers of the Six, including Italy, met to discuss this at Messina in Sicily in June 1955 and set up a committee under Spaak. Britain sent a representative but withdrew from the Spaak committee in November 1955. Fearing as usual a threat to its sovereignty and to economic ties with the Commonwealth, Harold Macmillan as Conservative Foreign Secretary, then Chancellor of the Exchequer, came up with an alternative which he presented in June 1956. This was the Plan G, which proposed a free trade area for all OEEC states, and free entry for all Commonwealth goods. Prime Minister Eden met his opposite number Guy Mollet in Paris on 27 September 1956. Eden said that Britain would 'like to draw close to Europe but that we must contrive to do so without losing the Commonwealth'. Mollet expressed an 'immense hope' that the United Kingdom would 'take her place in Europe and indeed lead the movement towards European unity'. Macmillan told the Conservative Party Conference on 12 October that Plan G was now government policy.[66] At this point, however, everything was thrown into the air by the Suez Crisis.

## The Suez Crisis

Between 22 and 24 October 1956 a top-level secret meeting was held at a villa in the otherwise unspectacular Paris suburb of Sèvres. The villa had been used as a safe house by French Defence Minister Maurice Bourgès-Maunory when he had been in the Resistance. With him on the French side were Foreign Minister Christian Pineau and Prime Minister Guy Mollet. On the British side was Anthony Eden's Foreign Secretary Selwyn Lloyd. Most unusual was the arrival of a delegation from Israel: Prime Minister David Ben-Gurion, Director-General of the Defence Ministry Shimon Peres and Chief of Staff

General Moshe Dayan, hero of the 1948 war. The parties signed a protocol for action on 24 October under which the Israelis would launch an attack on Egypt on 29 October and the British and French governments would issue ultimatums the following day, ordering the belligerents to cease fire. If either party rejected the ultimatums, British and French would themselves attack early on 31 October.[67]

For both France and Britain, the Suez intervention was a desperate attempt to shore up their empires. The balance of power in North Africa and the Middle East was tipped in 1952 when Gamal Abdul Nasser led a military coup that toppled the pro-British regime. In his *Philosophy of Revolution* he imagined Egypt at the intersection of three circles – the African, to which Egypt was the 'northern gateway', the Arab, and an Islamic circle stretching from the Near to the Far East. These were the energies on which he might draw in a showdown with the West.[68] He negotiated a treaty with Britain on 18 October 1954 under which the British would withdraw their forces from the Suez Canal base by 18 June 1956, although they might return if Egypt was attacked by another country. Nasser had been invited to a congress of twenty-nine Asian and African countries held at Bandung in April 1955 by Sukarno, president of Indonesia, who declared that all the countries present were united by 'the common experience, the experience of colonialism'. They did not have 'serried ranks of jet bombers' but were 1,400 billion strong and could exercise 'the Moral Violence of Nations'.[69] Nasser countered this lack by procuring weapons from the Soviet Union in September 1955, thus linking the challenges of decolonisation and the Cold War.

France's war to retain possession of Algeria had not been going well. On 20 August 1955 the FLN intensified the conflict by massacring about 120 Europeans at Philippeville in the Constantine region, to which the French Army replied by killing between 3,000 and 5,000 Algerians. A state of emergency was declared across the country. Fearing a 'Saint-Bartholomew of Europeans' the *pieds noirs* settlers began to group in self-defence militias, such as the Union Française Nord-Africain of Robert Martel and Joseph Ortiz.[70] Guy Mollet, the new socialist prime minister, visited Algiers on 6 February 1956 and was pelted with tomatoes by the settlers, who feared that he was going to make peace with the FLN.[71] He capitulated to the settlers and on 12 March 1956 asked the National Assembly for emergency powers to deal with the crisis, which were agreed upon and voted through even by the Communist Party. Soldiers called up for National Service were sent out to reinforce the professional army and, even more controversially, those who had already completed military service were recalled to the colours. Riots broke out from Le Mans to Grenoble as soldiers protested at being loaded onto trains and crowds attempted to stop trains leaving in scenes reminiscent of attempts to stop forced labour convoys to Germany leaving in 1943.[72]

The French were convinced that the FLN was being supplied and supported by Nasser. Foreign Minister Pineau declared that 'France considers it more important to defeat Colonel Nasser's enterprise than to win ten battles in Algeria', and the French began to supply Israel with arms, including Mystère jets, as another bulwark against Egypt.[73] In anticipation that Egypt might be lost, the British built up their military base on Cyprus and dealt with Greek Cypriot opposition by declaring a state of emergency on 26 November 1955, later deporting their charismatic leader Archbishop Makarios to Mombasa.[74] In the United States, President Eisenhower and Secretary of State John Foster Dulles were obsessed by the threat of Soviet expansion in the Middle East and constructed against it a so-called Northern Tier of allies including Turkey, Iraq and Pakistan. When they discovered that Nasser was receiving weapons from the Soviet Union they withdrew funding from Nasser's Aswan High Dam project. This provoked Nasser to nationalise the Canal on 26 July 1956. On the other hand the Americans had no time for colonial wars. Dulles was sent to London on 30 July with a message from Eisenhower to the British and French foreign ministers on 'the unwisdom even of contemplating military force at this point'. Pineau replied to Dulles that 'according to the most reliable intelligence services we have only a few weeks in which to save North Africa', and that this 'would then be followed by that of Black Africa'.[75]

Rather than thinking in Cold War terms, Britain and France were obsessed by the need to hold on to their colonies. They also seemed to be repeating the crises of the Second World War. They regarded humiliation by Egypt as a repetition of the humiliation of the 1938 Munich crisis, which by saving the peace appeased the dictators and handed them the opportunity for aggression.[76] The British government was also under pressure from the Suez Group set up in 1953 to defend 'Britain and Empire' and in particular its 'new Empire' in the Middle East.[77] 'The people', trumpeted *The Times* on 27 August 1956, 'still want Britain great again'.[78] The French were desperate not only to avoid Munich but to avert a defeat on the scale of 1940 that had ushered in the Vichy regime. Many of the key players on the French side, such as Bourges-Maunory and Pineau, had been involved in the French Resistance and were members of de Gaulle's elite Compagnons de la Libération.[79]

Intervention took place according to the plan devised at Sèvres. But the Suez intervention very rapidly became the Suez Crisis. The British press was divided. *The Daily Express* welcomed the action designed 'to safeguard the life of the British Empire' while *The Daily Herald* berated 'this lunatic aggression'.[80] In the House of Commons on 31 October, Labour leader Hugh Gaitskell denounced Eden's threat to reoccupy the Canal Zone as 'an act of disastrous folly whose tragic consequences we shall regret for years'.[81] On 1 November, Tony Benn told MPs that 'no country has committed as many crimes against Egypt as this country has', while Aneurin Bevan attacked 'the bankruptcy of statesmanship'.[82]

In the United Nations, at the behest of Dulles, on 31 October the Security Council called for an emergency session of the General Assembly. This was opposed by Britain and France but the General Assembly met overnight on 1–2 November. The Indian delegation led the charge behind a resolution that called for a ceasefire and for the withdrawal of all forces behind armistice lines. This was carried by 64 votes to 5, opposed by Britain, France and Israel, with the paltry support of Australia and New Zealand. On 3 November, as Anglo-French planes bombed Egyptian targets, Gaitskell accused the British government of defying a UN resolution passed by the largest ever majority, while Labour MP Dennis Healey declared that 'our action has shattered the pillars on which British policy has rested since 1945', that is, solid and secure relations with the Commonwealth and the United States. Both men called on Eden to resign.[83] On Sunday 4 November Dag Hammersskjöld, the secretary-general of the United Nations, wrote to Eden calling on Britain to end hostilities on pain of a sanctions resolution being passed against Britain and France. That afternoon, a huge demonstration for 'Law not War' took place in Trafalgar Square, organised by the Labour movement and the Movement for Colonial Freedom. Bevan harangued the crowds, saying that Eden was 'too stupid' to be prime minister and the crowds marched on Downing Street, shouting 'Eden must go!'[84] The same day the Soviet Union took advantage of the crisis to send its forces into Hungary and pro-voked a parallel crisis in the United Nations. Marshal Bulganin wrote to Eden, Mollet, Ben-Gurion and Eisenhower on 6 November threatening military action if they did not end the war in Egypt.[85] The British ambassador to the United Nations advised on 5 November that British legitimacy had been shot away: 'We are inevitably placed in the same low category as the Russians in their bombing of Budapest. I do not see how we can carry much conviction in our protests against the Russian bombing of Budapest if we are ourselves bombing Cairo.'[86] Britain duly caved in and called a ceasefire in the early hours of 7 November.

Although they were partners in the same crime, the conse-quences for Britain and France were very different. Eden survived a vote of no confidence on 8 November but then left the country. The weight of political opinion forced him to resign on 9 January 1957 and he was replaced by Harold Macmillan. In the French National Assembly on 18–20 December Guy Mollet was attacked by the Communists for not learning that 'imperialists cannot defeat peoples in revolt against colonial oppression'.[87] He riposted that the Egyptian crisis had been fomented by the Algerians and that the real issue was the Algerian War. He also declared to loud applause that appeasement was not an option. 'The weakness and indecision of the democracies', he said, 'allowed Hitler to climb, step by step, to the height of his power. France did not have the right to make the same mistake twice.'[88] He won his vote of no confidence by 372 to 213.

France and Britain also drew very different conclusions from Suez. Julian Amery of the Suez Group called it an imperial Waterloo and the list of setbacks for Britain was considerable.[89] Egypt, the northern gate to Africa, was lost, and with it the Suez route to what remained of the Empire. Nasser's reputation in the Middle East allowed him to make a brief union with Syria and to benefit from the overthrow of the pro-British regime in Iraq. Britain parted company with much of the Commonwealth, led by India, which disapproved of its action. Even Australia, which had stood by Britain in the United Nations, looked more towards the Pacific and concluded a trade deal with Japan. The General Assembly of the United Nations, in which colonial powers were now outnumbered by former colonised countries in Asia and Africa, voted a Declaration on Granting Independence to Colonial Countries and Peoples in November 1960 and now regarded Britain as 'public enemy number one'.[90] The Soviet Union tightened its grip on the East European Communist bloc and saw prospects for its influence in Africa open up. The United States filled the power vacuum left by the evaporation of Anglo-French power in the region. The Eisenhower Doctrine announced to Congress on 5 January 1957 invited any Middle East country to request economic or military assistance from the United States if they were threatened by armed aggression by another state, by which was plainly understood the Soviet Union. Denis Healey later wrote that 'Suez was a historic signal to the world that European imperialism was finished, and that the United States was the only Western power that really counted.'[91]

The French reaction was different. It had lost control of Suez in 1882 and its main concern was Algeria. No holds were now to be barred in the war waged by France to hold on to what, after all, was constitutionally part of metropolitan France and had a settler population a million strong. The victory of Nasser, seen as a grey eminence behind Algerian rebels, made the Algerian situation even more desperate. What was in the minds of the politicians and military was no longer Munich but Dien Bien Phu. Another such defeat in Algeria was beyond contemplation. Whereas the British concluded after 1956 that it must sail close to United States foreign policy, France decided the opposite: that it should be wary of a power that might dominate France and did not have its best interests at heart. Instead, France returned to the negotiations for a European Economic Community, which might in time evolve its own foreign and defence policies, and on 25 March 1957 signed the Treaty of Rome.[92]

## Apotheosis or Colonial Crime?

In January 1957 General Salan, who had been commander-in-chief in Indo-China, was given full powers to destroy the FLN. Five parachute regiments under Jacques Massu, who had fought with the Free French under Leclerc and under Salan in Indo-China, were sent into the labyrinth of the kasbah to eliminate terrorism in what became known as 'the battle of Algiers'. Hundreds of suspects were arrested and subjected to torture to reveal the names of their accomplices. 'The strength of this division', said Salan, 'was in its cohesion. All knew each other as members of the same cohort or brothers in arms in Indochina.'[93] Among the colonels was Marcel Bigeard, who had survived an FLN assassination attempt and was described by Massu as 'an animal of action' and 'the ace of his generation'.[94] Bigeard recalled that 'Every evening we sat around under the light of a few paraffin lamps, talking about Dien Bien Phu and our dead comrades, how we felt at the time. We also spoke of the present war and how we needed to win it very quickly.'[95] Bodies of suspects dropped from helicopters into the bay of Algiers became known as 'Bigeard prawns'.[96]

The brutality of the French Army in Algeria was accepted by most French people, insofar as they knew about it, as legitimate force against benighted and bloodthirsty terrorists. A minority nevertheless thought that the French were behaving like an army of occupation and now using against Algerian resisters the torture that only a decade before the Nazis had used against them. Jacques de Bollardière, who had graduated with Massu from Saint-Cyr and had been parachuted into the Ardennes in 1944 to work with the maquis, told Massu in March 1957, 'I scorn what you are doing'. Bollardière was promptly sent back to France, court-martialled and sent to a military prison.[97] Germaine Tillion, a former ethnographer and resister who had been deported to Ravensbrück, returned to Algeria in the summer of 1957 on behalf of the International Commission against the Concentration Camp Regime. 'Among the witnesses of the sufferings of this foreign people', she said, 'were some French people who had endured the same crushing experiences twenty years ago' and shared 'a friendship through torture'.[98] Denunciations of torture by the French Army grew in volume. Pierre-Henri Simon, who had spent most of the war in a German POW camp, argued that 'With their methods the Germans were little boys next to us', while the practice of reprisals was justified by the French 'in exactly the same way as the Germans justified Oradour'.[99] After Maurice Audin, a young communist assistant lecturer at the University of Algiers, was arrested by paratroopers in June 1957 and tortured to death, his prospective thesis examiner, mathematician Laurent Schwartz, and philosopher Pierre Vidal-Naquet, set up an Audin Committee to broadcast the crime and rally intellectuals around the cause.[100]

The French government carried on regardless with its war in Algeria, until it committed one massacre too many. On 8 February 1958 it ordered an air attack on Sakiet Sidi Youssef in Tunisia, from which FLN rebels were undertaking attacks on French forces in Algeria. This raid killed 75 and wounded twice as many. The government was overthrown by the National Assembly. A final withdrawal from Algeria by the decrepit Fourth Republic looked possible, but the army would have none of it. General Salan wrote to President of the Republic, René Coty, on 9 May, to say that 'the French army would unanimously feel the abandonment of this national territory as an outrage. Its reaction of despair could not be accounted for.'[101] That reaction came on 13 May 1958 when a combination of the military and *pieds noirs* seized power in Algiers to prevent this imminent 'abandonment'. Salan and Massu formed a Committee of Public Safety to restore order and called upon de Gaulle to take the reins of power in what became the Fifth Republic.

This is sometimes seen as an apotheosis, when the former Free French came together with the Army of Africa and the Algerian population in a momentary vision of what might have been a new Algeria. The so-called apotheosis, however, involved the ceremonial unveiling of Muslim women, who had long been considered governed by Islamic law and outside the pale of French citizenship, but were now going to become voting citizens for the first time. Raymond Dronne, the first soldier of General Leclerc's Second Armoured Division into liberated Paris on 24 August 1944, said it was a 'brilliant sign of reconciliation and an act of faith in France'.[102] 'Ceremonies' were organised in Algiers and other cities on 16 May 1958 in which Muslim women removed their veils, but the use of force was thinly disguised. Frantz Fanon, who had worked in a psychiatric hospital outside Algiers and witnessed the effects of torture on Algerian suspects, saw the veil as a battleground between coloniser and colonised, linked to rape and colonial domination. He wrote:

> This woman who sees without being seen frustrates the coloniser. She does not surrender, give herself, offer herself [. . .] Each veil torn away presents colonists with horizons until then obscured, and exposes Algerian flesh piece by piece [. . .] The occupier sees in each Algerian woman newly unveiled an Algerian society whose defence systems are being dislocated, opened, kicked in.[103]

It seemed for a moment that violence would save French Algeria for another day. In British Africa, on the other hand, violence ushered in the end of empire. On 3 March 1959 there were two massacres, one in Kenya, the other in Nyasaland. In the Hola internment camp in Kenya eight Mau Mau prisoners were beaten to death by their warders. In this case, news did get out and Colonial

Secretary Alan Lennox-Boyd had to explain himself before the House of Commons. He called the Mau Mau 'forest terrorists' who indulged in 'sexual and sadistic aberrations [...] murder and cannibalism'. Of the 63,000 Kenyans rounded up under the 1954 Operation Anvil, he said that only 13,000 were still interned because they were 'classed as "Z", that is not responding to rehabilitation'.[104] Against him was mobilised the Movement for Colonial Freedom and Labour MP Barbara Castle, who called for his resignation. 'We shall not lay the foundations for the multi-racial society in which we on this side believe, because we believe in the equality of men of every race and colour', she argued, unless 'we react as completely to any outrage against Africans as we would to any outrage against white men'.[105]

Also on 3 March 1959, forces of the King's African Rifles opened fire on a demonstration at Nkhata Bay, Nyasaland, killing thirty-three demonstrators. Nyasaland was part of the Central African Federation set up by the British in 1953 as a barrage against Pan-Africanism. The prime minister of the Federation was Sir Roy Welensky, the son of a Lithuanian Jewish father and Afrikaner mother. He defended the apartheid that operated because the country was 'only seventy years removed from barbarism', which was approximately when his father came to Southern Africa looking for diamonds, but had 'carried out an imperial mission it need never feel ashamed of', providing law, order and justice.[106] This regime was challenged by the African National Congress which had branches in all parts of the Federation. It was led by former railway worker Joshua Nkomo in Southern Rhodesia, teacher Kenneth Kaunda in Northern Rhodesia and medical doctor Hastings Banda in Nyasaland. After an open-air meeting on 25 January 1959 Banda was accused by the authorities of planning a massacre of whites. A state of emergency was declared, the Congress was banned and Banda was arrested. Riots broke out and the Nkhata Bay massacre followed. Outcry forced the appointment of a commission of inquiry under High Court judge Patrick Devlin. This reported in July 1959 that the so-called 'murder plot' was a fabrication that Lennox-Boyd had encouraged and that the government in Nyasland had used unnecessary and illegal force to crush discontent. Confronted by this report and the outcry over the Hola camp massacre Lennox-Boyd tendered his resignation. However, to defend the colonial service and with a general election coming up, Premier Macmillan refused to accept it.[107] These massacres proved to be a turning point in Britain's relationship with its colonies. Pressure was building up in the Commonwealth, led by Nehru and Nkrumah, for progress towards black majority rule. Following the October 1959 elections won by Macmillan's Conservatives, the new Colonial Secretary, Iain Macleod, brought the parties in Kenya to talks at Lancaster House, London. The first step was to secure agreement for a one-seat African majority on the Legislative Council. The second was to release Jomo Kenyatta from prison, allow him to take over the Kenya African National Union (KANU) and make him a minister. The third, in May 1963, was to hold free elections, which were won by KANU. Kenyatta became prime minister but his cabinet included whites and there was no mass exodus of settlers, as there were from Algeria in 1962.

The twin myths of a peaceful transfer of power by the British to former colonial authorities and of the French Empire defending itself by violence, seems clear from these narratives. All was not so simple. Ian Cobain has chronicled how in May 1961 Colonial Secretary Iain Macleod ordered that all documents that might embarrass the military, police, intelligence services and Her Majesty's Government in general, or be used 'unethically' by a post-independence government, should be kept secret. This order was developed in 1962 as Operation Legacy and in December 1963, just before independence, Kenyan files were flown back to Gatwick, while others were said to have been dumped in the sea. These 'migrated' archives were kept in Hayes and then in a purpose-built facility in Hanslope Park, but it was not until 2011, when Mau Mau victims were pursuing compensation claims in British courts, that the government admitted to the existence of 1,500 Kenya files.[108]

The fifteen years after the Second World War are often seen as founding the process of decolonisation. The liberation of Europe from Nazism became a model for the liberation of the rest of the world from colonialism. Indian and African soldiers who had fought in Allied armies returned home in the knowledge that empires were not invincible. The song of the United Nations was about the equality and self-determination of nations. France in particular, founding a new republic, had the opportunity to rethink relations with its overseas possessions. And yet precious little rethinking happened. France and Britain, having nearly lost their empires, were desperate to rebuild them.

The Dominions looked to Britain for emigrants while settler populations in Kenya, South Africa or Algeria became even more desperate to hold on to their privileges when indigenous populations took up the fight against their power and privileges. The onset of the Cold War increased the strategic value of colonies and enabled regimes to ban nationalist movements as communist. Past humiliations haunted present leaders. The urge to avoid another Munich led to Suez. The refusal to contemplate another Dien Bien Phu justified an eight-year war in Algeria. Modern thinking was going on and for many the way forward already lay in a European Community. But while France still managed to reconcile Europe and empire, Britain snubbed Europe in 1957 because it preferred the Empire. It would come to have form with this preference for empire over Europe.

# 4 NEO-COLONIALISM, NEW GLOBAL EMPIRE

On 16 September 1959 de Gaulle announced that once peace was established in Algeria the men and women of Algeria would be offered a referendum on their self-determination. Nothing was said about the special position of the settlers, whose control of the political process had been challenged by five years of war. This time, the majority would decide. His vision for France's Empire, called the French Union under the Fourth Republic, was now the French Community, a new structure in which former colonial countries would acquire autonomy in association with France.[1] A few months later, on 3 February 1960, the British Prime Minister Harold Macmillan, addressed the parliament of the Union of South Africa in Cape Town. He welcomed the fact that South Africa was part of the 'Free World' in the global struggle against communism and saluted the first African nationalism created by people from Europe. But he was also critical of apartheid and prophetic about the growth of nationalism among the African peoples. He quoted the words of Selwyn Lloyd to the United Nations the previous September, when he had said that the British 'reject the idea of any inherent superiority of one race over another. Our policy is non-racial.' In conclusion he observed that 'The wind of change is blowing through this continent and, whether we like it or not, this growth of national consciousness is a political fact.'[2]

Once again, decolonisation was at the forefront of the international agenda. Seats taken up by newly independent countries entirely changed the profile of the United Nations. The Bandung conference of 1955, dramatising the presence of the Third World, pressed for UN membership for countries such as Libya, Ceylon, Laos, Cambodia and Vietnam. Thirteen new members joined that year and twenty-three more by 1961. On 14 December 1960 a Declaration on the Granting of Independence to Colonial Countries and People in the General Assembly of the United Nations was voted by eighty-nine countries, with none against, but with Britain, France, Belgium, Spain, Portugal, the United States, South Africa and Australia abstaining. Fears that Pan-Asianism and Pan-Africanism, exploited by the USSR, might take over the United Nations put pressure on Britain and France to offer independence to their African colonies, on the understanding that they would continue to vote with them and with the Western bloc in the United Nations.[3]

There were, nevertheless, two major obstacles in the way of rapid and effective decolonisation. The first was the position of the European settler colonists, especially in French North Africa and British Central and Southern Africa. They considered themselves not as outsiders but as pioneers who had 'made' the colonies what they were over generations and were 'at home', with as much claim as those indigenous populations who were demanding independence and self-government. Their actions and their pressure had guaranteed the support of metropolitan governments and they were prepared to keep up the pressure to preserve the status quo; anything else was betrayal.

The second factor was the concern of metropolitan governments themselves to secure their strategic and economic interests. These remained as important as ever; the only question was how they might be secured. Clearly the territorial governance that had been imposed since the 'scramble for Africa' in the 1880s was no longer viable. The alternative was to revert to the model of 'informal empire' under which those interests were guaranteed by local rulers, who were kept in line by a combination of financial and military dependency. Although formally independent they looked to the former colonial power to secure their power against rivals by money and arms. This would be a new edition of the 'armed trade' which had served the European powers so well in the eighteenth and for most of the nineteenth centuries. In 1965 Kwame Nkrumah of Ghana called this new order 'neo-colonialism: the last stage of imperialism'.[4] Such an informal empire generally worked well for the Western powers until the oil crisis of 1973. The crisis shifted the balance of power from Europe and the United States to many former colonial countries, and required the more resolute elaboration of a global financial empire along the lines of Adam Smith's 'great mercantile republic' or Cain and Hopkins' 'gentlemanly capitalism'.

## Losing Algeria, Gaining *Françafrique*

What the metropolitan governments learned in short order was that the settler communities were not going to give up easily the ascendancy over colonial peoples they had so painstakingly built. In the French case it was particularly painful because they took the view that their actions with the French Army on 13 May 1958 had brought de Gaulle to power precisely in order to save French Algeria. On 4 June 1958, invested as the last prime minister of the Fourth Republic, the General stood in front of a vast crowd at the Place du Forum of Algiers, raised his arms above his head and declared, 'Je vous ai compris' (I understand you). While the European settlers wanted him to shout 'Vive l'Algérie française', he concluded with 'Vive la République! Vive la France!'[5] De Gaulle now founded the Fifth Republic, of which he became president, and had plans nurtured during twelve years in the political wilderness to make France great again. Vast oil resources had been discovered in the Algerian Sahara in 1956 and it was in the Algerian Sahara that in February 1960 the French first tested their nuclear weapon. De Gaulle came to Constantine on 3 October 1958 to launch a plan to develop Algeria through industrial and infrastructural development, rural land reform and education. On the military front three million rural inhabitants were herded into settlement camps under military supervision, to prevent them supporting rebels, while General Challe undertook a combing of the maquis from west to east to flush the rebels out.[6]

The problem for the new Fifth Republic was that the international situation was changing. The UN General Assembly was due to call for Algerian independence on 15 September 1959. The United States feared that France would find itself in a war with the whole of North Africa, whose nationalists would be supported by the Soviet Union. President Eisenhower flew to Paris for talks with de Gaulle on 3 September 1959.[7] Two weeks later de Gaulle made his speech offering a referendum on the self-determination of Algeria. However, he had another plan up his sleeve in order to protect France's interests in Africa, a model that was subsequently dubbed *Françafrique*.

De Gaulle's promise of a referendum sent a shock wave through the French settlers and the French Army in Algeria. 'That day', recalled Jean-Marie Le Pen, then a young right-wing deputy, 'the partisans of French Algeria began their movement of refusal and resistance'.[8] Right-wing settlers' leaders worked closely with the French Army of Africa, which was commanded mainly by generals such as Salan, Jouhaud, Challe and Zeller, who had remained loyal to Vichy against de Gaulle in 1940, and remained suspicious of him, but also by generals like Massu, who had joined the Free French but were hardened by years of war against the FLN. On 24 January 1960, when Massu was recalled to Paris for criticising de Gaulle's policy in a German newspaper, the settlers threw up barricades in the streets of Algiers and fought pitched battles with the authorities for a week.[9]

The question of the principle of self-determination in Algeria was put to the voters of both France and Algeria on 8 January 1961. In metropolitan France, 75 per cent of voters approved of self-determination, while the Algerians were divided 70 per cent for and 30 per cent against. The settler population obviously voted against and looked to their allies in the Army of Africa to resolve the question by force. Generals Salan, Jouhaud, Challe and Zeller organised a putsch in Algiers on 22 April 1961. Unlike in 1958, their aim was not to bring in de Gaulle but to overthrow him. De Gaulle appeared on television in his general's uniform, asserting his role as commander-in-chief, denouncing the 'handful of generals' who had launched this *'pronunciamiento'* and calling on the military not to follow them. The putsch collapsed after only a few days, but opposition to the French strategy of abandonment was continued by the Organisation de l'Armée Secrète (OAS), for which Salan and Jouhaud provided military leadership.[10] The OAS had wide support among the *pieds noirs* population, which it called out for saucepan-banging rallies, cars honking 'Al-gé-rie fran-çaise' and strike action.[11]

In its last pulsating phases the Algerian War was fought not only in Algeria but on the streets of French cities, especially Paris. The OAS launched bomb attacks both in Algeria and on the French mainland to provoke civil war and force the French Army to intervene to defend French Algeria, killing 2,400 people in the process. In Paris students demonstrated against the 'fascist' OAS and clashed with police. The French state used lethal force both against those protesting for peace and an Algerian Algeria and

Figure 4.1 Colonial violence in Paris: racist reaction to the Algerian demonstration of 17 October 1961.
Getty Images / Keystone-France / Gamma-Keystone / 107421806

those in revolt for a French Algeria. In Paris, the most brutal force of a colonial nature was used against Algerian immigrants who marched to the city centre on 17 October 1961 at the call of the French Federation of the FLN. They were stopped by the Paris police under Maurice Papon, a former Vichy official who had deported Jews in 1942 and in 1956–8 was regional prefect in Algeria, where he had fought the FLN. Now, in Paris, up to 300 Algerians were beaten to death and their bodies thrown into the Seine (Figure 4.1).

This was all concealed; at the time much more attention was given to a left-wing demonstration in Paris on 8 February 1962 that was attacked by police by the Charonne Metro station, killing eight communists, and to the mass protest and general strike that followed on 13 February.

Peace between the warring parties was finalised in the spa town of Evian on 19 March 1962. *Pieds noirs* who continued to claim betrayal were no longer supported by the French Army which now turned on its own citizens. In the rue d'Isly in Algiers on 26 March 80 settlers were killed and 200 injured. They became martyrs to a lost cause which gouged a trench of hatred between the *pieds noirs* and de Gaulle.[12] Generals Jouhaud and Salan were arrested and court-martialled; Salan was given a life sentence and Jouhaud was sentenced to death. *Pieds noirs* women gathered in church to pray for his pardon and his death sentence was in fact commuted.[13] A final flourish came with an attempt to assassinate General de Gaulle on 22 August 1962. Its perpetrator, 35-year-old lieutenant-colonel Jean Bastien-Thiry, was not pardoned by de Gaulle for this treason and was executed by firing squad on 11 March 1963.

Algeria had been lost after eight bloody years of war. French forces killed about 150,000 rebels and lost 24,000 men, including *harkis* or Muslim auxiliaries. The FLN killed 2,800 Europeans and 16,400 Muslims. Between 75,000 and 100,000 *harkis* were massacred as traitors in Algeria. This did not mean that France was going to let go of her African Empire. On the contrary, she was going to fight to preserve it and by foul means if necessary.

Meanwhile the new framework for the French Empire – the French Community – came into force. French colonies were consulted by referendum on 28 September 1958 about whether they wished to be members. The only country to vote 'no' and claim full independence was Guinea, whose nationalist leader Sékou Touré, had told de Gaulle when he had visited Conakry a month earlier, 'We would rather have freedom in poverty than richness in slavery.'[14] De Gaulle reacted badly and threatened to starve them of trade and credit, so that they would not become an example. In the event, even those countries who voted 'yes', such as Madagascar and French Sudan, now Mali, gained independence within the Community in 1960 and the Community faded like the Cheshire cat's smile.

Behind that smile, however, the French were busy developing *Françafrique* as they wanted it. The system was organised not by the Ministry of 'Cooperation', which replaced the Colonial Ministry, nor by the Quai d'Orsay, but by the Secretary-General of African and Malagasy Affairs, Jacques Foccart, who had an office in the Élysée Palace and met daily with General de Gaulle. Nicknamed 'Monsieur Afrique', he recalled that when he was offered the post de Gaulle had said, 'France has lost Indochina and that is that. Our situation in Algeria has been ruined by too many mistakes, too much blood and suffering. There remains Black Africa where decolonisation is in train but must be a success, maintaining friendship and guiding the people in those countries. That will be your job.'[15] He understood too that Africa was a pillar of de Gaulle's policy of grandeur and must be defended from the incursions of other countries. According to Jean-Marie Soutou, who was in charge of African affairs at the Quai d'Orsay, Foccart played on 'the enduring effect of the Fashoda syndrome, which determined reactions to the British and a sort of paranoia about Anglo-Saxons in Africa'.[16]

Foccart ran his own network of spies, agents and hit men. His people were in all the right places, whether missions to African countries, embassies or oil companies. Former colonial officials 'advised' government departments in the new states. The French oil company Elf-Aquitaine was a strong arm of *Françafrique*. Foccart had close personal relations with all African leaders in the French sphere, and operated through cronyism, bribery and bullying. Leaders who supported French interests were rewarded and their families likewise. Those who were seen as unreliable were denounced as 'communist' or 'terrorist', removed in short order and replaced by someone more pliable. More than one attempt was made by Foccart's agents to kill Sékou Touré in 1960.[17]

A prime example of how the Foccart system operated was in French Cameroon. A Union of Cameroon Populations (UPC) had been set up in 1948, based on trade unions, farmers' associations and village communities, led by a low-grade civil servant Ruben Um Nyobé. When it demanded independence in 1955 it was immediately banned by the French government. A Cameroon National Liberation Army (AFLK) was formed which launched a guerrilla war on the French. In response the French sent in forces under Lieutenant-Colonel Jean-Marie Lamberton, who deported villagers to internment camps, tortured rebels and threw them over waterfalls. Ruben Um Nyobé was murdered on 13 September 1958. This opened the way to independence under Ahmadou Ahidjo, dubbed the 'African Pétain', who was prepared to accept independence under the terms demanded by the French – control of foreign policy, defence, police and justice, finances and economic resources. AFLK rebels continued the fight but the French replied savagely, not least with bombing raids, leaving 20,000 dead. Because there were no conscripts from France who could write home, as in Algeria, the news blackout on the atrocities perpetrated was total. UPC leader Félix Moumié fled abroad but was assassinated by a French agent in Geneva on 13 October 1960. A month later the 'cooperation agreement' which gave France full powers of tutelage was signed in the Cameroon capital, Yaoundé.[18]

Figure 4.2 The brutality of colonial supremacy: the Sharpeville massacre,
21 March 1960.
Getty Images / Universal History Archive /UIG / 513686235

## Leaving Southern Africa, Recovering Informal Empire

Just as de Gaulle's speech of 16 September 1959 had set the cat
among the French settlers and the military in Algeria, so Macmillan's
'wind of change' challenged the South African Prime Minister Hendrik
Verwoerd and the Afrikaners. Verwoerd declared that South Africa
was a bulwark against international communism and that the
Afrikaner mission was grounded in Christianity. He also declared
that they were Europeans only in the sense that they were white.
'We call ourselves Europeans. But actually, we represent the white
men of Africa. They are the people, not only in the Union, but throughout major portions of Africa, who brought civilization here [...] And
particularly we, in this Southern-most portion of Africa, have such
a stake here that this is our only motherland. We have nowhere else to
go.'[19]

The apartheid regime was prepared to defend itself by force.
Six weeks later, on 21 March 1960, the Pan-Africanist Congress
(PAC), as if responding to recognition of the legitimacy of African
nationalism, decided that the time was ripe to overwhelm apartheid
by a campaign of massive non-collaboration. They marched without
passes on police stations in Sharpeville, a township outside
Johannesburg, and invited arrest, with the aim of triggering further
protest. They were met by police gunfire and sixty-nine protesters
were killed (Figure 4.2). Further protest marches and strikes took

place from Cape Town to Durban. The South African government declared a state of emergency, banned the ANC and PAC, and arrested 2,000 African political leaders.[20]

There was an international outcry. United Nations Security Council resolution 134 on 1 April 1960 condemned the killings and called upon South Africa to abolish apartheid. On 14 December 1960 the UN General Assembly resolved that 'all peoples have the right to self-determination' and that 'all armed action or repressive measures of all kinds directed against dependent peoples shall cease'. In Britain a movement to boycott South African goods that developed in 1959, as a direct result of Sharpeville, became the anti-apartheid movement. On 27 March 1960 a rally of 15,000 people in Trafalgar Square wearing black sashes and badges marched on South Africa House, demanding its expulsion from the Commonwealth.[21] In the face of international opprobrium, and to shut down pressure for majority rule, the Pretoria government held a referendum on 5 October 1960 'to unite and keep South Africa white' by declaring a republic, which was carried by 52 per cent.

A crisis point was reached for Britannic nationalism. Pretoria was still keen to remain in the Commonwealth but a meeting of the Commonwealth nations in London in March 1961 was dominated by the newly independent Asian and African countries, whose representatives threatened to walk out if South Africa was not expelled. Whether the Commonwealth remained a club of the white dominions or a multiracial forum was at stake. Australia and New Zealand supported South Africa. Australian Prime Minister Menzies declared himself 'very unhappy' when South Africa was asked to withdraw and later wrote to Macmillan, 'I ask myself what benefit we of the Crown Commonwealth derive from having a somewhat tenuous association with a cluster of republics, some of which like Ghana are more spiritually akin to Moscow than to London.'[22] On the other hand Canada's John Diefenbaker broke rank and sided with the Asian and African countries.

Out of the Commonwealth, the South African regime no longer had a brake on its policy of repression. It inaugurated what has been called 'high apartheid' or 'second wave apartheid'.[23] Between 1960 and 1982, 3.5 million Africans were tractored off white farms or driven out of townships and dumped in camps in the Bantu homelands in what may only be described as ethnic

cleansing.[24] 'In the second richest country in Africa we are reprodu-
cing the living conditions of nineteenth-century famine victims
allowed to labour under sufferance in a another country', wrote
Nadine Gordimer, 'we [...] have created encampments of people
living like the homeless refugees of Palestine, Biafra and
Vietnam'.[25] The days of non-violent opposition were over and the
banned ANC and PAC switched to armed struggle through secret
organisations respectively called the Spear of the Nation and Poqo.
Nelson Mandela visited FLN bases in Morocco in order to learn
guerrilla fighting techniques.[26] The South African authorities fought
back against what it called communism and terrorism. Mandela was
arrested in August 1962 and most of the rest of the ANC underground leadership was caught at Rivonia farm outside Johannesburg
in July 1963. At the so-called Rivonia trial in 1964 they were in
danger of hanging, but the regime was not prepared to make martyrs
of them and the accused were sent to Robben Island for life.

From the point of view of empire, it suited British capitalism
that South Africa imposed security at home and provided a welcoming
environment for trade and investment. The more liberal prime ministership of John Vorster after the assassination of Verwoerd in 1966 made it
an ideal place for multinational companies such as Citibank, Barclays,
General Motors and Ford to invest. Gold production increased in
response to rising gold prices in 1971–80 and coal production trebled in
1970–85. Investments increased after 1963 and reached a peak in
1976.[27] Harry Oppenheimer, the Oxford-educated chairman of the
Anglo-American Corporation and chair of De Beers Consolidated
Mines, was in many ways the heir of Cecil Rhodes. He controlled the
gold mines and developed into chemicals, explosives, textiles, plastics,
steel and newspapers. Anglo-American investments extended throughout Africa and income dwarfed that of many emerging African states.
He was on the board of the UK-South African Trade Association
(UKSATA), founded in 1966, which acted as a powerful lobby for
South African trade and investment.[28] The anti-apartheid movement
developed globally and campaigned for international sanctions to be
imposed on South Africa, but these did not bite until the later 1970s, and
there were always many loopholes.[29] Besides, the South African government responded to arms sanctions by building up its own arms industry
through the Armaments Development Production Company (Armscor),

set up in 1968, the better to respond to African nationalism within and outside its own borders.[30]

The settler problem for Britain was not over. It posed an enormous challenge in the Central African Federation. Desperate to avoid its own Algerian War, Britain embraced the policy of moving towards black majority rule and the construction of a black majority Commonwealth. It negotiated a new constitution for Nyasaland, which paved the way to an electoral victory for Banda's Malawi Congress Party in August 1961. Northern Rhodesia was under pressure to go the same way but Roy Welensky, president of the Federation, resisted in the name of a Britannic nationalism that Britain was in danger of betraying. He made frequent visits to London and cultivated allies in the Conservative Monday Club. He told the Institute of Directors that 'the Federation is the direct descendant of British imperialism' and quoted an 1892 speech by Cecil Rhodes which warned even then that 'there is a party of "scuttle" in England whose idea is to retire from every portion of the globe'.[31]

The white settlers of the Rhodesias were Britain's *pieds noirs*, but they were not able to exercise the same influence over the metropolis as their French opposite numbers. One factor was public opinion. 'What do I care about the fucking settlers?' exclaimed one Tory MP in private, 'Let them bloody well look after themselves!'[32] A second was the fact that Macmillan was not prepared to send in military forces or alienate the United Nations or Commonwealth. 'In Algeria the French have a million men under arms', he told Welensky in March 1962, 'and they have now suffered a humiliating defeat. It is too simple a view of history to think that you can exercise control simply by the use of power.'[33] Northern Rhodesia went the same way after a constitution was agreed and elections took place in October 1962. The Central African Federation was wound up on 31 December 1963; Nyasaland became Malawi and Northern Rhodesia became Zambia.

The last stand of white minority rule was in Southern Rhodesia. It had a distinct profile – self-governing since 1923, wealthy and with its own armed forces which had come to the aid of Britain in the Second World War. Only foreign policy was controlled by London but a governor of the Crown was resident in Salisbury. The United Nations had put South Rhodesia under pressure to concede majority rule and the British government tried to force a new constitution that provided for this in July 1961. The African opposition was stifled, its main party banned on three occasions in 1959, 1961 and 1962. The 1962 elections were won by the Rhodesian Front, representing hard-line settlers – farmers and artisans – under Ian Smith, whose family had emigrated from Scotland and who had served in the RAF during the war. He was keen to invoke Churchill to legitimate his view of the British Empire, arguing that 'he had not fought in Churchill's war, and Churchill had not had that war, to promote black majority rule of any kind of black mischief'.[34] He enjoyed considerable support among his 'kith and kin' in Great Britain, and the Monday Club hosted a London reception for him in 1964.

Ian Smith's Rhodesia Front was adamant that it would not accept independence on the basis of African majority rule. That was the sticking point. The coming to power of a Labour government in October 1964 made little difference to Britain's approach. Rhodesia was frozen out of Commonwealth meetings of heads of state and when Smith came to London for Winston Churchill's funeral on 30 January 1965 he was shown into Downing Street for talks with Harold Wilson through a side door. To break the deadlock, Smith and the Rhodesian government unilaterally declared independence (UDI) on the basis of a white majority constitution on Armistice Day, 11 November 1965. This was the last stand of the settlers, British-style. Unlike in the French scenario of 1962, there was no British involvement to support them. Neither did they send forces to bring the settlers to heel. A blockade was as far as they would go. Wilson was aware of the sympathy Smith enjoyed in some British circles. He was also aware of the strength of the Rhodesian Security Forces, which had seen action in Egypt, Burma and Malaya. Above all, he had no desire to repeat the mistakes of Suez, as *Daily Mirror* chairman Cecil King noted in his diary.[35] Wilson in fact let the cat out of the bag on 30 October 1964, twelve days before UDI, when he broadcast to the nation: 'If there are those in this country who are thinking in terms of a thunderbolt hurtling through the sky and destroying the enemy, a thunderbolt in the shape of the Royal Air Force, let me say that this thunderbolt will not be coming.'[36]

Having declared independence unilaterally, Smith's regime was thrown to the wolves. It was left to fight the rising tide of African nationalism on its own. Zimbabwean opposition movements formed guerrilla units outside the country and appealed to communist regimes in Czechoslovakia, the Soviet Union and China for help. The first attacks across the border into Rhodesia in the so-called Bush War came in March and July 1968. The Rhodesian Security Forces, African soldiers and NCOs officered by whites, were joined by French Foreign Legion forces and American and Australian Vietnam veterans fighting as mercenaries. Rhodesia also appealed for military support to South Africa, the United States and the Portuguese, who were fighting liberation movements in Angola and Mozambique. A dramatic reversal took place in 1974, when the Portuguese dictatorship was overthrown and wars of liberation reached a new intensity in Angola and Mozambique, with additional support from revolutionary Cuba. The Zimbabwe African National Liberation Army (ZANLA) under Robert Mugabe, based in Mozambique, was supported by the Chinese Communists, while the Zimbawe People's Revolutionary Army (ZIPRA) under Joshua Nkomo, based in Zambia, was backed by the Soviets.[37] About 48,000 white Rhodesians, repeatedly under attack, left the country between 1976 and 1980. Ian Smith, remaining at his post, saw himself as fighting a war that the British were now too decadent to assume. For him the Empire continued at its outposts, even if the metropolis was prepared to abandon them. 'If Churchill were alive today', he declared in September 1976, 'I believe he'd probably emigrate to Rhodesia, because I believe that all those admirable characteristics of the British we believed in, loved and preached to our children, no longer exist in Britain.'[38]

## Britain's Settler Colony: Northern Ireland

Britain may have been prepared to abandon its settlers to the forces of black nationalism in Africa. In Northern Ireland, however, it was a different matter. Ireland, even before India, had been partitioned, and Northern Ireland was given self-government within the Union under the 1921 Government of Ireland Act. The Protestant minority, many of whom were of Scottish origin, supported union with Great Britain and upheld a very Britannic nationalism, were challenged by a majority of Catholic nationalists who demanded a united Ireland. 'The hatred between colonized and colonizers', wrote young Catholic activist and politician Bernadette Devlin, 'was underlined by the difference in their religions, and the Irish were persecuted not only for being natives but on the basis of being Catholics as well.'[39] The Protestants maintained their power in town councils by a property franchise and gerrymandering. This ascendancy was defended by security forces comprising the Royal Ulster Constabulary (RUC), which was 88 per cent Protestant in 1961, and the part-time Ulster Special Constabulary or B Specials, who were exclusively Protestant. These official police forces were supplemented by and often perceived to be in league with irregular Unionist terrorists of the Ulster Volunteer Force, founded in 1965, who murdered Catholic troublemakers.[40]

This hegemony was challenged by the Catholic and nationalist community which set up a Northern Ireland Civil Rights Association, inspired by the American model, in 1967. A first march was organised from Coalisland to Dungannon on 24 August 1968 and another in Derry on 5 October 1968, which was brutally broken up by police. The initiative now shifted to People's Democracy, formed by Queen's University Belfast students, which organised a march from Belfast to Derry in January 1969, imitating the Civil Rights march from Selma to Montgomery in 1965. It was violently stopped at Burntollet Bridge by Unionist thugs and B Specials under former British officer 'Major' Ronald Bunting.

Catholic discontent grew and riots broke out in Belfast in August 1969. Claiming that a sniper was firing from the Divis Flats at the bottom of the Catholic Falls Road the RUC Army fired a machine gun from an armoured car, killing nine-year-old Patrick Rooney. The Queen's Regiment of the British Army, formed in 1966 from battalions that had seen action in Burma, Kenya and Aden, was now deployed to enforce a peace line between the Falls and Protestant Shankill Road. Tariq Ali of the International Marxist Group (IMG) was quick to see the colonial parallel: 'British troops are seen once again in action, this time not killing wogs in Aden but brutalizing Catholics in Ulster.' 'Ireland', he concluded, 'could thus turn out to be the Achilles heel of European capitalism, a Cuba in Europe'.[41]

The Catholic community in Belfast clashed with the British Army early in 1971 and riots broke out, while attacks by the Irish Republican Army (IRA) increased. The British government prorogued the Stormont parliament and introduced internment camps for suspected IRA members. On 30 January 1972, which became known as Bloody Sunday, British forces opened fire on Catholic demonstrators in Derry, killing thirteen. For Enoch Powell, Ulster Loyalists were on the front line of a war and Unionism was 'the assertion of British nationality, the claim to be part of the whole British nation'.[42] These were British *pieds noirs* which would not, as in Algeria, be sacrificed to indigenous nationalism.[43] On the other hand British rule might be described as neo-colonialist in the sense of a willingness to resort to massacre in defence of a settler minority.

## Neo-Colonialism Again: Falklands and New Caledonia

By the final third of the twentieth century it seemed clear that empire was finally at an end. The last colonial remnants were being abandoned. Building a new Europe had moved to the centre of the agenda. The Labour government of Harold Wilson determined that British troops would be withdrawn from 'east of Suez' – that is, Singapore, Malaya and the Persian Gulf – and on 30 November 1967 the Union flag was lowered in Aden, which now became the People's Republic of South Yemen.[44] The following year Foreign Office Minister Lord Chalfont travelled 8,000 miles to the Falkland Islands in the South Atlantic, Pacific, to warn the 2,000 islanders that 'keeping the Falklands British in 1968 meant something very different from what it might have meant in 1900; Britain was no longer a great nineteenth-century imperial power.'[45] The message was that the settlers would not be defended in the event of external aggression. A decade later, in December 1979, soon after Margaret Thatcher came to power, a Lancaster House Agreement brought white Rhodesia finally to an end and paved the way to the Republic of Zimbabwe.[46]

Similar developments took place in France, where for the first time in the Fifth Republic, a socialist president, François Mitterrand, and a socialist government were elected in 1981. 'Let us apply the same rule to everyone', declared Mitterrand on a visit to Mexico in October 1981, after paying homage to the heroes of the 1911 Mexican Revolution and affirming 'the same right to non-interference, the self-determination of peoples, peaceful conflict resolution, a new international order'.[47] As minister for cooperation – the new name for the minister for colonies – he appointed Jean-Pierre Cot, son of Pierre Cot, who had been a minister in the 1936 Popular Front government and a fervent partisan of decolonisation in 1945.[48] The new minister wanted to make a complete break with the neo-colonial practices of *Françafrique*. Instead of sending in French force to support local despots, he would respond directly to the demands of the Third World, propagate human rights and democracy, and deliver aid and development.[49]

These decolonising agendas, however, came up against two great obstacles: settler campaigns for protection and the importance of the metropole's economic and strategic interests. The Thatcher and Mitterrand regimes were prepared to use military might to defend both settlers and regional interests respectively in the Atlantic and the Pacific. In addition, particularly in the British case, intervention in the South Atlantic was powerfully driven by a fantasy that Britain still was an imperial power or that, if it was ceasing to be so, it must regain its former glory.

On 2 April 1982 Argentinian forces landed in the Falkland Islands. A semi-colony of Britain's for much of the nineteenth century, Argentina was now challenging British influence in the South Pacific. The British government was immediately in trouble for not having foreseen the event, and Foreign Minister Carrington resigned. Pictures of captured British marines lying face down in front of Government House in Port Stanley were published in the British press, and created a sense of national humiliation. Not since the Suez Crisis of 1956 had such a challenge to British power and international prestige been mounted. Not since Suez had Britain been confronted by the terrible decision: to intervene or not intervene. Each could be disastrous. The question of power and prestige was compounded by the question of commitment to the islanders. In 1968, after their demonstrations against Lord Chalfont's threat to abandon them and following a campaign by Conservative MPs and the popular press, it had been decided that the British would not surrender sovereignty over the islands against the wishes of the islanders. These thus became British *pieds noirs*, joined to the British people by ties of kinship and Britannic nationalism, an outpost of Greater Britain, holding the government fast to its promise not to let them go.[50]

Argentina was a country that switched on a regular basis between democracy and dictatorship, and since 1976 had been a military dictatorship. As in 1956, the analogy was made with the appeasement of dictators, a capitulation that was not going to be repeated after 1938. That is why the Second World War had been fought, and it was a sentiment that stirred much of the British Left as well as the Right. Addressing an emergency session of the House of Commons on 3 April 1982, Margaret Thatcher announced, 'We have absolutely no doubt about our sovereignty, which has been continuous since 1833. Nor do we have any doubt about the unequivocal wishes of the Falkland islanders, who are British in stock and tradition, and they want to remain British in allegiance.' Reviving the idea of Britannic nationalism in Churchillian terms, she declared that 'The people of the Falkland islands, like the people of the United Kingdom, are an island race.' Michael Foot, leader of the Labour opposition, was a longtime anti-colonial campaigner but had also written a tirade against the appeasers, *Guilty Men*, in 1940. He urged that 'foul and brutal aggression', like that of Hitler and Mussolini, had to be stopped, otherwise 'there will be a danger not only to the Falkland Islands but to people all over this dangerous planet'.[51]

During the two months of the war the press evoked and sustained a nationalism that was wider and deeper than anti-fascism. It created a fantasy of British greatness that briefly overlay a deeper sense of national decline. The Task Force that set sail for the islands was likened to the Armada and played on the myth of British naval supremacy (Figure 4.3). The sinking of the Argentinian battleship *Belgrano* was famously greeted by *The Sun* newspaper with the headline *Gotcha!* The air war was portrayed as a rerun of the Battle of Britain, with the Harrier fighter pilots the new 'Few' of 1940, while the landings at San Carlos became a new D-Day landing.[52] The home front in the Second World War was evoked in images such as Carl Giles' *Sunday Express* cartoon picturing Grandma clearing out the old air-raid shelter. Margaret Thatcher was likened to Kitchener, Nelson or Wellington, her features drawn onto Britannia, portrayed as a warrior-queen leading her people into battle against tyranny.[53] Addressing the Conservative Party conference in Brighton to eager applause on 10 October 1982 she declared that 'the spirit of the South Atlantic was the spirit of Britain at her best. It has been said that we surprised the world, that British patriotism was rediscovered in those spring days. Mr. President, It was never really lost.'[54]

While most of the country seemed delighted that there was a war on again, and one that they were likely to win, other voices, standing a little outside the fray, took the view that nationalist and imperialistic rhetoric had been dredged up in a quite anachronistic way. Historian E. P. Thompson, returning to Britain at the end of April 1982, said that it was 'like passing through a time warp into an earlier imperial age'. Ian McEwan wrote a play about an amateur historian researching Suez in the midst of the Falklands

Figure 4.3 Margaret Thatcher portrayed as a pirate in the Argentinian press, 30 April 1982.
Getty Images / SSPL / 90764586

War. He called it *The Ploughman's Lunch* because, he said, like the lunch, the hype around the war was 'a completely successful fabrication of the past'.[55]

In France, attempts to lay the colonial past to rest were also challenged. Jean-Pierre Cot's attempt to develop a Third World agenda in Paris came up squarely against the perennial methods of *Françafrique*: pursuing French economic and strategic interests with the help of local African rulers, no matter how brutal they might be. He was obliged to resign on 8 December 1982 and later reflected that 'decolonisation means not only the modernisation of French structures of cooperation but contributing to the changes hoped for by our partners in the Third World, by putting in place a new economic order'.[56]

After Cot's departure France reverted to business as usual in *Françafrique*. The former French colony of Chad was central to its strategy. Divided between an African population in the south and an Arab Muslim population in the north and east, it was vulnerable to predators such as Colonel Gaddafi of Libya, who invaded it in 1982. Cot had been reluctant to respond but after his departure Mitterrand sent in French forces to support Hissène Habré as the useful local leader. Gaddafi's forces were finally driven out in 1987, but Habré turned out to be a brutal ruler, with the bodies of 40,000 victims found after his overthrow in 1992. Meanwhile Cot's successor as minister of cooperation, the *pied noir* Christian Nucci, became involved in financial scandals. Aid money was regularly diverted to pay for arms supplies to local rulers or to finance their luxuries, but only rarely was this found out. Nucci set up a private company, the Carrefour du Développpment, to finance the perennial summit of African leaders, due to be held in Burundi in December 1984. He siphoned off large amounts of state funds not only for the summit but to entertain African leaders in the Alpine town where he was mayor, and to pay for his own election expenses.[57] This was discovered after the socialists lost power in 1986, and he was sent for trial. Far from signalling a change of course, there was a return to traditional *Françafrique* as the new right-wing government of Jacques Chirac recalled Jacques Foccart to his old post running African affairs.

As it happened, the long history of France's colonial brutality was not yet over. It was belatedly repeated in the late 1980s in its Pacific Territory of New Caledonia. Its history echoed in miniature some of the elements of the Algerian experience, but lessons learned from defeat in the Algerian War were put to good use. The New Caledonia affair may be seen as France's Falkland Islands, 10,000 miles away from the metropolis, but in this case there was no obvious rallying of national sentiment around the cause.

Seized by the French in 1853, New Caledonia was initially used as a penal colony and was the grim destination of many insurgents condemned after the Paris Commune of 1871. In the 1960s it became part of the 'nuclear colony' of French Polynesia selected for testing France's nuclear weapons. After the loss of Algeria many *pieds noirs* moved there to develop a new settler colony, taking land from the indigenous Melanesian or Kanak population and growing rich on the 1970s boom in nickel which the island produced for steel and armaments. The French state paid the wages or salary of half the Caldoches or European population of New Caledonia but, unlike in Algeria, they become the majority population, squeezing the Melanesians to only 42 per cent in 1976. As in colonial Algeria, the political system, including sending two deputies to Paris, was controlled by the Caldoches, and in 1984 Kanak activists led by the former priest Jean-Marie Tjibaou belatedly launched a national liberation movement: the Front de Libération Nationale Kanak et Socialiste (FLNKS). Rather than adopt the armed struggle of the Algerian FLN, Tjibaou was educated in the practice of non-violence by the former 1968 activists and sheep farmers of the Larzac plateau who had won a ten-year battle to prevent their expropriation by a French military base, but not all his followers agreed with him. In December 1984 a provisional government of the Kanaky Republic was declared and the next day ten militants, including two of Tjibaou's brothers, were killed by Caldoche thugs.

The other lesson learned by settlers from the Algerian case was the need to retain the support of the French government. The socialist government offered a mix of 'independence-association' on the *Françafrique* model in 1985 but this was not enough for the Kanaks and too much for the Caldoches. The formation of the Chirac government in 1986 was a boost for the settlers. Chirac and Bernard Pons, his minister for Overseas Departments and Territories sided squarely with the Caldoches and were hostile to independence. They conceded a referendum in September 1987 with only three years' residency qualifying to vote. The Kanaks boycotted the referendum as rigged and 98 per cent of the minority who did vote wanted to stick with France. After this the French came down hard on the FLNKS, which was treated as an illegal secessionist movement, while those accused of killing Tjibaou's brothers and associates were acquitted by the courts in October 1987. Marginalised and hunted, the FLNKS responded with force two days before the first round of the 1988 presidential elections, in which Chirac was running against Mitterrand. They kidnapped twenty-seven gendarmes who were held in a cave on Ouvea Island. On 6 May, two days before the second round of the presidential elections, crack French troops stormed the cave on the orders of Chirac and Foccart, killing nineteen Kanak militants while losing two of their own. This action was defended in almost Thatcherian terms by Bernard Pons as 'a matter that engaged the honour of France, the honour of the French army and the honour of the gendarmerie'. Tjibaou called Pons the 'gravedigger of the Kanak people'. In France, the Left and trade unions demonstrated in favour of independence for Kanaky and 'no to a second Algerian War'.[58]

If New Caledonia was Chirac's Falklands, his strong-arm tactics did not pay off in the same way. On 8 May 1988 he lost the presidential election to François Mitterrand, who secured a second term. The New Caledonia question was not settled in a defined way, as in the Falklands. The centre-left government of Michel Rocard negotiated an agreement in Paris between Tjibaou and the Caldoche leader, which made some concessions to the Kanaks and promised a new referendum on independence in 1998. This divided the Kanaks and Tjibaou was assassinated on 4 May 1989 by one of his own followers for allegedly selling out. Meanwhile, in 1989, the French were celebrating not nationalism or empire but the bicentenary of the French Revolution. They were taken up by internal wranglings about whether the Revolution had been a good or a bad thing. On 14 July 1989 the Communist newpaper *L'Humanité* denounced the 'savage and ruthless' bourgeoisie in the world, responsible for crushing the Paris Commune and for endless colonial wars. All eyes were nevertheless on the triumphal parade mounted in Paris by Jean-Paul Goude, culminating in the Place de la Concorde where black American singer Jessye Norman, draped in a vast tricolour flag, led the singing of the *Marseillaise*.[59]

## The Global Financial Republic: A New Imperialism?

The challenges to British and French interests from settler populations in the South Atlantic and Pacific were in many ways marginal to their global economic and strategic interests. Decolonising movements threatened those interests but in many cases the metropolitan governments were able to impose their will on developing countries through a combination of networking, bribery and military intervention. The balance of power was clearly in favour of the North.

Things did not always stay that way. The oil crisis of 1973 dramatically changed the economic balance of power between North and South. Influence shifted to the oil-producing countries. In Africa these included Algeria and Nigeria, linked to Middle East countries such as Saudi Arabia, Iran, Iraq, Kuwait, the United Arab Emirates and Libya, together with Venezuela, which exerted leverage through the Organization of Petroleum Exporting Countries (OPEC). Meanwhile, the United Nations Conference on Trade and Development

(UNCTAD), which met in New Delhi in 1968, Santiago de Chile in 1972, Nairobi in 1976 and Manila in 1979, provided a forum for developing countries to push for a 'new international economic order' in which they could become industrial and trading partners on the same level as the industrialised countries. Planning, industrialisation and import substitution successfully took place in the 1970s in countries such as Algeria, Malaysia, Thailand, Indonesia and the Philippines. The economic push was linked to a political offensive through the non-aligned movement that had been launched at the Bandung conference of 1955. In 1979 it met in Havana, where Fidel Castro had increased his Third World prestige by sending Cuban troops to Angola to defeat the dying Portuguese Empire.[60]

These challenges could not be ignored by the industrialised countries. They looked for a push-back against the developing world. What emerged was a new version of the global financial republic which reasserted its dominance of the global South not by military intervention but by exploiting its greatest asset: Third World debt. This global republic may be seen as a new form of imperialism in that it used that debt to impose controls on developing countries that were financial and economic. Multinational companies were contemporary versions of the trading companies with sovereign powers that had extended empire in the eighteenth and nineteenth centuries. Their hidden strings were much less obvious than the formal trappings of empire, but they were no less effective.

A first response was the formation in 1975 of the Group of Seven (G7) at a meeting in Rambouillet hosted by French president Giscard d'Estaing, involving the United States, Canada, the United Kingdom, France, Italy, West Germany and Japan. They were closely linked to the governing councils of the World Bank, which was designed to help countries with long-term development, and of the International Monetary Fund (IMF), which provided short-term loans to tide governments over short-term crisis. In 1976 the British Labour government, amidst economic crisis, had to go cap-in-hand to the IMF for $3.9 billion and implemented severe budget cuts. After 1980, however, the developing world plunged into crisis. Commodity prices fell, gravely affecting developing countries which relied on the export of raw materials and primary produce, making it increasingly difficult for them to repay loans. Argentina, in the aftermath of the Falklands War, had a foreign debt of $45 billion in 1983 which consumed over half its export earnings. The economies of Venezuela, Mexico, Nigeria and even Saudi Arabia were also in trouble.[61]

In October 1985 the US Treasury Secretary James Baker told an IMF meeting in Seoul that henceforth loans to debtor countries would require deep structural adjustments in the direction of the free market. The argument was that if they could not repay loans they had adopted the wrong policies and must change, whatever the local conditions. Tariffs which allowed them to push ahead with industrialisation had to go, state-owned industries had to be privatised and allow in foreign capital, public expenditure and taxes had to be cut and trade union rights had to be weakened in order to make labour more 'flexible'. This restructuring, as it happened, suited the international investors and traders of the industrialised world. This new strategy, agreed with the World Bank, became known as the 'Washington consensus'.[62]

These draconian conditions were extremely beneficial to international banks looking to invest and to multinational companies keen to massify production and export at the lowest cost. The number of multinational companies increased from 18,500 in the mid-1980s to nearly 50,000 in the mid-1990s. Among them, Walmart, BP, Royal Dutch Shell and Exxon ranked among the world's top fifty economies. The structural adjustments forced on struggling countries in Latin America, Africa and Asia allowed multinationals easy access to raw materials such as precious minerals, oil and timber. Global supply chains were established by corporations such as Nike, whose shoes were manufactured in Vietnam, Indonesia and China. The migration of labour increased from country to town and from deprived areas to new centres of production in East Asia and the Gulf. In the United Arab Emirates at the end of the century three-quarters of the population were migrants, sending back to their families at home a proportion of their pay. Meanwhile, in the period 1975–2005 about thirty million people, often women and children, were trafficked for labour from Asia and the Pacific, amounting to nothing less than the return of the slave trade. The exploitation of raw materials such as timber deforested hills and made regions more vulnerable to flooding. Rural poverty increased, especially in areas such as Latin America where land distribution was unequal and peasants were driven off the land by large landowners and business oligarchs keen to develop export crops. Low-regulation economies led to industrial disasters such as the toxic gas leak from the Union Carbide plant in Bhopal, Madhya Pradesh, India, in December 1984, killing 8,000 people within two weeks, another 8,000 subsequently and affecting over half a million people. Poverty increased, with the population living on less than a dollar a day rising from 70 million in the late 1970s to 290 million in 1998. Meanwhile, in order to avoid taxes, profits made by investors were regularly deposited in offshore bank accounts, many of which were situated in island paradises such as Bermuda that were the last remnants of the British Empire.[63]

In most cases, exploited populations were unable to fight back against this global domination. But resistance there was. Some came in the form of a rural resistance, championed by Marxist activists who were veterans of earlier national liberation struggles, and constituted the beginning of the anti-globalisation movement. The Landless Workers Movement developed in Brazil after 1984 against landlords and businesses that had displaced and now exploited them in order to grow and export coffee, sugar, soya and oranges. In the same year Rafael Sebastián Guillén Vicente, a Jesuit-educated former lecturer arrived in the southern Mexican region of Chiapas, where the local Mayan people were being driven off the land by big producers. Calling himself Subcomandante Marcos, he organised them into a Zapatista Liberation Army which went into action in 1994, occupying seven of Chiapas' main towns.[64] The uprising ended with a negotiated peace with the Mexican government. Not all rebels in similar situations were as fortunate, as the global financial empire used local rulers to impose its will, as in the heyday of informal empire.

The period from the 1960s to the 1990s thus saw a process of formal decolonisation, as Britain and France conceded independence to their former colonies. Settlers who clung on to their privileged position against the demands of indigenous revolt and independence movements were, in the end, sacrificed to the greater interest of the metropolis. Formal colonialism was replaced in the first instance by a neo-colonialism which, behind the façade of formal independence, defended and extended the strategic and economic interests of the metropole, often in alliance with multinational companies. The creation of *Françafrique* with all the fraud and brutality deemed necessary was one good example of this. The use of violence to defend French settlers and French interests in New Caledonia is another. Most of these interventions were conducted under the radar, and with no thought of legitimation. The exception was the Falklands War, where heavy news censorship coexisted with carefully orchestrated propaganda that this was a war for Greater Britain that was of no less consequence than the Second World War.

Increasingly, neo-colonialism was marginalised in favour of a global financial empire of which the United States was the senior partner. It relied less on force than on economic leverage, exploiting debt in order to impose liberal economic frameworks on developing countries that benefited the World Bank, the IMF and multinational companies. Populations in those countries became the serf labour of this new feudalism, virtually unfree labour paid miserable wages and prey to dangerous risks. If protest broke out local governments in hock to the global empire could generally be relied on to put it down. The end of the Cold War meant that even Russia became part of this neo-liberal, corporate regime. There was, however, one emerging force that could not be dealt with by financial measures alone. Resistance to the globalising West and its reinvented imperialism came after 1979 from a new source: political Islam.

# 5 COLONISING IN REVERSE AND COLONIALIST BACKLASH

Louise Bennett, a Jamaican poet, actor and broadcaster who first came to London in 1945 on a scholarship to study at the Royal Academy of Dramatic Art, neatly characterised immigration from the colonies as 'colonizin' Englan in reverse'.

> What a joyfulness, Miss Mattie
> I feel like me heart gwine burs'
> Jamaica people colonizin'
> Englan in reverse
> What a devilment a Englan!
> Dem face war an brave de worse,
> But I'm wonderin' how gwine stan'
> Colonizin' in reverse.[1]

The notion of 'colonizin' in reverse' expressed the hopes of the immigrants coming to the United Kingdom for a better life. They were arriving at the fount of imperial civilisation, under the headship of the king or queen. They were keen to work hard and improve their lot. They wished to integrate with the host community as far as possible. However, Louise Bennett also wondered how the host community was going to stand 'colonizin' in reverse'. Until then colonisation had been 'out there', in the Americas, Australasia, Africa or India. International events and the rise of nationalist movements had forced the British to withdraw. Now the peoples of those colonised regions were coming 'over here' to live and work. What was felt like a defeat in the colonies was experienced at home as an invasion. Far from being welcomed, immigrant peoples were subjected to racial prejudice, racial discrimination, even to racial violence. Those who identified as British defined themselves as superior to those from the colonies and attempted to redraw colonial hierarchies. The working class might be at the bottom of the social pile but they were certainly not at the bottom of the racial or colonial pile. The presence of immigrant peoples likewise transformed the political landscape. A defensive nationalism defined itself as a 'white man's country' against former colonial subjects whose presence, it seemed, was a reminder of the country's former imperial greatness, now compromised. 'Without a thorough working-through of the decolonization trauma', wrote historian Anna Marie Smith, 'the black immigrant becomes the postcolonial symptom [. . .] the most visible symptom of the destruction of the "British way of life"'.[2]

## From *Windrush* to 'Rivers of Blood'

Immigration into Britain was long-standing and the impact of those from the Caribbean, Africa or the Indian subcontinent took some time to be felt. In Britain, after the war, as before, the largest immigrant nationality was the Irish, 350,000 of whom came in 1946–59.[3] In the period 1946–51, most of the 460,000 foreigners who arrived in Britain were Poles who had fought in armed forces, German or Italian POWs, refugees or displaced persons from war-torn Europe. About 91,000 so-called European Voluntary Workers – mainly Ukrainians, Poles and Latvians – were recruited by the Ministry of Labour in 1946–9 to work in key sectors such as mining.[4] On 22 June 1948 the *Empire Windrush* landed 500 Jamaican passengers at Tilbury Docks, downstream of London.[5] They impressed by their colour rather than by their number and only 30,000 immigrants per year in 1955 and 1956 came from the Caribbean.

The challenge to entrenched colonial hierarchies by this immigrant majority did not, however, take long to be felt. Race riots broke out in August 1958 in Notting Hill, London and in Nottingham, in response to white women being seen with black men. 'It comes as a shock', declared the *Manchester Guardian*, 'to hear the ugly phrase, "lynch him" on English lips in an English city'.[6] Jamaican-born Stuart Hall, who was teaching at a secondary modern school in Stockwell, later said that this reflected both 'the racial violence associated with the segregated states of the American South' and 'the persistence of colonial mentalities [...] into the postcolonial years'.[7] On 17 May 1959 Antiguan carpenter Kelso Cochrane, aged 32, was murdered by white youths in the Notting Hill area. This violence persuaded many Afro-Caribbeans that even if they tried to assimilate into British society they should at the same time cultivate their own identity and traditions. Claudia Jones, a Trinidadian activist who had been expelled from the United States as a communist, founded the *West Indian Gazette* in Brixton and launched what became the Notting Hill Carnival.[8]

The British Nationality Act of 1948, crafted with the white Dominions in mind, made citizens of the Dominions and colonies also citizens of Britain.[9] Increased immigration from West Indian and African countries between 1960 and 1964 dramatically changed attitudes to immigration. The Commonwealth Immigrants Act of 1962 aimed to restrict the influx from the former colonies but also provoked a rush of immigration to 'beat the ban'. Between 1955 and 1968 net immigration to Great Britain from the non-white countries that became known as the New Commonwealth was 670,000. This included 191,000 Jamaicans and 132,000 from the rest of Caribbean, but more significantly 200,000 Indians and 146,000 Pakistanis. Bengali Muslims came to Britain, fleeing first the violence associated with partition in 1946–8, then the violence of the 1971 war of liberation of Bangladesh against Pakistan.[10] The influx of immigrants of Asian origin increased with the quasi-expulsion of populations of Asian origin from the newly independent East African countries of Kenya and Tanzania after 1967. Fearing a haemorrhaging of working-class votes the Labour government announced on 22 February 1968 a Commonwealth immigrants bill further restricting immigration, but this in turn provoked an influx of 750 Kenyan Asians a day, seeking to 'beat the ban'.

Those immigrants who made it past restrictions at the border found themselves subjected to racial prejudice, discrimination and segregation. In Britain immigrants from the West Indies or subcontinent concentrated in certain suburbs of the large cities. In 1971 in the Handsworth district of Birmingham, for example, 11 per cent of the population was Caribbean and nearly 8 per cent from India, Pakistan or Ceylon.[11] Bengali migrants favoured Tower Hamlets, because Bengali sailors had come there in the First World War, and Oldham, because the mills used Indian cotton.[12] In Leamington near Coventry, by contrast, the overwhelming proportion of the immigrant population were Sikhs from the Indian Punjab, living in the less fashionable southern side of the town.[13] Immigrants searching for housing, education and jobs were systematically frustrated by overt and covert colour bars. In Leamington, when a Sikh was granted a council mortgage 1959, thirty residents sent a petition of protest to the town hall.[14] Sikhs found menial jobs in foundry and engineering works, in hospitals and also in the Midland Bus Company. There was an expectation that a non-white worker would not be appointed over the head of a white worker, so when an Indian was appointed as a bus inspector in 1961, the Transport and General Workers' Union (TGWU) complained.[15] A 1966 survey in the London borough of Tower Hamlets, where the docks provided much employment, found that the craft unions did their best to block Bengalis from getting jobs and did not help them when they were the first to be laid off in a recession.[16] A parallel survey in 1966–7 in the outer London suburb of Croydon found that staff employed in shops, banks and commercial sectors prevailed on employers to operate 'an almost total colour bar'. In department stores non-white staff were allowed to work in the backroom but not at the sales counter. It was 'a bit difficult to have coloured sales staff in Croydon', said one personnel officer, 'the public might mind'.[17]

For the most part British politicians distanced themselves from the politics of racism and upheld tolerant attitudes, but there were signs that a few already recognised that political capital could be made out of racial prejudice. After the 1958 riots Solihull MP Martin Lindsay asserted, 'we all know perfectly well that the core of our problem is coloured immigrants. We must ask ourselves to what extent we want Great Britain to become a multi-racial community. A question which affects the future of our own race and breed is not one we should leave merely to chance.' In this he echoed the sentiments put bluntly by Lincolnshire MP Cyril Osborne after 1955 that 'This is a white man's country and I want it to remain so.'[18] His concerns were intensified by the arrival of Kenyan Asians ten years later. He then exclaimed that 'It will not be long before there are more coloured than white people in Britain. The English people will be strangers in their own land.'[19]

This influx to the metropolis had a dramatic effect on domestic politics. The arrival of immigrants from the former colonies at the same time as colonies were granted independence was a visible reminder to the 'home' French and British people of the trauma of the loss of empire and of national decline. Colonial hierarchies seemed to be overturned as immigrants competed for homes and jobs and made the 'host' society feel as if it were being 'overrun' or 'swamped'. A paradigm-changing response in this respect was the 1964 general election in Smethwick, a Birmingham suburb next to Handsworth. Since 1951 the seat had been held by Patrick Gordon Walker, an Oxford-educated Fabian socialist, the son and grandson of officials of the Raj. His views were seen to be paternalistic and out of touch as immigration increased into the area. In 1964 he was challenged by Peter Griffiths, a local working-class grammar-school boy, who was greatly affected by the loss of empire and supported Ian Smith's white Rhodesia. Elected to Smethwick council in 1955, he co-founded in 1961 the Birmingham Immigrant Control Association that met in Smethwick's Red Cow Hotel, and sent regular petitions on immigration control to Sir Cyril Osborne. Against all expectations Griffiths beat Gordon Walker and Colin Jordan's rowdy National Socialist troops, who backed Griffiths, chased the car of the defeated Labour MP shouting, 'Take your niggers away!'[20]

The defeat of the Conservative Party in 1964, however, made it vulnerable to the challenge of racist politics. The key player here was Enoch Powell, who had served in the Indian Army during the war, was greatly affected by the 1947 loss of India, and was elected to Parliament for Wolverhampton in 1950. He joined the Suez Group in 1953 and was committed to defend the remnants of empire, notably Ian Smith's Rhodesia. Britain, it has been suggested, was two things: a hard external carapace of the United Kingdom, and a soft centre of an idyllic England.[21] In the face of immigration and a sense of national decline and immigration Powell descanted on the latter. 'The power and the glory of the Empire have gone', he reflected in an address to the Royal Society of St George on 22 April 1964, 'but in the midst of the "blackened ruins", like one of her oak trees, standing, growing, the sap rising from her ancient roots to meet the spring, [is] England herself'. 'This sentimental, rustic wonderland', he clarified, 'is embodied in three enduring principles of Englishness: its unity under the Crown in Parliament, its historical continuity, and its racial homogeneity'.[22] This Englishness had no place for immigrants from India, Pakistan, the Caribbean or Africa.

Powell was also keen to draw lessons from other countries of the threat of immigration and communal politics. In the United States, the Civil Rights movement exposed entrenched racial inequalities which exploded in riots in the black ghettos of northern cities during three hot summers in 1965–7. As shadow defence minister he visited the United States in October 1967 and commented on the race riots of July 1967 in Detroit. Early in 1968, when Sikh bus conductors marched through Wolverhampton against a ruling that they could not work in their turbans and beards, he made a speech in Walsall warning that 'communalism has been the curse of India and we need to be able to recognise it when it rears its head here'.[23]

The climax of Powell's campaign was his so-called 'Rivers of Blood' speech in Birmingham on 20 April 1968. It linked the influx of immigrants and the betrayal of the British working class to the loss of empire and perceived national decline. It defined a narrow British nationalism based on a sense of racial superiority masquerading as racial victimhood. He told the story of a 'white woman pensioner' who had lost her husband in the Second World War, and now kept a boarding house. Black immigrants moved into the street and harassed her, he said, pushing excrement through her letter box.[24]

Premier Edward Heath considered that he had gone too far and dismissed him from the shadow cabinet the next day. There was, however, a powerful popular response in his support. Three thousand London dockers came onto the streets on 25 April 1968 (Figure 5.1), and thousands more signed a petition asking the government 'to seriously consider the continuous threat to our living standards by this blind policy of unlimited immigrants being imposed on us'.[25]

Powell received a huge postbag, which often linked immigration to Britain's squandering of victory in the Second World War and the loss of empire. One anonymous letter of 22 April 1968 read:

Our British working classes have maintained this country, all down the years with the toil of our hand and the sweat of our brows, and shed rivers of blood in its defence, as you know. We have bled for it, fought for it, worked for it and paid for it. And now, two packs of the dirtiest traitors on God's earth [British politicians], for the sake of a rotten, old tradition of a dead empire [...] have wrenched our birth-right from us and handed our country over on a silver plate to millions of immigrants from all over the world [...] Our British working classes have been sacrificed on the altar of a dead colonialism.[26]

Figure 5.1 A show of colonial force in London: dockers march in support of Enoch Powell, 23 April 1968.
Getty Images / Evening Standard / Hulton Archive / Stringer / 3398988

The virulence of anti-immigration rhetoric was taken up in working-class communities and injected a new element of violence into local race relations. In the summer of 1969 a West Indian youth was murdered in Handsworth Park, Birmingham.[27] In London what became known as 'Paki-bashing' by white skinheads or 'bovver boys' took off in the winter of 1969–70. This culminated in the murder on 6 April 1970 of Tausir Ali, returning from work from a Wimpy Bar in the West End to his home in Bromley, by two 18-year-old white youths.[28] Other attacks on Asians took place in Luton and Wolverhampton in May 1970.[29] In Tower Hamlets, Pakistanis held mass meetings and set up self-defence groups, much to the concern of Trevor Huddleston, now Bishop of Stepney, who feared the eruption of South Africa-style racial violence in the British capital.[30]

## The Algerian War Comes to France

In France, the largest immigrant communities in 1946 were the Italians (28 per cent) and the Poles (25 per cent), followed by Spaniards (18 per cent), Belgians (10 per cent) and other nationalities (19 per cent).[31] Under plans for French reconstruction 310,000 immigrants were to be brought in by 1949, including 90,000 North Africans, and by 1954 there were 240,000 Algerian workers in France.[32]

A French survey of 1951 said that North African immigrants 'created miniature ghettos in the *bidonvilles* or shanty-towns they inhabited' and 'little *casbahs* in Paris, Marseille and Lyon'.[33] Attitudes to immigrants depended very much on where they came from. In France, Belgians were very well regarded. Poles, Italians and Spaniards were tolerated, but North Africans were suspected of harbouring disease and criminality; only German immigrants were disliked more.[34] At this stage, North Africans were cowed by the political oppression they had experienced at home: migrants from Sétif, who worked as unskilled labourers in gas and chemical factories at Champigny-sur-Marne, feared a repeat of the reprisals they had experienced in 1945.[35] When they did respond to Algerian nationalist agitation and demonstrated in Paris on 14 July 1953, they were confronted by police who shot six of them.[36]

The issue of immigration and colonialism in France was completely redefined by the Algerian War. After six years of bloody struggle, France abandoned its most important overseas possession and with it the white community.[37] A million *pieds noirs* were obliged to flee the newly independent Algerian state they had resisted ever materialising. They suffered the trauma of having lost what they considered *their* homeland in French Algeria and felt that they had been betrayed by the French government which in the end turned its guns on them. At the same time 140,000 *harkis* – the Algerian auxiliary troops who had fought alongside the French – fled to France on pain of being massacred as traitors. Having used them, the French now found them an embarrassment. They were herded into internment camps across the south of France that had previously been used to control 'dangerous' or 'undesirable' groups, such as Spanish republicans, foreign Jews, and in turn Italian, German, Vietnamese and Algerian POWs. After a few years they were moved to so-called transit camps where the men were put to work on forest plantations.[38] While numerous Algerians living in France returned to independent Algeria many others came to work in France under the Evian agreements that ended the war, so that by 1969 there were 608,000 Algerians in France. In Paris, these Algerian immigrant populations were relegated to slum districts like the Goutte d'Or, near Barbès Metro station, crammed several to a room or in cellars in hostels owned by so-called *marchands du sommeil* or 'sleep merchants'. Otherwise they lived in *bidonvilles* that sprang up around Paris at Nanterre, Saint-Denis and Champigny-sur-Marne and also around other large cities such as Lille, Caen, Marseille, Toulon, Nice and Toulouse. To deal with the hygiene and security risk of these encampments, vulnerable to Algerian nationalist propaganda, special hostels were built in the 1960s by the mainly state-owned National Society for the Construction of Accommodation for Algerian Workers (SONACOTRA). These were no more than barracks for Algerian workers and were largely run by staff who had served as soldiers or police in Algeria and had experience of controlling what was considered a lazy and subversive population, not least by torture.

French settlers in Algeria and indigenous Algerians who had been at each others' throats in Algeria now regarded each other with scarcely concealed hostility in France. Historian Benjamin Stora, a *pied noir* of Jewish origin who was forced to leave Algeria as a boy in 1962, speaks of a 'transfer of memory' across Mediterranean from Algeria to the metropolis. He argues that the *pieds noirs* cultivated a 'Southern' memory, resembling the memory of the Confederation cultivated by the 'poor whites' in the United States, with its myths, its heroes and its own 'French War of Secession', that is, the Algerian War. This was a narrow and exclusive French nationalism which was anti-Arab and anti-Muslim.[39]

The question of French and British relations with their colonies and with the Third World in general was shaken up and deepened by the events of 1968. French activists who made 1968 were shaped by opposition to French brutality in the Algerian War, especially the use of torture. Young communists were inspired either by Trotskyism, who argued that revolution would be made by a vanguard of intellectuals, like the Bolsheviks of 1917, or by the Maoism of the Chinese Cultural Revolution that took off in 1966. Benjamin Stora, studying at the University of Nanterre, himself became a Trotskyist in the aftermath of 1968.[40] Jean-Pierre Le Dantec, studying at the elite École Centrale in Paris, recalled that 'We got an anti-Soviet and anti-Stalinist version of the story of the conquest of power in China [...] there was a spiritual time bomb in Mao Tse-tung's saying that "a revolution is not a dinner party" [...] we liked Mao's idea that there had to be trouble.'[41] What these movements had in common is that they responded to revolutions against imperialism, whether American, European or Soviet, across the Third World – first Cuba, then Algeria, then China. The Vietnam War, which pitted American imperialism against the communist people and Vietcong fighters of North Vietnam, galvanised immense support among young people and gave protest movements a mass base. On 16 April 1967 a letter from Che Guevara was read to the Organization of Solidarity with the People of Asia, Africa and Latin America, otherwise known as the Tricontinental. He urged creating 'a Second or Third Vietnam, the Second and Third Vietnam of the world!' All local Third World conflicts could aspire to become Vietnams.[42] Che himself then went off to fight in Bolivia, where he was killed on 9 October 1967, a death which dramatised the global Third World revolution even more than his life had done.

The mantra of activists in Europe and the United States fired up by Third World revolution was that at some point they would be able to 'bring the revolution back home'. British activist John Hoyland, who had visited Castro's Cuba, thought that 'during the May events in Paris for ten days a revolution was very possible. I mean, the students were fighting the police. There were pitched battles every single night. They'd occupied the centre of Paris. And then there was a general strike. The workers went on general strike. I mean, you thought, "crikey it really is happening".'[43]

The defeat of the 1968 movement was not the end of the story. For some militants it was only a beginning. Alain Geismar, secretary of the lecturers' union and one of the key leaders in May 1968, became convinced that revolution proper was just over the horizon. He co-wrote *Towards Civil War* and was one of the founders of the clandestine Gauche Prolétarienne (GP) whose aim was 'the fusion of anti-authoritarian revolt and proletarian revolution'.[44] This linked up with a new wave of Third World revolution, generated this time among Palestinians.

The Six Day War of June 1967 was in some way Israel's revenge for the Suez Crisis. It defeated an Arab coalition of Nasser's Egypt, Jordan and Syria and settler colonialism was reinforced as Israel now occupied Egypt's Gaza Strip, the Golan Heights taken from Syria and the Left Bank of the River Jordan, taken from the Kingdom of Jordan. Over 300,000 Palestinians were uprooted and driven into exile, most notably into Jordan, where they crowded into refugee camps. The United Nations passed Resolution 242 in November 1967 calling for Israel to withdraw from the occupied territories, but the United States, which backed Israel as the only reliable pro-Western power in the Middle East, supported her refusal to withdraw.

The failure of the Arab states in war meant that leadership of the Arab struggle now passed to Palestinian *fedayeen* or freedom fighters, organised in the Palestine Liberation Organization (PLO). Solidarity with their cause was organised in 1969 through Palestine Committees which brought together Maoist students of the Gauche Prolétarienne on the one hand and students of Near East and North African origin on the other. The movement was galvanised by the Jordanian Army's attack on Palestinian refugee camps to root out PLO militants, in what became known as 'Black September' 1970. Pro-Palestinian activists attacked the Jordanian embassy in Neuilly on 23 July 1971, and hoisted the Palestinian flag, and demonstrations were held in the north Paris Arab heartland of the Goutte d'Or. An activist report on the work of the Palestinian Committees said that Algerian workers were now recast as Arab workers, fighting against imperialism, Zionism and 'the suffering and misery inflicted on them by French imperialism [...] The *bidonvilles* are inspired by the way the *fedayeen* have transformed refugee camps into resistance camps.'[45]

On 27 October 1971 a 15-year-old Algerian boy, Djellali Ben Ali, was murdered in the Goutte d'Or district by the husband of the concierge of the building where he lived. The killer clearly took the view that the Algerian War was still being waged and that he was entitled to use repressive measures on a daily basis. On the day of the boy's funeral, 7 November 1971, a demonstration 4,000 strong waved Palestinian and Algerian flags and sang FLN songs.[46] 'A police cordon, which had never been seen here since the Algerian War', said the *Nouvel Observateur*, was thrown around the demonstrators. On 27 November another demonstration was held and both Jean-Paul Sartre and Michel Foucault came to Barbès to show their solidarity.[47]

In the same period the state and municipalities began to bull-doze the *bidonvilles* and clear slums in order to build homes for more desirable residents. Immigrants were left homeless and began to occupy empty housing. A squatting movement began in Issy-les-Moulineaux in January 1972 and spread to miners' dwellings in Douai, where the pits were being closed.[48] In 1975 a rent strike swept SONACOTRA hostels in the Paris region, and in Dijon and Strasbourg. 'These hostels are veritable prisons and the managers are prison warders', declared the strike committee of a Saint-Denis hostel. They were not allowed to meet together or to receive visitors. 'The managers are always army veterans who have served in Indo-China and Algeria. They are racists and colonialists.'[49]

The so-called Marcellin-Fontanet circular of September 1972 tackled the problem of immigration and immigrant political activity at one and the same time. Immigration was restricted and jobs were reserved for French nationals and foreigners who had appropriate residence and work permits. Immigrants who were in trouble with the police for political activity were liable to be denied the right to stay. When immigrants without papers marched through Grasse in Provence on 12 June 1973 to protest they were scattered by fire-hoses ordered by the mayor. 'The Arabs are behaving in the old town as if in a conquered territory', the press reported. 'These people are very different from us. They live by night. It is very painful to be invaded by them.'[50]

Fears of this 'invasion' from the Third World were captured by the novel *The Camp of Saints*, written near Saint-Raphaël in Provence by Jean Raspail, who combined exploring the Americas with a Catholic and royalist hatred of the modern world, and published in 1973. Dystopian and darkly obsessive, it describes the landing of a 'last chance armada' of a hundred ships from Calcutta, carrying a million immigrants, which moors on the Mediterranean coast of France. As the French government fails to resist and the French population flees north, an ironic inversion of the defeat of 1940, and the United Nations in Hanoi fails to act, a Multiracial Popular Assembly takes power in Paris, a postcolonial version of the 1871 Paris Commune of Paris, while a Non-European Commonwealth Committee takes control in London. White women marry non-white men, spelling 'the death of the white race'.[51]

In this embattled climate, racist attacks became more and more frequent. These were often concentrated in Paris or the Marseille region, where both immigrants and *pied noir* populations were concentrated. On 25 August 1973 a French tram driver in Marseille was killed by an Algerian who had himself been the victim of a racist assault four years earlier. The local press was quick to denounce the evils that immigrants were bringing into the country, a consequence of the loss of Algeria. 'Enough Algerian thieves, Algerian rioters, Algerian big mouths, Algerian syphilitics, Algerian rapists, Algerian madmen', trumpeted *Le Meridional.* 'We have had enough of this scum from the other side of the Mediterranean. Independence has brought them only wretchedness, the opposite of what they were led to believe.'[52] Local French activists set up a Marseille Defence Committee which defended their community by killing at least ten Algerians. The Algerian community responded by forming an Arab Workers' Movement (MTA), and organised strikes in both the Marseille region and Paris in September 1973.[53] Former OAS militants and partisans of French Algeria now founded a club named after Charles Martel, who had held the Arabs at bay at the Battle of Poitiers in 732 AD. They launched a bomb attack on the Algerian Consulate at Marseille in December 1973, killing four and injuring twenty-two. They then issued a communiqué declaring that 'There are more Arabs in France than there were *pieds noirs* in Algeria. They expelled us by violence, we will expel them by violence. The cowardice of our pseudo-governments is responsible. Down with Algerian France!'[54]

Partisans of French Algeria supported extreme Right groups such as the Ordre Nouveau, which held a meeting at La Mutualité hall in Paris on 21 June 1973 with the demand 'stop uncontrolled immigration'. This was met by a counter-demonstration of the Trotskyist Communist Revolutionary League (LCR), which came onto the streets helmeted and armed with coshes. As a result of the violence that ensued the government banned both the Ordre Nouveau and the LCR. The banning of the Ordre Nouveau was counterproductive. It was a major constituent of the Front National, founded in 1972 by Jean-Marie Le Pen, who now had his hands free to convert the Front National from a street-fighting force to a powerful electoral organisation. His breakthrough took another ten years, and had to wait for the victory of the Left and the defeat of the traditional right-wing parties in 1981, but it was no less impressive than the transformation of British politics by Enoch Powell.

## Assimilation or Exclusion?

The immigrants who arrived in the 1950s and 1960s were often single male breadwinners who sent some of their earnings to their families back home. Immigration restrictions imposed by governments in the 1960s and 1970s limited new migration but stimulated families to join the breadwinner in the metropolis.[55] These families struggled against prejudice to try to find a place in the metropolis. The first generation of immigrants tended to work hard, remain close to their own community and to keep a low profile. The second generation, however, born in the 1950s and 1960s, were exposed to the powerful and exciting youth culture around them. They often wanted to break away from their immigrant roots, and integrate with the youth and youth culture of their own generation.

In Liverpool, said Colin McGlashen of *The Observer*, these young people were 'Afro-English, and more English than African. They speak Scouse. Most have white mothers.'[56] They saw the world as full of opportunities for themselves and refused to accept the lot their parents had to endure of being second-class citizens. In France the new generation of home-grown immigrants became known as Beurs, 'Arabs' written backwards in the Verlan slang of the suburbs. They were divided between their Algerian roots and French school and youth culture, not quite belonging to one or the other. One young woman, Fatima, aged 22, was Algerian but had always lived in France. 'My soul is much more Algerian than French', she declared. On the other hand, she was inspired by the myth of the French Revolution: 'It was the beginning of freedom of expression and the end of monarchy and oppression [...] It could begin again, on the estates where we live.'[57]

Unfortunately, young immigrants' desire to assimilate was too frequently met by colonial hierarchies and exclusions. These were clearly manifested in housing, education and employment. In Britain, as we have seen, black and Asian populations lived in poor districts of cities, such as Toxteth in Liverpool, Oldham in Greater Manchester, Handsworth in Birmingham, Tower Hamlets or Brixton in London. One junior school in Handsworth, where 75 per cent of the children were black, staged Gilbert and Sullivan's *HMS Pinafore* around 1970. According to Grenadian researcher Augustine John, the most common comment was, 'I think it's a bit rich to have all these black kids singing, "For he is an Englishman"'.[58] It did not occur to the school to stage anything less overtly nationalistic. Meanwhile, a Liverpool employment agency admitted in 1975 that an unofficial colour bar operated in the job market:

out of every hundred black people who come to Liverpool in search of jobs, only twenty succeed. The skilled ones find jobs as ship's cooks or in restaurants after taking a catering course at Liverpool College. Others, after training, as spray painters or mechanics. These are the few. The majority have to work as porters, dish-washers, cleaners, and even these jobs are hard to find because of the employers' preference for white employees.[59]

As a result of such discrimination, in Brixton in 1981 average unemployment stood at 13 per cent, but ethnic unemployment was nearly twice as high, at 25 per cent.[60]

In France, immigrant families were moved in the 1960s and 1970s from *bidonvilles*, inner-city slums or rural internment camps for *harkis* to high-rise flats on estates build on the fringes of large cities. In Azouz Begag's semi-autobiographical novel about an Algerian boy who moves in 1966 from the *bidonville* of Chaâba outside Lyon to a new housing estate and attends the lycée, the hero comes top of the class although he is 'the only Arab in it. In front of the French boys'.[61] And yet, as he confessed in an interview, his novel was 'a story of humour and suffering' because of forty friends from his *bidonville*, he was the only one who succeeded.[62] Among those who did not was Toumi Djaïdja, a *harki* born in Algeria in 1962. He was brought up in internment camps in the south of France until in 1971 his family was moved to a flat in Les Minguettes, an estate in Vénissieux, a suburb of Lyon. He left school to be apprenticed as a metalworker, reflecting ironically that 'all the immigrant and working-class youths who had had a patchy education became metalwork apprentices but it led nowhere. Isn't that curious?'[63]

Often unemployed, living on the streets, taking to petty crime, young immigrants were frequently in confrontation with the police that confirmed colonial hierarchies. Not only societies, but also politicians and governments made it difficult for young immigrants to integrate. Pressure continued to tighten controls on immigration from former colonies or the Commonwealth. Panic set in about the erosion of national identity by immigrants who, it was felt, could not be assimilated.

In Britain the rise of Margaret Thatcher signalled a fresh commitment to immigration control, the policing of immigrant communities, and the strengthening of national identity. In February 1975 Margaret Thatcher ousted Edward Heath from the leadership of the Conservative Party and was one of forty-four Tory MPs to oppose Labour's 1976 Race Relations Act. Interviewed on Granada television in 1978 she expressed her fears on immigration. Citing a prediction that 'if we went on as we are then by the end of the century there would be four million people of the new Commonwealth or Pakistan here', she continued, 'Now, that is an awful lot and I think it means that people are really rather afraid that this country might be rather swamped by people with a different culture.' After she came to power in 1979 she made a strong ally of the police force and it is no accident that the police operation to control racial unrest in British cities in 1981 was called 'Operation Swamp 81'. In Brixton the police imposed a systematic stop and search policy. Squads made 943 'stops' and arrested 118 people. Of these over half were black and two-thirds were under the age of 21.

Rejected by the so-called host society, young black immigrants had a tendency to fall back on a culture that defined a separate identity and expressed their struggle with the discriminating and brutal British system. This might be the Rasta cult of Ethiopia, symbol of black independence and escape from the Babylon of slavery. It might be reggae, popularised by the Jamaican singer Jimmy Cliff in the 1972 film *The Harder They Come*, with its line, 'So as sure as the sun will shine / I'm gonna get my share now of what's mine'.[64] Or it might be black power, modelled on the movement in the United States. Linton Kwesi Johnson, born in Jamaica in 1952, followed his mother to Brixton in 1963. While at Tulse Hill Comprehensive School he joined the Black Panthers. He expressed his anger in dub poetry, delivered to a reggae beat. It was a response to Louise Bennett's comic lyrics, expressing alienation and a desire for liberation. In 1980 he wrote 'Inglan is a bitch':

> Well mi dhu day work an mi du nite work
> Mi dhu clean work an me do dutty work
> Dem seh dat black man is very lazy
> But if yu si how mi wok you woodah seh me crazy
> Inglan is a bitch
> Dere's no escaping it
> Inglan is a bitch
> Dere's no runin fram it[65]

Black discontent exploded in the Brixton riots of 10–12 April 1981, which were echoed by riots in Handsworth and Toxteth in July 1981, when police used tear gas to quell disturbances.[66] Lord Scarman later reported that Operation Swamp was a 'serious mistake', undertaken without consultation with community leaders, demonstrating 'racial prejudice among officers' and a failure to adjust police methods to the needs of policing a multiracial society.[67] A German observer, Werner Glinga, noted in his 1983 book *Legacy of Empire* that 'racial hatred is not innate, it is incited. This is part of the legacy of colonialism.'[68]

The Falklands War, coming less than a year after the riots, generated a colonial nationalism that was also exclusionary. On 3 July 1982 Mrs Thatcher made a victory address to a Conservative rally in Cheltenham:

> We have learned something about ourselves, a lesson we desperately needed to learn. When we started out, there were the waverers and the fainthearts. The people who [...] thought we could no longer do the great things which we once did, [who] had their secret fears that it was true: that Britain was no longer the nation that had built an Empire and ruled a quarter of the world. Well, they were wrong. The lesson of the Falklands is that Britain has not changed and that this nation still has those sterling qualities which shine through our history [...] What has indeed happened it that now once again Britain is not prepared to be pushed around.[69]

On one level this apotheosis of the British nation might have included everyone within its shores. But as Bombay-born writer Salman Rushdie pointed out, built on empire and tempered by war, Britain was sharply defined against an 'other':

> She felt able to invoke the spirit of imperialism, because she knew how central that spirit is to the self-image of white Britons of all classes. I say white Britons because it's clear that Mrs Thatcher wasn't addressing the two million or so blacks, who don't feel quite like that about the Empire. So even her word 'we' was an act of racial exclusion, like her other well-known speech about the fear of being 'swamped' by immigrants.[70]

In spite of these conscious and unconscious colonial attitudes, some progress was made in the 1980s towards thinking about Britain as a multicultural society. Anthony Rampton, who had blamed racism for the underachievement of immigrant children, was sacked by the Thatcher government, but the Swann report of 1985 reiterated many of his findings in more moderate terms. It argued that 'Britain is a multiracial and multicultural society and all pupils must be enabled to understand what this means.' It stipulated that education was not for 'the reinforcement of the beliefs, values and identity which each child brings to school', but should develop 'multicultural understanding [in] all aspects of a school's work'.[71]

There was, however, opposition in some circles to the new thinking on multiculturalism. The old woollen town of Bradford had been defined by the Industrial Revolution, the birthplace of the Independent Labour Party, the proximity of the Brontë's Parsonage at Haworth, and the 1970 filming of *The Railway Children*. From the 1960s an immigrant population came to work in the textile mills, transport services and catering from Mirpur in Azad Kashmir, conquered by the British in the 1840s and part of Pakistan since 1947. Mohammed Ajeed, who came to Britain from Mirpur in 1957 with a degree from Karachi University, became lord mayor of Bradford in 1985, the first Asian mayor in Britain, but as the textile industry declined and unemployment increased, so racial tensions worsened.

Raymond Honeyford, the headteacher of Drummond Middle School in Bradford, where most children were of Muslim origin, was of Manchester working-class origin, his father wounded in the First World War and his mother from a family of Irish immigrants. Early in 1984 he complained in the right-wing *Salisbury Review* that he had had enough of a multiculturalism that required halal meat to be served in the canteen, separate swimming and PE lessons for Muslim girls and permitted non-participation in sex education lessons. He also argued that black pupils performed worse in school because of family breakdown and 'lefty teachers'. This provoked a 'Honeyford out!' campaign in 1984 by parents and the Muslim community, but Honeyford was defended by the white population of Bradford, Conservative MPs and the *Daily Mail* and he was even received in Downing Street by Mrs Thatcher in October 1985. His reinstatement provoked a boycott of the school by Muslim parents and the Bradford Council of Mosques. Mayor Ajeed, who supported them, received hate mail, his house was stoned and his wife and daughter received obscene telephone calls.[72]

In France, under a socialist president and government, things seemed to go in a different direction. A majority of the population, immigrants included, looked forward to a new era, defined by the egalitarian and universalist principles of the French Revolution. From housing estates like Les Minguettes, groups of Beurs descended into Lyon town centre to take expensive cars and indulge in an orgy of joy-riding. The party did not last. On 21 March the police had their revenge, chasing a gang into a block of flats at Les Minguettes and using extreme violence to arrest them. For once the youths did not reply with violence. They organised a sit-in at the Vénissieux town hall to protest at police violence and then began a hunger strike, visited by the archbishop of Lyon. On 20 June 1983, however, attempting to free a child from the jaws of a police dog, Toumi Djaïdja was shot in the stomach by an officer. Later he understood that he was being treated like 'residue of the Algerian War' by officers many of whom had fought in it.[73] Having recovered, he visited the Larzac plateau to learn about non-violent protest from former *gauchistes* and sheep-farmers who were resisting the extension of a military base.[74] He, his comrades and the local clergy organised a March for Equality, also known as the Marche des Beurs, which began in Marseille with twelve 'disciples' on 15 October 1983 (Figure 5.2). Along the way the van accompanying them played Bob Marley's 1975 'Get up, stand up'. In Paris on 3 December they were greeted by a crowd of 100,000, to whom Djaïdja replied, 'Bonjour à la France de tous les couleurs'. He was whisked off to the Élysée for an audience with President Mitterrand, who announced that the position of immigrants would now be regularised by a ten-year joint residency and work permit.[75]

The story did not end altogether happily, however. The police were keen to exact revenge and Toumi Djaïdja was arrested in October 1984, spending three months in prison. The cause of the Beurs was taken up by an organisation called SOS-Racisme, which distributed badges with the slogan 'Touche pas à mon pote' ('Hands off my buddy') and held a rock concert on the Place de la Concorde on 15 June 1985. It soon transpired, however, that SOS-Racisme was operated by the Socialist Party, and the Beurs withdrew their support.[76]

**Figure 5.2** The March for Equality from Marseille to Paris, 1983. Getty Images / Jean MUSCAT / Gamma-Rapho / 847658590

At precisely this time the Front National which had been formed in 1972 but to date had made little impact, made its first big electoral break-through. This may be explained by the defeat of the mainstream Right in 1981 and the victory of socialism. It may also be seen as a push-back by French people who had fought Algerian rebels in Algeria now having to deal with the increasing presence and profile of immigrant Algerians in metropolitan France. In the municipal elections of March 1983, Le Pen won 12 per cent of the vote in the populous Parisian 20th *arrondissement*. In the bleak town of Dreux, west of Paris, which had a large immigrant population, his closest ally, Jean-Pierre Stirbois, secured 17 per cent and, in a rerun of the election because of irregularities, formed a coalition with other right-wing parties and became one of three Front National assistant mayors of the town. This breakthrough was France's Smethwick election, but nearly twenty years later. On 13 February 1984 Le Pen was able for the first time to demonstrate his rhetorical skills and down-to-earth arguments to a national audience on the popular TV programme, *L'Heure de Vérité*. He explained simply that

> I apply a sort of hierarchy of sentiments and preferences. I prefer my daughters to my cousins, my cousins to my neighbours,

those I don't know to my enemies. Consequently I prefer French people, and have every right to do so. After that I prefer Europeans, then Westerners and as far as other countries in the world are concerned I prefer France's allies and those who like her. That seems a good rule to me.[77]

This gave rise to a book, *Les Français d'abord*, in which his analysis was more historical. 'In the second half of the twentieth century', he explained, 'the population explosion in underdeveloped countries, especially African and Asian countries, has driven Europe back to its frontiers of the Year 1000'. This linked a demographic phenomenon 'out there' to fears – as a result of government weakness – that decolonisation resulted in waves of immigrants 'over here'. In his own 20th *arrondissement*, he clarified, there were schools which had only 20 per cent French children. The result was a dramatic reversal of hierarchies: 'We are fighting an immigration policy', he concluded, 'that will make us, French people, enslaved foreigners in our own country'.[78] The Front National went on to win 11 per cent of the vote in the 1984 European elections and secured ten seats, including ones for Le Pen and Stirbois.[79]

Threatened by the rise of the Front National, the main-stream right-wing parties moved further to the right to retain a hold on its electorate. Charles Pasqua, the hard-line minister of the interior in the Chirac government of 1986, sponsored a law on the conditions of entry and residence of foreigners in France that made it possible to expel non-nationals by administrative order. The case was made that this was also an anti-terrorist measure. In October that year the press and television carried pictures of a hundred handcuffed Malians being manhandled onto a plane at Orly airport.[80] The rising panic about immigration translated into a debate about national identity. Alain Griotteray of *Figaro Magazine* argued that France was going the same way as Lebanon and even Great Britain, with its 'Pakistanis, Indians and Jamaicans'. They had triggered race riots across the country in 1981, he argued, which 'broke completely with the basic principles of British civil order'. 'A France with a substantial black or North African population', he concluded, 'would no longer be France. It would be something else: a European Brazil, an Arabia of the North or an Islam of the West.'[81]

Particular concern was felt about the children born to immigrants in France who, according to the current rules, would automatically become French nationals on their eighteenth birthday, whether they requested it or not. These children were felt to be as attached to their place of origin as to France and would become only 'French on paper'. It was argued that a quarter of young Algerians opted to do their military service in Algeria rather than France, although the call-up was for two years rather than one.[82] In 1988 a Nationality Commission was set up to look in particular at whether the French-born children should be required to opt for French nationality and demonstrate a sufficient degree of assimilation to things French. Giving testimony to it, Henry de Lesquen, president of the right-wing think tank the Club de l'Horloge, asked, 'Do we want a multi-cultural society or do we want to preserve our cultural identity? We will see France explode. There are too many historical precedents: Austria-Hungary, the Ottoman Empire, India.'[83] The Commission concluded that young people born in France of foreign parents should indeed be required to opt for French nationality, altough doing French military service should carry with it French nationality.

In both France and Britain 'colonisation in reverse' thus provoked a colonialist backlash. In an early phase this took the form of spontaneous racial prejudice and racial violence and the imposition of 'colour bars' that reproduced colonial hierarchies. These feelings were then exploited by politicians who linked loss of empire to immigration from former colonies and sought a populist base against what it saw as a weak-kneed establishment. That establishment responded by raising barriers to immigration and beginning to develop British and French identities that cast aside experiments in multiculturalism. Although the Labour government of 1964 also tried to limit immigration from the former colonies, its presence was a red rag to emerging populists. The survival of right-wing governments in France until 1981 kept the extreme Right longer at bay but, even though twenty years after Enoch Powell, the breakthrough of Jean-Marie Le Pen caused no less of a political earthquake.

# 6 EUROPE: IN OR OUT?

In the second half of the twentieth century both France and Britain were in search of reconciling the reinvention of empire with the development of an economic and political Europe. An observer in the 1960s might have thought it logical for both powers to move from historic empire to the modern European project. As the sun set on empires which reached their peak in the Victorian era or Third Republic so in the postwar world Europe held out new hopes for peace and prosperity. Things were not, of course, as simple as that. Ideas of empire never vanished but were constantly reinvented to deal both with challenges of international reach and of immigration from formerly colonised countries. Moreover, empire and Europe were for a long time seen not as 'either or' choices but as 'both and'. This juggling act was kept up longer by France than by Britain, which came to consider entry into Europe as a defeat of its imperial ambitions.

## 'The England of Kipling is Dead'

Harold Macmillan's wind of change speech, delivered in Cape Town on 3 February 1960, makes sense only if it is understood in connection with his thinking on Europe. The Empire was fast disappearing and, to his mind, the Commonwealth was no longer strong enough or united enough to sustain her world influence. Britannic nationalism was a thing of the past. 'You and I were born into a very different world', he told Robert Menzies in February 1962, 'Queen Victoria, the Jubilee, Kipling'. 'And now here we are, my dear Bob, two old gentlemen, prime ministers of our respective countries, sixty years on, rubbing our eyes and wondering what has happened.' The old Commonwealth, he continued, was 'like a small intimate house party. Now it is becoming a sort of miniature United Nations, with various groups; the Afro-Asian strength strongly organised.'[1] The time had come to catch up with the European Economic Community, which had already been in existence for five years.

De Gaulle had for a long time been hostile to Europe. He had opposed the proposed European Defence Community in 1952–4 on the grounds that the French army would fall under the command of the United States and revive German militarism.[2] When he returned to power in 1958, however, he realised that a Europe composed of France, the Benelux countries, the Federal Republic of Germany and Italy, could in fact be a vehicle for French domination of Western Europe. To some, the EEC looked surprisingly like Napoleon's domination of Europe which included the Low Countries, the Rhineland, the Confederation of the Rhine and Italy. He saw no contradiction between France's role in Europe and France's role in its former empire, which in its African heartland was now branded *Françafrique*. Having imposed peace brutally on Cameroon, de Gaulle symbolically used its capital Yaoundé in July 1963 as the venue where the European Community signed a convention with the Associated African States.[3]

Negotiations between France and Britain were opened, despite the divergence of their goals. De Gaulle came to Britain on a state visit in April 1960 and Macmillan went to Paris on 27 January 1961, ahead of a meeting of foreign ministers of the Six. The *Daily Mail* explained very succinctly what was at stake in the dance between empire and Europe:

> At any time in the postwar decade Britain could have had the leadership of Europe. She rejected it, because she continued to regard herself as an imperial and oceanic power. Now, the empire has almost gone and Britain is one among a number of equal, sovereign Commonwealth states. In the meantime Europe has forged ahead.[4]

Macmillan told the House of Commons on 31 July 1961 that the government had decided to seek entry into the European Community. The Commons endorsed this on 4 August by 313 votes to 5, with Labour abstaining. At no stage did Britain envisage exchanging the

Commonwealth for Europe: the vision was to keep both. Lord Privy Seal Edward Heath announced in Paris on 10 October 1961 that he was seeking special provisions for the Commonwealth in relation to Europe. It would not do that an excluded Commonwealth drifted towards communism and in any case, he pointed out, French, Dutch, Belgian and Italian colonies had become Associated Overseas Territories with access to the Common Market.[5]

When Macmillan met de Gaulle at Château de Champs-sur-Marne on 2 June 1962, he began by saying, as he had said to Menzies, that 'the England of Kipling is dead'. The old British Empire was no more. De Gaulle was concerned about Britain coming in with its Commonwealth, while Algeria had just become independent. It was not, however, on the question of relations with its former empire that de Gaulle built his main objections to British membership of the EEC. He argued that Britain was 'too intimately tied up with the Americans' and would act as a Trojan horse for American influence in Europe. There was a history of humiliation here which de Gaulle wished to reverse. He had been summoned by Churchill on 4 June 1944 and told that no French forces would take part in the D-Day landings, which would be a purely 'Anglo-Saxon affair'. When he protested, Churchill had replied that 'if I had to choose between you and Roosevelt, I would always choose Roosevelt. When we have to choose between the French and the Americans, we always prefer the Americans.' D-Day was less about liberation than about the Americans coming to France as 'a conquered land', 'a second occupation'.[6]

De Gaulle's second concern was that while France could dominate the Europe of the Six, this would be changed if Britain came in. 'In the Six as they existed', he told Macmillan when they met again at Rambouillet in December 1962, 'France had some weight and could say no, even to the Germans. Once the United Kingdom and the Scandinavians entered the organisation things would be different. The result would be a sort of free trade area which might be desirable in itself, but would not be European.'[7] Not only did the Europe of the Six closely resemble the core of the Napoleonic Empire, but Napoleon tried to defeat Britain by corralling European countries into a Continental System to prevent the British trading with Europe. Macmillan saw this as well, and told President Kennedy that 'De Gaulle is trying to dominate Europe. His idea is not a partnership, but a Napoleonic or Louis XIV hegemony.'[8]

De Gaulle formally vetoed Britain's application to join the European Community on 14 January 1963. He called Britain an 'insular and maritime power', which would drag the United States into Europe and make it into a 'huge Atlantic community'.[9] The Labour government of Harold Wilson renewed the British application in May 1967, but France was then redefining its grandeur by scorning the United States. On 21 February 1966 de Gaulle announced that France was withdrawing from the integrated command structure of NATO and required the Americans to remove their thirty bases and 26,000 soldiers from French soil. Speaking in the Cambodian capital, Phnom Penh on 1 September 1966, as the Vietnam War escalated, he passed over France's colonial past in the region and denounced the militarism and imperialism of the United States in the name of the self-determination of peoples. The failure of Britain's second application was a fall-out of this anti-Americanism. De Gaulle simply repeated the point that British access would transform the EEC into 'an Atlantic zone that would deprive our continent of any real personality'.[10]

The success of the British application had to await de Gaulle's resignation in 1969 and Edward Heath's election in 1970. Georges Pompidou, the new French president, reflected that 'England could no longer put up with the Europe of the Six, which must have reminded her of Napoleonic Europe and the Continental Blockade.'[11] The place of the Commonwealth was perfunctorily assured by special provisions for New Zealand's butter and lamb exports and the *Daily Mail* declared on 24 July 1971, 'Britain's future lies inside the family of Europe.'[12] The House of Commons passed the EEC bill on 28 October 1971, opposed by a fifth of Conservative MPs and a minority of anti-European Labour MPs. Enoch Powell called the terms 'a humiliating surrender. Wilhelm II could not have demanded so much. I doubt if Hitler would have demanded more. I can still only half believe that I was myself an unwilling witness to my country's abnegation of its own national independence.'[13] Once again, Europe was portrayed as an empire seeking to control them, but this time it was seen as German rather than French.

Great Britain formally became part of the EEC on 1 January 1973, but Enoch Powell did a secret deal with Harold Wilson, whose policy was to renegotiate the deal, to get rid of Edward Heath in the next election. Labour renegotiated terms in a modest way and put the result to a referendum on 6 June 1975. During the referendum campaign precious little was said about the glories of empire, which seemed to have vanished, or even about the Commonwealth, which seemed to be unruly and divided between the former Dominions and newly independent African states over the question of apartheid. There was a powerful head of steam behind the idea of Britain's future in Europe. *The Sun* declared that 'After years of drift and failure, the Common Market offers an unrepeatable opportunity for a nation that lost an empire to gain a continent.'[14] Even Enoch Powell was resigned to the loss of the Empire and thought the Commonwealth 'a farce'. As he repeatedly told the Society of St George, he was much more interested in the project of England with its racial homogeneity, historical continuity and parliamentary sovereignty. 'For a nation such as we are', he told a meeting in Sidcup on the eve of the referendum, with 'our whole history dominated by the evolution of Parliament and our very existence inseparable from parliamentary self-government', the question was 'nothing less than whether we shall remain a nation at all'.[15]

In the event, the British public voted 67.2 per cent to stay and 32.8 to leave. 'We are all Europeans now. Let us make sure that we are good Europeans', trumpeted *The Sun*.[16] In the event, although Britain was now part of Europe, it was a reluctant member. It was not a founding father of postwar Europe, but had boarded the train when it had already left the station. More than that, joining Europe in itself felt like a defeat. Britain had built an empire on which the sun never set, and which it had ruled without being answerable to any other power, but now it was falling apart. It had won the Second World War and – albeit with the United States and USSR – been able to dictate terms to the defeated European countries, but this now counted for nothing. Henceforth Britain was part of a Europe in which she was not the leading power and could not dictate the rules. Enoch Powell put his finger on the pulse of this popular discontent when he told Tony Benn of a conversation with a taxi driver who had voted No. The taxi driver said, 'there was some talk of a European Parliament and I was not prepared to see the British Parliament put under a European parliament'.[17]

## 'Up Yours, Delors!'

Britain's scepticism towards the European project continued and even intensified in the Thatcher era. France, under President

Mitterrand, continued to develop the European project, not only as a vehicle for French influence but as the best way to lock in the ever more powerful Federal Republic of Germany. When German reunification took place in 1990, memories of France's historic defeats by Germany came flooding back, but it became even more important to the French to keep Germany under supranational controls. For many in Britain, by contrast, Europe seemed simply to move from a French to a German hegemony.

In the early years of her prime ministership Margaret Thatcher pursued a tireless offensive against the amount the United Kingdom contributed to the EEC budget. She repeatedly demanded a rebate until she was finally given what she wanted at the Fontainebleau summit of June 1984. That same month she attended the fortieth anniversary commemoration of the D-Day landings in Normandy, at which the keynote speech was given by US President Ronald Reagan. Commemorating the Second World War was always a good way of reminding the Europeans who had been victorious. Federal German Chancellor Helmut Kohl was not invited to the ceremony while François Mitterrand was left to rue how the French had not been invited to take part in the landings in 1944. Kohl and Mitterrand chose the commemoration of the Battle of Verdun, in which 700,000 French and German soldiers had died, now to join hands in a gesture of renewed Franco-German friendship. 'Europe is our shared fatherland', said their joint declaration, 'The union of Europe is our common goal and we will work towards it in a fraternal future.'[18] This Franco-German axis would be at the centre of the European project as it was now relaunched, while the United Kingdom would remain very much on the sidelines.

In January 1985 Jacques Delors, Mitterrand's former finance minister, became president of the European Commission. He was an admirer of Pierre Mendès-France because, like him, he was in favour of 'decolonisation, the modernisation of France and the deepening of democratic participation'.[19] He wanted to broaden the EC, including Spain and Portugal, which had recently rejected their dictatorships, and to deepen it both economically and politically, to control West Germany and ensure that it did not move closer to communist Eastern Europe and the Soviet Union. He argued that 'France will become greater through Europe'.[20] Mitterrand, back in Paris, was also keen to develop Europe militarily, overcoming the failure of the European Defence Community in 1954 by making France and West Germany a European pillar of

NATO, while ensuring that Germany did not become once again an independent great power. 'France has no better or solid partner in Europe' than West Germany, he wrote in 1986. 'Germany is part of Europe, without Germany there would be no Europe, and there will be no German greatness outside Europe.'[21]

Delors' first step was to propose to European leaders a Single European Act, which would achieve a single market in Europe without customs barriers by the end of 1992. It would also end the system by which one power could veto an EC decision by moving to a system of qualified majority voting. He wished to take advantage of the economic recovery and the embrace of more liberal economic principles by France and Britain, as well as West Germany. The Act was signed in Luxembourg and The Hague in February 1986 and came into force on 1 July 1987. Meanwhile, in Brussels in May 1986, Jacques Delors unveiled the new twelve-star European flag and sounded the new European anthem, Beethoven's *Ode to Joy*.[22]

This was already a step too far for Margaret Thatcher, but it was only the beginning for Jacques Delors. In February 1987 he proposed that the EC budget should be set for five years. In February 1988 he proposed to double EC structural funds and move towards an economic and monetary union (EMU) with a single currency, together with a social charter that would soften some of the shifts towards a free market. In July 1988 Delors also suggested that in ten years 80 per cent of economic legislation, and possibly also financial and social legislation, would come from the EC.[23]

After her third general election victory in June 1988, Mrs Thatcher felt that she could push back against the developing European project. 'Britain counts for something good again', she had announced earlier that year. 'For the first time since the Second World War our energies as a people are now concentrated on improving our national standing.'[24] Jacques Delors was her bugbear, and the fact that the British trade movement embraced the social charter sorely antagonised her. After Delors came to England and addressed the TUC conference in Bournemouth on 7 September 1988, and was greeted by chants of *Frère Jacques*, she decided to make Britain's position clear. Until now, she had been quite pragmatic in her negotiations with Europe, but this was an ideological offensive against what she called 'the federalist express' or 'the Babel express' which drew on all the weapons of her armoury: freedom, sovereignty, nationhood and British relations with the wider world.[25]

Addressing the College of Europe in Bruges on 22 September 1988, Margaret Thatcher argued that modern Europe was not created in the 1950s but had a much longer history in which Britain had played a central part:

> We British have in a very special way contributed to Europe. Over the centuries we have fought to prevent Europe from falling under the dominance of a single power [...] We have fought and we have died for her freedom [...] And it was from our island fortress that the liberation of Europe itself was mounted.

This political liberation, she argued, had also brought economic freedom, as collectivist projects were seen off and deregulation, privatisation and free markets had been promoted. Britain had pioneered this work through privatisation, the Big Bang (deregulation of financial markets) and (though she did not mention it) dismantling the power of trade unions and crushing the miners:

> We have not successfully rolled back the frontiers of the state in Britain, only to see them re-imposed at a European level with a European super-state exercising a new dominance from Brussels.

The European Community, she continued, should not be thought of as moving towards a federation or a United States of Europe. That was anathema to her. Instead, it should be a

> willing and active cooperation between independent sovereign states [...] Let Europe be a family of nations, understanding each other better, appreciating each other more, doing more together but relishing our national identity no less than our common European endeavour [...] Europe will be stronger precisely because it has France as France, Spain as Spain, Britain as Britain, each with its own customs, traditions and identity. It would be folly to try to fit them into some sort of identikit European personality.[26]

Lastly, Britain's commitment to Europe had to be balanced by its commitment to the Commonwealth, to NATO for defence and above all to the special relationship with the United States.

> Let us have a Europe which plays its full part in the wider world, which looks outward not inward, and which preserves that Atlantic community – that Europe on both sides of the Atlantic – which is our noblest inheritance and our greatest strength.

Strong stuff though this was, Foreign Secretary Geoffrey Howe had to persuade Mrs Thatcher to cut some phrases, such as proclaiming the British 'more successful colonialists than any other European countries' and 'forget a United States of Europe, it will not come'.[27] At the Madrid summit of the European Council in June 1989 he battled valiantly to keep the prime minister on course for monetary union, but was increasingly unable to control her anti-European outbursts. He feared the growing isolation of Great Britain from the European Community. In June 1989 they both attended a European summit in Madrid at which the pressure was increased both for monetary union and the social charter, which she described as 'quite simply a socialist charter'.[28] On 14 July 1989 Thatcher attended the French Revolution celebrations in Paris, giving an interview to *Le Monde* in which she claimed that with Magna Carta the English, not the French, had invented liberty, and pointedly giving Mitterrand a copy of *A Tale of Two Cities*.[29] On her return, on 24 July 1989, she sacked Geoffrey Howe as Foreign Secretary. A few days later François Mitterrand announced that it would be quite possible to enact a treaty on greater union without Britain.[30]

British scepticism about Europe crashed into a higher gear after the fall of the Berlin Wall on 9 November and steady progress towards German reunification, which was finalised in August and September 1990. Mitterrand too was anxious about the revival of the German threat. A Pancho cartoon in *Le Monde* depicted Mitterrand saying to Kohl, 'You haven't said anything about the Oder-Neisse line' and Kohl teasing, 'Nor about Alsace-Lorraine'.[31] For Margaret Thatcher and some of her Cabinet colleagues it was as if all the lives lost in the First and Second World War had been sacrificed in vain. 'We must not forget. We have had two world wars, haven't we?' she asked in July 1990.[32] Her Trade and Industry Secretary, Nicholas Ridley, was even more explicit. In an interview to *The Spectator* he said of monetary union, 'This is all a German racket designed to take over Europe. I'm not against giving up sovereignty in principle, but not to this lot. You may as well give it to Adolf Hitler.'

The ensuing furore obliged Ridley to resign but arguably, in private, Mrs Thatcher shared his thoughts.[33]

For Jacques Delors the answer to German reunification was deeper European union. Appearing on *L'Heure de Vérité* on 23 January 1990 he expressed hope that Europe would become a 'true federation' by the end of the millennium.[34] Matters came to a head at a meeting of the European Council in Rome on 27–28 October 1990, when agreement was reached about progress towards a European Union with greater powers and a timetable for further monetary union, with a central bank by 1994 and a single currency by 1997. The United Kingdom was unable to sign up to these developments and in the House of Commons on 30 October 1990 Margaret Thatcher reported that 'The President of the Commission, Mr Delors, said at a press conference the other day that he wanted the European Parliament to be the democratic body of the Community, he wanted the Commission to be the Executive and he wanted the Council of Ministers to be the Senate. No. No. No.' In reply to a challenge from Liberal Democratic leader Paddy Ashdown that the prime minister 'no longer speaks for Britain – she speaks for the past', Mrs Thatcher replied:

> Oh dear, it seems that there must be quite a lot of late parrots in cloud cuckoo land, judging by the right hon. Gentleman coming out with that stuff [. . .] I take it that the right hon. Gentleman's policy is to abolish the pound sterling, the greatest expression of sovereignty [. . .] That matter is one to be decided by future generations and future Parliaments. Parliament is supreme, not the right hon. Gentleman, the Leader of the Liberal Democrats.[35]

The verdict of *The Sun* on 1 November 1990 was somewhat more succinct: 'Up yours, Delors'. That day, Geoffrey Howe, now leader of the House, resigned. As a backbencher, on 13 November 1990, he explained that the prime minister had made compromise impossible by asserting 'a false antithesis' between 'independent sovereign states' and 'a centralised, federal super-state'. 'I have fought too many battles in a minority of one', he regretted, intimating that Mrs Thatcher had no problem with standing alone, as Britain had in 1940. He concluded:

The tragedy is – and it is for me personally, for my Party, for our whole people and for my Right Honourable Friend herself, a very real tragedy – that the Prime Minister's perceived attitude towards Europe is running increasingly serious risks for the future of our nation. It risks minimising our influence and maximising our chances of being once again shut out. We have paid heavily in the past for late starts and squandered opportunities in Europe. We dare not let that happen again. If we detach ourselves completely, as a Party or a nation, from the middle ground of Europe, the effects will be incalculable and very hard ever to correct.[36]

This was the beginning of the end of the Thatcher era. Other Cabinet ministers came out against her and a leadership election was called. Although she topped the poll her majority was not enough to avoid a second round, and on 28 November 1990 she resigned. It seemed for a moment that the pro-Europeans had won the battle. But Geoffrey Howe was reminded ruefully of Dukas' *The Sorcerer's Apprentice*, which exposes the danger of conjuring up powerful spirits: 'Where Margaret had drawn the first bucket of Euro-scepticism from the well, others were only too ready to follow.'[37]

## The Breakthrough of Euroscepticism

Plans for greater monetary and political union promoted by President of the European Commission Jacques Delors came to a head with the Maastricht Treaty on European Union, signed by leaders on 7 February 1992. This renamed the EC the European Union, introduced citizenship of the Union, added steps towards political union in foreign, security and internal affairs and paved the way to the introduction of the euro in 1997. The governments of François Mitterrand and John Major supported the treaty but this had to be ratified by national parliaments or by referendum. There was a good deal of opposition to Maastricht in both France and Britain. Ghosts of past domination of Europe by Germany and fears of its return were conjured up. On this occasion the French and British behaved differently: the former swallowed the treaty in order to retain a dominant role in Europe, while among the latter Euroscepticism took long strides forward.

'I love Germany so much', French writer François Mauriac once wrote, 'that I am delighted there are two of them'. After 1990 there was only one, with a population of 80 million. France relived the painful memories of 1870, when the first German unification was built from the defeat of France, and even closer to home, memories of the defeat of 1940 and the German occupation of France. The message of 1940, however, was that France could only survive in a united Europe. During the parliamentary debates of May 1992, socialist Prime Minister Pierre Bérégovoy said that his experience as an adolescent in 1940 of the defeat of France had made him more European, not less. As a left-wing European, moreover, he was able lovingly to quote Victor Hugo on the future United States of Europe.[38] However, not all socialists voted the same way. Jean-Pierre Chevènement, whose constituency of Belfort had famously not been taken by the Germans in 1870, denounced what he called 'the new American-German Holy Alliance of capital' and the emergence of a new Bismarckian Reich.[39]

On the Right, the leadership of the Gaullist Rassemblement pour la République (RPR) was in favour of the treaty, but Philippe Séguin, who had written a biography of Emperor Napoleon III, who had made France great again in the nineteenth century, feared that the French would lose their sovereignty in the new German-dominated Europe. In terms of national identity, he said, they would be left 'only their cheeses, a few of their customs, because folklore doesn't upset anyone [...] perhaps the *Marseillaise*, so long as we change the words'.[40] There was much debate over whether General de Gaulle would have approved Maastricht. His former prime minister, Michel Debré, aged 80, argued that the treaty subjected France to collaboration with a dominant Germany, as in 1940–4, so that 'Laval would have said "yes", de Gaulle would have said "no"'.[41]

The treaty was approved by the French National Assembly on 13 May 1992 by 398 votes to 77, with 99 abstentions, but the country was far more reserved. Its feeling would be gauged in a referendum on 21 September 1992. During the campaign François Mitterrand argued for 'a strong France in a strong Europe', which would reach out to the former communist states of Eastern Europe.[42] Giscard d'Estaing, leader of the centre-right Union de la Démocratie Française (UDF), visiting the peace memorial at Caen, told a female voter to support Maastricht 'for Franco-German reconciliation, Madame'.[43] Later he told young UDF activists at Vincennes that they had launched today's Europe: 'There is too much negativity in this campaign. People are conjuring up fear and advising retreat. But this idea of Europe came from France. Imagine how other countries would see us if we tore up our own work with our own hands?'[44] On the eve of the vote, Bérégovoy warned that 'victory for the "no" vote would be victory for the Front National'.[45] In the event, the vote was very close, 'yes' 51 per cent and 'no' 49 per cent. Large cities and those with high levels of education and high incomes voted in favour, but the *banlieues*, the deindustrialised regions of the Nord Pas-de-Calais and Normandy and towns on the south coast from Perpignan to Nice (which were indeed Front National strongholds) were against.[46] The danger of a France closing in on itself and fearing wider engagement was commented upon, but for the moment France's commitment to Europe was safe.[47]

There was no referendum in Britain to ratify the Maastricht Treaty; what mattered was the vote in Parliament. Parliamentary opposition to Maastricht was led by the so-called Bruges Group who hailed Mrs Thatcher's speech of 1988 as the gospel of Euroscepticism. Norman Tebbitt argued that 'Britain still carries the burdens (and some residual benefits) of the imperial past' and warned that in the European Union 'the British Chancellor of the Exchequer's powers will be comparable to those of the treasurer of a permanently rate-charge-capped local authority'.[48] More pithily, in *The Sunday Telegraph* Boris Johnson denounced a 'Delors plan to rule Europe'.[49] Whereas the French were refighting the wars of 1792 and 1870, the British were refighting the Second World War. Bill Cash, one of their key affiliates and chair of the Conservative Backbench Group on European Affairs, declared that Germany had 'long wanted to establish a German-centred united Europe, based around a Deutsche [sic] Mark zone and a federal union modelled on herself'.[50] 'Britain and its democracy in Westminster', said Cash, 'played an absolutely fundamental role in the Second World War in saving Europe from German hegemony and dictatorship'. Once again they were fighting the 'Battle for Britain'.[51]

Although there was no Maastricht referendum in Britain, Eurosceptic opinion was stirred up by the debates and pressure to hold one was demanded by a Referendum Party set up in 1994 by millionaire James Goldsmith. It secured a modest 2.6 per cent of the vote in the 1997 general election. Goldsmith died shortly afterwards but his campaigning opened the way to the United Kingdom Independence Party (UKIP), which would have much more of a future. UKIP was a 1993 rebranding of the Anti-Federalist League founded in 1991 by Alan Sked, a lecturer at the London School of Economics and former pupil of historian A. J. P. Taylor. It secured 3.7 per cent of the vote in the 1994 European elections and attracted the likes of City financier Nigel Farage, whose view of Europe was shaped by visits to First World War battlefields and who favoured Bomber Command ties. After UKIP was squeezed to 0.3 per cent of the vote in 1997, Sked was ousted by a group including Farage, who wanted a less constitutionalist and more populist approach, playing on monocultural British nationalism and hostility to immigration. Sked denounced Farage as a racist who was once quoted as saying, 'We will never get the nigger vote. The nig-nogs will never vote for us.'[52] The popular appeal of Farage was undoubted, and he and his party emerged as a powerful Eurosceptic voice, exerting huge pressure on the Conservative Party and British politics more widely.

By the 1990s the issue of Europe was becoming a real problem in Britain. Whereas the French embraced the European project as a way of extending French power and reducing the threat of Germany by locking her into federal institutions, the British increasingly saw those institutions as a threat to national sovereignty. Britain had a very different experience of the Second World War from France. For France, 1940 meant defeat and occupation, while Britain was entranced by the fantasy of 'standing alone' against Hitler, like the dome of St Paul's rising above the smoke of the Blitz. If she had been rescued it was by the United States, not by Europe; indeed Britain claimed that along with the Americans she had liberated Europe from Fascism and Nazism. Isolation from Europe carried no fears because of the 'special relationship' with the United States. Besides, Great Britain's calling historically had been outside Europe, a Greater Britain of white Dominions and an empire stretching from the Caribbean to India. In her empire she had been supreme; she had not had to take rules from anybody. As the European option became less palatable, so a fantasy of a global Britain that was in some way a reincarnation of her empire became more attractive.

# 7 ISLAMISM AND THE RETREAT TO MONOCULTURAL NATIONALISM

Thinking about empire was radically changed in the last ten or twenty years of the twentieth century by a powerful phenomenon: the rise of global Islamism. This was the eruption onto the world stage of a political Islam with universalist claims.[1] Its first breakthrough was the Iranian Revolution of 1979, its second the war in Afghanistan against the Soviet invasion of that year. It came to the fore after the end of the Cold War which, it was hoped in the West, would lead to the triumph of democracy and human rights. Instead, it provoked a new phase of neo-imperialism by the Western powers, drawing on fantasies of their colonial past. These battles were fought not only along what had been the north-west of India and in the Middle East; they affected immigrant communities in the metropolis, who increasingly identified as Muslims. This perceived threat fired Islamophobia in the host societies and the refinement of monocultural national identities which excluded Muslims, much as they had done in the colonial era but now alienating or radicalising them.

## The Rise of Global Islamism

The Iranian Revolution of 1979 toppled the Shah who had been backed by American power. It opened the way to the return of Ayatollah Khomeini and the foundation of the Islamic Republic.[2] This confronted the West not on the economic battlefield, although it paid US$8 billion for the release of the fifty-two Americans taken hostage during the revolution, but on the religious and cultural battlefield, where Islam was used to define opposition to America and the West, and to mobilise mass movements. In his September 1980 Message to the Pilgrims Khomeini declared of the 'Great Satan' that 'America is the number one enemy of the deprived and oppressed people of the world. There is no crime America will not commit in order to maintain its political, economic, cultural and military domination.' He announced that 'Iran is a country effectively at war with America' and its stooges and that its Revolutionary Guard was ready for combat.[3]

Iran's riposte began with demonstrations but moved on to armed attacks. After Israel invaded Lebanon in 1982, 400 Revolutionary Guards were sent to support the Islamist militant group Hezbollah, and forced Israel out. They then organised devastating suicide attacks on the US embassy in Beirut on 18 April 1983, killing 63 people, including 17 Americans, and on a barracks in Beirut on 23 October 1983, killing 241 American and 58 French servicemen.[4] Palestinians on the West Bank, suffering intensified Israeli occupation and settlement, but fired up by Islamist actions and led by those whom Yasser Arafat called 'generals of the stones', launched an *Intifada* or revolt in December 1987.[5]

A second dimension of the Islamist movement was triggered by the Soviet invasion of Afghanistan in 1979. A holy fightback or jihad was mounted by Afghan guerrillas, the *mujahideen*, who were reinforced by volunteers drawn widely from the Islamic world, including Palestinian refugees, Egyptians, Algerians and Saudis.[6] Like the International Brigades who went to fight fascism in Spain in 1936, they were inspired by a desire for justice and bound together as brothers in arms. One of the recruits was Osama bin Laden, the son of a Syrian mother and Saudi businessman who died in a plane crash when he was a child. He decided not to follow his brothers who went to study in Britain and the United States but graduated from university in Jeddah in 1979. In 1984 he went to Peshawar on the Pakistan–Afghan border, formerly a key garrison of the British Empire on the North-West Frontier, to recruit and train *mujahideen* for the war against the Soviets.[7] The Soviets finally withdrew from Kabul on 15 February 1989, and Osama bin Laden and his comrades later claimed that their guerrilla action was responsible not only for the Soviet defeat in Afghanistan but also for the subsequent implosion of the USSR (Figure 7.1). For them it was an anti-imperial victory on the scale of the defeat of the Sassanid Empire in 651 or the Byzantine Empire

**Figure 7.1** Global Islamism: *mujahideen* fighter with rocket-launcher advancing on Jalalabad, Afghanistan, March 1989.
Getty Images / David Stewart-Smith / Hulton Archive / 76309285

in 1453, and the next target would be what it saw as the American Empire and its allies.[8]

The end of the Cold War was supposed to hand undisputed victory to the West, now supreme over its old enemy, the communist USSR. A forty-year struggle under the threat of nuclear destruction was over and the following decade was later dubbed 'the holiday from history'.[9] The way seemed open for the United States and its allies to promote a new world order of liberal democracy, the rule of law, human rights, the free market and peace, without fear of opposition. If there were opposition, intervention to promote these goals would be justified on liberal or humanitarian grounds, especially if the United Nations offered it sanction, to safeguard or extend that new world order.[10]

In the event, things did not turn out so simply. The threat of communism was immediately replaced by the threat of global Islam. The British orientalist and Princeton academic Bernard Lewis wrote a piece on 'The Roots of Muslim Rage' for *The Atlantic* in September 1990. The cover picture was of a turbaned figure, staring out at the reader with anger.[11] Harvard professor Samuel Huntington argued in 1993 and more fully in 1996 that after the Cold War the conflicts of the future would be clashes of civilisations, fired by opposing religious and cultural identities.[12] The doctrine of liberal interventionism was all too soon displaced by a neo-imperialism which resurrected the methods and fantasies of former empires.

It was in the Persian Gulf that promises of the new liberal world order came up against neo-colonial realities. One of the vestiges of Britain's colonial power was Kuwait, a hub of the oil trade on the Gulf, which it had ruled as a protectorate from 1899 and regarded as its sphere of influence even after it became independent in 1961. Saddam Hussein's Iraq invaded Kuwait on 2 August 1990. Under the cover of UN economic sanctions against Iraq, the Americans and British exploited their new-found confidence and resolved to take firm action. 'Out of these troubled times', President George Bush told the US Congress on 11 September 1990, 'a new world order can emerge' in which 'the rule of law supplants the law of the jungle'.[13]

For many Britons intervention was less about upholding the rule of law and more about reliving the heroics of the Second World War. Veterans of the Desert War against Rommel were asked to give advice to British troops dug in on the Saudi/Iraqi border, while Battle of Britain pilots sent goodwill messages to their heirs in the Gulf.[14] The French were much less happy with a war that looked too much like a repeat of the Suez Crisis. French Defence Minister Jean-Pierre Chevènement, who had witnessed the evils of the Algerian War as a young administrator, and opposed American imperialism, pressed for a negotiated solution. As late as 14 January François Mitterrand tried to convince the UN Security Council to hold an international conference that would broker an Iraqi withdrawl from Kuwait and attempt to solve the Israel–Palestine question.[15] This was opposed by both Great Britain and the United States, who extracted Resolution 678 from the Security Council requiring Iraq's unconditional withdrawal from Kuwait by 15 January 1991, or else face war. Saddam Hussein was a secular, not a Muslim leader, but three days before the UN deadline he played the Islamic card, having 'Alallahu Akbar', God is great, placed between the three stars on the Iraqi flag.[16]

Operation Desert Storm began on 16 January 1991, with bombs and cruise missiles raining down on Kuwait and Baghdad. To those on the ground it seemed less like liberal intervention than neo-colonial aggression. The Americans committed 540,000 troops, the British 35,000 and the French 10,000. Chevènement resigned on

**Figure 7.2** The 'clash of civilisations': an American soldier inspects the carbonised bodies of Iraqi soldiers on the 'highway of death' from Kuwait to Baghdad, February 1991.
Getty Images / Peter Turnley / Corbis Historical / VCG / 640507099

29 January, criticising the 'big stick applied on a scale not seen to date' and the 'Victorian hypocrisy of the world establishment' which, he claimed, concealed the right of the strongest behind the rights of man.[17] This had no effect on the 'shock and awe' tactics of the allied forces who drove the Iraqis out of Kuwait on 23 February. The Americans attacked retreating Iraqi forces along what became known as the 'highway of death' (Figure 7.2). General Colin Powell, chair of the Joint Chiefs of Staff, said he had 'no idea' how many Iraqis had been killed and, he continued, 'I don't really plan to undertake any real effort to find out'. Greenpeace estimated that between 70,000 and 115,000 Iraqi troops and between 72,000 and 93,000 civilians had been killed.[18]

That said, the Gulf War never really ended as the United States and United Kingdom tightened the blockade on Iraq, encouraged hopeless revolts by Shiites and Kurds, imposed 'no-fly zones', and bombed Baghdad in Operation Desert Fox in December 1998. One calculation is that between 1991 and 1998 half a million Iraqi civilians died.[19]

After defeating the forces of the Soviet Union and fired anew by the brutality of the United States and its allies in the Gulf War, the Muslim 'International Brigades' that had gone to fight in Afghanistan fanned out to engage in other actions. These included the war in Bosnia against the Serbs in 1992–5 following the breakup of Yugoslavia, the 1994–6 war in Chechnya against the Russian Federation and the civil war in Algeria following the coup of 1992. One individual who went to fight in Afghanistan and then fought for the Bosnian Muslims was Mustafa Kamel Mustafa, the son of an Egyptian army officer, and who studied civil engineering at Brighton Polytechnic College. He later became more commonly known as Abu Hamza.

In Algeria, the government of Colonel Chadli, a veteran of the FLN, began a programme of economic liberalisation in 1986 and political liberalisation from 1989. But free elections benefited the Islamic Salvation Front (FIS) which aimed at founding an Islamic state. The FIS won over 80 per cent of the seats contested in December 1991 and looked set to win most of the rest of them in January 1992. Encouraged by France and the United States, the Chadli government mounted a coup on 11 January 1992, dissolving parliament, cancelling the elections, declaring a state of emergency, banning the FIS and arresting its leaders.[20] Secretary of State James Baker later explained that upholding the rule of law and democracy was tempered by the challenge of dealing with global Islamism:

> Generally speaking, when you support democracy, you take what democracy gives you. If it gives you a radical Islamic fundamentalist, you're supposed to live with it. We didn't live with it in Algeria because we felt that the radical fundamentalists' views were so adverse to what we believe in and what we support and to what we understand the national interests of the United States to be.[21]

The military coup against democracy gave Islamists no alternative but to turn to armed struggle. An Islamic Armed Movement (MIA) was set up by Saïd Mekhlofi, a veteran of the Afghan War and the FIS's former head of security, and its members wore stolen army uniforms. The Armed Islamic Group (GIA) formed in the summer of 1992 also involved Afghan veterans and adopted Afghan-style beards, shaved heads and loose-fitting clothes. Algeria now descended into civil war as these armed groups attacked local authorities and police, seized control of tax revenues and massacred their opponents in the name of jihad.[22] These opponents included the French, who were seen to be backing the Algerian dictatorship. The GIA killed five French people in Algiers on 3 August 1994 and on Christmas Eve 1994 hijacked an Air France airbus at Algiers airport, demanding the release of imprisoned comrades. The plane was stormed two days later by French forces after it arrived in Marseille and the hijackers were killed.

## *The Satanic Verses* and the Crisis of British Identity

The rise of global Islamism and the return of neo-colonial conflict had a profound impact on immigrant communities in France and Britain. To date, even if they had a Muslim background, these had identified as North African or Arab, as Indian, Pakistani or East African Asian. Increasingly, these minority communities now identified themselves as Muslim and were identified as such by members of the host communities who embraced Islamophobia.

The underlying issue in both countries was the extent to which immigrant populations could be integrated into metropolitan society. How much would they have to transform their values, leaving behind beliefs brought from their country of origin, and how far could they retain these while living in the host society? Equally, how far were metropolitan societies prepared to accommodate difference and diversity by reinventing themselves as multi-ethnic, multicultural spaces, and how far would they retreat into a defensive, monocultural and indeed colonialist nationalism which stigmatised and excluded immigrant populations?

In Britain, these questions were played out in a famous 1989 *cause célèbre*. Salman Rushdie's book *The Satanic Verses* was published in September 1988 and shortlisted for the Booker Prize, but the Muslim community felt deeply that it insulted the Prophet. Matters came to a head in the Yorkshire city of Bradford. Many of the immigrant population had come from Mirpur in Azad Kashmir to work in the woollen industry. When factory jobs disappeared they set up businesses instead and those who made money built places of worship; the Bradford Council of Mosques was founded in 1981. Industrial decline, however, also sharpened the hostility of the white community and conflict flared up locally and nationally with the Honeyford case of 1984–5.[23]

Four years later the storm that swept the city was international. In *The Satanic Verses* Gibreel, a Bombay film star, who has survived a plane crash, imagines himself to be the Archangel Gabriel, abandoned by God. He speaks diabolic verses to the sleeping Prophet Mohammed which are dictated to the English-educated author, a thinly-disguised Rushdie, who confesses, 'there I was, actually writing the Book, or rewriting, anyway, polluting the word of God with profane language'. Bradford Muslims considered that atheists were portrayed in a good light while people of faith were mocked. They petitioned the publisher, Viking/Penguin, to have the book removed, only to be told that it was a work of fiction, universally acclaimed by literary critics. In response they took to direct action, and on 14 January 1989 two thousand angry people in Bradford publicly burned the book. Similar book-burnings took place in Rushdie's home town of Bombay and in Kashmir, Dacca and Islamabad. A month later, on 14 February 1989, Iranian leader Ayatollah Khomeni issued a *fatwa* enjoining true Muslims to kill the author and his publishers, 'so that no one will dare insult the sacred beliefs of Muslims henceforth. And whoever is killed in this cause will be a martyr.' Rushdie went into hiding under the protection of the Special Branch and the British government broke off diplomatic ties with Iran.[24]

The debates triggered by these incidents were ostensibly about freedom of speech. At a deeper level, however, they were about British national identity. The case was made that freedom of speech had been won over the centuries by Protestant reformers and Enlightenment thinkers and defended against tyranny and totalitarianism in two world wars. *The Daily Mail* called the Bradford book-burning a reaction 'in the fashion of the ayatollahs'. *The Independent* argued that the Muslim book-burning followed 'the example of the Inquisition and Hitler's National Socialists', and that if Rushdie were killed, 'it would be the first burning of a heretic in Europe in two centuries'.[25] Shabbir Akhtar, a Cambridge graduate who was Community Relations Officer in Bradford and spokesman of its Council of Mosques, received hate mail calling him 'a Fascist, the British Ayotollah seeking to establish a theocracy in the middle of Yorkshire', and telling him to leave the country.[26]

For British Muslims, on the other hand, the debate was about their right to practise their faith in the host society without fear of attack, and to feel that the host society genuinely welcomed them. Akhtar criticised what he called the 'Liberal Inquisition' of the intellectuals and press that was legitimating popular and often violent attacks on 'Muslim Fanatics':

> The word 'Muslim' became a term of abuse [...] mosques were stoned [...] There was talk of deporting Muslims who publicly supported the fatwa. Muslims were regularly portrayed as trouble-makers refusing to assimilate while other ethnic groups were appropriately applauded for their good sense and cooperation. Many leader writers openly began to doubt the very possibility, let alone the wisdom, of creating a multicultural society in the first place.[27]

He was not the only Muslim who, caught between their family and culture of origin, and the intellectual life of their adopted country, now felt alienated from the latter. Yasmin Alibhai Brown, of Ugandan Asian heritage, who wrote for the *New Statesman*, said that she was

> shocked by the way that liberals, who proclaimed their belief in freedom of thought and expression, were completely unwilling to listen to the voice of very powerless people who were offended by the book. These supposedly dangerous people were my mum, my aunts and my uncles [...] But it was not just the hatred that angered me. It was also the way liberals totally misunderstood people's continuing need for religion. Particularly among members of Muslim groups who are still finding it hard to find their place in British society.[28]

The debate soon moved on explicitly to what it meant to be British. In 1991, of a total British population of 50 million, 3,625,000 or 7.2 per cent were foreign-born. But how many, Conservative politicians wished to know, were *really* British? In April 1990 Norman Tebbit, formerly a minister under Mrs Thatcher, gave an interview to the *Los Angeles Times* in which he registered concern about how far Asian immigrants might be considered British. He applied what he called the Test Match 'cricket test' and observed, 'A large proportion of Britain's Asian population fail to pass the cricket test. Which side do they cheer for? It's an interesting test. Are you still harking back to where you came from or where you are?'[29]

Tariq Modood, a young researcher of Pakistani origin, took issue with Tebbit, underlining how British nationalism and the weight of its colonial past served to exclude Commonwealth immigrants from British society rather than to integrate them.

> Many young Asian people – especially if they have visited the country of their parents and grandparents – know how thoroughly they are a part of British society, outside of which they would be lost. Yet they do not, indeed cannot, glory in their Britishness. For what, after all, is their status here? How can they when they are constantly told, not least by the Tebbits of this country, that they are not really British, that they do not belong here [...] If we care for social harmony and national unity, the priority must be to dismantle the legacy of imperial racism and to develop some forms of Britishness that go beyond narrow nationalism. What we don't need are facile tests of loyalty that reinforce the social divisions they are supposed to eliminate.[30]

The debate delicately sidestepped the underlying question of Islam, but this was rapidly made explicit. Charles Moore, an Eton-educated journalist, made a deliberate contrast between the barbarians who had overrun the Roman Empire and those who were now at the gates of what remained of the British Empire. He argued in October 1991 that 'the foundation of any British immigration policy should be that immigration is a positive good, but only if it enhances, and does not undermine Britishness. You can be British without speaking English or being Christian or being white', he went on, 'but nevertheless Britain is basically English-speaking, Christian and white, and if one starts to think that it might become basically Urdu-speaking and Muslim and brown, one gets frightened and angry'. If Europeans did not have enough babies, he warned, 'the hooded hordes will win, and the Koran will be taught, as Gibbon famously imagined, in the Schools of Oxford'.[31]

Debates about free speech and Islam generated renewed obsessions about immigration and national identity. After 1981, when the British Nationality Act withdrew the concept of citizenship of the United Kingdom and Colonies, migration from the Commonwealth became much more difficult. The main route now tried was to request asylum under the 1951 UN Convention on Refugees of which Britain was a signatory. Numbers of asylum seekers rose from under 4,000 in 1988 to nearly 45,000 in 1991. The Asylum and Immigration Act of 1993 tried to deal with this and in 1995 Peter Lilley, the Secretary of State for Social Security, told the Conservative Party Conference that he would 'deter the hordes of people who were arriving in these shores under the guise of students or tourists, only to announce later that they were refugees'. This gesture was described by one journalist as attempting to close 'the gates of Fortress Britain'.[32] Asylum seekers whose applications were turned down, or other illegal immigrants arrested for minor offences without proper documentation, were likely to be interned and deported. In 1993 an Immigration Removal Centre was opened at Campsfield House in Kidlington outside Oxford, built like a prison with razor-wire topped walls, surveillance cameras and guard dogs, run by a private security service. This was the first instance of a British gulag, entrusted to the private sector, in which unwanted immigrants of non-European origin were held arbitrarily for undefined periods, stigmatised and often maltreated.[33]

Debates about British national identity often revolved around two fantasies: the beneficence of the Empire and the 'good' Second World War. Rushdie's *Satanic Verses* was in fact as critical of Britain's view of its colonial past as it was of religious fundamentalism. In the novel, the whisky-drinking film producer S. S. Sisodia asserts that 'the trouble with the Engenglish is that their hiss hiss history happened overseas, so they dodo don't know what it means'. Meanwhile for Gibreel, London was 'a wreck, a Crusoe-city, marooned on the island of its past, and trying, with the help of a Man-Friday underclass, to keep up appearances'.[34] Britain continued to wallow in nostalgia about the beneficent Empire, particularly the Raj. In 1984 Granada Television had a huge success with *The Jewel in the Crown*, based on the novels of Paul Scott, who had served in the British Army in India during the Second World War, while E. M. Forster's *A Passage to India* hit the screen as a major film by David Lean.

The Second World War had been fought to defend that Empire and the British habitually fell back on the narrative of victory in the Second World War to boost their sense of national and indeed imperial pride. The fiftieth anniversary of the Normandy landings in June 1944 and of VE Day in 1995 provided opportunities to rehearse this story. 'This year we will commemorate the 50th anniversary of the landing of the Allied armies', Norman Tebbit told the Bruges Group on its fifth anniversary, 'overwhelmingly English-speaking armies, from the United States of America, the Empire and the Kingdom itself, which liberated Western Europe from the Nazi darkness'. This narrative, however, was not the experience of immigrants whose families had fought in the Allied armies. The independent fortnightly Muslim paper, *Q News*, founded in 1992, pointed out that 'A large proportion of the armed forces of the British Empire was made up of Muslims, with some very famous Army regiments containing a high percentage.' Moreover, it continued, 'the Free French had North and West African troops, most of whom were Muslim'.[35]

## 'No More Paki. Me a Muslim'

The generation of young immigrants born around 1970 in Britain and France faced alienation on two sides. On the one hand they were increasingly part of a global culture which was defined by the mass media and expanding higher education and they felt estranged from their families and communities who seemed narrow-minded and traditional. On the other hand these young immigrants were repeatedly told that they were not fully French or British because of their origin in former colonies or other parts of the developing world. They were antagonised by what remained of colour bars, by religious discrimination and growing Islamophobia, and by national narratives of empires and wars that divided them from the host country. Immigrants of Muslim origin who had often been attacked as Arabs or Muslims now found that the teaching of Islam gave them a powerful sense of identity, honour and mission. In Hanif Kureishi's 1995 novel *The Black Album*, a young man, Chad, asks a friend, 'Earlier, did you say Paki to me? [...] No more Paki. Me a Muslim. We don't apologise for ourselves neither.'[36]

This turn to Islam might have reconciled older and younger generations but too often they clashed when the pragmatism of the former came up against the idealism of the latter. At a UK Islamic Mission conference in Bradford in 1991 Bangladeshi vice-president Dr Wasti called for practical measures against discrimination in housing, education and jobs, Muslim schools and accommodation with Muslim law, while also voting for mainstream parties in the forthcoming 1992 election. He was confronted by Munir Ahmed, Bradford president of Young Muslims UK. He scorned what he called 'petty little things' and 'reforms' and instead offered 'the greatest gift, Islam and the Qur'an, a light for all to "save ourselves and the whole of humanity from the fire"'.[37]

New music bands sprang up expressing protest and resistance, such as Fun-da-mental, led by Bradford-born Haq Qureshi, otherwise known as Aki Nawaz.[38] It hit the scene at the 1991 Nottingham Carnival with its mixture of hip-hop and bhangra combined with an overtly political stance. A *Melody Maker* review said that 'their live performances are more like political rallies than gigs. Samples of Louis Farrakhan, Malcolm X and Enoch Powell's famous "Rivers of Blood" speech, and the fact that a couple of the group dress like PLO fighters further fuel the excitement.' Their tracks offended Muslim elders and were banned from two Asian television channels because they openly supported the *fatwa* against Salman Rushdie. Haq retorted:

> Forget the image of Asians as passive, happy people. Listen man, there are gangs of young Indians and Pakistanis like us on the streets of Bradford, Birmingham, Manchester, every-where, who refuse to put up with the shit our parents and grandparents have lived with for years [...] But this group aren't just speaking for Asians in Britain, we're speaking for all non-whites all over the world. Black people have been fucked over for centuries, and it has to end. If the western powers don't back off, we are heading for one huge war. Maybe not just yet, maybe not for another twenty years, but at some stage in our lifetime.[39]

In reality the war came more quickly than anticipated. Second- or third-generation immigrants who had previously identified as British might now identify with Pakistan and the struggles that were being played out there. For example, Moazzam Begg was born in Birmingham in 1968. His mother died when he was six and while he was still a child he travelled to meet an aunt in Karachi. Back in Birmingham, as a teenager he joined the Lynx gang of English, Irish, Indian, Afro-Caribbean but mostly Kashmiri youths who battled against local racists and neo-Nazis. After leaving school he worked in his father's estate agency but thought of becoming a soldier, since his father had told him that 'Begg' meant leader or chief, and that 'We are the descendants of Tatars, Mongols who settled in Central Asia and established the Great Mughal Empire in India.' He then worked for the Department of Social Security (DSS) and took a part-time law degree. The 1991 Gulf War politicised him. He took to wearing a Palestinian scarf and returned to Pakistan in 1993 where he met *mujahideen* who were fighting in Afghanistan. Becoming a practising Muslim, he took part in a relief convoy to embattled Muslims in Bosnia. He converted to the idea of the jihad as a Muslim obligation, left the DSS, learned Arabic and in 2001 travelled to Afghanistan, where al-Qaeda was now active. He would be waiting when the British and American forces arrived.[40]

## The Veil Controversy and the Crisis of French Identity

In France also there was a *cause célèbre* in 1989. On 3 October that year three female Muslim pupils, aged between thirteen and fifteen, were excluded by Ernest Chenière, headteacher of the Collège Gabriel Havez in Creil. Forty miles north of Paris, Creil was an unremarkable town of 32,000 inhabitants established in the nineteenth century on the railway line to Belgium. Its immigrant population from North Africa was attracted by the availability of industrial work and concentrated in the poor neighbourhoods of Rouher and Les Cavées. As in Bradford, industrial decline from the 1970s made life tougher but Creil was one of the many *banlieues d'Islam* drawn to the attention of the public by political scientist Gilles Kepel in his 1987 book of the same name. He showed that in 1965 there were only four Muslim places of worship in France but prayer rooms multiplied in factories, SONACOTRA hostels and the council flats of the suburbs, and by 1985, promoted by missions from Pakistan and oil money from the Middle East, there were nearly a thousand. They were concentrated in the north-east of Paris and old industrial towns in the Paris region and provincial cities where North African and sub-Saharan Muslims concentrated.[41]

The Collège Gabriel Havez was in an educational priority area, ethnically mixed and described by the head himself as 'a social dustbin'.[42] The pupils, however, were excluded not for educational underachievement but for refusing to take off their headscarfs in the school. Chenière argued that this garment violated the principle of *laïcité*, the doctrine that the republican school was a religiously neutral space. He cited an education circular of 1937 that declared: 'State education is secular. No form of proselytism is permitted in its schools.' The young women replied that the Qu'ran forbade them from showing their hair in order to preserve their purity. Politicians and the media backed the teacher. *Le Monde* agreed that the school of the Republic must be 'the same for everyone' and warned against what looked like an attack on it: 'French people see fanaticism in anything that looks, even from a distance, like a *chador*.'[43] The French Muslim community rallied around the girls and on 22 October about a thousand Muslims, veiled women followed by men, marched from Barbès in northern Paris to the Place de la République, demonstrating in defence of their right to wear the veil. Film footage showed some of them wearing Khomeini masks, which encouraged fears that the Islamic revolution was coming to France.[44]

Ostensibly, this was a debate about the republican principle of *laïcité* or secularism. Secular education was pioneered by the Third Republic in the 1880s as a way of clipping the wings of Catholic education, which had supported the rival regimes of monarchy and empire and had destroyed the republics of 1792 and 1848. It required children to leave their religious identities at the door of the republican school in order to learn to become citizens, to put their own beliefs and interests behind them in pursuit of the common good of the Republic. The doctrine had often been mitigated in the interests of Catholics, not least in June 1984 when the socialist government was forced to withdraw plans to abolish state subsidies to private Catholic schools after a million Catholics came onto the streets to demonstrate. *Laïcité*, however, overlay much deeper issues about French national identity and indeed colonialism, which were challenged by Islam. Whereas compromises had been possible with Catholicism, and whereas the Jewish minority had generally espoused the principles of *laïcité*, with Islam things were different. It was argued that no compromise was possible because Islam was essentially a foreign religion and tolerance of Islamic practices in public spaces prevented the integration of immigrant communities. Journalist Christian Jelen said that 'frightening pictures' of the 22 October 1989 demonstration 'made it look as though Paris was one or two metro stops from Teheran or Beirut'.[45]

There were traditionally two forms of *laïcité*, one which allowed religions to flourish freely in the private sphere and another that was hostile to religion as such. The socialist Education Minister Lionel Jospin accepted that the school was a neutral space in terms of religion. However, he said that *laïcité* should not be 'a *laïcité* of combat'. On the contrary it should be 'a benevolent *laïcité*, designed specifically to avoid wars, including wars of religion!'[46] This weaker version was not to the taste of French intellectuals. Alain Finkielkraut joined forces with Régis Debray, who had campaigned during the Bicentenary of the French Revolution for a return to revolutionary values, and Elisabeth Badinter, who had just published a book on the Enlightenment philosopher Condorcet, to write an open letter to Jospin on 2 November entitled, 'Teachers, don't capitulate!' 'The future will tell', it began, using powerful references to France's disastrous Second World War, 'whether the year of the Bicentenary will have witnessed the Munich of the republican school'. If France was not to become 'a mosaic of ghettos', the republican school must be a neutral space in which its citizens were forged. 'Neutrality is not passive, nor is liberty tolerance [...] Should we abandon what you call '*laïcité* of combat' in favour of kindness just when religions are spoiling for a fight? *Laïcité* is and remains a battle by its very nature.'[47]

Although it was barely articulated, there was also a colonial dimension to this struggle. In colonial Algeria, to be Muslim and a French citizen was almost a contradiction in terms. Before 1946 only a thin stratum of Arabs who set aside their Muslim 'personal status' and accepted the Code Civil became citizens. After 1946 Muslim men were given the vote but treated like second-class citizens in a separate electoral college. Muslim women were not given the vote until 1958 when, as we have seen, they were also pressured to remove their veils. This was seen to be a precondition of their integration but it was also the violence of the coloniser over the colonised. As Frantz Fanon had observed in 1959, 'The occupier sees in each Algerian woman newly unveiled an Algerian society whose defence systems are being dislocated, opened, kicked in.'[48] The insistence that young Muslim women remove the veil was arguably a repetition of the same gesture, thirty years on.

## The Return of the Algerian War

The veil controversy reignited conflicts that could be traced back to the Algerian War. Some politicians held that thirty years was enough time to get over the Algerian War. Centrist François Bayrou claimed that 'the conflict no longer had any significance today', while right-wing Nicolas Sarkozy thought that the legacy of the war had been 'rapidly digested' and did not have a lasting political impact on French political life.[49] Against this, however, Benjamin Stora, an Algerian of

Jewish origin who had left Constantine aged eleven in 1962, argued in *La Gangrène et l'oubli* (1991) that the traumas of the Algerian War had not been forgotten but merely repressed. They were made manifest by the presence of first- and second-generation immigrants who in 1999 made up 17 per cent of the French population, nearly 28 per cent of whom were of North African origin.[50] The Right, argued Stora, could not endure the presence of Algerian Muslims on French territory. This 'intrusion' constantly reminded them of their colonial defeat and yet persuaded them that the colonial regime in Algeria was the natural order of things:

> The intrusion of the former colonised person in the metropolis is experienced as a ghastly inversion, seen as him colonising the territory of 'civilized' people [...] Far from inducing a sense of failure the loss of Algeria produces a pride and certainty that the French were right during the colonial period. This narcissistic scar is evident in the will to keep replaying, repeating and reviving the war years, perpetuating the disappointment that the war was lost.[51]

The pain of the Algerian War years was replayed in a very dramatic way in 1991, the thirtieth anniversary of the massacre of pro-FLN Algerians in Paris on the orders of police chief Maurice Papon. To commemorate this, a director of Algerian origin, Mehdi Lallaoui, made a film about the massacre, *Le silence du fleuve*. On 17 October 1991 a procession of 10,000 marched from the Canal Saint-Martin, where so many Algerians had been drowned in racist attacks, to the Rex cinema, where the film was screened.[52] The story of the massacre was also publicised by radical historian Jean-Luc Einaudi in his *La Bataille de Paris, 17 October 1961*.[53] He explored the connections between the repressive actions of Maurice Papon – from deporting Jews under Vichy and firing on Algerian demonstrators in Paris on 14 July 1953 to ordering torture and summary executions as super-prefect in Algeria in 1956 – and the 1961 massacre for which he was responsible as Paris prefect of police.

In 1997 Maurice Papon was brought to trial. This was not for his role in the 1961 massacre, because the amnesty laws passed in the 1960s prevented prosecutions for acts committed during the Algerian War. Instead he was tried for deporting Jews from Occupied France. The trauma of the Algerian War was nevertheless stirred up again by the trial. Einaudi took the opportunity to denounce Papon for the massacre. Papon sued for libel, but lost. Then, on 10 June 1999, the French National Assembly officially recognised that what had taken place in Algeria for eight years was not an internal police problem but war. A debate was reopened about the use of torture against Algerian rebels by the French security services. On 31 October 2000 twelve former French resisters from the 1940s and actors in the campaign against torture in the 1950s and early 1960s appealed to President Chirac and Prime Minister Jospin in the Communist daily *L'Humanité* to condemn the torture that had been undertaken in the government's name.[54] One of the signatories was Simone de Bollardière, whose soldier husband Jacques had been cashiered and imprisoned for his opposition to torture in Algeria. She explained that 'the army is like the Church, you don't criticise it. It is *la grande muette*. It does what it wants but you must not say so.'[55] Meanwhile the historical evidence for torture in Algeria was provided by Raphaëlle Branche, the book of whose thesis, *La Torture et l'Armée pendant la Guerre d'Algerie*, was published in December 2001 and attracted very wide reviews.

It might be imagined that the evils of torture and massacre committed during the Algerian War would now be universally condemned. But this was far from the case. Airtime was given to General Paul Aussaresses who, with a patch over one eye, boasted about having personally tortured to death twenty Algerians.[56] The Jospin government attempted to pass a law dedicating the date of the 1962 ceasefire, 19 March, to the memory of all victims of the Algerian War. This, however, was opposed by a 'Manifesto of the Generals' signed by 521 generals who had served in Algeria. They argued that they had themselves fought 'with honour and dignity' against 'all forms of torture, murder and crimes that were ideologically inspired and methodically organised'. The dilemma they occasionally faced, they claimed, was either 'to dirty their hands by harshly interrogating those who really were guilty or to accept the certain death of innocent people'.[57] In this way, not only were the battles of the Algerian War still being fought but the partisans of French Algeria and the conduct of the French forces in that bloody war had not given up the fight.

Together, the rise of global Islamism and the resurgence of the colonial past challenged attempts to build a contemporary multicultural society. Nationalist and even extreme nationalist movements gained ground. The French governments, like the British, clamped down on immigration and defined more closely who was French and who was not. In March 1993 the socialist government lost the election to the right-wing and tough Interior Minister, Charles Pasqua, who ordered sweeping arrests in *banlieues* of Algerian immigrants thought to favour the GIA.[58] Measures were taken to tighten immigration controls and immigrants without proper documentation – the so-called *sans-papiers* – faced arrest and deportation. In August 1996 a group of *sans-papiers* under threat undertook a hunger strike in the church of Saint-Bernard, in the Goutte d'Or, but police used axes to smash the doors of the church and arrest and deport them. Meanwhile, the government implemented the recommendation of the Long Commission that the acquisition of French nationality by French-born children of immigrants should not be automatic. As a result the Beur generation which had marched for equality in 1983 now faced the possibility of not being granted French nationality.

A powerful reason for firm action by the government was the rise of the Front National. In 1995 the presidential election was won by Jacques Chirac, and Jean-Marie Le Pen won 15 per cent of the vote. The Front National made breakthroughs in towns along the Mediterranean coast from the Pyrenees to the Côte d'Azur together with the deindustrialised towns of northern and eastern France. Much of this was explained by the ongoing battles of the Algerian War and by the influx of immigrants from North Africa. The link between the Algerian War and the Front National was clear. Le Pen had fought and allegedly tortured rebel suspects in Algeria; he was one of the few politicians to publicly support the *pieds noirs*. Former leaders of the OAS ran for the Front National: Pierre Sergent was a deputy in the Pyrénées Orientales in 1986–8, Jean-Jacques Susini stood in elections in Marseille 1997, although without success. The *pieds noirs* had settled along the Mediterranean coast, opposite their old homeland, and supported those who had fought to defend French Algeria. A survey of 2002 showed that 90 per cent of *pieds noirs* and their children who voted for the Front National still preferred to have held on to French Algeria.[59] The *pieds noirs* nevertheless made up only a small proportion of the Front National vote. In the formerly industrialised towns of the Nord Pas-de-Calais and Lorraine, where *pieds noirs* did not live, the white working-class electorate had traditionally voted communist but now switched to the extreme Right. The main reason was their opposition to North African immigrants who were portrayed by the Front National as the scapegoat for all France's ills: unemployment, crime, drugs and national decline. Political scientists had to find new terms for this and variously called it 'Left Le Penism', 'Labour Le Penism' or 'social nationalism'.[60]

As French national identity became more restrictive so young people of North African origin defined themselves more sharply as Algerian and Muslim. There was an enthusiasm for Raï music which contested both French colonialism and conservative Islam. Raï came from the bars and bordellos of the port city of Oran in Algeria, appealing to a deracinated population exposed to many influences. A new generation of singers in the 1980s such as Cheb Khaled, born in Oran in 1960, appealed to the Beurs of the *banlieues* of Paris, Lyon and Marseille. Banned as dissolute by the FIS, the singers exiled themselves to France although one of them, Cheb Hasni, was murdered in Oran by Islamist extremists in 1994. More aggressive were rappers such as Malek Brahimi, known as Malek Sultan and later Freeman, born to an Algerian family in Marseille, who joined the rap group IAM with musicians of Neapolitan and Malgache origin and infused Arab heritage with black consciousness.[61]

Those who committed to young Muslim movements were a minority, but no less influential. A Union of Muslim Youth (UJM) was founded in Lyon in 1987 by Yamin Makri, born in Lyon in 1963 and in charge of a small publishing outfit, Tawhid, denoting the oneness of the faith. The Young Muslims of France (JMF), founded in 1993, was particularly strong in Marseille and Nice. Of North African origin but born and educated in France, they did not attend traditional mosques where Arab was spoken by their elders, and they wanted to move beyond what they called the 'tribalism' of neighbourhoods in a more universal project.[62] Increasingly, young Muslims identified with the global community (*ummah*) of Islam, whose militants challenged first the global reach of Soviet communism through the *mujahideen* in Afghanistan, then US imperialism in Iraq, and finally the pro-Western governments through the activities of Groupes Islamiques Armés.

As in Britain, youths who combined French and Algerian identities might prefer to espouse the latter and then buy into the violence of the Algerian civil war. One extreme individual was was Khaled Kelkal, born in Algeria in 1971, brought up in the Lyon suburb of Vaux-en-Velin, and imprisoned as a petty criminal in 1990–2. In prison he was radicalised into Islam and learned Arabic. In July 1995 he exploded a bomb at the Saint-Michel Metro station, killing eight and wounding 117. Shot by police in October 1996, he was vilified in the press as a 'young delinquent from Vaux-et-Velin' and 'an Islamic terrorist born in Mostaganem in Algeria'. What was significant, however, was precisely how a young immigrant with some delinquent tendencies from a Lyon *banlieue* could be radicalised as what was now called a Muslim terrorist.[63]

## A Multicultural Moment?

In spite of the reach of global Islamism and the retreat to monocultural nationalism there were still moments when French and British societies seemed to be open to more multicultural solutions. Ethnic minorities were treated more equally and religious and cultural diversity was celebrated. Unfortunately there were limits to such shifts in thinking. French intellectuals and politicians never accepted the concept of multiculturalism, which they regarded as 'Anglo-Saxon'. A national identity, they argued, could not be forged from a melting pot of different ethnic communities. In Britain, there were more serious attempts to bring in multicultural policies and attitudes. Repeatedly, however, these collided with the unspoken assumption that there were colonial hierarchies which had existed 'out there' and were now reproduced 'back here'.

Between 1997 and 2002 France was under the socialist government of Lionel Jospin. It gave some thought to bringing back the principle that immigrants born on French soil should automatically become French when they reached their majority, but decided that the stigmatisation of 'paper French people' was too strong and the danger of socialists weakening national identity too great.[64] The great achievement of multicultural France was the 1998 World Cup victory of a French team that included a Beur, Zidane, a Senegalese, Patrick Vieira, a Kalmuk, Youri Djorkaeff, an Armenian, Alain Boghossian, and a Kanak from New Caledonia, Christian Karembeu. This was widely praised as the black-blanc-beur team which reflected contemporary France. The Swiss daily, *Le Temps*, said that while France had lost an empire she had 'regained her rank on another field'.[65] This diversity was not, however, to all French people's taste. Alain Finkielkraut, a passionate supporter of the principle of *laïcité*, regretted that commentators were constantly referring to the footballers' origins whereas what mattered was that they were all French. 'This obsession with ethnicity distances us from the republican ideal and takes us closer to multicultural America. The message now is *metissage*, diversity replaces culture.'[66] For most French intellectuals, multiculturalism was never a goal, and French culture must prevail.

There was a brief multicultural moment in Britain after the murder of 18-year-old Stephen Lawrence on 22 April 1993 at a bus stop in Eltham, south London. Stephen's parents had come to Britain from Jamaica in the 1960s, and one of his five white assailants asked him 'what, what, nigger?', before stabbing him to death. The police failed to arrest any suspects for two weeks and a court case against them collapsed for lack of evidence. Stuart Hall, Jamaican-born professor of sociology at the Open University, provided evidence to the Macpherson inquiry set up by the Labour government in 1997. His distinction between 'formal' and 'informal' variants of British racism fed into the ultimate report which indicted the Metropolitan Police for its 'institutional racism'. In 1997 Hall sat on a Runnymede Trust commission on *The Future of Multi-Ethnic Britain*, which demanded that all forms of racism be addressed and put equality and diversity at the centre of the public agenda. The Home Secretary, Jack Straw, gave his blessing to the commission, but when its recommendations were greeted by 'comprehensive outrage', said Hall, Straw 'publicly rubbished our work' and 'went scurrying back to the writings of George Orwell – containing a sort of love letter to a certain version of Englishness – in order to establish the virtues of English nationalism'.[67]

Journalist and writer Yasmin Alibhai Brown commented forcefully on the structural defects in the British imagination. She argued that it was not 'catching up with a globalized world' but was 'still locked into an imperial past'. She criticised both the 'white Oxbridge men' who staffed the Foreign Office and the 15-year-old British National Party supporter who declared, 'This is a white country. We ruled these monkeys before they came here with their horrible smells.' The British, she said, should pay more attention to the perspectives of the people they once ruled.

> This country could learn so much from the diverse people who now live here. For centuries, we, the colonized peoples of the world and those who came to stay and lay their claim on their

mother country, have been told that we have everything to learn from and nothing to teach our ex-masters. That in spite of decolonization – maybe in revenge for it – that power relationship of cultural dominance can never be shed by either side.[68]

Racial conflicts still racked British towns, but at the turn of the century the new dynamics of global Islamism changed their meaning. The riots that broke out in Bradford on 7 July 2001 began as a conventional fight by Pakistani youths joining an anti-Nazi march to defend their neighbourhood against a National Front rally. Those who remained on the street were surrounded by the police in riot gear and began to throw missiles at them. Hundreds of arrests were made and of 144 charged, 107, overwhelmingly Asian Muslims, with a few Afro-Caribbeans, were given harsh prison sentences for riot. Although their parents' generation had taken part in the burning of the *Satanic Verses* in 1991, these youths were keen to hit back with force against discrimination and humiliation. 'In those days people used to call 'em monkeys or raisins. Me dad used to tell me how it used to be, even me mum', said one youth in prison. 'This country is a very racist country. Now the Asian people, Jamaicans, won't stand for it, know worra mean?'[69]

What began as a conventional race riot, however, became for some a laboratory of Muslim extremism. Offenders claimed that they been sentenced for up to ten years for the more serious offence of riot, instead of violent disorder, 'because of the colour of their skin', said one prisoner. British Asians were still being treated by the police, courts and popular press as colonial subjects. The experience of prison caused some of the youth to convert to Islam. They grew beards and were mocked by prison guards as 'Taliban'. The riots happened before 9/11 but the global jihadism that provoked the attack and the subsequent War on Terror were keenly felt in prison. 'I watch the news, Muslims getting' killed all over the world', one young prisoner complained, 'no one gives a toss'.[70]

The rise of global Islamism, which was in part a response to American and Soviet imperialism, thus derailed the hopeful new order of liberal interventionism and launched a new phase of neo-colonialism with the Gulf War of 1991. In both Britain and France culture wars broke out over the issue of Islam. Immigrants of Arab or Pakistani origin identified increasingly as Muslims, while host communities panicked about invading 'hordes' and defined national identities which rejected multiculturalism and espoused monoculturalism. In Britain, there was a cult of beneficent imperialism and the Second World War while in France, painful memories of the Algerian War returned to haunt and divide. Immigrant communities felt alienated and excluded, and the young generations abandoned assimilation and defined themselves more radically as Muslims, loyal to a global Muslim community. Racial and religious tensions and violence increased, both at home and internationally, opening a road that would lead to 9/11.

# 8 HUBRIS AND NEMESIS: IRAQ, THE COLONIAL FRACTURE AND GLOBAL ECONOMIC CRISIS

At 8.45 a.m. on Tuesday 11 September 2001, American Airlines Flight 11 flew into the North Tower of the World Trade Center of New York City. At 9.03 a.m. United Airlines Flight 175 crashed into the South Tower. A third plane, American Airlines Flight 77, flew into the Pentagon while a fourth, in which the passengers fought back against the terrorists, came down in a field in Pennsylvania. These targets represented the financial centre of global capitalism and the nerve centre of US military power. The towers collapsed at 9.59 and 10.28 a.m. respectively. In the four attacks 3,000 people were killed and 6,000 injured. The core group of attackers belonged to the 'Hamburg cell' of Middle Eastern activists who had gone to study at the Hamburg Technical Institute in 1992–6, trained in Afghanistan with Osama bin Laden in 1999, and went on to the United States in June 2000. The pilots of the deadly planes were Mohammed Atta, born in Cairo in 1968, Marwan al-Shehhi, born in Beirut in 1975, and Ziad Jarrah, born in the United Arab Emirates in 1978. 'Muscle' to control the passengers was provided by veterans from Saudi Arabia who had fought in Bosnia such as Khalid al-Mihdhar, born in 1975, and Nawaf al-Hazmi, born in 1976.[1]

The events of 9/11 were followed by four overlapping crises that shook the first decade of the twenty-first century. First, the displacement of liberal or humanitarian interventionism by new ambitions of empire, masquerading as a War on Terror which set aside all rules and provoked blowback from the regions invaded. Second, the alienation of immigrant communities at home by the pursuit of pseudo-colonial wars and the demonisation of Muslims as terrorists, so that some young immigrants came to identify less with the host community but with former oppressed colonial peoples or with global Islam. Third, a crisis of global capitalism, as global financial flows in pursuit of ever greater profits became unsustainable. The burst of the financial bubble in 2008 provoked economic recession, fiscal crisis and austerity, and inflicted pain on populations from the developing world and Europe to the United States. Fourth, increased and defensive nationalisms triggered a renewed crisis over Europe, this time over the proposed European constitution of 2004. This was rejected in a French referendum of 2005, which excused Britain from having to hold its own referendum, but only postponed her crisis by ten years.

## 'American Empire (Get Used to It)'

9/11 was a watershed in global history. 'History starts today', said US Deputy Secretary of State Richard Armitage.[2] While still governor of Texas, in November 1999, George W. Bush asserted that the goal of American foreign policy was 'to turn this time of American influence into generations of democratic peace. America has never been an empire. We may be the only great power in history that had the chance, and refused – preferring greatness to power and justice to glory [...] Let us reject the blinders of isolationism, just as we refuse the crown of empire.'[3] Once elected president in 2000, however, Bush was surrounded by a group of neo-conservative politicians with other ideas. The Cold War had been won and nothing, logically, stood in the way of the United States imposing its will globally. A think tank founded in 1997 called the Project for the New American Century, whose leading lights included Dick Cheney, Donald Rumsfeld, Paul Wolfowitz and Colin Powell, argued that the United States might take unilateral action in pursuit of its goals and use force preventively, before potential enemies could launch an attack. In 1998 they had put pressure on President Clinton to remove Saddam Hussein from power, but did not prevail. In the Bush administration, however, they called the shots as respectively Vice-President, Secretary of Defence, Under-Secretary of Defence and Secretary of State. In the days and weeks after 9/11 they decided that Osama bin Laden had plotted the attacks, declared a War on Terror and made plans to invade those countries that were said to be harbouring terrorists, first Afghanistan, then Iraq.[4]

The Bush administration was supremely confident that it had the right answers and challenged the international community to follow its lead or, like the League of Nations, face historic oblivion. Bush told Congress on 20 September 2001 that the War on Terror had started and that 'Every nation, in every region, now has a decision to make. Either you are with us, or you are with the terrorists. From this day forward, any nation that continues to harbour or support terrorism will be regarded by the United States as a hostile regime.'[5] British Prime Minister Tony Blair was certainly with Bush. After they first met in February 2001 Blair basked in Bush's announcement that Britain was 'our strongest friend and closest ally'.[6] Blair attended the 20 September session of Congress and was welcomed as a 'friend'.

Billed as a War on Terror, and later as a war on the Axis of Evil which included Iraq and Iran, the American offensive appeared very much a war on Islamism and even on Islam. In his 20 September Congress address Bush explained that 'The terrorists' directive commands them to kill Christians and Jews, to kill all Americans and make no distinctions among military and civilians, including women and children.' This black and white division of the world allowed Israel to show the United States that she too was signed up to the War on Terror against Palestinian 'terrorists'.[7] On 19 September 2001 Premier Ariel Sharon visited the Temple Mount in Old Jerusalem, a site which included the Al-Aqsa Mosque. Stones were thrown at him by angry Palestinians and this moment has been seen as the beginning of the Second or Al-Aqsa Intifada. On 23 November, Sharon visited Ground Zero, the site of the Twin Towers, and returned home saying that America and Israel were fighting the same War on Terror. In March, June and September 2002 the Israelis attacked the Palestinian National Authority in Ramallah, reducing much of it to rubble. They also built an Iron Wall to contain the Palestinians, cutting off villages from their fields and wells.[8] The injustice and humiliation suffered by Palestinians were witnessed by Muslims worldwide on their TV screens and computers and provided a powerful incentive to take the fight to imperialists and Zionists.[9] 'For me, the most important thing is Palestine', said 31-year-old Nabil, a Muslim held in a French prison. 'There have been too many massacres. Frankly, I hate the Jews [. . .] I live near Belleville in Paris. It is a Jewish area and I have Jewish friends, but when I get out, I'll ditch them.'[10]

The United States was reluctant to let go of the liberal interventionist idea that it was fighting to bring democracy and the rule of law to the world. 'Write this down', Bush told Republican governors at the White House on 2 September 2002: 'Afghanistan and Iraq will lead that part of the world to democracy. They are going to be the catalyst to change the Middle East and the world.'[11] This suggested that the liberation of Kabul and Baghdad would be like the liberation of Paris in 1944, replacing dictatorship by democracy. What struck observers, however, was the scale and ferocity of the American attack on Afghanistan which began on 7 October 2001, after the Taliban refused to hand over Osama bin Laden, who was alleged to be in their hands.

'These people were fascinated by historical examples of might', Harvard professor Stanley Hoffmann said of the neo-conservatives around Bush, 'the Roman Empire, or eighteenth- or nineteenth-century Great Britain, an admiration that is rather scarce in American history'.[12] The model of British imperialism was picked up by journalist Max Boot. 'It is striking and no coincidence', he wrote in October 2001, 'that America now faces the prospect of military action in many of the same lands where generations of British colonial soldiers went on campaigns. Afghanistan, Sudan, Libya, Egypt, Arabia, Mesopotamia (Iraq), Palestine, Persia, the Northwest Frontier (Pakistan). Afghanistan and other troubled lands today cry out for the sort of enlightened foreign administration once provided by self-confident Englishmen in jodhpurs and pith-helmets.'[13] Publicly the claim was made that the Americans were helping Afghanistan rebuild itself as a democratic nation, through the good offices of Karzai, who became the country's interim president. Not everyone was fooled. According to Canadian academic Michael Ignatieff in the *New York Times* on 28 July 2002:

> In Washington they call this nation-building lite. But empires don't come lite. They come heavy, or they do not last. And neither does the peace they are meant to preserve. Call it peacekeeping or nation-building, call it what you like – imperial policing is what is going on in Mazar. In fact, America's entire war on terror is an exercise in imperialism. This may come as a shock to Americans, who don't like to think of their country as an empire. But what else can you call America's legions of soldiers, spooks and Special Forces straddling the globe?[14]

Six months later Ignatieff made the point even more strongly. The cover story of the *New York Times* on 3 January 2003 was 'American Empire (Get Used to It)'. In his article on the burden of the American Empire, he warned, 'What every schoolchild also knows about empires is that they eventually face nemeses. To call America the new Rome is at once to recall Rome's glory and its eventual fate at the hands of the barbarians.'[15]

Empire, in reality, was not only imperial glory but colonial brutality. The provisos of liberal interventionism were punctured as early as 17 September 2001 when Bush announced, 'there are no rules'. The War on Terror brought with it massacres, prisons, torture and the strengthening of the security state at home. In Afghanistan 500 Taliban forces who had surrendered were imprisoned in the fortress of Qala-i-Jangi. On 25 November 2001, as Americans moved in to root out al-Qaeda sympathisers among them, the POWs rose in revolt. They were ruthlessly put down by US bombing and only eighty-six survived.[16] The struggle in Afghanistan became a magnet for young Muslims from the West to join the jihad against American and British imperialism. Many of them were captured and became part of the network of prisons being developed by the Americans and British – Bagram in Afghanistan, Guantanamo Bay in Cuba – where they could be held indefinitely and interrogated secretly. Three young British Muslims from the Birmingham area – Ruhal Ahmed and Asif Iqbal, aged 20, and Shafiq Rasul, aged 24 – later known as the Tipton Three, were seized in Afghanistan in 2001. They were transferred to US military custody as enemy combatants and imprisoned in Guantanamo. Meanwhile Birmingham-born Moazzem Begg, now aged 33, who had been living with his family in Kabul and moved to Pakistan for safety, was arrested in February 2002 as an alleged member of al-Qaeda, held and tortured in Bagram prison, and transferred to Guantanamo a year later. The British offensive in Afghanistan also had the effect of alienating and radicalising groups of young Muslims back in Britain. Many young Pakistanis who had been imprisoned for their part in the July 2001 riots in Bradford, 82 per cent of whom were Muslim, came to identify with the struggle of their Muslim brothers while serving their term.[17] The government responded to such threats by an Anti-Terrorism, Crime and Security Bill which was introduced in Parliament on 19 November 2001 and became law on 14 December. It allowed foreign nationals suspected of terrorism to be detained indefinitely without charge. Many of those arrested were held without charge in Belmarsh Prison in London, the United Kingdom's response to Guantanamo.

War in Afghanistan was one thing; war against Iraq was another. It could be argued that al-Qaeda was being sheltered in the former but the case for war against the latter was more difficult to make. It would be necessary for the United Kingdom and United States to act together to persuade – indeed to mislead – the United Nations and worldwide public opinion. At a meeting with Vice-President Dick Cheney on 11 March 2002, Tony Blair said that 'it was highly desirable to get rid of Saddam. The UK would help so long as there was a clever strategy.'[18] The centre-piece of this strategy was to demonstrate that Iraq had weapons of mass destruction (WMD). The commitment to work together was explicit in Blair's note to Bush of 28 July 2002 which began, 'I will be with you, whatever'. The rest, and there was much of it, simply flowed from that. 'If we recapitulate all the WMD, add his attempts to secure nuclear capability, and, as seems possible, add on the al-Qaeda link', continued Blair, 'it will be highly persuasive over here. Plus the abhorrent nature of the regime.' On 12 September 2002, the first anniversary of 9/11, Bush addressed the United Nations General Assembly. He denounced Iraq's refusal since 1991 to meet UN demands for its disarmament, and indeed her development of 'weapons of mass destruction'. This was less a request for solidarity than a threat that if they did not act the United Nations would be finished. Tony Blair immediately slapped him on the back: 'Dear George, it was a brilliant speech. It puts us on exactly the right strategy to get the job done. The perception has been very positive with everyone challenged to come up to the mark.'[19] On 8 November 2002 UN Security Council Resolution 1441 duly gave Iraq 'a final opportunity to comply with its disarmament obligations', but it was less than clear that this resolution authorised military action if it did not.

This close conspiracy of the United States and United Kingdom had a chilling effect on their relations with other European countries, which were much less enthusiastic about the drive to war. France, together with Germany, Russia and China, wanted to give UN weapons inspectors more time to verify whether the Iraq regime did indeed have weapons of mass destruction before war was unleashed. On 22 January 2003 President Chirac welcomed German Chancellor Helmut Schroeder to Paris to celebrate the fortieth anniversary of the

Élysée Treaty between General de Gaulle and West German Chancellor Konrad Adenauer which had cemented the two powers as the heart of the European Community. They agreed to stand up to the Americans, only to be denounced by Secretary of Defence Rumsfeld as representatives of 'old Europe'.[20] At its meeting on 14 February the Swedish head of weapons inspection Hans Blix reported that his inspectors had not yet found the cast-iron evidence of WMD they needed. The French Foreign Minister, Dominique de Villepin, turned the dismissal of 'old Europe' against the Americans by pointing out that Europe also stood for historical experience and solidarity. To loud applause he offered America, a new and brash power, the advice that

> an old country, France, an old continent, Europe, which has known wars, occupation, barbarism, is telling you this today. A country that has not forgotten what it owes to the fighters for freedom who came from America or elsewhere. Which has not ceased to stand strongly in the eyes of History and of men. It wishes to remain faithful to its values and act resolutely with all members of the international community. It believes in our ability to build a better world together.[21]

On behalf of the Americans, the British drafted a Security Council resolution that effectively imposed an ultimatum on Iraq to disarm by 17 March or face war. This required the support of nine of the fifteen members of the Council, but France, Germany, Russia and China were not on board. Three of the undecided members were African and two, Guinea and Cameroon, were former French colonies whose bids for liberation France had done its best to frustrate. Villepin nevertheless drew on the remaining influence it enjoyed in *Françafrique* to make a lightning tour of these states on 9 March 2003. In Cameroon, Villepin announced that 'France would not let a new resolution pass that would open the way to war in Iraq.'[22]

Worldwide, there was a powerful swell of public opinion against war. Huge demonstrations took place on 15 February 2003 in 600 cities from Toronto, Montreal, Seattle, Los Angeles, San Francisco and New York to Barcelona, Rome, London, Glasgow, Dublin, Paris, Brussels, Amsterdam, Copenhagen, Oslo, Helsinki, Berlin, Warsaw, Budapest, Athens and Tokyo.[23] Robin Cook, who had been Labour Foreign Secretary in the 1997 government and was Leader of the Commons after 2002, responded to the verdict of public opinion and the dangers of Blair 'going to war as Sancho Panza to George Bush's Don Quixote' by resigning from the Cabinet on 17 March. Free to speak his mind, he told the Commons:

> The longer that I have served in this place, the greater the respect I have for the good sense and collective wisdom of the British people. On Iraq, I believe that the prevailing mood of the British people is sound. They do not doubt that Saddam is a brutal dictator. But they are not persuaded that he is a clear and present danger to Britain [...] they are uneasy at Britain going out on a limb on a military adventure without a broader international coalition and against the hostility of many of our traditional allies.[24]

This speech, in the short term, was in vain. Tony Blair brandished the spectre of appeasement, the last refuge of all British politicians seeking a mandate for war. He warned the British people not to repeat the experience of the 1930s and 'the almost universal refusal, for a long time, of people to believe Hitler was a threat'. Later he clarified, 'I was careful not to conflate Saddam and Hitler and specifically disowned many of the glib comparisons between 2003 and 1933. But I did mention how joyful people had been at Munich when they thought action had been avoided.'[25] This feat of oratory secured a Commons majority of 412 to 149 for a war that had not been sanctioned by the United Nations.

## 'Another World is Possible'

On 21 July 2001 an estimated 300,000 demonstrators gathered at the G8 – that centre of global economic and political power. Hosted by Silvio Berlusconi, the Italian media mogul and prime minister, and attended by Bush and Blair, it was held in a barricaded red zone behind a massive police presence to keep demonstrators at bay. After 9/11 nothing was left to chance, and even the anti-globalisation movement, which was opposed to violence, was seen as a threat. The *carabinieri* were not so restrained and 23-year-old protester Carlo Giuliani was shot dead from the back of one of their Land Rovers and run over.[26]

'The issue is not how to stop globalisation', Blair told the Labour Party Conference the following October. 'The issue is how we use the power of community to combine it with justice.'[27] The anti-globalisation movement present at Genoa was not going to leave global justice to governments. It gained traction in opposition to the ambition of multinational companies, facilitated and legitimised by the neo-liberal project of the governments of the industrialised North, to impose their will and conditions on the global South. The first drama was the 'Battle for Seattle' on 30 November 1999, when protesters disrupted a ministerial conference of the World Trade Organization. One of the leading demonstrators was José Bové, a French activist who had dismantled a McDonald's restaurant at Millau, at the base of the Larzac plateau, and was photographed at his trial in France holding his chained hands above his head like the Gallic hero Vercingétorix.[28] The lessons learned from Seattle were fed into the World Social Forum which brought 10,000 people to a first meeting in Porto Alegre, Brazil, in January 2001. It was timed to challenge the annual closed meeting of the global political and corporate elite at Davos in Switzerland, and was open to activists from all social movements, trade unions, political parties and NGOs which shared its values. It was masterminded by the Association for the Taxing of Financial Transactions to Help Citizens (ATTAC), set up by French intellectuals around *Le Monde diplomatique*, and by a cluster of Brazilian trade unions and associations. Its Charter of principles, approved in April 2001, said that it was 'a plural, diversified, non-confessional, non-governmental [space where], in a decentralised fashion, interrelated organisations and movements engage in concrete action at levels from the local to the global in order to build another world'. It saw the neo-liberal project as a form of imperialism, opposed 'neoliberalism and [...] domination of the world by capital and any form of imperialism', and condemned 'all forms of domination and all subjections of one person to another'.[29]

The 9/11 attacks forced the World Social Movement to take a stand on global jihadism and the War on Terror. Its second meeting at Porto Alegre in January 2002, attended by 55,000 people, 'absolutely condemn[ed] the terrorist attacks' but also criticised the launch of 'a permanent global war to cement the domination of the US government and its allies. The war reveals another face of neoliberalism [...] Islam is being demonized, white racism and xenophobia are deliberately propagated.' Antonio Negri, a veteran of the Italian Red Brigades, and American radical Michael Hardt had argued in 2000 that imperialism, which had a power centre and boundaries, was being replaced by empire, which had no centre or territory.[30] It now seemed that the global financial empire was showing its teeth. The World Social Movement was behind the massive success of the worldwide demonstrations of 15 February 2003 against the war being driven by Bush and Blair. It was, according to Negri and Hardt, a push-back against 'a common enemy – whether it be called neoliberalism, US hegemony, or global empire'.[31] In the short term the protest failed, but in the medium term it isolated the US and UK governments, who were held responsible for a war based on deceit and whose consequences had not been thought through.

## Nemesis 1: 'Everything Falls Apart' in Iraq

About 130,000 American and 28,000 British forces attacked Iraq on 19 March 2003. The rhetoric of Operation Iraqi Freedom did little to hide the reality of 'Shock and Awe'. Massive air strikes were launched on Iraqi cities before ground forces went in. The initial fighting lasted no more than three weeks. British troops entered Basra during the night of 6–7 April while US troops took Baghdad on 9 April. Two or three thousand Iraqi fighters were killed in the attack on Baghdad but total casualties from the invasion in the first eighteen months including civilians were estimated by *The Lancet* at 98,000.[32]

The Americans and British had been preparing a long time for this war. Militarily, they were effective at knocking out the Iraqi Army, but they were not prepared for what might happen next. In his note to Bush of 28 July 2002 Blair had mentioned 'unintended consequences':

> Suppose it got militarily tricky. Suppose Iraq suffered unexpected civilian casualties. Suppose the Arab street [Arab public opinion] finally erupted [...] Suppose that, without any coalition, the Iraqis feel ambivalent about being invaded and real Iraqis decide to offer resistance.[33]

On 6 September 2002 he foresaw 'a danger of Iraq blowing up in the absence of a serious opposition figure to take power'.[34] On 10 February, only five weeks before the offensive, Blair received advice from the Joint Intelligence Committee that 'the threat from al-Qaeda will increase at the onset of any military action in Iraq'. The same committee warned him again on 17 February that 'the threat from Islamic terrorists, including al-Qaeda, will increase in the event of war with Iraq'.[35] The first ministerial meeting about post-conflict planning was held by

Blair on 6 March 2003, two weeks before the invasion, and that only to request a plan from the Ministry of Defence and the Department for International Development, which could not in any case agree between themselves.[36]

If one failing of the British government was not to listen to intelligence or to plan for post-conflict, another was not to envisage the situation from the perspective of the Iraqis and of Arab and Muslim populations, for whom this was simply a more brutal repeat of age-old colonial violence. Iraq had been a British mandate between 1921 and 1932 and a sphere of influence long after that. The bombing of Iraq by the British in 1920 was engraved on the Iraqi consciousness. As the bombs fell again in 2003, Sadiq, who worked for the Antiquities service in Baghdad, had a flashback to a massacre of a family wedding in 1920, when 'a two-winged plane suddenly came over the horizon and dropped a fireball among the celebrations'. Men and women had been separated for the occasion and half the men were killed or maimed. Now, in 2003, he sighed:

> It's the British again. They have been bombing my family for over eighty years now. Four generations have lived and died with these unwanted visitors from Britain who come to pour explosives on us from the skies. It first began in 1920 [...] I often wonder how they would feel if we had been bombing them in England every now and again from one generation to the next, if we changed their governments when it suited us. They say that their imperial era is over now. It does not feel that way when you hear the staccato crack of fireballs from the air. It is then that you dream of real freedom – *in shaa' allah* – freedom from the RAF.[37]

The trauma suffered in 1920 by Iraqi populations now returned. Pictures of the atrocities instantly relayed across the world had a powerful impact on the *ummah*, the whole body of Muslim believers. On 21 March, the day after the offensive began, protest marches were held in Egypt, Jordan, Yemen, Kenya, Nigeria, Pakistan and Indonesia.[38] Journalist Jonathan Raban described how a wound inflicted by the invasion on one part of the Muslim body was felt by members of the same body hundreds or thousands of miles away. For many decades Muslim suffering had focused on Palestine; now Iraq was the seat of pain.

To see the invasion of Iraq as a brutal assault on the Ummah, and therefore on one's own person, is not the far-fetched thought in the Islamic world that it would be in the west. For weeks the *Jordan Times*, like every other newspaper in the region, carried front-page colour pictures of civilians killed or wounded in Operation Iraqi Freedom [...] On April 2, the picture was of an Iraqi father in a dusty grey jellaba, arms spread wide, screaming at the sky in grief, while at his feet, in a single barewood open coffin, lay huddled the three small, bloodied bodies of his children. His rage and despair can be seen exactly mirrored in the faces of Egyptian demonstrators in Tahrir Square, as the Ummah bewails the injuries inflicted on it by the western invaders.[39]

The invasion was presented by the Americans and British as the liberation of the oppressed Iraqi people from the tyranny of Saddam Hussein, whose statue was filmed being ritually toppled. According to Mark Steel official reports were designed to convey this message: 'Iraqis only count if they're dancing in the streets'.[40] On 1 May, standing on the deck of the aircraft carrier USS *Abraham Lincoln*, George W. Bush declared 'mission accomplished'.

In fact, the mission was far from accomplished and a new version of what Chalmers Johnson called 'blowback', and what Tony Blair had feared might be unintended consequences, began only too soon. The liberation of Iraq was actually its occupation by military forces under a Coalition Provisional Authority headed by diplomat Paul Bremer, who had the power to rule by decree. One of his first acts was to disband the defeated Iraqi Army, lest it become a tool of resistance. The immediate result of this, however, was the breakdown of law and order and widespread looting. Journalists were quick to make comparisons to other war zones and failed states. 'Baghdad has turned into Afghanistan faster than Afghanistan', wrote one; 'Palestinisation of Iraq as Iraqis throw stones at troops', said another.[41] Blair himself visited Iraq and reported back to George Bush on 2 June 2003 that Bremer was 'doing a great job'. That said, he admitted:

the task is absolutely awesome and I'm not sure we're geared for it. This is worse than rebuilding a country from scratch. We start from a really backward position. In time, it can be sorted, but time counts against us. My sense is, we're going to get there but not quickly enough. And if things fall apart, everything falls apart in this region.[42]

Resistance to the military occupation of their country might be spontaneous, such as riots in Basra against British occupation on 9 August 2003. Or it might be organised and targeted by groups which had never before worked together: former supporters of Saddam Hussein's regime, Sunni fighters belonging to Ansar al-Islam, which was linked to al-Qaeda, Shia Muslims of the Mahdi army of cleric Muqtada al-Sadr, and *mujahideen* drawn from outside the country.[43] Resistance attacks were brutally effective. A car bomb explosion at the Jordanian embassy on 7 August killed 23 people and injured 100, while a lorry bomb attack on the UN headquarters in Baghdad on 22 August killed 22 people, including the UN special envoy.[44]

As in Afghanistan, the military occupation involved the imprisonment and torture of captured 'terrorists' by the army and CIA in order to track down other members of their network. The main centre of this activity was Abu Graib prison. So long as what went on in violation of the Geneva Convention was kept secret only so much damage was done. In April 2004, however, pictures of the most degrading, humiliating and sadistic torture of prisoners were leaked to CBS News and broadcast across the world. It was alleged that Secretary of Defence Rumsfeld had authorised these practices. 'Abu Ghraib had become, in effect, another Guantánamo' reported *The New Yorker*, with 'enormous consequences [. . .] for the integrity of the Army and for the United States' reputation in the world'.[45]

Although France had opposed the war in Iraq, it was not against furthering its own neo-colonial ambitions. It had used its influence in *Françafrique* to reinforce its position on the Security Council. It was also more effective than the United States and Britain in undertaking military operations under the radar and away from public attention. This lesson it had learned while crushing the movement for Cameroonian independence behind the screen of the Algerian War. The issue in 2004 was to remove President Jean-Bertrand Aristide in Haiti, whom the French and Americans considered a thorn in the side, while the world's attention was focused on Iraq. Aristide was a radical priest who had countered the dictatorship of the Duvalliers, and enjoyed massive support among the black slum poor. He presented himself as the heir of Toussaint Louverture who had led a slave revolt against the French in the 1790s.

He challenged French and American interests in the Caribbean and wanted to obtain compensation from the French for the tyranny of slavery on the island. On 26 February 2004 he was denounced by Foreign Minister Villepin as a fomenter of disorder and during the night of 28–29 February the French orchestrated a coup to topple him. Just as Toussaint had been captured and sent to die in France, Aristide was kidnapped and flown to the Central African Republic.[46] France had demonstrated how to undertake regime change at its most clinical, without everything falling apart.

## Nemesis 2: The Colonial Fracture at Home

The metropolitan front was another matter. These invasions and occupations had a profound effect on immigrant communities in France and Britain, who too often felt humiliated, stigmatised and alienated. Those of Muslim origin were attacked as outside the national community and sympathetic to terrorists. In France a poll of 28 March 2003 registered that 78 per cent of respondents supported Chirac's line against intervention in Iraq. Another poll of 5 April 2003 revealed a gulf between Muslims and non-Muslims: a quarter of French people but two-thirds of French Muslims felt themselves on Iraq's side while a third of French but nearly three-quarters (72 per cent) of French Muslims did not want the United States to win.[47] A survey of British Muslims in 2005 found that 85 per cent were 'very proud to be Muslims'. Most did not justify violence but 29 per cent of those for whom being Muslim was very important said that there were circumstances in which acts of violence against non-Muslims could be justified, while 23 per cent justified violence against other Muslims.[48]

In both France and Britain national security was tightened up to deal with this threat. Egyptian-born preacher Abu Hamza was arrested on 26 August 2004 under the 2000 Terrorism Act. On 16 December 2004 the Law Lords ruled that the detention without trial of eight foreigners at Belmarsh Prison, known as the 'Belmarsh Eight', even under the 2001 Anti-Terrorism, Crime and Security Act, was unlawful, being incompatible with European and therefore domestic human rights legislation. To avert their imminent release emergency legislation was rushed through and became the 2005 Prevention of Terrorism Act. This provided the government with powers to place control orders on suspected terrorists. It brought an end to the so-called 'covenant of security' under which the British authorities had sometime tolerated Muslim radicals so long as they pledged not to organise attacks in the United Kingdom.[49]

In France, young men of Muslim origin who felt excluded from French society formed a large part of the prison population, but prison only too often increased their radicalism. In 2003 Muslims in Britain accounted for 3 per cent of the overall population in 2003 and 8 per cent of the prison population, whereas in France Muslims accounted for 7 per cent of the population but up to 70 or 80 per cent of prisoners.[50] Omar, a French Muslim prisoner of North African origin, aged 40, explained his predicament:

> I feel abandoned, cheated. They made me believe in [wonderful] things. I was told that I could be successful in France. But all this is false [...] You need a diploma to succeed. [...] As young people of Arab origin, we have always been mistreated in every respect; there was nothing for us, and it's even worse now for the young generations. This is why, with all the injustices that happen to us everywhere and which are getting even worse, it is good to have people like Bin Laden awakening the masses. The Arabs are asleep. [...] Bin Laden woke them up with what he did on September 11th.[51]

France's leading jihad university was Fleury-Mérogis prison south of Paris, the biggest prison in Europe. Djamel Beghal, also aged 40, was a radical preacher there, described by Gilles Kepel as 'a pure al-Qaeda product, a rare case for a Frenchman'.[52] Of Algerian origin, once a youth worker, he moved to Leicester in 1997 and then on to the Afghan jihadist camps. He was arrested on a return trip in 2001, accused of plotting an attack on the US embassy in Paris, and finished up in Fleury-Mérogis. There he became the mentor of two young men of the Buttes-Chaumont gang in Paris, Chérif Kouachi and Amédy Coulibaly, who ten years later would commit the *Charlie Hebdo* killings.

Heightened concerns about the failure of Muslims to integrate and about the threat they posed provoked a reaffirmation of national values. In France this triggered a return of the veil controversy that had broken out in 1989 but had not been settled definitively because the Conseil d'État encouraged the local negotiation of compromises. President Chirac took the opportunity of the approaching centenary of the 1905 Separation of Church and State to set up a commission to look into *laïcité* as a tool to strengthen the Republic and promote national unity. The commission reported on 11 December 2003, declaring that *laïcité* was 'the keystone of the republican model' and that 'conspicuous' religious signs should not be worn in state schools. Enacted by a law of 15 March 2004, it applied nominally to all religions but discriminated very plainly against the Muslim veil.[53]

Presumed threats to national identity also provoked a controversial rehabilitation of France's colonial past. The memory of the Algerian War, which had long been cultivated mainly by the extreme Right and by veterans' associations, was now resurrected officially in order to justify France's past as an empire but, as might have been anticipated, this proved even more divisive than before. France was now a postcolonial society but found itself fractured by conflicting experiences and memories of that war.

On 5 March 2003, just before the invasion of Iraq, Philippe Douste-Blazy, deputy and mayor of Toulouse, tabled a bill which eventually became law on 23 February 2005. Its key clauses were:

> Art. 1: The Nation expresses its thanks to the women and men who took part in the work undertaken by France in its former French departments of Algeria, Morocco, Tunisia and Indochina.
>
> Art. 4: University research programmes will give the place it deserves to the history of the French presence overseas, especially in North Africa. School syllabuses will recognise in particular the positive role of the French presence overseas, notably in North Africa, and give the eminent place they deserve in history to the sacrifices of the soldiers in the French army that originated from these territories.[54]

Following a concerted campaign by intellectuals and academics, who refused to be dictated to about what they taught, the part of Article 4 concerning school syllabuses was withdrawn in February 2006, but the damage was already done.

There was a clear link between law on the veil and the law on colonial history which was provocative to young people of North African origin. Houria Bouteldja, born in Algeria in 1973 but studying in Lyon, was politicised by the 2003–4 debacle over the banning of the veil. She was keen to found a new organisation to articulate the views of young Muslims. Initially she thought of linking the new organisation to the twentieth anniversary of the Marche des Beurs in December 1983, but 9/11 and the wars in Afghanistan and Iraq had brought home that 'we are the children of colonisation' and that 'France is still a colonial state'. Her organisation was called Les Indigènes de la République, the Natives of the Republic. Its members identified with Algerians of Muslim faith who had been denied citizenship and refused independence without long and bloody wars. The date chosen to launch the movement was 8 May 2008, the anniversary of both VE Day and the Sétif massacre in Algeria. This was designed to expose 'the contradiction between the end of the [German] occupation and the rebirth of the Republic in the metropolis and the fact that, on the same day, a massacre was being committed in one of the French colonies. It was very important to us to mark the contradictions of the Republic then and now, a racial and inegalitarian Republic.'[55] The manifesto of the movement developed this theme, claiming that they, not those who went on to torture Algerians, were the true heirs of the French Resistance:

> Our agenda is the decolonisation of the Republic! The egalitarian Republic is a myth. State and society must undertake a radical reassessment of their colonial past-present [...] Our parents and grandparents were enslaved, colonised, animalised. But they were not crushed. They preserved their human dignity by the heroic resistance they undertook to shake off the colonial yoke. WE are their heirs, as we are the heirs of all those French people who resisted Nazi barbarism and joined the oppressed, demonstrating that the anti-colonial struggle cannot be divided from the fight for social equality, justice and citizenship. Dien Bien Phu was their victory. Dien Bien Phu was not a defeat but a victory for liberty, equality and fraternity.[56]

At the same time an alternative history of French colonialism was being pioneered by a research group called ACHAC (Colonisation, Immigration, Postcolonialism). This did not enjoy the legitimacy conferred by the French academy, which by and large defended the French colonial enterprise. ACHAC, on the other hand, argued that France needed to take critical responsibility for its colonial past, which had often been brutal and exploitative and the legacies of which were felt today, above all through the presence of immigrant populations whose family histories were marked by colonialism. They used the term 'colonial fracture' to argue that memories of the Algerian War were divided by the colonial experience – constructed in one way by the so-called *Français de souche*, but totally differently by the children of immigrants. The survey they undertook in Toulouse in 2003 demonstrated that the latter saw colonisation as 'a metaphor for oppression endured *today*': they feel like a 'child of the *indigène* or a child of colonisation', a way of thinking very like that of 'children of slaves' in France's overseas territories. Like the descendants of slaves, they did not see French national history as their own. For most '*Français de souche*', the problem of the Algerian Muslim was seen as proof that ex-*indigènes* from North Africa and their descendants could never be fully integrated into France.[57]

In Britain too there was redefinition of national identity which likewise proved divisive. *Laïcité* itself was not a consideration in British schools, where the teaching of religion was compulsory under the 1944 Education Act. The Labour government included citizenship education on the national curriculum in 2002, in response to the Crick Report on *Education for Citizenship* (1998). This encouraged socially responsible behaviour, service in the community and informed engagement with public life. However, after the 2001 Bradford riots and 9/11, fears increased that immigrant communities were not integrating sufficiently and living 'parallel lives'. The new mantra became 'community cohesion', in the words of Ted Cantle, who produced a report on this question, 'to create shared experiences and values, rather than continuing to entrench separatism and to recognise and reinforce differences'.[58]

Britain, like France, also developed its own version of the *roman national*, 'Our Island Story', which preached an unbroken history of strong government and national greatness. It emphasised the benefits brought to the world by the Empire, informed by a strong sense of British superiority to people in other parts of the world, and discarding its negative side of exploitation and violence. In 2003 historian Niall Ferguson presented a Channel 4 documentary on *Empire: How Britain Made the Modern World*, and published a book with the same title. 'There has never been a better time to understand how Britain made the modern world', through 'the biggest empire ever, bar none', he asserted from a boat on the Port of London. In his view the Empire brought global trade and finance, white settlement, law, order and good governance. It was a vehicle of both globalisation and 'Anglobalization'.[59] Ferguson went on to write *Colossus*, in which he argued that the

United States not only was an empire but must extend its imperium for the greater good of mankind.[60] In the same year American businessman James C. Bennett argued that the Anglosphere, as a network of countries sharing an English culture – in effect the British Commonwealth and the United States – should join together for the robust defence of Western values such as individual freedom, democracy and the rule of law.[61] British historian Andrew Roberts offered a demonstration from the past, arguing that 'the long hegemony of the English-speaking peoples' had seen off Prussian militarism, German Nazism, Soviet-led communism and was battling Islamic fundamentalism. Britain had passed the flame to the United States during the Second World War but 'working together for the good of Civilisation' they were 'the last, best hope for mankind'.[62]

This was not a narrative with which former colonial peoples in Britain could identify. 'Civilisation' had largely been on their backs, if not built with their bodies. Paul Gilroy, author of *The Black Atlantic*, warned in 2004 that 'the quality of the country's multicultural frame depends on what is now done with the hidden shameful store of imperial horrors'.[63] The brutalities committed by the British in Kenya in the 1950s and 1960s were now substantiated by historians of Africa. Caroline Elkins revealed that between 160,000 and 320,000 of the African population of 1.5 million in Kenya were held in the internment camps of 'Britain's Gulag', and most of the rest held in 800 enclosed villages, surrounded by spiked trenches, barbed wire and watchtowers, with the loss of 'tens of thousands, perhaps hundreds of thousands'.[64] David Anderson explained that while Mau Mau killed 32 European settlers and 1,800 African loyalists they lost 20,000 of their own in combat while 1,090 were hanged by the British. 'In no other place, and at no other time in the history of British imperialism', he said, 'was state execution used on such a scale as this, double that in Algeria'.[65] Such revelations powerfully undermined the narrative of peaceful British decolonisation and the benevolent Anglosphere.

Tighter security and remastered national identities did not help to assimilate young immigrant populations. Instead, they were radicalised by the renewed colonial wars of America, Britain and France. On 7 July 2005 three British-born Pakistanis and a Jamaican, who had converted to Islam after the atrocities in Iraq, blew themselves up on London's transport system, killing fifty-six people including themselves. Their leader, Mohammed Sidique Khan, aged 30, was the son of a foundry worker and had not practised Islam as he grew up in the Leeds suburb of Beeston. He called himself 'Sid', campaigned to get Pakistani children off drugs and worked as a teaching assistant in a local primary school. Things changed when a radical preacher, Abdullah el-Faisal, came to Beeston in 1999 and then 9/11 provoked the British invasions of Afghanistan and Iraq. Sidique Khan married a young Indian woman of the fundamentalist Deobandi tradition, against the will of his parents, and went with Shehzad Tanweer, whose family kept a fish and chip shop in Beeston, to Pakistan in order to contact jihadist groups.[66]

In a video released by al-Jazeera on 1 September 2005, nearly two months after his death, Sidique Khan explained the link between British wars and their own actions. First, he declared his friends' dedication to Islam. Second, he explained the unity of the *ummah* and the solidarity they felt with the global Muslim community. Third, he criticised the British government which was occupying Muslim lands and inflicting atrocities and the British people for condoning this:

> I and thousands like me are forsaking everything for what we believe. Our driving motivation doesn't come from tangible commodities that this world has to offer. Our religion is Islam – obedience to the one true God, Allah, and following the footsteps of the final prophet and messenger, Mohammed. This is how our ethical stances are dictated.
>
> Your democratically elected governments continually perpetrate atrocities against my people all over the world. And your support of them makes you directly responsible, just as I am directly responsible for protecting and avenging my Muslim brothers and sisters. Until we feel security, you will be our targets. And until you stop the bombing, gassing, imprisonment and torture of my people we will not stop this fight. We are at war and I am a soldier. Now you too will taste the reality of the situation.[67]

A *Daily Telegraph* poll published that day found that two-thirds of Muslim students in Britain agreed that British foreign policy had contributed to the 7/7 bombings. A *Guardian* poll nationally gave a figure of 64 per cent while a *Daily Mirror* poll put this as high as 85 per cent.[68]

The British government, however, was loath to make a connection between its foreign policy and the suicide attacks.

The first response was to step up arrests of British nationals who had gone to fight in Afghanistan and authorise torture, usually carried out in Pakistan. David Miliband, who became Foreign Secretary in 2007, was frequently asked by MI6 whether a person could be tortured: according to journalist Ian Cobain, sometimes he said 'no' but often he said 'yes'.[69] At the end of his premiership Tony Blair concluded that it was time to halt progress towards a multicultural society and assert staunchly British values. In a speech on 8 December 2006 on 'the duty to integrate' he argued that 'when it comes to our essential values – belief in democracy, the rule of law, tolerance, equal treatment for all, respect for this country and its shared heritage – then that is where we come together, it is what we hold in common; it is what gives us the right to call ourselves British'. He blamed the attacks on what he called 'a warped distortion of the faith of Islam' and 'a new and virulent form of ideology associated with a minority of our Muslim community'.[70] Sayeeda Warsi, who knew the Khan family and had unsuccessfully contested Dewsbury as a Conservative, explained that Blair's message of integration was once again a diktat of exclusion. 'The duty to integrate was firmly aimed at the non-white folk', she observed, the 'adopt our values or stay away' was aimed at the foreigner, the outsider. In reality it was a speech in response to 7/7 delivered with menace towards the Muslim community.[71]

In France also rising tensions were observed through a colonial lens and handled as such. Immigrant communities were consigned to the *banlieues*, the outer suburbs of major cities, without transport, services or ambitions. They were excluded from mainstream society, kept under a constant police surveillance and greeted by force if they protested.[72] On 19 June 2005, Sid-Ahmed Hammache, aged 11, was shot in a fight between two gangs in the Paris *banlieue* Courneuve. Interior Minister Sarkozy said 'tomorrow we will take a Kärcher to clean up the estate. We will use the forces and the time we need, but it will be done.' Under cover of the 'war against crime', the police entered these *banlieues* as if they were internal colonies. They undertook *ratonnades*, a term used for dealing violently with Algerians during the Algerian War, both in Algeria and Paris. Youths of immigrant origin were insulted as 'bastards' or 'scum', intimidated, searched, beaten up and arrested.[73] On 27 October two youths chased by the police in Clichy-sous-Bois fled and hid in a transformer, where they were electrocuted. Their comrades and neighbours claimed that their memory was insulted by

Sarkozy who alleged that they were criminals. Three days later police fired a tear-gas canister into a local mosque where women were marking Ramadan, which was seen as sacrilege by the Muslim community. Youths took to the streets in a chain of riots.[74] Tunisian-born Dhaaou Meskine, the imam of Clichy since 1984, said that they were 'not part of anything. They were without hope. They came knocking, a little too hard, true, at the door of the Republic, asking "Where is Equality? Where is Fraternity?"'[75]

The response of the authorities was once again that of a colonial power, this time explicitly. On 8 November 2005 Prime Minister Villepin invoked emergency powers going back to 1955, as the Algerian War escalated.[76] An individual named Hamza, of Turkish Muslim origin, reported that 'seeing helicopters over the HLM automatically reminds you of Pakistan. The comment you hear most often is, "Look, that's what our Palestinian brothers must experience".'[77] Not surprisingly, many of the young people became even more radicalised. Their manifesto, which they drew from the Internet, was the *Appeal to World Islamic Resistance* by Abu Musab al-Suri, who had gravitated around the Finsbury Park mosque in the 1990s, gone to Kandahar in 1997 and was widely regarded as Osama bin Laden's PR man. His message, which was perfectly designed for the *banlieues*, was that the new phase of the jihad should not be top-down and highly organised, like 9/11, but bottom-up and decentred, passing under the radar of the colonial power and turning its immigrant children against it.[78]

## Nemesis 3: The Rejection of the European Constitution

While colonial war was unfolding in Paris and London, crisis was engulfing the European Union. In 2004 the EU was enlarged to include ten new states – Estonia, Latvia, Lithuania, Poland, Hungary, the Czech Republic, Slovakia and Slovenia from the former communist bloc – together with Cyprus and Malta. Bulgaria and Romania were due to join in 2007. There was also talk of including Turkey in the not too distant future, although its Muslim identity and threat of immigration from Turkey provoked resistance. The difficulty of organising a Union of twenty-five states gave rise to a new European constitution, which would include a president of the Council, a president of the Commission, a foreign minister and a Supreme Court. This was adopted in June 2004 but had to be ratified by the member states. The spectre of referendums across Europe loomed.

France and Britain were both divided about the European project and how it was being broadened and deepened, but France held a referendum on the constitution while Britain avoided it. For Jacques Delors this was simply 'the logical result of the fall of the Berlin wall'. Most political leaders saw that the diplomatic influence of their countries depended on being part of the Union. Even Tony Negri and Michael Hardt saw Europe as a 'barrier against capitalist, conservative and reactionary economic unilateralism'.[79] There were, however, deep cultural and economic fears that national influence and national identities might be diluted in such a large and unwieldy Europe, that competition would increase from low-wage economies in the east to which corporations would move their plants, and that immigration would increase to high-wage economies in the west. Behind these concerns was a fear that Turkey might join Europe and that Europe was becoming less protective of social rights and more the vehicle of the 'Anglo-Saxon' neo-liberal project.

In France, opposition to the new constitution and the enlargement came from two sides. On the Left, an alliance of socialists moving to the left since electoral defeat in 2002, residual communists, Greens and anti-globalisers around ATTAC and peasants led by José Bové came together to fight the neo-liberal project that was blamed for dumping, low wages and reduced welfare and pensions. They were joined, decisively, by Laurent Fabius, who had been economics minister under Mitterrand and Jospin, and close to Blair as a moderniser, but was now battling with Jospin for control of the Socialist Party. He argued the changes would result in 'a real social fracturing, in two Frances'.[80] On the Right were those concerned about French sovereignty and identity, the 'delocalisation' of businesses to Eastern Europe, the possible inclusion of a Muslim Turkey in the Union and a wave of migrants from Turkey.[81] They included the Movement for France, founded in 1994 by Philippe de Villiers, a Catholic conservative politician from the Vendée region and promoter of the Puy du Fou show which recreated counter-revolutionary fantasies of French history.

On 29 May 2005, the French electorate voted against the European constitution by 55 per cent to 45 per cent. As with the Maastricht referendum, 'left-behind' France in the deindustrialsed north and west and along the Mediterranean, voted against, but this time they won. Communists claimed that it was a victory of 'the people', Philippe de Villiers that it came from 'the depths of the country'.[82] Tony Blair was on holiday in Tuscany when news of the French vote came through. He had announced in 2001 that Britain needed to be at the heart of Europe but he was exercised by the fact that the tabloid press was overwhelmingly Eurosceptic and he had never put his heart into making the case for the Union. 'I knew at once that was off the hook', he declared. 'It was true that that I fancied the fight, but it was also true that had I lost, it would have been au revoir. You could almost feel the waves of relief coming over the English Channel and making their way down to Italy.'[83]

The French 'no' vote was not taken as an answer by the European political class. It was decided that the main constitutional changes could be included in an intergovernmental treaty that could be ratified by governments, not by popular referendum. The Lisbon Treaty was duly signed on 13 December 2007. In order to avoid the ire of Eurosceptics, new Prime Minister Gordon Brown failed to appear at the ceremony and sent Foreign Minister David Miliband instead. Brown signed the document discreetly on a later occasion.[84] Britain had got away with it on this occasion, but it would not be the same nine years later.

## Nemesis 4: The End of the Global Financial Empire?

On Friday 7 September 2007 long queues formed outside branches of the Newcastle-based Northern Rock bank as ordinary people tried desperately to withdraw their savings before the bank collapsed. Such a run on a major bank had not been seen in Britain since 1866. Northern Rock was the first sign in Britain of a global financial earthquake, the epicentre of which was the United States. It gathered force as confidence in the system evaporated and banks refused to lend to each other. In September 2008 the New York investment bank Lehman Brothers, founded in 1850, filed for bankruptcy and the City of London Stock Market crashed.

The crisis, though unpredicted, reflected the structural flaws of the global commercial republic that had been relaunched in the 1980s. Those flaws were many. First, financial capitalism had become bloated, the driving force of the world economy, with an estimated 40 per cent of profits accruing to the financial sector. Mergers and acquisitions increased the size of global giants and reduced their ability to know what all their branches were doing. In pursuit of ever-higher yields the sector sold ever-more complex 'products' that were far removed from the productive process. Hedge funds basically bet on whether markets would go up or down and were supposedly geared to win either way. 'Subprime mortgages' were lent to people who did not have the income to pay them and then packaged as securities that could be sold to other investors. The decline in the US housing market after 2006 led to a collapse of this system.

Second, firewalls between commercial banks which took deposits and investment banks which speculated had been taken down. One of these firewalls, the US Glass–Steagall Act of 1932, was repealed in 1999. Northern Rock, a building society that was floated as a bank in 1997, began to borrow money to finance mortgages. Other regulations were removed or avoided, leading to 'casino banking' with ordinary savers' deposits. The City of London was generally less regulated or less policed than New York, earning it the name of the Guantánamo Bay of the banking system. Third, there was a lack of reinvestment in the economy as shareholders demanded higher returns and directors earned higher and higher bonuses. Fourth, and related to this, the takeout from the economy by capital increased at the expense of labour, which was steadily de-unionised, deskilled, delocalised and made precarious. Aggregate demand declined as social inequality increased, making it impossible to sustain economic and financial expansion. The bubble burst.[85]

There was immediate speculation about whether this was the end of the thirty-year era of neo-liberal or Anglo-Saxon financial capitalism. The financial crisis became an economic crisis, with falling outputs, declining wages and rising unemployment. The down-turn spread to the Gulf where 20,000 migrant workers from India were laid off and could no longer send remittances back to their families. As economies collapsed in Europe and the United States so demand for manufactured products from the developing world slumped. Clothing workers in India and Bangladesh – mostly female – also lost their jobs. The diamond-polishing industry in Surat (Gujarat) collapsed after Diwali in November 2008 and 200 workers committed suicide.[86]

The financial and economic crisis became a fiscal crisis. The banking crisis was stabilised by a combination of takeovers and bail-outs by governments which considered some banks as 'too big to fail'. Capitalism reinvented itself as what was dubbed 'Capitalism 4.0', which succeeded the 'Capitalism 3.0' of 1973–2008. On the other hand the cost of bail-outs and falling revenues as a result of the economic recession drove up government debt by 2010 to 8.6 per cent of national income in France, 10.7 per cent in the United States and 13.3 per cent in the United Kingdom.[87] Labour's chief secretary to the Treasury left an ironic note saying 'I'm afraid there is no more money' that was ruthlessly exploited by the Conservatives during the election campaign of 2010 that saw off thirteen years of Labour government.

Governments' response to the crisis was to pass on the pain to ordinary taxpayers, employees, students and pensioners. Public services were cut by austerity measures and taxes raised from easy targets while failing to chase corporate tax-avoiders. A sense of injustice triggered waves of protest across Europe and the United States. They began in Greece on 5 May 2010 when the government imposed savage cuts and tax rises in order to obtain emergency loans from the European Union and IMF, which imposed its neo-liberal agenda as a condition. In France, where the government decided to raise the retirement age, a fortnight of demonstrations took place in October 2010, supported by trade unions and strike action. In Britain, students demonstrated and occupied campuses against the tripling of student fees in the first significant student movement since 1968 while the UK Uncut movement targeted corporations that were not paying taxes.[88] In Spain, where unemployment was at 21 per cent, hundreds of thousands of young people occupied public squares in Madrid, Barcelona and other cities in May 2011. In New York the Occupy Wall Street movement took off on 17 September 2011 as young people protested under the slogan 'We are the 99%', against the 1 per cent who owned all the money and controlled the political system by 'legalised bribery'. It was influenced by events in Athens, Barcelona, Madrid and London and in turn inspired 'a mass movement of debt resistance across America' as well as occupations as far away as Bahia, Brazil and KwaZulu-Natal.[89] Fifty Chinese intellectuals and activists sent a message on 2 October 2011 declaring that 'the eruption of the "Wall Street Revolution" in the heart of the world's financial empire shows that 99% of the world's people remain exploited and oppressed – regardless of whether they are from developed or developing countries [. . .] The great era of popular democracy, set to change history, has arrived again!'[90]

In the first decade of the twenty-first century these four crises converged. The first was the overtaking of liberal interventionism by a new form of imperialism triggered and legitimated by 9/11 and the War on Terror. In Iraq it operated according to Bush's maxim that 'there are no rules' and instead of regime change destroyed the state, stirring up a hornet's nest of jihadist movements fighting Anglo-American occupation and driving waves of refugees out of the war-torn area. The second was a colonial fracture at home, dividing immigrant communities, particularly those of Muslim origin who felt stigmatised and excluded by the host society, which in turn defined French and British identities in ever more colonial and imperialist ways. Immigrant communities identified with the sufferings of their fellow-believers in regions attacked by the Western powers, and in the metropolis a small minority turned to riot and even terrorist attacks. Third, the global financial empire which kept the developing world and much of the developed world in thrall, and was challenged by anti-globalisation movements, experienced a meltdown in 2008. Financial institutions were bailed out by governments but the pain of austerity measures and tax rises was passed on to ordinary people who began to push back. Lastly, the development of a nationalism that was fearful of Islamism and migration and lauded the imperial past had a negative effect on the European project. Voters who were feeling the pinch of austerity were only too easily beguiled by politicians and the press into believing that the real enemy was not the global financial empire but Muslims, migrants and the European Union.

# 9 THE EMPIRE STRIKES BACK

## The Arab Spring and Multicultural Optimism

On 17 December 2010 a 26-year-old Tunisian street fruit and vegetable seller, Mohamed Bouazizi, whose wares were confiscated by the police because he was unwilling to bribe them to have a licence to sell, set fire to himself. His death in hospital from the burns he sustained on 4 January 2011 triggered protests against Zine el Abidine ben Ali, president of Tunisia since displacing Habib Bourguiba in a bloodless coup in 1987. These protests forced ben Ali to flee with his family on 14 January 2001 and, refused entry into France, he went to Saudi Arabia.

Protest movements against corrupt and dictatorial regimes spread across the Middle East in what became known as the 'Arab Spring'. In Egypt, rallies against the regime of Hosni Mubarak, who had been president since 1981, began on 25 January 2011. Clashes with Egyptian security forces resulted in the deaths of over 800 protesters before Mubarak resigned on 11 February and handed power to the armed forces. In August he was put on trial for failing to stop the killing of protesters. In Libya protests against the regime of Colonel Gaddafi, who had been in power since 1969 and remained there by the brutal repression of opponents, began on 15 February 2011 in the eastern city of Benghazi. Military intervention against the regime was authorised by the UN Security Council on 26 February and Western allies supported the rebels. In Syria, equally, protests against the Baathist regime of Bashar al-Assad, who had succeeded as president in 2000 after his father's thirty-year rule, began on 15 March 2011. Initially, the agitation was peaceful, but, like Mubarak, Assad was prepared to use lethal force against the protesters to secure his regime. In June 2011 the opposition took up arms and formed the Free Syrian Army in July 2011, taking control of Aleppo.[1]

In the West there was enthusiasm for the tentative arrival of democracy in the region. The Arab Spring was widely seen as a response to President Obama's speech in Cairo on 4 June 2009 in which he announced that he had come 'to seek a new beginning between the United States and Muslims around the world'.[2] In his State of the Union address on 25 January 2011 Obama declared that 'the United States of America stands with the people of Tunisia and supports the democratic aspirations of all people', and the Tunisian people were given a standing ovation by Congress.[3] On 5 March the French philosopher Bernard-Henri Lévy went to Benghazi to meet rebel leaders. He telephoned President Sarkozy and negotiations began for UN moves that cleared the way for air strikes by France and Great Britain in support of the rebels.[4] Six months later, on 15 September 2011, Nicolas Sarkozy and British Premier David Cameron were grandstanding as liberators in Tripoli. Gaddafi was captured and killed by opposing militiamen on 20 October. In somewhat patronising mode, the West congratulated the new arrivals at the table of democracy. The European Parliament awarded the Sakarov Prize for freedom of thought to five representative activists of the Arab Spring, including Mohamed Bouazizi posthumously, in October 2011, and in December the London *Times* made Bouazizi person of the year 2011.

The optimism of this period was reflected in a cautious hope that France and Britain might be able to strengthen their multicultural societies. The embrace of democracy by Muslim citizens in Arab countries seemed to diminish the threat of militant Islamism and held out hope for the integration of immigrant populations in Europe. Multicultural approaches nevertheless had constantly to battle against the push-back of simpler, overwhelmingly white, French or British national identities and their frailty was always likely to be demonstrated.

On 6 April 2011 Nicolas Sarkozy unveiled a plaque in the Panthéon to Aimé Césaire, the Martiniquais poet and political leader who had died at the age of 94 and praised him as a leader of France's black Caribbean territories.[5] On 1 January 2012 the Palace of the Porte Dorée, which in 1931 has been dedicated to the history of colonialism, reopened as a completely new project, a Museum of the History of Immigration. In Britain, on 27 July 2012, the opening ceremony of the London Olympics directed by Danny Boyle was a powerful dramatisation of the country's multicultural past and aspirations. England's Green and Pleasant Land was celebrated alongside the Industrial Revolution of Isambard Kingdom Brunel, the suffragettes and the National Health Service (NHS). Doreen Lawrence, the mother of the murdered black British teenager Stephen Lawrence, was among those carrying the Olympic flag. The arrival of the first Jamaican immigrants aboard the *Empire Windrush* in 1948 was recreated, and British West African rapper Dizzee Rascal and Zambian-Scottish Emei Sandé performed alongside Mike Oldfield and Simon Rattle. Tribute was paid to the victims of 7/7 but there was a confidence that such attacks could be withstood without narrowing national horizons. Inevitably, this was not to the taste of some Britons. Conservative MP Aidan Burley tweeted during the ceremony, 'Thank God the athletes have arrived! Now we can move on from leftie multicultural crap. Bring back Red Arrows, Shakespeare and the Stones!'[6]

## Jihadism, Refugees and Embattled Monocultural Nationalism

Within two years, regrettably, the optimism of the Arab Spring came crashing down and with it the chances of a confident, multicultural solution to the challenges faced by France and Britain. The Arab Spring turned to Autumn as hopes for democracy faded and civil wars broke out between partisans of dictatorship and fomenters of Islamist revolt. Jihadism intensified with the rise of the Islamic State of Iraq and Syria (ISIS), also known as Daesh. This attracted fighters for the cause from Europe and inspired attacks on military, civilian and Jewish targets in Europe. War in the Middle East and Africa drove hundreds of thousands of civilians to flee as refugees towards the relative safety of Europe. In Britain and France fears intensified about waves of immigrants who were often of Muslim origin and were portrayed as threats to national security and national identity. These were combined with fears about the alienation of populations of immigrant origin and the radicalisation of a small but deadly number of immigrants who identified with militant Islamism. Such fears sharpened the crisis of British and

French identity which discarded multicultural solutions as not only impossible but dangerous and intensified the construction of monocultural nationalisms. They generated an obsession with immigration which was seen as a threat to native Britons' access to jobs, housing and services, to national security and to British identity itself. This embattled nationalism, in turn, fuelled criticism of European institutions which were regarded as not doing enough to stop waves of migration and jihadism and which, at the same time, by their creeping federalism, were preventing nation states from 'taking back control' to deal with the problem themselves.

Of those countries that experienced the Arab Spring, only one reached the autumn of 2011 with democracy intact. In Tunisia elections to a National Constituent Assembly on 23 October 2011 were won by a coalition led by the democratic Muslim Ennaahda party, leading to the promulgation of a new Tunisian constitution on 26 January 2014.[7] In Egypt, the Freedom and Justice Party formed by the Muslim Brotherhood won parliamentary elections held between November 2011 and January 2012, and its leader, Mohammed Morsi, was elected president in May 2012. The pro-democracy movement feared a theocratic state and 13 million people demonstrated on 30 June 2013, calling for Morsi to resign. The military duly obliged, removing Morsi in another military coup on 3 July 2013 and violently crushing all opposition.[8] In Libya, things were even worse, as the state collapsed. A General National Congress formed in August 2012 was paralysed by conflict between secularists and Islamists and civil war broke out between competing militias. In Tripoli alone there were 150,000 militiamen. The door was opened to penetration by al-Qaeda, which gained the upper hand in Benghazi and attacked the US consulate there in September 2012.[9]

In Syria the regime of Assad held on by brute force, with over 8,000 Syrians killed in the first six months of 2012 alone. The democratic opposition in exile set up a Syrian National Council in Istanbul in August 2011 while the Free Syrian Army battled the regime on the ground. The limits of liberal interventionism now became clear. Obama and European leaders announced that Assad must go, but they feared another Iraq disaster even more and at this stage did not send in forces. The UN Security Council called for a ceasefire by both sides on 14 April 2012 but more effective intervention was vetoed by Russia, which backed Assad. As in Libya, civil war opened the way to an

Islamist resurgence in the non-governed areas of Syria and Iraq in 2012. The al-Nusra Front, a branch of al-Qaeda, was formed in Syria in January 2012, while its rival, ISIS, crossed the non-existent border from Iraq.[10] Many ISIS fighters emerged from American camps in Iraq such as the notorious Camp Bucca, and even from Syrian prisons, perversely released by the Assad regime in 2011 in order to enhance its image in the West as the only buffer against Islamic terrorism.[11]

These new Islamist organisations were generally manifestations of Salafism, a version of Islam that held particular appeal to young Muslims who were violently hostile both to the West and to Muslim elites and regimes that were seen to collaborate with it. It was an Islamic puritanism that required a return to the original simplicity of the faith and the role of an elite in the restoration of the Caliphate – the sacred empire of Islam in the Middle East that had been abolished in 1924, after the fall of the Ottoman Empire. This was centred on Mecca and extended from Yemen in the south to Greater Syria in the north. Fighters already active in Syria appealed to Muslim militants everywhere to undertake the *hijrah* or emigration to Syria, where the Last Battle against the West was foretold to begin at Dabiq, between Aleppo and the Turkish border.[12]

The military and religious prowess of Salafist fighters had a powerful influence on a small minority of Muslim youth who had difficulties integrating into European society and who criticised France and Great Britain for their violent interventions against Muslim populations from Iraq to Libya and Somalia and for their support of Israel against Palestinians. In the French case the Algerian War and civil war of the 1990s was also carried into the metropolis. Mohammed Merah was born in a Toulouse suburb in 1988 to a family which had migrated from Algeria in 1981 and were fanatical supporters of the Islamic Salvation Front (FIS) and the Armed Islamic Group (GIA). His parents divorced when he was five and Mohammed followed the example of his older brother Abdel Kader, who was imprisoned in 2003 and converted to Salafism by fellow Muslim prisoners. Excluded by French society Mohammed also went to prison and converted to Salafism in 2008. In 2010 he followed Abdel Kader to Egypt, travelling on to Pakistan and Afghanistan in 2011, hoping to make contact with al-Qaeda, but without success. Back in France, on 11 and 15 March 2012 he killed two French soldiers of North African origin and one of Guadalupian origin in Montauban and Toulouse, shouting 'That's Islam, brother. You kill

my brothers, I kill you'. Merah then killed three Jewish children and a
teacher at a Jewish school on 19 March before he was shot by police
after a siege in Toulouse on 22 March 2012.[13]

Nine months later, in December 2012, Mehdi Nemmouche was
released from prison in Toulouse. Of Algerian *harki* origin, born in the
northern industrial town of Roubaix in 1985 and brought up in care, he
became a petty criminal and spent five years in prison from 2007. There
he was converted to Islam and on leaving prison went to the Brussels
suburb of Molenbeek, which incubated many jihadists, and flew to join
ISIS in Syria. The prisoner Nemmouche became a gaoler, standing guard
over two French journalists taken hostage in June 2013 by ISIS.[14]
Nemmouche returned to Europe and on 24 May 2014 attacked the
Jewish Museum in Brussels, killing four people, including two Israeli
tourists.

Gaolers working for ISIS were also recruited in Britain.
Mohammed Enwazi was born to an Iraqi family in Kuwait in 1988
and came with them to the United Kingdom in 1994. He was brought up
in West London and graduated from the University of Westminster in
2009 with a 2/2 in Information Systems and Business Management. In
2006 he travelled to Somalia to join up with al-Shabab, a jihadist
organisation linked to al-Qaeda. When he tried to repeat this after
graduation he was arrested and interrogated by British police. Later in
Syria he became notorious as Jihadi John. Michael Adebolajo, a British
citizen of Nigerian origin, was brought up a Christian but converted to
Islam at the time of the Iraq War in 2003. In 2010 he also attempted to
join al-Shabab in Somalia but was arrested in Kenya and sent back
to Britain. On 22 May 2013, claiming to be exacting punishment for
British attacks on Muslims, he attacked and killed an off-duty soldier,
Fusilier Liam Rigby, who was returning to the Royal Artillery Barracks
at Woolwich.

These murders helped to crystallise a discourse that had been
developing for some time. This argued that terrorism was overwhelmingly the result of Islamic extremism and that it was present not only in
Iraq, Syria and North Africa but on the streets of France, Belgium and
Britain. It was used to demonstrate that radicalised youth were only the
sharp end of the broader problem. Immigrant populations, especially
those of Muslim origin, had failed to integrate and also failed to stop
their young people becoming radicalised. Immigrants were increasingly
denounced as 'illegal immigrants' who had no right to stay and should

be deported. The urgent priority was to defend the interests and identity of the French and British people.

In a speech delivered in Munich on 5 February 2011 David Cameron argued that there was a link between 'an ideology, Islamic extremism', which produced terrorists, and the problem that

> young men [...] find it hard to identify with Britain too, because we have allowed the weakening of our collective identity. Under the doctrine of state multiculturalism, we have encouraged different cultures to live separate lives, apart from each other and apart from the mainstream [...] We've even tolerated these segregated communities behaving in ways that run completely counter to our values.[15]

A dual response to this was necessary. On the one hand, British values must be clearly defined and immigrant communities required to adhere to them. On the other hand, much tougher measures must be adopted to prevent the radicalisation of young people, especially young men, into terrorist activity. The death of Osama bin Laden on 2 May 2011 seemed a good moment to take these measures and in June 2011, Home Secretary Theresa May announced her Prevent Strategy:

> Osama bin Laden may be dead, but the threat from Al-Qaeda-inspired terrorism is not. [...] That threat comes both from foreign nationals and terrorists born and bred in Britain. To tackle that threat – as the Prime Minister made clear in his speech in Munich earlier this year – we must not only arrest and prosecute those who breach the law, but we must also stop people being drawn into terrorist-related activity in the first place [...] Our new Prevent Strategy will challenge extremist ideology, help protect institutions from extremists and tackle the radicalisation of vulnerable people.[16]

A further challenge to multiculturalism was delivered by the riots of August 2011 that swept the suburbs of London, Handsworth in Birmingham and other run-down areas with high levels of immigrant populations, unemployment and social deprivation. Triggered by the police shooting of a mixed-race Briton, Mark Duggan, in Tottenham on 4 August 2011, the riots demonstrated that problems of integration affected not only Muslim minorities but black communities which still experienced exclusion and victimisation.[17] However, rather than engage with this kind of debate, David Cameron attacked the rioters as 'feral' and criminal while *Daily Mail* journalist Melanie Phillips took the opportunity to denounce 'the disaster of multiculturalism – the doctrine which held that no culture could be considered superior to any other because that was "racist"'; 'children were no longer taught about the nation in which they lived, and about its culture'.[18]

The response of politicians and much of the press to these challenges was not to seek to understand them but rather to ramp up social fears and to scapegoat minorities. British Pakistani Sayeeda Warsi, who served as minister of state for faith and communities in the Cameron government, recalled that after the Lee Rigby murder, 'We didn't discuss the two terrorists, their profile, their history [...] We didn't even take on board their own reasons, the words they spoke after the attack, or the note Adebolajo handed over as an explanation.'[19] Fear of terrorism was increased by the rise in refugees from Libya, Syria and Iraq from a million in March 2013, to two million in September 2013, half of them children, of whom a minority made attempts to reach safety in Europe, travelling by flimsy and overcrowded boats from Turkey to Greece or from Libya to Italy. However, rather than being recognised as asylum seekers from intolerable war zones, these refugees were attacked in the press as 'illegal' immigrants, who harboured criminals or terrorists in their midst, threatening the security, prosperity and identity of the home countries. Among the migrants Muslims were singled out as a particular threat, not least to whip up antagonism and fear. 'You know there's nothing better than a Muslim asylum seeker', said one British journalist off the record, 'that's a sort of jackpot I suppose [...] It's very much the cartoon baddy, the caricature [...] All social ills can be traced back to immigrants and asylum seekers flooding into this country.'[20]

Theresa May made the most of this in her speech to the Conservative Party Conference on 30 September 2013. She cited the Lee Rigby murder as a case of 'international terrorism' and argued that his killers wanted to 'start a war in London'. She sought approval for her treatment of 'foreign criminals' such as Abu Hamza, extradited to the United States on 5 October 2012, and Abu Qatada, deported to Jordan on 7 July 2013. She then related these cases to the question of illegal immigrants, who were deemed to be no better than 'foreign criminals'. As for foreign students, 'many of these people weren't students at all'. A new Immigration Act was promised which would stop illegal immigrants accessing jobs, housing or the NHS, and make it easier to deport them. This deliberately created a 'hostile environment' for immigrants, who all fell under some kind of suspicion. Their numbers must be cut and their life-chances diminished in order to protect the interests of the British people.

> It is a simple question of fairness. Because it's not the rich who lose out when immigration is out of control, it's people who work hard for a modest wage. They're the people who live in communities that struggle to deal with sudden social changes, who rely on public services that can't cope with demand, who lose out on jobs and have their wages forced down when immigration is too high. Only the Conservatives can be trusted to control immigration. Only the Conservatives can be trusted to get tough on crime. And only the Conservatives can be trusted to be fair for the hard-working, law-abiding majority [...] Let's remember that we share the values of the British people.[21]

Who, though, were the 'British people'? After a brief flirtation with Britain as a multicultural society, there was a general retreat to a monocultural version of British national identity which did not include but excluded minorities. This was explained by Jamaican-born and Oxford-educated cultural theorist Stuart Hall as a response to the decline of empire and to the challenge of immigration. He observed that in this context 'Englishness can feel more fragile, beleaguered and defensive than it once did', and that defensiveness led to the stigmatisation and marginalisation of those who could not or would not adhere to it.[22]

In 2014 the question of 'British values' was returned to by David Cameron. These were never clearly defined but it was presumed that they would be immediately recognised as common sense by people who identified as British while being alien to those who did not. These values, he claimed, writing in *The Mail on Sunday* on 15 June 2014, had been invented in Britain and exported to the rest of the world on the wings of empire.

> We should be proud of what Britain has done to defend freedom and develop these institutions – Parliamentary democracy, a free press, the rule of law – that are so essential for people all over the world. This is the country that helped fight fascism,

topple communism and abolish slavery; we invented the steam engine, the light bulb, the internet; and we also gave so much of the world the way of life that they hold so dear. As President Obama put it when he addressed MPs and peers in Parliament, 'What began on this island would inspire millions throughout the continent of Europe and across the world.'[23]

The exclusiveness of these British values did not go uncontested. Sayeeda Warsi, who resigned from the Cameron government in August 2014, described them as 'the space where we police views and thoughts, and we punish opinions which do not break the law'. They were a 'loyalty test' to demonstrate to Muslims that 'they didn't match up to our "British values": they didn't belong'. Their very vagueness allowed for responses that divided those who defined as British from immigrants. When schoolchildren were asked what 'British values' meant, said Warsi, they answered 'fish and chips', 'drinking tea', 'celebrating the Queen's birthday' and 'we need to get rid of these immigrants, they're taking our jobs'.[24]

Regardless, Cameron returned to the subject in a Birmingham school in July 2015, underlining even more strongly the exclusiveness of British values and denouncing the failed project of multiculturalism.

For all our successes as multi-racial, multi-faith democracy, we have to confront a tragic truth that there are people born and raised in this country who don't really identify with Britain – and who feel little or no attachment to other people here. Indeed, there is a danger in some of our communities that you can go your whole life and have little to do with people from other faiths and backgrounds.[25]

'British values' were a way of testing and policing immigrant communities and imposing the code of the former coloniser on the formerly colonised, as Kieran Yates, a young British writer of Punjabi origin, pointed out.

The message was clear: either you're on the side of Britain, of how we think, act and live, or you're against it. It's hard not to see that language as divisive. As a result, it's sort of become a buzzword for proving your allegiance to British identity, whatever that might mean. We should challenge that idea and make the point that British immigrant identities are great and funny and important to the social and cultural fabric. Who we are and what we value need to be visible.[26]

The instruction in British values was accompanied by a new syllabus on the teaching of British history. This was to tell a single, continuous history of the nation from the earliest times, highlighting national sovereignty and empire. In October 2010 Education Secretary Michael Gove told the Conservative Party Conference that

> The current approach we have to history denies children the opportunity to hear our island story. Children are given a cursory run through Henry VIII and Hitler without knowing how the vivid episodes of our past become a connected narrative. Well, this trashing of our past has to stop.[27]

Gove chaired a committee that rewrote the national curriculum and prescribed that pupils aged 11 to 14 should 'know and understand the history of these islands as a coherent, chronological narrative, from the earliest times to the present day: how people's lives have shaped this nation and how Britain has influenced and been influenced by the wider world'.[28] The credo was reprised by David Starkey, speaking to a teachers' conference in 2011. He argued that the continuous history of the British people was also that of the white British: 'Britain is a white mono-culture and schools should focus on our own history.'[29]

This conflation of continuity, oneness and whiteness which deliberately excluded non-white peoples, whether abroad or at home, was brilliantly critiqued by Stuart Hall, who explained that:

> Whiteness remains a signifier of a particular unique and uninterrupted progressive history, an advanced civilization crowned by a worldwide imperium. We are this *because* they are not. 'They', the blacks in our history, become the constitutive outside of this national story [...] And yet, this fantasy of a return to a reconstituted 'oneness' and to the elimination of difference, tends not to unify, heal and resolve but, on the contrary, it releases pathological impulses.[30]

Despite the constraints of the new syllabus, ways around it were found by a small number of academics and teachers committed to history as a way to integrate diversity and multiculturalism. Professors Claire Alexander and Joya Chatterji had completed a project called

*Bangla.stories*, based on interviews with Bengali Muslims caught up in the 1947 Partition, the Bangladesh War of Liberation and migration to Britain.[31] 'Who and what', they asked, 'are included in "British history" and who or what are excluded? How does "our island story" engage with centuries of migration to and from its shores? [...] Our island story is necessarily a globalized one, and has always been, and Britain itself has always been, ethnically, culturally and socially diverse.'[32] In 2014 they pioneered a 'History Lessons' project among schoolchildren in multi-ethnic cities – London, Manchester, Leicester, Sheffield and Cardiff. In their own families, in the classroom, on guided walks in the neighbourhood and in local museums the children explored stories of immigration. With the help of teachers, museum staff and film-makers they discovered histories that brought to life global trade, industry, empire, slavery, immigration and diversity. Far from being excluded from a monocultural national history, one London teacher reflected at the end of the project, children whose families came from overseas 'can see themselves reflected back in the history classroom'.[33]

In France too, the challenges of jihadism and immigration were reinforcing a monocultural, anti-Islamist nationalism. Jean Raspail's *Camp of Saints*, first published in 1973 and which foretold an armada of a thousand ships and a million migrants landing on the south coast of France, was republished in 2011 with a preface entitled 'Big Other'. This argued that Islam was a threat but was 'only the most organised and determined component of the submersion' that was threatening native French people (*les Français de souche*). 'The most exotic ethnic groups, tribes and nationalities are banging on our gates and when they have forced them their heritage is assured.' By 2050, he predicted, over 50 per cent of those living in France would be of extra-European origin and the only alternatives were a 'clash' or 'a sort of *Reconquista*'.[34] This book was the favourite reading of Front National leader Marine Le Pen, who recommended it to her supporters in 2015, and of Steve Bannon, co-founder of Breitbart News and chief strategist of Donald Trump.[35] In response to these immigration fears an organisation of French youth called Génération Identitaire, formed in September 2012, declared that it was 'the barricade manned by young people fighting for their iden-tity'.[36] Meanwhile another veteran reactionary, Renaud Camus, pub-lished *Le Grand Remplacement*, which issued the same warning that the French people were being 'replaced' by immigrants.[37] He gave a speech on 4 November 2012 at Orange in France in which he praised the courage and patriotism of these young people who the previous month had occupied the roof of a mosque being built in Poitiers, refighting the 732 Battle of Poitiers in which Charles Martel had checked the advance of the Muslim armies and thus achieved mythic status.[38]

The new socialist regime of François Hollande, elected president of the Republic on 6 May 2012, had to deal with these questions of jihadism, immigration, empire and French national identity. On 15 May 2012, the day of his inauguration, Hollande paid a visit to the statue of Jules Ferry in the Tuileries Gardens. Ferry was the architect in 1881–2 of free, compulsory lay education up to the age of 13 in the schools of the Republic, but he also presided over the expansion of the French Empire into Tunisia and Indo-China, and this had to be addressed in a progressive France. 'Every man is fallible', said Hollande of Ferry. 'I am not forgetting some of his political mistakes. His defence of colonisation was a moral and political error and, as such, must be condemned.'[39]

This regret was mealy-mouthed. It did not prevent France in practice from pursuing its neo-colonial policy in Africa. In January 2013 the Malian president appealed for French military support against a threat from the Salafist jihadist group Ansar Dine. There was little debate about this intervention. It simply repeated the conventional practices of *Françafrique*, according to which France supported African leaders who defended her interests. Moreover, on this occasion the intervention had the approval of the United Nations. French air and ground forces were duly deployed alongside Malian forces in Operation Servan to drive the jihadists back and on 2 February President Hollande made a lightning visit to Timbuktu, to be greeted by crowds as a liberator. 'Gunboat diplomacy is not a solution', argued a coalition of immigrant and anti-colonialist groups, including the Frantz Fanon Foundation and the Parti des Indigènes de la République, called 'Sortir du colonialisme', but this criticism was not widely shared.

Hollande was even more at ease ratcheting up Ferry's doctrine of *laïcité*. On 6 September 2013, a circular required a 'Charter of *Laïcité*' to be displayed in every school. Among its fifteen articles were (3) '*Laïcité* guarantees freedom of conscience for all. Each person is free to believe or not to believe' and (2) 'The lay Republic organises the separation of religions from the state. The state is neutral in matters of religious or spiritual conviction. There is no state religion.'[40] In a formal sense this doctrinal approach dealt even-handedly with all religions, but in reality it imposed a single ideology that was, at least implicitly, anti-Muslim.

Meanwhile French history was taught as the single story of the French nation from 'Our ancestors, the Gauls', to the present. In 2011 President Sarkozy had announced that a Museum of the History of France would be established in the National Archives, which in turn would be moved to the suburb of Saint-Denis.[41] He never set foot in the separate National Museum of the History of Immigration, which told immigrants' stories in a parallel and unofficial way. Hollande's socialist prime minister and mayor of the former slave port of Nantes, Jean-Marc Ayrault, suggested in November 2013 that the contribution of immigrants to French history should be incorporated into the official syllabus. This was more controversial than was tolerable. Front National leader Marine Le Pen headed a nationalist backlash, denouncing the proposal as 'a declaration of war against the French Republic, French history and French culture' and the proposal was withdrawn.[42]

The trouble was that the single story of the French nation included the story of the French Empire, above all of French Algeria. An official exhibition on 'Algeria 1830–1962' organised at the Invalides in Paris in the summer of 2012, which played down the role of army violence, was visited by 44,000 people.[43] Meanwhile French settlers forced to leave Algeria in 1962 and who had settled along the Mediterranean coast felt free to promote their own memories and values. Robert Ménard, whose family had left Algeria when he was nine years old, was elected mayor of Béziers in April 2014. The following July he unveiled a monument in honour of French settlers who had been massacred in Oran on 5 July 1962, as Algerians celebrated their independence. The settlers were cast not as colonial oppressors but as victims of decolonisation. Ménard then decided to remove the name of the Béziers street marking the Evian agreement of 19 March 1962, traditionally favoured by the Left to acclaim the end of the hated Algerian War, and to rename it in honour of Hélie Denoix de Saint-Marc, a former resister and professional soldier who had supported the generals' putsch of 1961 against an Algerian Algeria. Thus the most unreconstructed defenders of French Algeria were brought into the mainstream national narrative.

## War on the Caliphate and Jihadist Attacks at Home

The epicentre of trouble at this point for France, Britain and the United States was not Algeria but France's former mandate of Syria. The trouble was that it was difficult to establish who the real enemy was after the defeat of the democratic opposition to President Assad: was it the Assad regime or the rising threat of ISIS? The long shadow of the disastrous intervention in Iraq also hung over decision-making, for the overthrow of Saddam Hussein had plunged the country into civil war and the allied occupation had provoked multi-headed jihadist resistance.

A crisis point came in August 2013, when the Assad regime used chemical weapons on Ghouta, a suburb of Damascus held by the opposition, killing an estimated 1,400 people, including many children. The House of Commons voted narrowly by 285–272 against intervention on 29 August 2013. US National Security Adviser Zbigniew Brzezinski nevertheless remarked that the vote might have gone the other way because of the old colonial reflex. 'I am struck by how eager Great Britain and France appear to be in favour of military action', he said. 'And I am also mindful that both of these powers are former imperialist, colonialist powers in the region.'[44]

The opportunity for them to flex those imperialist, colonialist muscles was not far away. The situation changed dramatically in June 2014 when ISIS took Mosul and Abu Bakr al-Baghdadi duly proclaimed the Caliphate of Iraq and the Levant. The last US troops had left Iraq as recently as December 2011, and now it seemed that their work would have to start all over again. The United States launched air strikes against ISIS in Iraq on 8 August 2014, provoking an immediate retaliation by ISIS forces against the American hostages they held. On 19 August they published a gruesome video of the beheading of journalist James Foley and on 2 September one of the beheading of journalist Steven Sotoff. Both hostages appealed to the Americans to stop the bombing before they were executed by English-speaking Mohammed Enwazi, aka Jihadi John. The execution of British humanitarian David Haines followed on 13 September and of Alan Henning on 3 October 2014.

The American response was to step up retaliation. On 10 September 2014, President Obama announced that he would 'degrade and ultimately destroy' ISIS. 'I have made it clear that we will hunt down terrorists who threaten our country, wherever they are', he warned. Air strikes on 22 September were aimed at ISIS bases at Raqqa in Syria, even though there had been no invitation from the Syrian government. France had not joined in with other allies in the 2003 Iraq War but she now reverted to her former colonial pretensions. President Hollande was received by the Iraqi president in Baghdad on 12 September 2014, responding to a request for support against the jihadists, and French Rafale aircraft began attacking ISIS targets on 19 September.

At this point the danger of military intervention became clear. The French attacks provoked a jihadist response in metropolitan France and reopened divisions in French society along the lines of the 'colonial fracture'.

On 7 January 2015 two Islamist militants entered the offices of the *Charlie Hebdo* magazine in Paris and shot dead twelve cartoonists and journalists at their weekly meeting. *Charlie Hebdo* was part of the avant-garde of French political satire and had been pouring scorn for some years on the Prophet Mohammed. While for the magazine this was acting out the Enlightenment, which defined French intellectual life, for the Salafists it was simply blasphemy.

The leader of the attacks was Amédy Coulibaly, aged 32, the only male in a broken Malian family of ten children, whose hatred of the French state dated to the shooting in 2002 of his friend and accomplice in petty crime. Doing time in the prison of Fleury Mérogis, a notorious jihad academy, he fell under the influence of Algerian-born Djamel Beghal, who had been sentenced to ten years in prison in 2005 for planning an attack on the US embassy in Paris in 2001.[45] At Fleury Coulibaly met Chérif Kouachi, also of Algerian origin, brought up with his brother Saïd in the Paris suburbs and a member of the Buttes-Chaumont gang. The Kouachi brothers went to Yemen in 2011 to train with AQPA (al-Qaeda in the Arabian Peninsula). Meanwhile, out of prison, Coulibaly married Hayat Boumeddiene, an Algerian by background who had lost her job in a French supermarket for refusing not to wear the veil. The Kouachi brothers were responsible for the *Charlie Hebdo* killings, under instruction from Coulibaly. In a video he recorded probably on 8 January, Coulibaly described himself as a 'soldier of the caliphate' and explained, 'You attack the Islamic State, we will attack you. You are bombing regularly over there.' Then, addressing his Muslim brothers, he asked, 'What do you do when they directly violate the law of Allah? What do you do when they assault our

Figure 9.1  The colonial fracture: 'Nous sommes Charlie' demonstration in Paris, 11 January 2015.
Getty Images / Dan Kitwood / 461343474

sisters?'[46] On 9 January he took staff and customers hostage at a kosher supermarket in Vincennes and killed four of them before dying in the police assault. The Kouachi brothers were killed by police the same day.

The response of the French public to the *Charlie Hebo* massacres was immediate and dramatic. An estimated four million people demonstrated on Sunday 11 January, wearing badges with the words 'Je suis Charlie' (Figure 9.1). The fundamental values of freedom of thought and speech, *laïcité* and the Republic were declared. The Front National was not invited, lest anti-Muslim, xenophobic sentiments displace those of the Enlightenment. Intellectuals mobilised as during the Dreyfus Affair. Writer and cineast Gérard Mordillat argued that the cartoonists had committed no blasphemy: 'In the Republic it is perfectly possible to write, shout, proclaim that you couldn't care about God, Jehovah, Allah, Nanabozo the Giant Rabbit, Buddha, Father Christmas, Mickey Mouse, Harry Potter and all the other gods invented by man to cope with his fear of death.'[47]

The *Charlie Hebdo* and Jewish supermarket massacres, however, divided as much as they united. Immigrant populations in the *banlieues* did not take part in the marches. In Belleville they challenged demonstrators with shouts of 'Je ne suis pas Charlie' and sang Intifada songs.[48] The school of the Republic was also divided. Muslim schoolchildren shouted in corridors at school and refused to observe the minute's silence instituted by the government.[49] 'For many Muslims it was impossible to say "Je suis Charlie"', writer Karim Miské said later, 'because *Charlie Hebdo* attacked their prophet [...] To say "Je suis Charlie" would have been to say, "I submit to the white secular order, even though I think it is horrible"'.[50]

The *Charlie Hebdo* affair dramatised how fractured French society was between those who endorsed the values of the Enlightenment and *laïcité* and those who felt that these values served to marginalise them, discriminate against them, even stigmatise them. It underscored the rift between those who identified with France as a colonial power and had been able to assimilate and those who experienced discrimination and segregation and alienation as former subjects of that power and identified with the push-back by Islamist fighters (Figure 9.2). One reader of *Le Monde* from Conakry, in the former French colony of Guinea, pointed out that:

> France is a country curiously ill at ease with its cultural diversity. With very few exceptions, it is obvious that those from visible minorities do not get a good deal either in education or on the job market, because of different forms of segregation and a badly adapted policy of integration based on assimilating French people of overseas origin. It is utopian to try to assimilate people who, because of their circumstances, have different cultural and historical references. Because they cannot succeed, these people break with French society and in the end no longer have faith in the institutions of the Republic. Some of them join jihadist organisations where they recover their lost honour and a meaning of life.[51]

This interpretation was reinforced by sociologist Edgar Morin, whose radicalism went back to the Spanish Civil War and opposition to the Algerian War, and Patrick Singaïny, a writer from Réunion who had written a biography of Aimé Césaire. Immigrants of Arab and Muslim

**Figure 9.2** The colonial fracture: Senegalese Muslims declare 'Je ne suis pas Charlie', Dakar, 16 January 2015.
Getty Images / SEYLLOU / Stringer /AFP / 461637124

origin, they argued, were ghettoised in the *banlieues*, harassed by the police and became radicalised in prison, where paradoxically they were reborn. 'They could not become real French people, but they could become real Muslims.'[52] The rise of Daesh was a consequence of the destruction of Afghanistan and Iraq by military interventions led by the Americans, they claimed. 'France was present through its air force, through French Muslims who joined the jihad and came back from the jihad. It is now clear that the Middle East is now present in the heart of France.'[53]

This analysis that French Muslims, joined by Belgian Muslims in a similar situation, joined the jihad and returned from the jihad to undertake attacks in France was confirmed in Paris ten months later. Salim Benghalem, a former crane operator of Algerian origin from Cachan, outside Paris, met members of the Buttes-Chaumont group while in Fresnes prison in 2007 and travelled to Syria in 2013. He called on would-be French jihadists to join Daesh and defended the *Charlie Hebdo* assassins in a video. The French authorities launched a bombing raid on a Daesh training camp in Raqqa on 8 October 2015 in the hope of killing him, but without success. It is possible to trace a connection between this raid and the shootings and the suicide bombings in Paris on 13 November 2015, which killed 130 people. Omar Mostefai, aged 29, from Courcouronnes and Samy Amimour, aged 28, from Drancy, both in the Paris region, attacked the Bataclan concert hall. Three brothers, Brahim, Salah and Mohammed Abdeslam, Belgians of Moroccan origin from Molenbeek, shot at drinkers in the Bastille-Nation quarter of Paris. Meanwhile, Bilal Hadfi and Ahmed al-Mohammed blew themselves up at the Stade de France. The mastermind, to begin with, was thought to be Abdelhamid Abaaoud, a Belgian of Moroccan origin, who had travelled to Syria early in 2013, joined Daesh and returned to the Molenbeek suburb of Brussels in September 2013. Two months later, however, the mastermind was thought to be Salim Benghalem himself.[54]

After this second devastating attack on Paris in 2015, François Hollande declared a state of emergency in France and closed the frontiers. This time there were no marches in support of freedom of thought. Hollande, who three years earlier had paid tribute to the Algerians massacred in Paris in October 1961, now sent a small army into the northern Paris *banlieue* of Saint-Denis, a ghetto of segregation and exclusion, where Abdelhamid Abaaoud and two other terrorists had holed up. Over 1,500 projectiles were spent in the assault that killed the terrorists and made the building they were in uninhabitable. 'It was quite a trauma for us here, for the population', said local councillor Madjid Messaoudene. He complained that subsequently the police and army had occupied Saint-Denis, a multicultural melting pot, in which 135 nationalities lived side by side, like a foreign town.[55] It was as if the Battle of Algiers, fought to clear the kasbah of FLN terrorists in 1957, was now being fought in the *banlieues* of Paris.

As the colonial shutters came down in France a few voices suggested that France should take a hard look at the divisions that lay behind these terrible attacks. Edgar Morin traced France's ills to her foreign policy in the Middle East and to the effective exclusion of Muslims from French society. Much more thought, he said, had to go into how to integrate them:

> Make peace in the Middle East. Build a general coalition of the least barbaric powers (including Russia, Iran and ourselves) against the most barbaric of all [...] The war against Daesh will be won not only through peace in Syria but through peace

in the *banlieues*. Nothing in depth or over time has been done for a real integration of the nation by schools teaching that French history is multicultural and by confronting discrimination in society.[56]

Attempts to reach a new accommodation with Muslims, however, were unlikely after the attacks of 13 November 2015, and more or less unthinkable after the attack of 14 July 2016, when Tunisian-born Mohamed Lahouaiej-Bouhlel, aged 31, drove a highjacked truck into crowds celebrating Bastille Day on the Nice sea front, killing 86 people and injuring 458. Prime Minister Manuel Valls, coming to pay his respects the following day, was booed by the crowd for failing to provide adequate security against Islamist terrorism. Local authorities on the Côte d'Azur took their revenge that summer by banning the wearing of the full-body swimming costume, commonly known as the burkini, on their beaches. For republicans this was simply the imposition in public places of a *laïcité* that forbade the conspicuous display of religious affiliation, whereas for Muslims it was gratuitous discrimination. Given the predominance on the French Mediterranean coast of *pieds noirs*, who were reminded of their 1962 defeat and exodus by the Arab Muslim presence on French soil, it seemed like the reimposition of a segregation that would have been taken as read fifty years before, in colonial Algeria.

Initially, Britain was more cautious about military intervention against ISIS in Syria. It voted narrowly against intervention against the Assad regime in August 2013. It did not, like France, follow the lead of the United States in August and September 2014. Memories of the disastrous intervention in Iraq were still too painful. This did not mean, however, that it had worked through the consequences of military intervention in terms of alienating Muslim populations abroad and at home, creating waves of refugees from the war zone and inviting a jihadist response, and was therefore liable to make the same mistake as in Iraq.

The limits of official thinking were demonstrated when news came through on 15 June 2015 that Talha Asmal, a 17-year-old from Dewsbury in West Yorkshire, had blown himself up as a suicide bomber in Syria. On the BBC, Lord Alex Carlile, the head of Prevent, argued that the answer was better policing: intelligence services should be given greater powers to access communications between terrorists and those they were radicalising. Against him, former MP for Dewsbury Shahid Malik replied that to see radicalisation only through the lens of security and to criticise British Muslims for not doing enough to counter radicalisation was counter-productive. 'If we undermine the Muslim part of our population', he said, 'we are effectively undermining the front line against terrorism in the UK'.[57] His view made a good deal of sense, but was not sufficient to counter the official view that the Islamist threat must ultimately be conquered by force.

Meanwhile the refugee crisis intensified over the summer of 2015. Far from being moved to compassion the right-wing press ratcheted up scare stories. Writing in *The Sun*, Katie Hopkins dehumanised the refugees and proposed tried and tested nineteenth-century methods. 'Rescue boats?' she exclaimed. 'I'd use gunships to stop illegal immigrants. Make no mistake, these migrants are like cockroaches.'[58] One of those insects turned out to be Hamza, an English teacher from Syria who was interviewed when she reached Budapest in September 2015. Powerfully she exposed the contradiction between the West's bombing of Syria and its shutting the gates against the refugees it created. 'All the governments make this war on Syria. I don't know why', she said. 'They put their hands in everything, even in the war. And now they stop us, preventing us to go to their countries. I don't know why. So where we go, where we go? We can't stay in the war. The president there will kill us. They will do something bad to my children, to my daughters.'[59]

Intervention was about to intensify. On 2 December 2015, three weeks after the Paris attacks of 13 November, the House of Commons approved military intervention in Syria alongside the United States and France by 397 votes to 223. David Cameron argued that in the previous year British security services had 'foiled no fewer than seven different plots against our people [...] we will be safer and better off in the long term if we can get rid of the so-called Caliphate which is radicalising Muslims, turning people against us and plotting atrocities on the streets of Britain'. Labour leader Jeremy Corbyn riposted that British bombing, on the contrary, would 'increase the short-term risks of terrorist attacks in Britain'. Green Party MP Caroline Lucas agreed that bombing by what Daesh called 'the crusader West' was 'an incredibly effective recruiting sergeant' that had brought 30,000 volunteers from a hundred countries to fight in Syria. The debate, however, was turned by Labour Shadow Foreign Secretary Hilary Benn who argued somewhat perversely that ISIS was fascist and that in intervening against it Britain was not acting as a crusading or imperial power but in a time-honoured British anti-fascist tradition.

> What we know about fascists is that they need to be defeated. It is why, as we have heard tonight, socialists, trade unionists and others joined the International Brigade in the 1930s to fight against Franco. It is why this entire House stood up against Hitler and Mussolini. It is why our party has always stood up against the denial of human rights and for justice. My view is that we must now confront this evil. It is now time for us to do our bit in Syria.[60]

Benn lightly sidestepped the fact that volunteers who had fought fascism in Spain had been roundly criticised as communists by the pro-Munich establishment and that the last time Britain had intervened against a 'fascist' dictator in the Middle East was Suez.

Critics who warned that bombings in Syria, as in Iraq, would provoke jihadist responses were right, although the responses in Britain did not come until the US bombing campaign Operation Inherent Resolve led by Donald Trump in the spring of 2017. In the meantime, however, immigration and fear of terrorist attacks intensified an embattled British nationalism that fed directly into Brexit.

## Brexit: The Revenge of Colonial Nostalgia

The redefinition of British and French identities, largely in response to perceived threats from Islamist jihadism and mass migration from the Near East and North Africa, which reached a high point in the summer of 2015, had a powerful impact on the relations of these two countries with the European Union. Of course, Eurosceptic attitudes had a history and dynamic of their own, and had been gathering force since Margaret Thatcher's Bruges speech and the Maastricht Treaty, but they were reinforced by colonialist and imperialist sentiments that were shaped by these global factors.

In both Britain and France extreme nationalist parties gained traction since 2010, hammering away on issues of national difference, national sovereignty, and national ambitions apart from and outside what was seen as the European Union 'superstate'. This success had an influence on mainstream parties of both right and left which feared the slippage of their vote to the nationalist Right. At this point, however, the national narratives parted company. The British Conservative Party opted to deal with divisions within its own ranks by offering a referendum on membership of the European Union, while in France a new presidential candidate and movement emerged, independent of the mainstream parties, to take on and defeat the challenge of the nationalist Right.

Speeches delivered by Nigel Farage to the UKIP party conference in Birmingham in September 2013 and by Marine Le Pen to her supporters in Marseille the same month were strikingly similar in argument and rhetoric. They were hostile to immigration, defensive of sovereignty and rooted in a proud history. According to Farage:

> The fact is we just don't belong in the European Union. Britain is different. Our geography puts us apart. Our history puts us apart. Our institutions produced by that history put us apart. We think differently. We behave differently [...] I believe that leaving the Union and reclaiming our destiny will create the most exciting opportunity for national renewal in our lifetime [...] We get our money back. We get our borders back. We get our Parliament back. We get our fisheries back. We get our own seat in on the bodies that actually run the world [...] There are those who say we can't go it alone. That our global influence will decline because we are small. Those are the true voices of Little England. We speak for Great Britain.[61]

In Marseille Marine Le Pen spoke likewise of French independence and exceptionalism, while using more abstract terms such as liberty and appealing to very French tropes such as 'honour and glory':

> First of all, France must regain her liberty. Her liberty as a state and as a nation. A free France is a sovereign and independent France [...] To regain our sovereignty is to regain our liberty to make laws instead of having most of them made in Brussels without our knowledge or against our will. It is to regain control over our budget and control over our currency [...] It is to regain our frontiers at last [...] All that, my friends means immediately rethinking our relationship with the European Union [...] The policy of independence that I proclaim has its

models and its previous incarnations that have often covered the history of our country with honour and glory.[62]

Conservative leader David Cameron told his first party conference in 2006 that Conservatives would regain power only when they 'stopped banging on about Europe'. Euroscepticism, however, would not go away, and was the lifeblood of the right wing of his party. The European Union was seen as a foreign power, a German empire, with federalist pretensions that disregarded British national interests. European institutions were deemed to be unelected, bureaucratic and opposed to popular sovereignty. Matters were made worse by the Eurozone crisis after 2009, which required bail-outs of struggling Mediterranean economies by central European institutions, and by the rising tide of migrants who, once in Europe, could not be stopped until they reached the Channel.[63] In a bid to silence the Eurosceptic Right once and for all, Cameron announced in his Bloomberg speech of January 2013 that a new Conservative government would negotiate a new settlement with its European partners on the basis of which there would be an in/out referendum on Britain's membership of the European Union.[64] This did not prevent and even encouraged the rise of UKIP, which topped the poll in the European elections of 25 May 2014 with 27.5 per cent of the vote, just as the Front National topped the poll in France with 17.9 per cent.

The arguments of those wishing to leave the European Union combined an uneasy mixture of Little Englandism and a global version of Britannic nationalism. The Brexit mantra was to 'take back control' of Britain's laws, money and borders. Immigration was the main concern, both as a material threat to jobs and demands on the NHS and schools, and as a cultural threat to British national identity. Overall, the ambition was for Britain to regain the national unity and greatness that she had last enjoyed in the Second World War. Many of these sentiments were captured by the roving reporters of the national press and BBC. In the West Midlands town of Dudley, where 10 per cent of the population was foreign-born, mainly Asian, a local Briton interviewed in a pub asserted the superiority of the white British over non-white migrants. 'At the end of the day they are guests here. This is a historic country for England', he said, meaning no doubt 'for the English'.[65] A year later, on the eve of the referendum, three generations of a family were interviewed on a council estate in Hull, elected UK City of Culture in 2007, also with an immigrant population of 10 per cent and one of the most deprived cities in the country. The grandmother, aged 88, was said to have 'survived the war'. Sharon, her daughter, said that she would not vote for Nigel Farage because 'you always see UKIP as racist. But I like what he says, that British bit. He's not saying, "let's kick them all out", he's saying, "stand on your own two feet and get on with it"'. 'Like we used to be,' added her husband Geoff, 'stand by ourselves again'.[66]

A global version of Britannic nationalism was also powerful in the argument for Brexit. The referendum, it was felt, would finally resolve the tension between membership of Europe, with its inconvenient rules, and leadership of the empire or Commonwealth. This debate had been raging since the days of Churchill, Bevin and Macmillan. Because the decline of the Great Britain seemed to coincide with her entry into Europe as well as with decolonisation, it was argued that to leave Europe would open the way to the recovery of some kind of imperial role. What this might mean covered a number of possibilities. One was to refashion the 'great commercial republic' of which Adam Smith had spoken and which had been the driving force of empire in the eighteenth and early nineteenth centuries. Even David Cameron told *The Independent* on 19 March 2016 that he wanted Britain to be 'a swashbuckling, trading, successful buccaneer nation of the twenty-first century', but 'within the EU'.[67] Terms such as 'swashbuckling' and 'buccaneer' were especially dear to Brexiteers, an empire seen through the lens of *Pirates of the Caribbean* but also alluding to the reality of a trading empire underpinned by the man-of-war and gunboat. This option was not lost on City bankers, who occasionally played at the limits of the rules. They imagined, according to one of them, that 'the UK can thrive by "reverting" to the model of an entrepôt trading and financing island-nation. Behind this is the notion that Britain's imperial, trading DNA still flows through the veins of places like Singapore and Hong Kong.'[68] There was no doubt in the mind of the Brexiteers that this was possible, given Britain's illustrious history. 'We used to run the biggest empire the world has ever seen', boasted former Mayor of London Boris Johnson in February 2016. 'Are we really unable to do trade deals?'[69]

Another idea of empire was that of Greater Britain, the white settler Dominions, which had been the heart of the Commonwealth and were now to be revived in a new incarnation, the 'Anglosphere'. These Dominions had criticised Britain when Macmillan engaged in talks to join the European Community, for fear of losing their trade deals with Britain. Now the boot was on the other foot, and Britain was looking for trade deals with former Commonwealth countries. Visiting Melbourne in 2013 Boris Johnson cited the case of a teacher in London of Australian origin who had been sent home as an

> infamous consequence, as we all know, of a historic and strategic decision that this country took in 1973. We betrayed our relationships with Commonwealth countries such as Australia and New Zealand, and entered into preferential trading arrangements with what was then the European Economic Community [...] By a fluke of history [Australia] happens to be intimately cognate with Britain. I don't just mean that we once supplied them with the dregs of the Victorian penal system, or that we have cricket and rugby in common. I mean that we British are more deeply connected with the Australians – culturally and emotionally – than with any other country on earth.[70]

This quasi-apology for the 'betrayal' of 1973 asserted a common identity and destiny of the English-speaking peoples, based on a shared culture and history, a spirit of enterprise and free institutions, all of which were different from what was found in continental Europe. Early in 2016 David Davis, who had lost out to Cameron in the race for the Conservative Party leadership in 2005, reinforced the point:

> We must see Brexit as a great opportunity to refocus our economy on global, rather the regional, trade. This is an opportunity to renew our strong relationships with Commonwealth and Anglosphere countries. These parts of the world are growing faster than Europe. We share history, culture and language. We have family ties. We even share similar legal systems. The usual barriers to trade are largely absent.[71]

A third fantasy of empire, which would come to be called Empire 2.0, was nostalgia for lost colonies in India and Africa. A rose-tinted image of the British Raj had been nurtured by many a Merchant-Ivory film, and a new but familiar take on the Raj, *Indian Summers*, with British officials and businessmen and their flowery wives gathered in Simla, away from the heat and dust, was screened in the springs of 2015 and 2016. A public opinion poll of July 2014 found that 59 per cent of UK respondents thought the empire was 'something to be proud of' against 19 per cent who said it was a source of shame; 49 per cent thought that former colonies were better off as a result of British rule against 15 per cent who did not; finally 34 per cent wished that Britain still had an empire.[72] This was nevertheless a divisive issue. Only 48 per cent of young people were proud of the empire against 65 per cent of those aged over 60. And when Shashi Tharoor, former UN undersecretary-general and Indian Congress politician, argued before students in the Oxford Union on 28 May 2015 that 'Britain's rise for two hundred years was financed by its depredations in India' and that 'We were denied democracy, so we had to snatch it, seize it from you', the video of his speech on YouTube went viral.[73]

There were, however, contradictions between the campaign for a Little England and that for a global Britain. Many of those who voted to leave the EU were in parts of England that felt 'left behind' by globalisation. The development of the global economy had wrecked the staple industries of coal and cotton, steel and shipbuilding, which had underpinned empire in its heyday and kept their communities together. They then found themselves paying for the global economic crash of 2008 by nearly ten years of austerity through cuts to social services, education and benefits. They took out their anger on the Cameron–Osborne government which was seen to be allied to the global elite and had imposed that austerity. They also took it out on the EU, which was seen to be allied to the same elite and which at the same time was letting immigrants penetrate its borders in the Mediterranean and Balkans.

The referendum vote of 23 June 2016 was a victory for those who subscribed to Little England, orchestrated by those who believed in global Britain, a rebooted fantasy of the British Empire. While London voted by 60 per cent to remain in the EU, England-without-London voted by 55.4 per cent to leave. Wales voted narrowly to leave but Scotland voted by 62 per cent and Northern Ireland by 56 per cent to remain.[74] Leave voting was heavy in former manufacturing areas 'left behind' by globalisation and deindustrialisation, such as Stoke-on-Trent (69 per cent leave) and Sunderland (61 per cent leave) but also in seaside resorts like Scarborough (62 per cent leave) and Eastbourne (57 per cent leave) who felt 'left out' by the liberal elites of London and Brussels. Among those hostile to immigration fully 80 per cent voted to leave.[75] Hostility to immigrants was acted out before and after the vote. A week before the referendum pro-Remain Labour MP Jo Cox was killed in Birstall, Yorkshire, by a local man shouting 'This is for Britain!' On 25 June, *The Sun* proclaimed, 'Goodbye Germany, France and the rest [...] a new Britain is rising from the ashes'. Inside it published a picture of African refugees adrift on a rubber boat with the caption, 'It's business as usual in the Med'.[76] In the eight weeks after the referendum 2,300 racist incidents took place as white Britons told East European migrants and Muslims to 'get the fuck out of our country' or physically assaulted them, aiming to reclaim 'their' country.[77]

And so the Empire struck back. First, in response to the allied bombing of Syria, in the shape of jihadist execution of Western hostages and attacks on soldiers and Jews in mainland France and Britain. Second, also as a result of war in the Middle East and more widely, in the form of a wave of immigrants into Europe that reached a peak in the summer of 2015. The response of Britain and France was to pull up the drawbridge against immigration, to tighten security and to redraw the boundaries of national identity even more tightly. This had the effect of excluding and alienating immigrant population, especially those of Muslim origin, a tiny minority of which took up arms to punish the colonial aggressor. The strengthening of national identity, including in the British case renewed fantasies about a global Britain free of the EU, together with the anger of those suffering the effects of the global economic crisis, often blamed on immigration, were driving forces in the June 2016 vote for Brexit.

# 10 FANTASY, ANGUISH AND WORKING THROUGH

On 13 July 2016, the day she became prime minister, Theresa May announced that 'As we leave the European Union, we will forge a bold new positive role for ourselves in the world, and we will make Britain a country that works not for a privileged few, but for every one of us.' She vowed to fight 'burning injustice' which meant that 'If you're black, you're treated more harshly by the criminal justice system than if you're white.' She understood that 'if you're from an ordinary working class family [...] you can just about manage but you worry about the cost of living and getting your kids into a good school'.[1] This combined a number of promises that were in tension with each other. Brexit would break the shackles that supposedly prevented Great Britain from acting as a sovereign power on the world stage and permit her to 'take back control' in order further to restrict immigration. Restrictions on immigration in the name of monocultural nationalism were one of the main Tory levers for defending the interests of the white working class. However, those same restrictions inflicted 'burning injustices' on non-white populations who were increasingly considered to be illegal immigrants. These contradictions did not appear straight away but gradually they would be exposed.

Although she had personally voted Remain, Theresa May gave the whip hand in government to leading Brexiteers: Boris Johnson was appointed to the Foreign and Commonwealth Office, Liam Fox took International Trade, and David Davis became Secretary of State for Exiting the European Union. On 29 March 2017 May formally announced Britain's intention to leave the EU under Article 50 of the

Figure 10.1 'Make Britain great again': Brexit supporter at UKIP conference, 16 September 2016.
Getty Images / Matt Cardy / Stringer / 606180624

Treaty of Lisbon: 'I want Britain to be what we have the potential, talent and ambition to be – a great, global trading nation that is respected around the world and strong, confident and united at home.'[2] She clearly enjoyed the support of much of the British public. That morning, a woman in the former colliery town of Hetton-le-Hole, Sunderland, interviewed for Radio 4, said, 'I think it's the right thing that we leave and build our better Britain back to where it used to be. You know, make Britain great again.'[3] May's Brexit agenda tapped into the sense that while the British Empire had declined, even fallen, it might be conjured back into existence by a historic sense of superiority and entitlement that only increased as that decline took place (Figure 10.1).

It did not take long for the hollowness of those fantasies to be revealed. In the first place, Britain followed the American lead in a renewed campaign of bombing against ISIS in Syria and Iraq. This provoked a backlash of terrorist attacks in London and Manchester that were inspired by ISIS. Second, the civil service leaked ironic comments about Britain's bid to found an Empire 2.0, a balloon that was rudely burst by former subjects of Empire 1.0 or their descendants. Third, it became clear that the 'global trading nation' was a new incarnation of the neo-liberal, low-regulation, low-tax empire that had been developed since the 1980s and in which many leading Brexiteers had a financial interest. Fourth, the idea was propounded that while Britain would restore ties with old friends in the Commonwealth, her friends in the former white Dominions were more solicited than those in the Caribbean.

The US-led bombing attacks on ISIS, codenamed Operation Inherent Resolve, was stepped up under President Trump in March 2017, with the aim of destroying ISIS bases in both Mosul and Raqqa. British, French and American planes bombed Mosul on 17 March, killing at least 150 civilians. On 18 March a mosque near Raqqa was destroyed, killing fifty-two, while on 20 March a school being used as an air-raid shelter was destroyed at al-Massoura, near Raqqa, killing thirty-three people, including children.[4] Back in London on Wednesday, 22 March, a driver drove a car into pedestrians on Westminster Bridge, killing five people, and then knifed a police constable guarding the Palace of Westminster. The perpetrator was Adrian Elms, 52, the mixed-race son of a teenage white mother, who had been bullied as 'black Abe' at school in Tunbridge Wells and been sentenced to prison in 2000 and 2003 for slashing local men he quarrelled with in Wales and Eastbourne. In prison for the second time in the wake of 9/11 he converted to Islam and became Khalid Masood. He was known to MI5 but regarded as a 'peripheral figure'.[5] No attempt was made to link his deeds to the coalition raids that had taken place only days earlier.

Two months later, on Monday, 26 May 2017, a suicide bomber blew himself up at a pop concert in Manchester Arena, killing twenty-two and injuring fity-nine, mostly young people. It was a British Bataclan. The bomber was Salman Abedi, aged 23, a Libyan whose family had fled the Gaddafi regime in 1980 but who had returned briefly with his father to fight against Gaddafi with the Libyan Islamic Fighting Group in 2011. While his father remained in Tripoli, Salman returned to Manchester where he first 'went off the rails' with vodka and cannabis, then converted to Islam, wearing traditional Arab dress. No link was made to the British intervention in Libya in 2011, effectively destroying the state, until Jeremy Corbyn argued that 'many experts, including professionals in our intelligence and security services, have pointed to connections between wars our government has supported or fought in other countries and terrorism at home'. Prime Minister Theresa May sharply scolded him for suggesting that 'terror attacks in Britain are our own fault [...] there can never be an excuse for terrorism'.[6]

An Islamophobic backlash was not slow in coming. Katie Hopkins immediately tweeted '22 dead – number rising [...] We need a final solution'.[7] On 18 June Darren Osborne, aged 47, who had been radicalised by the propaganda of the English Defence League and Britain First, drove a truck into a group of Muslims outside Finsbury Park mosque, shouting 'I want to kill all Muslims'. He killed one and injured eleven and was saved from lynching by the crowd only by the intervention of the imam. Outside Downing Street Theresa May returned to the charge: 'As I said here two weeks ago, there has been far too much tolerance of extremism in our country for many years, and that means extremism of any kind, including Islamophobia.' The problem was that she had called the Manchester attack 'terrorism' while the Finsbury Park attack was mere 'extremism'. For journalist Nesrine Malik the attack on Muslims was a function of both incitement to hate crime and of the 'normalisation' of such crimes which now simply 'feel part of the scenery'.[8]

Meanwhile the coalition forces stepped up their bombing of Raqqa and Mosul with thirty-five attacks on 15–16 June alone and *The Observer* ran a leader entitled 'We are part of a coalition dealing death in Syria and Iraq'.[9] A week later, on Saturday night, 23 June 2017, a group of three led by Pakistan-born Muslim convert Khurum Shazad Butt, aged 27, who had once worked on the London Underground, mowed down pedestrians on London Bridge and ran amok in Borough Market, killing seven and injuring forty-eight people. Theresa May responded like a headteacher, declaring 'Enough is enough' and again that there was 'far too much toleration of extremism in our country'. She then adopted a colonialist position, arguing that extremism would be defeated only when 'we turn people's minds away from this violence and make them understand that our values – pluralist British values – are superior to anything offered by the preachers and supporters of hate'.[10]

This arrogance extended to dealing with international criticism of the coalition offensive. In July 2017 Amnesty International reported that coalition forces were using unnecessarily powerful weapons, killing many thousands of civilians, and committing human rights violations and possibly war crimes. Its spokesman rejected the claim of the Ministry of Defence that the RAF bombing of Mosul had caused no civilian casualties.[11] The task of rejecting the reports as 'irresponsible and naïve' was left to General Rupert Jones, the deputy commander of the Combined Joint Task Force and most senior British commander involved. 'The sad reality', he said, 'is that you cannot take a city like Mosul without risk. This is probably the toughest urban fight that has been fought since the Second World War.' He had reason to defend the reputation of British armed forces, being the son of Colonel H. Jones who was posthumously awarded the Victoria Cross for gallantry leading the 2nd Battalion of the Parachute Regiment at the Battle of Goose Green on 28 May 1982.[12]

Intervention in Syria and Iraq, which was supposed to demonstrate that Britain was still a great power, was accompanied by the revival of claims that Britain would return even more convincingly to being an imperial power after Brexit. The term Empire 2.0 was originally ironic in its conception, coined by civil servants sceptical about Trade Secretary Liam Fox's aim of building closer trading ties with African Commonwealth countries.[13] One of them suggested that this was a revival of Cecil Rhodes' dream of joining up the British Empire from the Cape to Cairo. Liam Fox dismissed the term, although it was later pointed out that he had chosen to hang a portrait of Cecil Rhodes in his Whitehall office.[14]

There were astonished reactions to this magical thinking from those who had experienced the reality of Empire 1.0. Shashi Tharoor, whose criticisms of the British Empire has taken the Oxford Union by storm in 2015, published *Inglorious Empire*, a sustained attack on the British Raj, in March 2017. He pointed out that 'the British public is woefully ignorant of the realities of the British Empire, and what it meant to its subject peoples' and urged that 'the need to temper British imperial nostalgia with postcolonial responsibility has never been stronger'.[15] Joining the media debate, he warned that in India, which was currently celebrating seventy years of independence from Britain, the notion of Empire 2.0 would go down 'like a lead balloon'. Quoting Tharoor, David Olusoga, author of *Black and British*, underlined that empire was discussed by the British only on their own terms.

> [T]he national conversation about the lost empire is too often an internal monologue, largely focused on what 'we' did or did not do, and whether or not 'we' should be proud of it. What 'they' – the peoples of the former empire and current Commonwealth – felt about it then and think about it now, rarely enters the solipsistic debate [...] Empire 2.0 is a fanciful vision of the future based on a distorted remembering of the past. It's a delusion and, like all delusions, has the potential to lull us into a false sense of security and lead us to make bad decisions.[16]

Examples of how this delusional thinking might lead to inappropriate views and bad decisions were not long in coming. Boris Johnson, visiting a pagoda in Myanmar, formerly Burma, in January 2017, began to recite Kipling's line, 'Come you back, you British soldier; come you back to Mandalay!', and had to be stopped by the British ambassador before he got to the insulting 'Bloomin' idol made o' mud / Wot they called the Great Gawd Budd'.[17] When Spain announced that it would reassert its claim to Gibraltar if Britain left Europe, former Conservative leader Michael Howard tendentiously reminded viewers of *Sky News* on 2 April 2017 that:

> thirty years ago this week another woman prime minister sent a task force half way across the world to defend the freedom of another small group of British people against another Spanish-speaking country. And I'm absolutely certain that our current prime minister will show the same resolve in standing by the people of Gibraltar.[18]

The idea of the 'great, global trading nation' was the centrepiece of the Leave argument. Only a hard Brexit, leaving the single market and the customs union, could give Britain the free hand to make her own free trade treaties. Outside Europe, Britain would be able to restore the 'great commercial republic' of which Adam Smith had spoken, or in David Cameron's words, make it the 'swashbuckling [...]

buccaneer nation' it once had been. Meanwhile Nick Timothy, Theresa May's Joint Chief of Staff, proposed that the new hero of Brexit should be Joseph Chamberlain, a Unionist who broke with the Liberal Party over its policy of Home Rule for Ireland, becoming Colonial Secretary in the Salisbury government of 1895. This case was attacked by former Permanent Secretary of the Treasury, Nicholas Macpherson, who argued that Chamberlain's 'imperialist vision of a Greater Britain proved to be a fantasy'. His 'provocations led to the outbreak of the Boer War' while his project to make the empire into a protectionist area split the Conservative Party. Timothy was obliged to resign from Downing Street after the Conservatives' poor performance in the June 2017 elections.[19]

First attempts by the British government to do its own trade deals did not meet with great success. Theresa May travelled to India with a large trade delegation in November 2016 but her enthusiasm for free trade was contradicted by her obsession with reducing immigration numbers, which greatly affected Indian students coming to study in the United Kingdom. There was a strong sense that Britain was interested in India's business but not in her people. Headlines in India when she was Home Secretary ran 'Take our money and then get out'.[20]

Meanwhile it became increasingly clear that the 'great, global trading nation' free from EU red tape and the European Court of Justice that was the dream of Brexit ministers and their business friends was a Singapore-style low-regulation, low-tax, low-wage financial and commercial empire that exploited workers in developing countries and was designed to hide profits where the taxman would not find them. The leak of the so-called Paradise papers in November 2017 revealed that global businesses like Nike, registered in Portland, Oregon, employed low-paid workers in Vietnam and Indonesia to make their shoes, which were warehoused in Belgium. The UK profits of Nike were hidden in Bermuda, a British overseas territory where the law firm Appleby serviced an offshore tax haven for many other global companies. One of them, the UK company Serco, ran immigration detention centres for the Australian government at Christmas Island in the Indian Ocean and for the British government at Yarl's Wood immigration removal centre for women in Bedford, where numerous cases of sexual abuse were reported. What The Guardian called a 'globally mobile republic' was a hydra of multinational corporations and webs of the super-rich making money out of slave-like labour and desperate migrants of the developing world and using some of the oldest parts of the British Empire in order to avoid taxes.[21]

This neo-liberal project demonstrated the vacuity of promises to tackle 'burning injustice'. Ironically, the Conservative electorate was being kept on board by promises that Brexit would deal with social issues by reducing immigration, rather than any social investment or social reform. On 2 December 2017, Alan Milburn, former Labour minister, resigned from his chairmanship of the Social Mobility Commission, taking the rest of the Commission with him. In his letter to Theresa May he said that 'whole communities and parts of Britain are being left behind economically and hollowed out socially. The growing sense that we have become an us and them society is deeply corrosive of our cohesion as a nation [...] more and more people are feeling that Britain is becoming more unfair rather than less'.[22] Four weeks later Andrew Adonis, chair of the National Infrastructure Commission, also resigned, telling Theresa May that her government was 'hurtling towards the EU's emergency exit with no credible plan for the future of British trade and European cooperation, all the while ignoring [...] the crises of housing, education, the NHS, social and regional inequality which are undermining our nation and feeding a populist upsurge'.[23] Increasingly it appeared that while growing inequalities had fuelled the vote against the EU, leaving the EU risked making those inequalities worse.

The plan that Britain would leave Europe and become a more global power through its ties with the Commonwealth was highlighted by Boris Johnson in September 2017. 'We will be able to intensify old friendships around the world, not least with fast-growing Commonwealth economies, and to build a truly global Britain', he declared, finishing with, 'I believe that we can be the greatest country on Earth'.[24] One burning question was, of which Commonwealth was he thinking? Was it the white Dominions, which had become known as the Anglosphere, which he had praised during his 2013 visit to Australia? Or was it the Commonwealth in general, including India and former colonies in Africa and the Caribbean? For Philip Murphy, director of the Institute of Commonwealth Studies, there was little doubt. He argued that 'Eurosceptics, currently in the ascendant, are implicitly rehabilitating the racialized, early twentieth-century notion of the Commonwealth as a cosy and exclusive Anglo-Saxon club', and in this was providing 'new clothes' for the British Empire.[25]

Opening the Commonwealth Games on the Australian Gold Coast on 4 April 2018, Prince Charles declared that 'over forty years these friendly games have shown the potential of the Commonwealth to connect people of different backgrounds and nationalities'. Unfortunately, some backgrounds and nationalities were excluded. Indigenous Australians protesting with chants of 'Always was, always will be Aboriginal land' were driven away by mounted police.[26] Back in Britain, a scandal broke over the 'Windrush generation' of immigrants from the Caribbean, many of whom had come as children and also as British subjects in the 1950s and 1960s. It became clear that, to quote Theresa May's speech on taking office, 'If you're black, you're treated more harshly [. . .] than if you're white.' In the 'hostile environment' she had created British Caribbeans were now being classed as illegal immigrants in order to meet its draconian target of reducing immigration to 100,000 per year. Because of multiple checks on their status as British citizens for which they could not provide documentation many of the Windrush immigrants had lost their jobs or been refused accommodation or NHS treatment. Under a policy of 'deport first, appeal later', an undisclosed number had been sent to detention centres ahead of deportation. The Reverend Guy Hewitt, High Commissioner of Barbados, said that 'Seventy years after Windrush we are facing a new wave of hostility. This is about people saying, as they said seventy years ago, "Go back home". It is not good enough for people like this who gave their lives for this country, to be treated like this.'[27] David Lammy, born in London to Guyanese parents and MP for Tottenham, told Home Secretary Amber Rudd that 'this is a day of national shame and it has come about because of the "hostile environment" policy that was begun under the prime minister'.[28]

Salman Rushdie argued in 1982 that the notion of 'the British people' silently excluded non-white populations. Despite the racism they encountered on their arrival and confrontations with the police in 1981 the 'Windrush generation' acquired a privileged status as the pioneers of postwar immigration. Amber Rudd was forced to resign but the relegation of the Caribbean immigrants to the status of illegal immigrants demonstrated the pervasiveness of the colonial mentality. Keith Mitchell, prime minister of Grenada, attending the Commonwealth Heads of Government Conference in London, said 'I think we have been making the point that Britain, being our former colonial masters, has not necessarily treated us in the postcolonial period in the way we expected.'[29] 'I'll be crucified for saying this', responded Jamaican-British poet Linton Kwesi Johnson, who had lived in South London for fifty-five years, 'but I believe that racism is very much part of the cultural DNA of this country, and probably has been since imperial times'.[30]

The rhetoric of Empire 2.0, the global trading nation, did not translate into a global profile for Great Britain for a simple reason: the fantasy sought to cover the country's international weakness and isolation. A good example of this was Theresa May's decision to participate with the United States on 14 April 2018 in air strikes on the chemical facilities allegedly used by President Assad of Syria to attack the population of the Damascus suburb of Douma, said to be harbouring rebels. This was a replay of the crisis of 29 August 2013 when Parliament had discussed retaliation against Assad for his bombing of Ghouta, but decided against it. Theresa May joined the air strike without recalling Parliament and was accused of being 'Mr Trump's poodle'. Grilled by the Commons after the event, she claimed that she was acting to 'uphold and defend the global consensus' against chemical weapons and that not to intervene would have been 'a stain on our humanity'. Her critics suggested that global consensus required consulting the United Nations while humanitarianism should have dictated a generosity towards Syrian refugees fleeing the bombing that the government had refused for five years.[31] The sole plausible justification for air strikes was to make Britain appear like the vestige of a great power.

In the period after June 2016 France might have gone the same way as Britain. She might have embraced a narrow nationalism in order to defend her borders and her national identity, and distanced herself from a Europe regarded as a superstate run by Germany. This defensive attitude would have made it difficult for her to play a significant world role. In the event, France took a different path from Britain. She embraced Europe and saw no contradiction between a leading role in Europe and her global ambitions. She also began to work through the difficult legacy of the French Empire, making an apology for the evils of colonialism in order to act with a freer hand on the world stage.

The day after the Brexit vote Marine Le Pen had herself photographed with a poster reading, 'Brexit, and now France!'[32] There was plenty of evidence of ordinary people in France struggling with globalisation and immigration. Brittany had voted on the Left and for Europe in recent times but Fougères, a former shoe-making town near the border with Normandy, was suffering from the closure of factories, agricultural crises

**Figure 10.2** Emmanuel Macron as Napoleon: carnival float in Mainz, 12 February 2018.
Getty Images / FABIAN SOMMER / AFP / DPA / 917363126

and threats to jobs. In late June 2016, Louis Pautrel, mayor of a nearby rural commune, said that the Front National was polling up to 35 per cent in local elections. 'People feel very abandoned', he said, 'a Frexit vote would get 60% here, easily'.[33]

Frexit required Marine Le Pen to become president of France in elections scheduled for May 2017. The victory of a populist politician in France seemed a strong possibility after Brexit, and even more so after the election of Donald Trump in November 2016. In France, however, there was a political earthquake which catapulted Emmanuel Macron to power as the youngest ever president of the French Republic. Not beholden to any of the old parties, he had a free hand to remake France's destiny. If he had a guiding star it was that of Charles de Gaulle, or even Napoleon Bonaparte (Figure 10.2).

Macron had pursued an elite trajectory: a graduate of the École Nationale d'Administration and member of the corps of financial inspectors, he switched to merchant banking and then moved into politics, working for François Hollande in the Élysée and appointed minister for the economy and industry in 2014. Calculating that the Socialist Party would crash in the 2017 presidential elections, he resigned from the government and announced his candidature for the presidency in November 2016. He founded his own movement, largely of young people, called En Marche! (Forward!) and took on the established parties. In the first round of the presidential elections, in April 2017, he saw off the conservative Republican François Fillon, the Socialist Benoît Hamon, who secured a derisory 6.4 per cent of the vote, along with the left-populist candidate Jean-Luc Mélanchon. Pitted in the second round against Marine Le Pen of the Front National, he defeated her by 66 per cent to 34 per cent, taking nearly 90 per cent of the votes in Paris. In the end struggling but hopeful Fougères voted 23 per cent for Le Pen and 77 per cent for Macron.[34] En Marche! now became a political party, La République en Marche, which took 308 of the 577 seats in the National Assembly on 18 June 2017. This enabled Macron to choose a new direction for France, appealing particularly to young people.

The first task of Macron was to challenge the narrowly nationalistic, Eurosceptic views of Marine Le Pen and to make a bid for a French leadership of Europe. In the televised debate before the second round of presidential elections, Le Pen declared, 'I am the candidate of the nation, which protects jobs and the security of our frontiers, which protects us against undercutting and the rise of Islamic fundamentalism.' The restoration of national sovereignty would allow the French to decide 'who comes in to our country and who does not'. Macron riposted: 'I reject the Front National's defeatism and hatred. We have always been a generous, open country [...] I am the candidate of a strong France in a Europe that protects', for only Europe could protect France against superpowers such as Russia and China.[35]

Once elected, Macron set about proposing reforms for the EU. He accepted that there was a crisis of confidence about the EU, both because of the austerity measures it had imposed to deal with debt in countries such as Greece, and because of what was perceived as a democratic deficit. On 4 July 2017 he told a joint meeting of the National Assembly and Senate that the solution was to 'go back to the beginnings of Europe [...] to rediscover the original meaning of the European project'. He developed these ideas talking to students at the Sorbonne on 26 September 2017. 'At this moment I am thinking of Robert Schuman who, in Paris on 9 May 1950, dared to advocate building Europe', he told them. Schuman had declared, 'we failed to build Europe and we got the war'. Today, said Macron, was not the time for 'retreat or timidity, but for boldness and a sense of history'. His bold idea was a more centralised and effective EU, equipping the Eurozone with a common budget, a common finance and economics minister, and a Eurozone parliament to which he or she would be accountable.[36]

In setting out such an agenda, Macron was making a bid for French leadership in Europe. The moment was propitious. The British government was embroiled in Brexit negotiations and Theresa May lost her overall parliamentary majority on 8 June 2017. In Germany, Angela Merkel lost her dominant position in the Federal elections of 28 September 2017, when the far right Alternative für Deutschland made a breakthough, and took six months to put together a coalition government. Merkel was resistant to Macron's reforms of the Eurozone, which threatened to be a drain on Germany's finances, while Britain had voted to leave the EU altogether. Macron's answer was a two-speed Europe: an inner circle of Eurozone countries and an outer circle of countries outside the Eurozone which wished to move at a slower pace.[37] This was reminiscent of Napoleon's European empire, an inner core based on a Greater France including Belgium, the Netherlands, western Germany and northern Italy and an outer circle including southern Italy, Spain and Poland.[38] It was also reminiscent of the original Europe of the Six, which from 1958 to 1969 was dominated by General de Gaulle. Pointedly, on the 55th anniversary of de Gaulle receiving Chancellor Adenauer at the Élysée Palace in January 1963, Macron in his young pomp welcomed an Angela Merkel whose star was beginning to sink.[39]

While asserting his claim to lead Europe, Macron was also obliged to deal with France's colonial past. De Gaulle had seen no contradiction between France as a European power and France as a global power, drawing in the first place on the resources of Africa. But just as de Gaulle had been obliged to abandon Algeria before building *Françafrique*, so Macron had to deal with the painful debate over French colonialism before he could move on. A master of cultural diplomacy, he announced on 14 February 2017 while visiting Algiers, that French colonialism was 'a crime against humanity, a real barbarity. It is a past that we must confront squarely and apologise to those we have harmed.'[40] This was the sharpest of breaks from the law of 2005 that enjoined schools and universities to teach the 'positive role' of French imperialism and demonstrated a commitment to begin to work through what others saw as a toxic inheritance. This was bound to be controversial. On 6 April, he was asked by a history teacher from Rouen, Barbara Lefebvre, who turned out to be working for François Fillon, how she was going to tell her pupils that French heroes such as Jules Ferry and Marshal Lyautey, proconsul of Morocco, had committed crimes against humanity. Macron replied that 'sixty years on we have to open our eyes. Memories have been profoundly traumatised by the Algerian War [...] There is a problem of divided memories. We have to reconcile memories.'[41]

The masterful cultural diplomacy of Macron often made it difficult to separate symbol from substance. Was his rejection of colonialism purely rhetorical, or was he going to uproot all remnants of the French Empire? Houria Bouteldja of Les Indigènes de la République suggested in July 2017 that Macron 'denounced the crimes of the past to win over French postcolonialists the better to pursue his imperialist project'. She argued that only deeds would reveal France's commitment to the global South.[42] Macron indeed had very ambitious plans. On 28 November 2017 he addressed 800 students from the University of Ouagadougou in Burkina Faso, formerly the French colony of Upper Volta. He told them that the neo-colonialist days of *Françafrique* were over, and that archives concerning the murder in 1987 of Thomas Sankara, the revolutionary president of Burkina Faso, would be declassified. He announced that France would develop the education of girls, allow students to circulate between Africa and France and back with long-term visas, invest in infrastructure projects and train local forces to combat Islamist terrorism.[43]

While on his African tour Macron revived the concept of Francophonie. This had been established in the late 1960s to gather former French colonies and mandates in Africa, the Near East, Far East and Pacific, together with Canada. From 1986 its representatives met at an annual summit to debate policies but the summit was undermined by association with African dictators, rivalry for leadership with Canada and the threat of Islamist organisations which spoke for Arab-speaking masses against French-speaking elites.[44] To recentre Francophonie on France and to reboot the project Macron hosted a conference under the sacred portals of the Institut de France on 20 March 2018. He proposed a French 'archipelago of language' that would, without the trappings of empire, challenge the British Commonwealth and the Anglosphere.

> Today, from Maradi [Niger] to Séoul, from Yaoundé to Ulan Bator, from Nouméa [New Caledonia] to Buenos Aires, the world hums with our language. It resonates through its literature, its poetry, its songs, its theatre and cinema, through cookery, sport and philosophical debate [...] It is the language of journalists, dissidents, bloggers, poets in so many countries where people fight for freedom in French.

For Macron, the French language was a vehicle of soft power that far outstripped the borders of her former colonies. It was taught to young women in Africa menaced by 'terrorism and obscurantism' and to refugees who sought asylum in France. It was taught in 200 international schools across the world and he wanted this number increased to 500 by 2022. He also wanted to take advantage of Brexit to raise the profile of French in Brussels.[45]

France, like Britain, had claims to be a global trading nation. The difference was that for France this was not sold as an alternative to trade with the EU, but to complement it. In order to further trade Macron made an art of his cultural diplomacy. Donald Trump was invited to Paris on 14 July 2017 to watch the military display on the Champs Élysées and was dined half way up the Eiffel Tower. When Macron visited Chinese President Xi Jinping in January 2018 he flew over a horse from his own Republican Guard, as from one great republic to another, together with a harness from the 1870s and engraved sabre. He even countered traditionally anti-French sentiment in Britain by offering to lend her the Bayeux Tapestry. All this was linked to the promotion of France's international profile and to the assertion of France's importance as a global player. In March 2018 Macron visited India for talks with Prime Minister Narendra Modi. His gift was a 1922 French translation of the ancient Hindu scripture *Bhagavad Gita*. This prefaced the sale of arms and nuclear reactors but also talks on joint strategic interests in the 'Indo-Pacific' region and a co-chairing a conference of the International Solar Alliance. Not concerned about migration from India, he came away with much more than Theresa May, with the additional irony that all this was going on in the former British Raj.

Macron's popularity was significantly greater internationally than at home. He was prepared to drive through modernising legislation to weaken the power of the railway trade unions and to make French universities more competitive by introducing greater selection of students. This provoked a wave of strikes and university occupations in April 2018 and a sense that France was once again fighting the battles of May 1968, fifty years later. For Macron, born in 1977, 1968 was only history, not memory. He was also prepared to court hostility by a policy on immigration that did enough to keep future votes away from the Front National. A bill on asylum and migration was passed through the National Assembly in April 2018, with some unhappiness and even rebellion from the République en Marche party.

All this, however, was at the service of France's presence on the world stage. Rather that kow-tow to President Trump's America First policy and Israel's settlement policy, Macron was prepared to speak his mind in favour of a more secure and more just world order. On 10 December 2017, making a serious claim to speak for Europe in the Middle East, he received Benjamin Netanyahu at the Élysée and told him that US recognition of Jerusalem as the capital of Israel was a threat to peace and urged him to 'freeze the colonisation' of the occupied territories.[46] France took part in the air strikes on Assad's chemical plants on 14 April 2018 but persuaded Donald Trump to limit the strikes rather than to 'decapitate' the regime and urged a political solution to the Syrian problem that would involve Russia and China.[47] On 25 April 2018, addressing a joint session of the American Congress, he criticised 'isolation, withdrawl and nationalism' and implicitly the foreign policy of Donald Trump. The alternative was not necessarily internationalism, for the United Nations had largely ceased to function as a global policeman, but it should be multilateral:

We can build the twenty-first century world order on a new breed of multilateralism, a more effective, accountable and results-based multilateralism. This requires more than ever the United States' involvement, as your role was decisive in creating and safeguarding today's free world. The United States invented this multilateralism, you are the one now who has to preserve and reinvent it [...] The United States and Europe have a historic role to promote our universal values, to express strongly that human rights, the rights of minorities and shared liberty are the true answer to the disorders of the world.[48]

In the aftermath of the Brexit vote, then, the British and French governments' approaches to power and prosperity were strikingly different. One proposed withdrawal from Europe to recover the fantasy of a global empire while the other embraced internationalism and multilateralism as the best way to defend French interests. One said 'either, or' to Europe and the world, the other said 'why not both?' One made threats if it did not get what it wanted, the other perfected the use of soft power. One was trapped in its own past, the other was inspired by its best examples but had its eyes resolutely on the future.

# CONCLUSION

Empire, then, has been a fantasy of glory and a chronicle of anguish. As an empire in the mind, it continues to be both. And yet in the twenty-first century, in order to move forward, European countries must recognise the anguish caused by empire and lay to rest fantasies of rebuilding empire in ever more dubious reincarnations.

Historically, empires were built up from trading networks, from colonies of settlement and from territorial possessions from which huge amounts of tributes, taxes and soldiers could be raised. They were portrayed to the metropolitan publics as the free enterprise of buccaneering seamen, the farms of vigorous farmers and bejewelled realms in which everyone knew their place in the hierarchy. Yet, as we have seen, the most prosperous trade was in plundered slaves, trading corporations such as the East India Company fielded large armies, trading concessions were forced on unwilling partners by gunboats and unequal treaties, and credit made over to local rulers was used to tighten the screws of imperial control. Colonies of settlement were not virgin lands but already inhabited by indigenous peoples who were driven off, expropriated and often massacred to make way for European colonists. Territories under metropolitan control were accorded a degree of control if they were peopled by Europeans; otherwise they were ruled in an authoritarian way by a European bureaucracy. Strategies of partition and divide and rule prevented ethnic and religious groups coming together, indigenous peoples were segregated, subjected to arbitrary justice and punishment, and any passive or active resistance was met with lethal force.

Empire was always established by fraud or force or a combination of both. It was always opposed by dominated or colonised peoples, whether by fight or flight, passive or active resistance. Imperial rule constantly looked to legitimate itself, in the eyes both of its subject peoples and of publics in the metropolis who were often opposed to the brutality and cost of empire. Empire was said to bring capitalist exchange to far-flung parts of the world whose riches were as yet untapped or whose people languished in poverty. It was said to bring civilisation to benighted peoples, a natural order in which, in the words of Jules Ferry, 'superior races' did their duty to 'inferior races' or, in the words of Kipling, shouldered the 'white man's burden'. This legitimation fulfilled itself in what W. E. B. Du Bois called 'the religion of whiteness' which underpinned European empires and justified the worst oppressions, exclusions and atrocities.

The language of legitimacy, meanwhile, could be turned against the imperial powers. Hundreds of thousands of soldiers recruited from the British and French colonies were told that they were fighting for freedom against the tyranny of the enemy and came to think that they might enjoy some of that from their colonial masters. The United States, intervening in 1917, and the League of Nations proclaimed the principle of the equality of all nations and their right to self-government. Educated leaders of Arab and Asian peoples duly turned up in Paris and London, demanding their slice of freedom and self-government. This was a wonderful occasion on which the imperial powers might have acknowledged the change of historical era and the appropriation of legitimacy by the subject peoples, and granted them the liberty they craved. The opportunity was missed. Concessions were debated for Algeria and India but then shelved, and protesters at Amritsar were duly massacred. Former German colonies became mandates under the League of Nations but were administered by France and Britain like their other colonies, and aerial bombardment was tested in Iraq in 1920 and Syria in 1925. A new generation of colonial subjects was radicalised: Ho Chi Minh became an anti-colonial communist while Sayyid Abdul Ala Mawdudi published his *Jihad in Islam* in 1927.

The Second World War brought the colonial powers to their knees. In 1940 France was defeated and occupied by the Germans and the Japanese occupied its Indochinese Empire. In 1942 the British colonial citadel of Singapore fell to the Japanese. The same principles of freedom and equality that had been proclaimed in 1917–19 were announced in the Atlantic Charter of 1941 and above all by the United Nations Charter of 1945. Decolonisation was now firmly on the agenda. But it was precisely the trauma of almost losing their empires which made France and Britain desperate to reclaim them after the defeat of Germany and Japan. On VE Day, 8 May 1945, the French massacred Algerians demanding independence at Setif. They returned to Indo-China and fought a long and bloody war against Ho Chi Minh until they were overwhelmed at Dien Bien Phu in 1954. Losing Indo-China made them even less willing to lose Algeria, where settlers held the whip hand, and they committed themselves to a six-year war, resorting to torture and massacre. The British abandoned India and handed Palestine over to the State of Israel, which became a new colonial power. They were determined, however, to hold on to their possessions in the Middle East and Africa, especially in Eastern and Southern Africa where settlers demanded protection from indigenous revolt.

In the 1960s the Third World exploded in colonial revolt. Anti-colonial wars of liberation rocked Latin America, Africa, the Middle East and Asia. Newly independent countries asserted themselves in the 1955 Bandung Conference and in the United Nations. The colonial powers were still not prepared to give up. The Suez intervention of 1956 has been seen as a last attempt at colonial intervention against a nation demanding independence, except that it was far from being the last attempt. Gestures were made in de Gaulle's offer of an Algerian referendum in September 1959 and Macmillan's 'wind of change' speech in February 1980, but the public drama of decolonisation concessions concealed the private development of neo-colonialism. France abandoned its Algerian settlers but promoted *Françafrique* under the radar. Britain let its settlers in Kenya and Rhodesia go but continued to pursue its economic and strategic interests in South Africa which, outside the Commonwealth, intensified the apartheid regime. Troops from the British Empire were repatriated to defend Protestant settlers in Northern Ireland, and then dispatched across the Atlantic to defend a small number of sheep farmers but above all Britain's self-image as an imperial power.

There were two moments at which neo-colonialism might have evolved into something less destructive and less divisive. The first was after the oil crisis of 1973 when the balance of power shifted back to those Third World countries that were oil-producing. Countries like Algeria began to speak of a new economic order in which they took back control of the productive forces through nationalisation and trade controls. The reaction of the leading industrial countries was to exploit Third World debt in order to impose a global financial empire, forcing privatisation and dismantling trade restrictions in order to benefit their governments and multinational corporations. It was in many ways a reinvention of the informal empires of the nineteenth century. Dealing with local opposition could be devolved to local governments who were heavily indebted to the West. A worldwide anti-globalisation movement which took off in 1999 made more serious challenges but was sidelined after the Iraq War of 2003.

The second moment was the end of the Cold War and the global triumph of the United States. This allowed the United States to claim that it was furthering a new world order based on the market economy and democracy and operating a strategy of liberal or humanitarian intervention only when that order was challenged. Unfortunately, what was seen as the 'Great Satan' American imperialism was challenged by the Iranian Republic after 1979 while Soviet imperialism in Afghanistan was resisted by Islamist guerrillas. Each were vehicles of a global Islamism that culminated in 9/11 and drove the United States and its allies to launch what was called the War on Terrorism. This was none other than a neo-imperialist movement, fought with massive military superiority in Afghanistan, Iraq and Libya, and against the Islamic State that rose from the rubble of Iraq and Syria in 2014. Very little thinking was done about the cost of military interventions in these regions, which were seen locally as simply repeating the colonial crimes of earlier eras. They produced a 'blow-back' of Islamist attacks in Britain and France, including the 7 July 2005 bombings in London, the *Charlie Hebdo* and Bataclan attacks in Paris in January and November 2015 and attacks in London and Manchester in the spring of 2017.

Colonial violence in the metropolis reached a crescendo in 2015–17, but the effects of colonialism on metropolitan society had manifested themselves for decades. Colonisation produced what Louise Bennett called 'colonising in reverse' or, as Sri Lankan writer Ambalavaner Sivanandan put it, 'we are here because you were there'.

Many migrants from the colonies and former colonies had fought in the armed forces of Britain and France and had been encouraged to rebuild the economies there after the Second World

War. Far from being welcomed into the host societies, however, these migrants were subjected to racial discrimination and racial violence. This may been seen not as pure racial antagonism but as the re-establishment 'back here' of colonial hierarchies that had existed 'out there'. It involved segregation in inner cities or specific *banlieues*, exclusion from decent housing, jobs and education, and subjection to police harassment and violence. The loss of empire by Britain and France produced in the metropolis a sense of having been defeated not only in the colonies but also on home ground, prompting hostility to immigration as 'swamping' or 'invasion'. Political movements sprang up to reassert the supremacy of white populations. Although sporadic attempts were made to develop multiracial, multicultural societies, these were generally seen as a threat to the host societies which defended themselves by recourse to monocultural nationalism. Behind the rhetoric of free speech that greeted the burnings of Salman Rushdie's *Satanic Verses* and the rhetoric of *laïcité* that greeted the wearing of veils by Muslim students lay colonialist strategies to redefine British and French identities in ways that excluded minorities who identified with Islam.

Although generations of immigrants tried to assimilate with the host society, espousing their values and attitudes, exclusion forced them to develop their own identities in opposition to those of the country they were living in. Their alienation was increased by each lethal military intervention in Afghanistan or the Middle East, by each tightening of immigration and detention rules, by each announcement of 'British values' or combative *laïcité* and by each police offensive against immigrant *banlieues*. Colonial wars and oppression were replayed in their minds. 'I get angry when I hear that word "empire"', said poet Benjamin Zephaniah, turning down an OBE after the Iraq War. 'It reminds me of slavery, it reminds me of thousands of years of brutality, it reminds me of how my foremothers were raped and my forefathers brutalised.' In France the term 'colonial fracture' was coined to describe the opposition of those who identified as makers of empire and those who identified as the heirs of the colonised. When the French parliament passed a law in 2005 requiring schools and universities to teach the benefits of French colonial rule, especially in North Africa, it provoked the formation of Les Indigènes de la République by a group of young French citizens of North African origin, who announced that the French massacre of Algerians in Sétif in 1945 was their founding moment and that for them Dien Bien Phu was a victory.

The fantasies and anguish of empires had a powerful effect on the European project. The construction of Europe first as an economic, then as a political entity, coincided with the process of decolonisation. Colonies were lost, but a new future in Europe beckoned. France and Britain had very different experiences of this challenge. France took the initiative in building the new Europe, and Charles de Gaulle actually saw it as a continental French empire that would keep Britain out. France also saw no contradiction between her neo-colonial ambitions and her ambitions in Europe. Britain, by contrast, was absent from the first phase of European integration. When she finally joined in 1973 it was felt in some quarters as timely modernisation but in others as a defeat, a poor alternative to her Empire and a Europe over which she had precious little influence.

The reunification of Germany in 1990, it is true, provoked similar feelings of disquiet in both France and Britain. There were fears that Germany would seek to dominate Europe, as she had in 1870, 1914 and 1939. France had nightmares about the Franco-Prussian War and the defeat of 1940, Britain about winning the Second World War in vain. Right-wing nationalist parties in both countries opposed not only immigration but also European integration. The French solution to the challenge, however, was very different to the British. France promoted federalism as a way to contain Germany, but Britain regarded federalism as vehicle of European empire, controlled first by the French, then by the Germans. Eurosceptical attitudes steadily gained traction, appealing to the defence of British sovereignty, British national identity defined against immigration, and British ambitions which had historically been less European and more 'global'.

The anguish of losing an empire and the fantasy of rediscovering it came to a head with the referendum of 2016. Britain, it was said, would leave the European Union but she would not be alone. She would rediscover her past as a 'swashbuckling [...] buccaneer nation', free to make trade treaties of her own design across the world. She would commune again with the 'Anglosphere' of the white Dominions which she had cruelly betrayed in 1973 but which had always been kith and kin and spoke the same English language. She would found an Empire 2.0 with countries like India, once the Raj, now partners, but also linked by deep historical connection and understanding. France, meanwhile, under Emmanuel Macron, brought up with no memories of the French Empire, was able to draw France's twenty-first century ambitions on a clean sheet. He apologised for colonialism as a 'crime against humanity' in order to placate those who condemned France's colonial past but moved swiftly on in order not to antagonise unduly those who were still nostalgic for it. He jettisoned the baggage of imperial fantasy while promoting strategic projects in Africa and reviving the concept of Francophonie in which France was one among equals. Above all he saw no contradiction between ambitions to lead in Europe and ambitions to do business with world leaders, mobilising the charm of soft diplomacy.

Britain and France stand at a crossroads in their history. They both have proud imperial pasts and a legacy of colonial challenges. Neither of them is any longer a world power; they are both still permanent members of the UN Security Council but they are medium-sized powers who cannot seriously compete with the United States, Russia and China. They have been sustained in their belief that they are still great powers by fantasies of empire which they have repeatedly attempted to recreate. These fantasies have been shadowed by the anguish of the loss of empire. The anguish of the former colonisers, however, is of little weight compared to the anguish of former colonial peoples who have come to live and work in the metropolis, both about the exclusion and oppression their families suffered in the colonies and the exclusion and oppression they too often encounter in the metropolis today.

The challenge for both France and Britain is to work through their colonial pasts. No one history of empire will ever be agreed; the colonial and the postcolonial approaches are defined against each other. Each side, however, must listen to the other's story, the other's history, and seek to understand it. As Emmanuel Macron said to Rouen schoolteacher Barbara Lefebvre, 'There is a problem of divided memories. We have to reconcile memories.' Connections between what happened 'out there' and what has happened 'back here' have to be thought about. Salman Rusdie was probably right that the British were ignorant of much of their history because it happened 'out there'. The 'radicalisation' of young people of immigrant origin may be explained by the impact of Western military strikes against insurgents in the Middle East or Afghanistan and the suffering of civilian victims with whom they identify. Racist attacks in the metropolis on those of immigrant origin may be an acting out of the colonial superiority felt by white people. The final challenge is one of equality, that in society and politics all individuals and all communities should be considered as entitled to the same rights, the same respect and the same justice. This was something colonialism manifestly and repeatedly failed to do. To remedy this, it is never too late.

# ACKNOWLEDGEMENTS

This study began as the 2013 Wiles Lectures, delivered in Queen's University Belfast. I am very grateful to John Gray, Professor of Modern Irish History at Queen's, and to the sponsors of the lectures. Their generosity made it possible to invite a wonderful group of colleagues to come to Belfast to discuss the lectures, notably Manu Braganca, Emile Chabal, Hannah Diamond, Laurent Douzou, Julian Jackson, Christopher Lloyd and Guillaume Piketty.

I am deeply indebted to Michael Watson of Cambridge University Press, who has overseen the project from the beginning. His vision, patience, clarity and encouragement to detail have been crucial in seeing it to completion. I am also grateful to Ruth Boyes, Lisa Carter and Chris Burrows at Cambridge University Press for their good-humoured professionalism, and to Joanna North for her impeccable copy-editing.

A first draft was the subject of a 'monograph workshop' in June 2017. This experiment in collective critique by colleagues expert in a range of fields was a landmark in its development. Profuse thanks are due to Joya Chatterji, Patricia Clavin, Richard Drayton, Margret Frenz, James McDougall, Guillaume Piketty and to International Relations doctoral student Angharad Jones Buxton.

My doctoral students working in the field provided invaluable inspiration and advice. Particular thanks are due to Hannah al-Hassan Ali, Gabrielle Maas, Avner Ofrath, Alex Paulin-Booth and Sarah Stokes.

Many other colleagues offered support and advice over the course of this project. Among them I must thank Paul Betts, Andrea Brazzoduro, Ludivine Broch, Rebecca Clifford, Aurélie Daher, John Davis, Jennifer Dueck, Martin Evans, Sudhir Hazareesingh, Dan Hicks, Daniel Lee, Karma Nabulsi, Ed Naylor, Kalypso Nicolaïdis, Lyndal Roper, Nick Stargardt, Martin Thomas, Imaobong Umoren and Natalya Vince.

The enthusiasm of undergraduate students has been uplifting. I am especially grateful to those I worked with on Oxford History Faculty's 'Global Twentieth Century' option and to those active in the Common Ground and Oxford and Colonialism initiatives.

As ever, my family has been unstinting in their generosity and encouragement. Their diverse projects to make the world a better place inspire me. Thank you Lucy-Jean, Rachel, Georgia, William and Adam.

# The Wiles Lectures

The Wiles Lectures, given at The Queen's University of Belfast, is a regular, occasional series of lectures on an historical theme, sponsored by the University and published (usually in extended and modified form) by Cambridge University Press. The lecture series was established in the 1950s with the encouragement of the historian Herbert Butterfield, whose 1954 inaugural lecture series was published as 'Man on his Past' (1955). Later lecture series have produced many notable Cambridge titles, such as Alfred Cobban's 'The Social Interpretation of the French Revolution' (1964), J. H. Elliott's 'The Old World and the New' (1970), E. J. Hobsbawm's 'Nations and Nationalism since 1780' (1990), and Adrian Hastings' 'The Construction of Nationhood' (1997).

A full list of titles in the series can be found at: www.cambridge.org/wileslectures.

# NOTES

## Introduction

1 www.ibtimes.co.uk/eu-referendum-boris-johnson-warns-risks-leaving-eu-will-be-exaggerated-uk-better-off-out-1545161.

2 www.lemonde.fr/election-presidentielle-2017/article/2017/02/16/pour-macron-la-colonisation-fut-un-crime-contre-l-humanite_5080621_4854003.html.

3 www.youtube.com/watch?v=ohe-6E2L3ks.

4 Patricia Lorcin, *Algeria and France, 1800–2000. Identity, Memory, Nostalgia* (Syracuse, NY: Syracuse University Press, 2006); Claire Eldrige, '"Le symbole de l'Afrique perdue": Carnoux-en-Provence and the *pied noir* Community', in Kate Marsh and Nicola Frith (eds.), *France's Lost Empires. Fragmentation, Nostalgia and* la fracture coloniale (Lanham, MD: Lexington Books, 2011), 125–30.

5 Charles-André Julien and Charles-Robert Ageron, *Histoire de l'Algérie contemporaine* (2 vols., Paris: PUF, 1964, 1979).

6 Charles-Robert Ageron, 'L'Exposition Coloniale de 1931. Mythe républicain ou mythe impériale?', in Pierre Nora (ed.), *Les Lieux de Mémoire I. La République* (Paris: Gallimard, 1984), 561–91.

7 Peter Mathias, *The First Industrial Nation. An Economic History of Britain, 1700–1914* (London: Methuen, 1969), 93, 97.

8 Ronald Robinson and John Gallagher, with Alice Denny, *Africa and the Victorians. The Official Mind of Imperialism* (London: Macmillan, 1967), xi, 5.

9 Hugh Trevor-Roper, 'The Rise of Christian Europe', *The Listener*, 70/1809, 28 Nov. 1963, 871, republished with small qualifications in *The Rise of Christian Europe* (London: Thames & Hudson, 1965), 9.

10 Niall Ferguson, *Empire. How Britain Made the Modern World* (London: Allen Lane, 2003); Niall Ferguson, *Colossus. The Rise and Fall of the American Empire* (London: Allen Lane, 2004).

11 See for example Stuart Hall with Bill Schwarz, *Familiar Stranger. A Life between Two Islands* (London: Allen Lane, 2017); Afua Hirsch, *Brit(ish). On Race, Identity and Belonging* (London: Jonathan Cape, 2018); Nedjib Sidi Moussa, *La Fabrique du Musulmam* (Paris: Éditions Libertalia, 2017).

12 Chris Bayly, *Imperial Meridian. The British Empire and the World, 1780–1830* (London: Longman, 1989); Chris Bayly, *The Birth of the Modern World, 1780–*

1914. *Global Connections and Comparisons, 1780–1914* (Oxford: Blackwell, 2004).

13 Frederick Cooper and Ann Stoler, 'Between Metropole and Colony: Rethinking a Research Agenda', in Cooper and Stoler (eds.), *Tensions of Empire. Colonial Cultures in a Bourgeois World* (Berkeley, CA: University of California Press, 1997).

14 Catherine Hall and Sonya O. Rose (eds.), *At Home with the Empire. Metropolitan Culture and the Imperial World* (Cambridge University Press, 2006), 5; Bill Schwarz, *Memories of Empire. The White Man's World* (Oxford University Press, 2011), 13; Todd Shepard, 'Thinking between Metropole and Colony: The French Republic, "Exceptional Promotion" and the "Integration" of Algerians, 1955–1962', in Martin Thomas (ed.), *The French Colonial Mind I. Mental Maps of Empire and Colonial Encounters* (Lincoln, NE: University of Nebraska Press, 2011), 300.

15 Gayatri Chakravorty Spivak, 'Can the Subaltern Speak?' in Cary Nelson and Lawrence Grossberg (eds.), *Marxism and the Interpretation of Culture* (Urbana, IL: University of Illinois Press, 1988), 271–313.

16 Bill Ashcroft, Gareth Griffiths and Helen Tiffin, *The Empire Writes Back. Theory and Practice in Post-Colonial Literature* (London and New York: Routledge, 1989).

17 Joya Chatterji, *Bengal Divided. Hindu Communalism and Partition, 1932–1947* (Cambridge University Press, 1994); Joya Chatterji, *The Spoils of Partition. Bengal and India, 1947–1967* (Cambridge University, 2007); Claire Alexander, Joya Chatterji and Annu Jalais, *The Bengal Diaspora. Rethinking Muslim Migration* (London: Routledge, 2015).

18 Caroline Elkins, *Britain's Gulag. The Brutal End of Empire in Kenya* (London: Pimlico, 2005); David Anderson, *Histories of the Hanged. Britain's Dirty War in Kenya and the End of the Empire* (London: Weidenfeld & Nicolson, 2005). See also Ian Cobain, *Cruel Britannia. A Secret History of Torture* (London: Portobello Books, 2012).

19 Richard Drayton, 'Where Does the World Historian Write From? Objectivity, Moral Conscience and the Past and Present of Imperialism', *Journal of Contemporary History*, 46/3 (2011), 685.

20 Pascal Blanchard and Armelle Chatelier, *Images et colonies, 1880–1962. Nature, discours et influence de l'iconographie coloniale liée à la propagande coloniale et à la représentation des africains et de l'Afrique en France, de 1920 aux indépendances* (Paris: Association Connaissance de l'histoire de l'Afrique contemporaine/Syros, 1994).

21 Pascal Blanchard, Nicolas Bancel and Sandrine Lemaire (eds.), *La Fracture coloniale. La société française au prisme de l'héritage colonial* (Paris: La Découverte, 2005).

22 Achille Mbembe, 'La République et l'impensé de la "race"', in Blanchard, Bancel and Lemaire, *La Fracture coloniale*, 139–50 (139); see his *On the Postcolony* (Berkeley, CA: University of California Press, 2001).

23 Derek Gregory, *The Colonial Present* (Oxford: Blackwell, 2004), xv.

24 Paul Gilroy, *After Empire. Melancholia or Convivial Culture?* (Abingdon: Routledge, 2004); Gregory, *The Colonial Present*, 110.

25 John Darwin, 'Memory of Empire in Britain', in Dieter Rothermund (ed.), *Memories of Post-Imperial Nations. The Aftermath of Decolonization, 1945–2013* (Cambridge University Press, 2015), 32.

26 Andrew Thompson, *The Empire Strikes Back? The Impact of Imperialism on Britain from the Mid-Nineteenth Century* (Harlow: Pearson Longman, 2005); Schwarz, *Memories of Empire*; Jordanna Bailkin, *The Afterlife of Empire* (Berkeley, CA: Universary of California Press, 2012); Sandra Halperin and Ronen Palan (eds.),

*Legacies of Empire. Imperial Roots of the Contemporary Global Order* (Cambridge University Press, 2015); Kalypso Nicolaïdis, Berny Sèbe and Gabrielle Maas (eds.), *Memory, Identity and Colonial Legacies* (London and New York: I. B. Tauris, 2015); Elizabeth Buettner, *Europe after Empire. Decolonization, Society and Culture* (Cambridge University Press, 2016).

27 Benjamin Stora, *La Gangrène et l'oubli. La mémoire de la guerre d'Algérie* (Paris: La Découverte, 1991); Benjamin Stora and Mohammed Harbi (eds.), *La Guerre d'Algérie, 1954–2004, la fin de l'amnésie* (Paris: Robert Laffont, 2004); Benjamin Stora with Alexis Jenni, *Les Mémoires dangereuses, suivi d'une nouvelle édition de Transfert d'une mémoire* (Paris: Albin Michel, 2016).

28 Todd Shepard, *The Invention of Decolonization. The Algerian War and the Remaking of France* (Ithaca, NY and London: Cornell University Press, 2006); Marsh and Frith, *France's Lost Empires*.

29 See below, pp. 198, 251, 259.

30 Nicholas Draper, *The Price of Emancipation. Slave-Ownership, Compensation and British Society at the End of Slavery* (Cambridge University Press, 2010); Catherine Hall, Nicholas Draper, Keith McClelland, Katie Donington and Rachel Lang, *Legacies of British Slave-Ownership. Colonial Slavery and the Formation of Victorian Britain* (Cambridge University Press, 2014).

31 John Newsinger, 'Why Rhodes Must Fall', *Race & Class*, 58/2 (2016), 70–8.

32 Anthony Lemon, '"Rhodes Must Fall": The Dangers of Re-writing History',*The Round Table*, 105/2 (2016), 217–19.

33 www.qub.ac.uk/schools/happ/Discover/WilesLectureSeries/WilesLectures2013.

34 David Andress, *Cultural Dementia. How the West has Lost its History and Risks Losing Everything Else* (London: Apollo, 2018), 2, 29.

35 Sigmund Freud (1914). 'Remembering, Repeating and Working-Through (Further Recommendations on the Technique of Psycho-Analysis II)', in *The Standard Edition of the Complete Psychological Works of Sigmund Freud XII (1911–1913)* (London: Hogarth Press and the Institute of Psycho-Analysis, 1914).

36 Jacques Bigeard, *Pour une Parcelle de gloire* (Paris: Plon, 1975), 229–30.

# 1 Empires Constructed and Contested

1 Adam Smith, *The Wealth of Nations*, Book IV, 1 (London: Dent, 1977), 389; John Darwin, *The Empire Project. The Rise and Fall of the British World-System, 1830–1970* (Cambridge University Press, 2009), 112–43.

2 Jack Gallagher and Ronald Robinson, 'The Imperialism of Free Trade', *Economic History Review*, 6/1 (1953), 1–15; P. J. Cain and A. G. Hopkins, *British Imperialism, 1688–2000* (Harlow: Longman, 2002), 37–67.

3 K. N. Chaudri, 'The East India Company in the 17th and 18th Centuries: A Pre-Modern Multinational Organisation', in Leonard Blussé and Femme Gaastra (eds.), *Companies and Trade. Essay on Overseas Trading Companies in the Ancien Regime* (Leiden University Press, 1981), 31.

4 C. L. R. James, *The Black Jacobins. Toussaint Louverture and the San Domingo Revolution* (London: Secker & Warburg, 1938); Michael Duffy, Soldiers, Sugar and Sea Power. *The British Expeditions to the West Indies and the War against Revolutionary France* (Oxford: Clarendon Press, 1987), 149–217; J. R. McNeill, *Mosquito Empires. Ecology and War in the Greater Caribbean, 1620–1914* (Cambridge University Press, 2010), 242–58. Sudhir Hazareesingh is writing a new biography of Toussaint Louverture.

5  www.theguardian.com/world/2015/mar/04/east-india-company-original-corporate-raiders.

6  Henry Weber, *La Compagnie Française des Indes, 1604–1875* (Paris: Arthur Rousseau, 1904), 346–79; Jean Meyer, Jean Tarrade, Annie Rey-Goldzeigeur and Jacques Thobie (eds.), *Histoire de la France coloniale I. Des origines à 1914* (Paris: Armand Colin, 1991), 140–3; P. J. Marshall, *Bengal. The British Colonial Bridgehead, 1740–1828* (Cambridge University Press, 1987), 49–93.

7  C. A. Bayly, *Indian Society and the Making of the British Empire* (Cambridge University Press, 1988), 79–105.

8  Cain and Hopkins, *British Imperialism*, 343–7.

9  James McDougall, *A History of Algeria* (Cambridge University Press, 2017), 58–72.

10 Saint-Arnaud, letter to his brother, 15 Aug. 1845, in *Lettres II* (Paris: Michel Lévy, 1855), 37; Benjamin Claude Brower, *A Desert Named Peace. The Violence of France's Empire in the Algerian Sahara, 1844–1902* (New York: Columbia University Press, 2009), 35–47.

11 Ferdinand de Lesseps, *Souvenirs de quarante ans* (2 vols., Paris: Nouvelle Revue, 1887), II, 31–2, 223–45, 759–67.

12 André Demaison, *Faidherbe* (Paris: Plon, 1932), 17.

13 Jonathan Spence, *In Search of Modern China* (New York and London: Norton, 1999), 122.

14 Spence, *In Search of Modern China*, 149–66, 180–3.

15 Meyer et al., *Histoire de la France coloniale I*, 487.

16 Patrick Wolfe, 'Settler Colonialism and the Elimination of the Native', *Journal of Genocide Research*, 8/4 (2006), 387–409.

17 Edward Gibbon Wakefield, *Letters from Sydney* [1829] in M. F. Lloyd Pritchard (ed.), *The Collected Works of Edward Gibbon Wakefield* (Glasgow and London: Collins, 1968), 165–6.

18 Marjory Harper and Stephen Constantine, *Migration and Empire* (Oxford University Press, 2010), 41–54.

19 Lyndal Ryan, *The Aboriginal Tasmanians* (St Lucia and London: University of Queensland Press, 1981), 112, 174, 265–76.

20 Jennifer Sessions, *By Sword and Plough. France and the Conquest of Algeria* (Ithaca, NY and London: Cornell University Press, 2011), 278–95.

21 A. Prévost-Paradol, *La France nouvelle* (Paris: Michel Lévy, 1868), 415–19.

22 Leonard Thompson, *A History of South Africa* (New Haven, CT and London: Yale University Press, 1990), 77–93.

23 Olive Patricia Dickason with David T. McNab, *Canada's First Nations. A History of Founding Peoples from the Earliest Times* (Oxford University Press, 2009), 186–200, 229–35; Harper and Constantine, *Migration and Empire*, 11–24.

24 Cain and Hopkins, *British Imperialism*, 229–34; Dickason and McNab, *Canada's First Nations*, 215–20.

25 A. G. Hopkins, 'Rethinking Decolonization', *Past & Present*, 200/1 (2008), 212–18.

26 Ayesha Jalal, *Partisans of Allah. Jihad in South Asia* (Cambridge, MA: Harvard University Press, 2008). 119–33.

27 Bayly, *Indian Society*, 120–7, 183–95; David Gillard, *The Struggle for Asia, 1828–1914* (London: Methuen, 1977), 43–133; Bernard S. Cohn, 'Rethinking Authority in Victorian India', in Eric Hobsbawm and Terence Ranger (eds.), *The Invention of Tradition* (Cambridge University Press, 1983), 165–209.

28 McDougall, *History of Algeria*, 118–25, 95–100; Avner Ofrath, 'Demarcating the cité française: Exclusion and Inclusion in Colonial Algeria under the Third Republic' (Oxford DPhil thesis, 2017), chs. 1 and 2.

29 Jules Ferry, preface to *Le Tonkin et la Mère Patrie* in *Discours et Opinions V. Discours sur la politique extérieure et coloniale* (Paris: Armand Colin, 1897), 555.

30 Félix Ponteil, *La Mediterranée et les puissances depuis l'ouverture jusqu'à la natio-nalisation du Canal de Suez* (Paris: Peyot, 1964), 48–52; Jean Ganiage, 'France, England and the Tunisian Affair' and Agatha Ramm, 'Great Britain and France in Egypt', both in Prosser Gifford and William Roger Louis (eds.), *France and Britain in Africa. Imperial Rivalry and Colonial Rule* (New Haven, CT and London: Yale University Press, 1971), 35–72 and 73–119, respectively; Cain and Hopkins, *British Imperialism*, 313–17.

31 Joseph Galliéni, *Voyage au Soudan Français* (Paris: Hachette, 1885); Marc Michel, *Galliéni* (Paris: Fayard, 1989).

32 Winfried Baumgart, *Imperialism. The Idea and Reality of British and French Colonial Expansion, 1880–1914* (Oxford University Press, 1982), 60–2.

33 Cain and Hopkins, *British Imperialism*, 324–35; Darwin, *The Empire Project*, 227–32.

34 Joseph Galliéni, *Galliéni Pacificateur. Écrits coloniaux de Galliéni*, eds. Hubert Deschamps and Paul Chauvet (Paris: PUF, 1949), 14.

35 Roger Glenn Brown, *Fashoda Reconsidered. The Impact of Domestic Politics on French Policy in Africa, 1893–98* (Baltimore, MD: Johns Hopkins University Press, 1969); Darrell Bates, *The Fashoda Incident of 1898. Encounter on the Nile* (Oxford University Press, 1984).

36 Bernard Taithe, *The Killer Trail. A Colonial Scandal in the Heart of Africa* (Oxford University Press, 2009). I am grateful to Rob Lemkin for this reference.

37 Jules Ferry, speech of 31 Oct. 1883 in *Discours et Opinions V*, 282–3.

38 Dennis Duncanson, *Government and Revolution in Vietnam* (Oxford University Press, 1968); Pierre Brocheux and David Hémery, *Indochina. An Ambiguous Colonization, 1858–1954* (Berkeley, CA: University of California Press, 2009), 75–82; Spence, *In Search of Modern China*, 220.

39 Chushichi Tsuzuki, *The Pursuit of Power in Modern Japan, 1825–1995* (Oxford University Press, 2000), 100–31.

40 Cain and Hopkins, *British Imperialism*, 369–71.

41 Spence, *In Search of Modern China*, 221–2, 229–33.

42 Cain and Hopkins, *British Imperialism*, 319–20; Darwin, *The Empire Project*, 225.

43 J. P. Fitzpatrick, *The Transvaal from Within* (London: Heinemann, 1899); Darwin, *The Empire Project*, 232.

44 Marilyn Lake and Henry Reynolds, *Drawing the Global Colour Line* (Cambridge University Press, 2008), 213; Darwin, *The Empire Project*, 239–53.

45 Lake and Reynolds, *Drawing the Global Colour Line*, 222–6.

46 Darwin, *The Empire Project*, 145–8, 155–6, 243–4.

47 J. R. Seeley, *The Expansion of England. Two Courses of Lectures* (London: Macmillan, 1885), 45, 47, 185, 191.

48 Lake and Reynolds, *Drawing the Colour Line*, 144.

49 Lake and Reynolds, *Drawing the Colour Line*, 9.

50 Lake and Reynolds, *Drawing the Colour Line*, 116–21.

51 Quoted by Imanuel Geiss, *The Pan-African Movement* (London: Methuen, 1974), 182–92.

52 W. E. B. Du Bois, 'The Souls of the White Folk' [1910] in *Dark Water. Voices from within the Veil* (London and New York: Verso, 2016), 18, 24; Lake and Reynolds, *Drawing the Colour Line*, 2.

53 Jules Ferry, speech of 30 June 1881 in *Discours et Opinions V*, 20.

54 Jules Ferry, speech of 28 July 1885 in *Discours et Opinions V*, 210–11.

55 David Prochaska, *Making Algeria French. Colonialism in Bône, 1870–1920* (Cambridge University Press, 1990), 87, 146–53.

56 Sylvie Thénault, 'Les Débuts de l'Algérie algérienne' and 'Le code de l'Indigénat', both in Abderrahamane Bouchène, Jean-Pierre Peyroulou, Ounassa Tengour and Sylvie Thénault, *Histoire de l'Algérie à la période coloniale* (Paris: La Découverte, 2012), 159–84 and 200–6; McDougall, *History of Algeria*, 123–8.

57 Prochaska, *Making Algeria French*, 183–203; McDougall, *History of Algeria*, 105–6; Ofrath, 'Demarcating the *cité française*', ch. 4.

58 Alice Conklin, *A Mission to Civilize. The Republican Idea of Empire in France and West Africa, 1895–1930* (Stanford University Press, 1997), 77–91.

59 Conklin, *A Mission to Civilize*, 51–119.

60 Pierre Lyautey, *L'Empire colonial français* (Paris: Les Éditions de la France, 1931), 143–52; William A. Hoisington, *Lyautey and the Conquest of Morocco* (Basingstoke: Macmillan, 1995), 37–48.

61 Darwin, *The Empire Project*, 185–201.

62 Curzon, speech to the Royal Societies Club, London, 7 Nov. 1898, in George Nathaniel Curzon, *Lord Curzon in India. Being a Selection of his Speeches as Viceroy and Governor-General of India, 1898–1905*, ed. Thomas Raleigh (London: Macmillan, 1906), 8.

63 Darwin, *The Empire Project*, 205–9.

# 2 Empires in Crisis: Two World Wars

1 Virginia Woolf, 'Thunder at Wembley' [June 1925], in *The Captain's Death Bed and Other Essays* (London: Hogarth Press, 1950), 203–6; Hermione Lee, *Virginia Woolf* (London: Chatto & Windus, 1996), 461–2.

2 John Mackenzie, *Propaganda and Politics. The Manipulation of British Public Opinion, 1880–1960* (Manchester University Press, 1984), 107–12; Andrew Thompson, *The Empire Strikes Back? The Impact of Imperialism on Britain from the Mid-Nineteenth Century* (Harlow: Pearson Longman, 2005), 86–7; Daniel Stephen, *The Empire of Progress. West Africans, Indians and Britons at the British Empire Exhibition, 1924–25* (New York: Palgrave Macmillan, 2013), 14, 23, 86–8, 123.

3 Charles-Robert Ageron, 'L'Exposition Coloniale de 1931: Mythe républicain ou mythe impérial?', in Pierre Nora (ed.), *Les Lieux de Mémoire I. La République* (Paris: Gallimard, 1984), 561–91; Jacques Thobie, Jean Meyer, Jean Tarrade and Anne Rey-Goldzeiger, *Histoire de la France coloniale II. 1914–1990* (Paris: Armand Colin, 1990); Martin Thomas, *The French Empire between the Wars. Imperialism, Politics and Society* (Manchester University Press, 2005), 91, 200–2, 228–30.

4 Joan Beaumont, *Broken Nation. Australians in the Great War* (Sydney: Allen & Unwin, 2013), 17.

5 John Darwin, *The Empire Project. The Rise and Fall of the British World-System, 1830–1970* (Cambridge University Press, 2009), 333–46.

6 *The Worker*, 5 Oct. 1916, cited in Beaumont, *Broken Nation*, 229.

7 David Olusoga, *The World's War. Forgotten Soldiers of Empire* (London: Head of Zeus, 2014), 158.

8 Abderrahamane Bouchène, Jean-Pierre Peyroulou, Ounassa Tengour and Sylvie Thénault, *Histoire de l'Algérie à la période coloniale* (Paris: La Découverte, 2012), 230–58; Thobie, *Histoire de la France coloniale II*, 76–100; Alice Conklin, *A Mission to Civilize. The Republican Idea of Empire in France and West Africa, 1895–1930* (Stanford University Press, 1997), 143–67; Olusoga, *The World's War*, 158–64, 190–7.

9  Olusoga, *The World's War*, 217–31.

10  Pierre-Jean Luizard, *La Formation de l'Iraq contemporain* (Paris: CNRS, 1991), 325–7.

11  Leonard Stein, *The Balfour Declaration* (London: Valentine Mitchell, 1961), frontispiece and 664.

12  Jonathan Spence, *In Search of Modern China* (New York and London: Norton, 1999), 258–77.

13  Chushichi Tsuzuki, *The Pursuit of Power in Modern Japan, 1825–1995* (Oxford University Press, 2000), 185–91.

14  Erez Manela, *Wilsonian Moment. Self-Determination and the International Origins of Anticolonial Nationalism* (Oxford University Press, 2007), 35–8.

15  James McDougall, *A History of Algeria* (Cambridge University Press, 2017), 152; Manela, *Wilsonian Moment*, 5, 67–75, 163–6; Margaret Macmillan, *Peacemakers. The Paris Peace Conference of 1919 and its Attempt to End the War* (London: John Murray, 2001), 398; Pierre Brocheux, *Ho Chi Minh. A Biography* (Cambridge University Press, 2007), 10.

16  McDougall, *History of Algeria*, 152.

17  Manela, *Wilsonian Moment*.

18  Judith Brown, *Modern India. The Origins of an Asian Democracy* (Oxford University Press, 1985), 198–202, 211–14.

19  Brocheux, *Ho Chi Minh*, 17–27.

20  Macmillan, *Peacemakers*, 325–30; Manela, *Wilsonian Moment*, 113–15.

21  Marilyn Lake and Henry Reynolds, *Drawing the Global Colour Line* (Cambridge University Press, 2008), 305.

22  Spence, *In Search of Modern China*, 299–308, 317–18; Rana Mitter, *A Bitter Revolution. China's Struggle with the Modern World* (Oxford University Press, 2004), 15–40, 71–129.

23  Joe English, 'Empire Day in Britain, 1904–1958', *Historical Journal*, 49/1 (2006), 247–76.

24  Marjory Harper and Stephen Constantine, *Migration and Empire* (Oxford University Press, 2010), 18, 58.

25  P. J. Cain and A. G. Hopkins, *British Imperialism, 1688–2000* (Harlow: Longman, 2002), 579–82; Harper and Constantine, *Migration and Empire*, 17–30, 58–9; Dane Kennedy, *Islands of White. Settler Society and Culture in Kenya and Southern Rhodesia, 1890–1939* (Durham, NC: Duke University Press, 1987), 22–3, 44–72; C. J. D. Duder, 'The Settler Response to the Indian Crisis of 1923 in Kenya: Brigadier-General Philip Wheatley and "Direct Action"', *Journal of Imperial and Commonwealth History*, 17/3 (1988–9), 349–73.

26  J. C. Smuts, *Africa and Some World Problems* (Oxford: Clarendon Press, 1930), 77–98; Darwin, *The Empire Project*, 457–60.

27  Merlin to Sarraut, 26 Mar. 1921, cited in Conklin, *A Mission to Civilize*, 189.

28  Albert Sarraut, *La Mise en Valeur des Colonies Françaises* (Paris: Payot, 1923), 101–4.

29  William A. Hoisington, *Lyautey and the Conquest of Morocco* (Basingstoke: Macmillan, 1995), 185–204.

30  McDougall, *History of Algeria*, 154–74; Avner Ofrath, 'Demarcating the *cité française*', ch. 6.

31  Susan Pedersen, *The Guardians. The League of Nations and the Crisis of Empire* (Oxford University Press, 2015).

32  Michael Provence, *The Great Syrian Revolt and the Rise of Arab Nationalism* (Austin, TX: University of Texas Press, 2005), 109–29.

33  Luizard, *La Formation de l'Iraq*, 390–414; Peter Sluglett, *Britain in Iraq. Contriving King and Country* (London and New York: I. B. Tauris, 2017), 34–47.

34  Darwin, *The Empire Project*, 379–82; Michael J. Cohen, *Palestine: Retreat from the Mandate. The Making of British Policy, 1936–1945* (London: Paul Elek, 1978), 10.

35  Ayesha Jalal, *Partisans of Allah. Jihad in South Asia* (Cambridge, MA: Harvard University Press, 2008), 242–65.

36  Brown, *Modern India*, 266–306.

37  Spence, *In Search of Modern China*, 314–59.

38  Pierre Brocheux and David Hémery, *Indochina. An Ambiguous Colonization, 1858–1954* (Berkeley, CA: University of California Press, 2009), 308–19; Brocheux, *Ho Chi Minh*, 36–57.

39  Rana Mitter, *China's War with Japan, 1937–1945. The Struggle for Survival* (London: Allen Lane, 2013), 49–135; Susan Pedersen, 'Empires, States and the League of Nations', in Glenda Sluga and Patricia Clavin (eds.), *Internationalisms. A Twentieth-Century History* (Cambridge University Press, 2017), 131–2.

40  Dominique Leca, *La Rupture de 1940* (Paris: Fayard, 1978), 235.

41  www.winstonchurchill.org/resources/speeches/1940-the-finest-hour/their-finest-hour/.

42  Myron Echenberg, *Colonial Conscripts. The Tirailleurs sénégalais in French West Africa, 1857–1962* (Portsmouth, NH and London: Heinemann, 1991), 88; Raoul Salan, *Mémoires. Fin d'un empire I: Le sens d'un engagement* (Paris: Presses de la Cité, 1970), 11, 32, 76.

43  Anthony Clayton, *France, Soldiers and Africa* (London: Brassey's Defence Publishers, 1988), 255–6.

44  Charles de Gaulle, *Lettres, Notes et Carnets. Juin 1940–Juillet 1941* (Paris: Plon, 1981), 15.

45  Eric Jennings, *La France Libre fut africaine* (Paris: Perrin, 2014), 25.

46  De Gaulle, *Lettres, Notes et Carnets*, de Gaulle to his wife, 28 Sept. 1940, 127.

47  Sébastien Verney, *L'Indochine sous Vichy. Entre révolution nationale, collaboration et identités nationales, 1940–1945* (Paris: Riveneuve, 2012), 191–3.

48  Marc Ferro, *Pétain* (Paris: Fayard, 1987), 312.

49  James Barr, *A Line in the Sand. Britain, France and the Struggle that Shaped the Middle East* (London: Simon & Schuster, 2011), 207–17.

50  Jean-Louis Crémieux-Brilhac, *La France libre. De l'appel du 18 juin à la Libération* (Paris: Gallimard, 1996), 156–61.

51  Gamal Abdel Nasser, *Philosophy of Revolution* (Buffalo, NY: Economica Books, 1959), 30.

52  Cited by Darwin, *The Empire Project*, 503.

53  William Langer and S. Everet Gleason, *The Undeclared War, 1940–1941* (New York: Harper & Brothers, 1953), 687–8.

54  Cited by Christopher Bayly and Tim Harper, *Forgotten Armies. Britain's Asian Empire and the War with Japan* (London: Penguin, 2005), 142.

55  Winston Churchill, *The Second World War IV. The Hinge of Fate* (London: Cassell, 1951), 81.

56  J. C. Smuts, *Thoughts on the New World* (London: Empire Parliamentary Association, 1943), 6–17.

57  Amartya Sen, *Poverty and Famines. An Essay on Entitlement and Deprivation* (Oxford: Clarendon Press, 1981), 212, 215; Paul R. Greenough, *Prosperity and Misery in Modern Bengal. The Famine of 1943–1944* (Oxford University Press, 1982), 237; Sri Manjari, *Through War and Famine. Bengal 1939–45* (New Delhi: Orient Black Swan, 2009), 95–102, 161–8.

58  Fred Saito and Tatsuo Hayashida, 'To Delhi! To Delhi! 1943–1945', in Sisir K. Bose (ed.), *A Beacon across Asia. A Biography of Subhas Chandra Bose* (New Delhi: Orient Longman, 1973), 148–9.

59  Cited by Bayly and Harper, *Forgotten Armies*, 146.

60  Peter Clarke, *The Cripps Version. The Life of Sir Stafford Cripps, 1889–1952* (London: Allen Lane, 2002), 305.

61  Martin Thomas, 'Imperial Backwater or Strategic Outpost? The British Takeover of Vichy Madagascar, 1942', *Historical Journal*, 39/4 (1996), 1049–74; Eric Jennings, 'Angleterre, que veux-tu à Madagascar, terre française? La propaganda vichyste, l'opinion publique et l'affaire anglaise sur Madagascar 1942', *Guerres mondiales et conflits contemporains*, 246 (2012), 23–39.

62  Cited by Siân Nicholas, '"Brushing up your Empire": Dominion and Colonial Propaganda on the BBC's Home Services, 1939–45', *Journal of Imperial and Commonwealth History*, 31/2 (2003), 215.

63  Cited by William Roger Louis, *Imperialism at Bay, 1941–1945. The United States and the Decolonization of the British Empire* (Oxford: Clarendon Press, 1979), 158.

64  *Life*, 12 Oct. 1942, 34, partially cited by Louis, *Imperialism at Bay*, 198.

65  Cited by Louis, *Imperialism at Bay*, 200.

66  Cited by Louis, *Imperialism at Bay*, 164.

67  Archives Nationales, Paris, 72AJ 220/1, testimony of Pierre Billotte, 4 and 11 July 1950.

68  *Tribune*, 13 Nov. 1942; Michael Foot, *Aneurin Bevan. A Biography I. 1887–1945* (London: MacGibbon & Lee, 1962), 404.

69  British National Archives, REM 3/442/9, Roosevelt to Churchill, 17 Nov. 1942.

70  Robert D. Murphy, *Diplomat among Warriors* (New York: Doubleday, 1964), 215–16.

71  Scott L. Bills, *Empire and Cold War. The Roots of US–Third World Antagonism, 1945–47* (London: Macmillan, 1990), 31.

72  Ferhat Abbas, *Guerre et Révolution d'Algérie* (Paris: Julliard, 1962), 114, 135–9.

73  Echenberg, *Colonial Conscripts*, 88; Julie Le Gac, *Vaincre sans gloire. Le corps expéditionnaire français en Italie, novembre 1942–juillet 1944* (Paris: Les Belles Lettres, 2013), 56.

74  Robert Merle, *Ahmed Ben Bella* (Paris: Gallimard, 1965), 24–59.

75  Jacques Frémeaux, 'Les Contingents impériaux au cours de la guerre', *Histoire, économie et société*, 23/2 (2004), 220.

76  Barnaby Phillips, *Another Man's War. The Story of a Burma Boy in Britain's Forgotten African Army* (London: One World, 2014), 17–41; Rita Headrick, 'African Soldiers in World War II', *Armed Forces and Society*, 4/3 (1978), 508.

77  Timothy Parsons, *The African Rank-and-File. Social Implications of Colonial Military Service in the King's African Rifles, 1902–1964* (Portsmouth, NH: Heinemann, 1999), 203–6.

78  Ashley Jackson, *Distant Drums. The Role of Colonies in British Imperial Warfare* (Brighton: Sussex Academic Press, 2010), 203–18.

79  La Conférence Africaine Française, Brazzaville (30 janvier–8 février 1944) (Algiers, 1944), 27, 35. See also Paul Isoart, 'Les Aspects politiques, constitutionnels et administratifs des recommendations', in Institut Charles de Gaulle/IHTP, *Brazzaville, janvier–février 1944. Aux sources de la decolonisation* (Paris: Plon, 1988), 81.

80  Crémieux-Brilhac, *La France libre*, 836; Robert Gildea, 'Myth, Memory and Policy in France since 1945', in Jan-Werner Müller, *Memory and Power in Postwar Europe* (Cambridge University Press, 2002), 61.

81 Churchill to General Ismay, 6 July 1944, cited by Andrew Buchanan, *American Grand Strategy in the Mediterranean during World War II* (Cambridge University Press, 2014), 188.

82 Jennings, *La France Libre*, 155.

83 Claire Miot, 'Le retrait des tirailleurs sénégalais de la Première Armée française en 1944', *Vingtième Siècle*, 125 (2015); Echenberg, *Colonial Conscripts*, 101–3; Julien Fargettas, 'Le révolte des tirailleurs sénégalais de Tiaroye', *Vingtième Siècle*, 92 (2006), 17–30.

84 Léopold Sédar Senghor, 'Tiaroye', in *Oeuvre poétique* (Paris: Points, 2006), 91.

85 W. E. B. Du Bois, *Color and Democracy. Colonies and Peace* (New York: Harcourt, Brace & Co, 1945), 4.

86 Glenda Sluga, *Internationalism in the Age of Nationalism* (Philadelphia, PA: University of Pennsylvania Press, 2001), 89.

87 Sluga, *Internationalism*, 91.

88 Quoted by Charles-Robert Ageron, 'La survivance d'un mythe: La puissance par l'Empire colonial, 1944–1947', in René Girault and Robert Frank (eds.), *La Puissance française en question, 1945–1949* (Paris: Publications de la Sorbonne, 1988), 32.

89 McDougall, *History of Algeria*, 180.

90 L'Humanité, 11 May 1945, cited in Grégoire Madjarian, *La Question coloniale et la politique du Parti Communiste Français, 1944–1947* (Paris: Maspéro, 1977), 103.

91 Bills, *Empire and Cold War*, 38. Letter forwarded by US Consulate in Algiers, 3 July 1945.

92 *Journal officiel de la République Française. Débats de l'Assemblée Consultative provisoire. Séance du mardi 19 juin 1945* (Paris, 1945), 1114, 1138, 1143.

93 Charles de Gaulle, *Mémoires de Guerre III. Le Salut, 1944–1946* (Paris: Plon, 1959), 189, 196–7; Barr, *A Line in the Sand*, 305–6.

94 Alan Bullock, *Ernest Bevin. A Biography* (London: Politico's, 2002), 432.

95 Shabtai Teveth, *Ben Gurion. The Burning Ground, 1886–1948* (London: Robert Hale, 1987), 872.

96 William Roger Louis and Robert Wilson Stookey (eds.), *The End of the Palestine Mandate* (New York and London: I. B. Tauris, 1986), 83.

97 Ho Chi Minh, *Selected Works, vol. 3* (Hanoi: Foreign Languages Publishing House, 1960–2), 17–21.

98 Archimedes Patti, *Why Vietnam? Prelude to the American Albatross* (Berkeley, CA: University of California Press, 1980), 307–17.

# 3 The Imperialism of Decolonisation

1 Quoted in Donald Moggridge, *Maynard Keynes. An Economist's Biography* (London and New York: Routledge, 1992), 774; M. W. Kirby, *The Decline of British Economic Power since 1870* (London: George Allen & Unwin, 1981), 93.

2 *New York Times Magazine*, 3 Mar. 1946, in S. Gopal and U. Iyengar (eds.), *The Essential Writings of Jawaharlal Nehru II* (Oxford University Press, 2003), 222–4.

3 George Padmore, *Gold Coast Revolution* (London: Dobson, 1953), 62; Kwame Nkrumah, *Autobiography* (Edinburgh: Nelson, 1959), 20–8, 40–5.

4 https://lematin.ma/journal/2003/56e-anniversaire-du-voyage-historique-de-S-M–Mohammed-V-a-Tanger–un-tournant-majeur-dans-l-et-8217Histoire-du-Maroc/27817.html.

5 D. A Low and John Lonsdale, 'East Africa: Towards the New Order, 1945–1963', in D. A. Low (ed.), *Eclipse of Empire* (Cambridge University Press, 1991), 198; William

Roger Louis and Ronald Robinson, 'The Imperialism of Decolonization', *Journal of Imperial and Commonwealth History*, 22/3 (1994), 462–511; John Darwin, 'Was There a Fourth British Empire?' in Martyn Lynn (ed.), *Empire in the 1950s. Rethink or Renewal?* (Basingstoke: Macmillan, 2006), 16–31; A. G. Hopkins, 'Rethinking Decolonization', *Past & Present*, 200/1 (2008), 211–47.

6 Randall Hansen, 'The Politics of Citizenship in 1940s Britain: The British Nationality Act', *Twentieth Century British History*, 10/1 (1999), 67–95.

7 Darwin, 'Was There a Fourth British Empire?', 26.

8 Reg Appleyeard, *The Ten Pound Immigrants* (London: Boxtree, 1988), 27–31, 160; A. James Hammerton and Alistair Thomson, *Ten Pound Poms. Australia's Invisible Migrants* (Manchester University Press, 2005).

9 Hopkins, 'Rethinking Decolonization', 224–5.

10 Quoted in Stuart Ward, *Australia and the British Embrace. The Demise of the Imperial Ideal* (Melbourne University Press, 2001), 20–7.

11 R. J. Moore, *Escape from Empire. The Attlee Government and the Indian Problem* (Oxford: Clarendon Press, 1983), 86–9.

12 Joya Chatterji, *Bengal Divided. Hindu Communalism and Partition, 1933–1947* (Cambridge University Press, 1994), 227–65.

13 John Darwin, 'Memory of Empire in Britain', in Dieter Rothermund (ed.), *Memories of Post-Imperial Nations. The Aftermath of Decolonisation, 1945–2013* (Cambridge University Press, 2015), 23–4.

14 Camilla Schofield, *Enoch Powell and the Making of Postcolonial Britain* (Cambridge University Press, 2013), 70.

15 Ian Talbot and Gurharpal Singh, *The Partition of India* (Cambridge University Press, 2009), 62–96.

16 Joya Chatterji, *The Spoils of Partition. Bengal and India, 1947–1967* (Cambridge University Press, 2007), 111–67.

17 Louis Mountbatten, *Reflections on the Transfer of Power and Jawaharlal Nehru* (Cambridge University Press, 1968), 20.

18 John Gallagher, *The Decline, Revival and Fall of the British Empire* (Cambridge University Press, 1982), 144–6.

19 William Roger Louis, 'British Imperialism and the End of the Palestine Mandate', in William Roger Louis and Robert Stokely (eds.), *The End of the Palestine Mandate* (London and New York: I. B. Tauris, 1986), 16.

20 Michael J. Cohen, 'The Zionist Perspective', in Louis and Stokely (eds.), *The End of the Palestine Mandate*, 85–7.

21 Ritchie Ovendale, *Britain, the United States and the End of the Palestine Mandate, 1942–1948* (London: Royal Historical Society, 1989), 184.

22 Ilan Pappé, *The Making of the Arab–Israeli Conflict, 1947–51* (London and New York: I. B. Tauris, 1992), 32–60, 154; Benny Morris, 'Revisiting the Palestinian Exodus of 1948', in Eugene Rogan and Avi Shlaim (eds.), *The War for Palestine* (Cambridge University Press, 2007), 37–56; Derek Gregory, *The Colonial Present* (Oxford: Blackwell, 2004), 84–8.

23 I am grateful to Dr Karma Nabulsi for these insights.

24 Nkrumah, *Autobiography*, 106–7.

25 Richard Wright, *Black Power* (New York: Harper, 1954), 53, 65.

26 Fenner Brockway, *Why Mau Mau? An Analysis and a Remedy* (London: Congress of Peoples Against Imperialism, 1953), 2–15.

27 Don McCullin, *Unreasonable Behaviour* (London: Vintage, 1992), 35.

28 Caroline Elkins, *Britain's Gulag. The Brutal End of Empire in Kenya* (London: Pimlico, 2005).

29  *Peace News*, 977, 8 Mar. 1955. The letter appeared originally in the *Tribune*, 4 Mar. 1955.

30  See his autobiography: Fenner Brockway, *Towards Tomorrow* (London: Hart-Davis, 1977); Stephen Hale, *Anticolonialism in British Politics. The Left and the End of Empire, 1918–1964* (Oxford: Clarendon Press, 1993), 169–203.

31  Hale, *Anticolonialism*, 233–4.

32  Barbara Castle, *Fighting all the Way* (London: Macmillan, 1993), 264–88.

33  Saul Dubow, *Apartheid, 1948–1994* (Oxford University Press, 2014), 34–62.

34  Dubow, *Apartheid*, 42–4.

35  Dubow, *Apartheid*, 68–73.

36  Dubow, *Apartheid*, 51.

37  Dennis Austin, *Britain and South Africa* (Oxford University Press, 1966), 126–7.

38  De Gaulle, speech at Constantine, 27 Aug. 1946, in *Discours et messages II 1946–1958* (Paris: Plon, 1970), 18–19.

39  *Journal Officiel de la République Française. Débats de l'Assemblée Nationale Constituante*, 11 Apr. 1946, 1718.

40  *Débats de l'Assemblée Nationale Constituante*, 11 Apr. 1946, 1713–15.

41  *Débats de l'Assemblée Nationale Constituante*, 27 Aug. 1946, 3333–7.

42  Grégoire Madjarian, *La Question coloniale et la politique du Parti Communiste Français, 1944–1947* (Paris: Maspéro, 1977), 193.

43  Institut d'Études Politiques (IEP), Paris, Centre d'Histoire, 'Témoignages sur la Guerre d'Algérie'. Interview with Claude Bourdet, conducted by Odile Rudelle, 5 Apr. 1979.

44  Jean de Lattre de Tassigny, *Ne pas subir. Écrits, 1914–1952* (Paris: Plon, 1984), 482.

45  Jacques Tronchon, *L'Insurrection malgache de 1947* (Paris: Maspéro, 1974), 28.

46  Tronchon, *L'Insurrection malgache*, 120–5.

47  I am grateful to Professor Guillaume Piketty for this information.

48  Martin Thomas, *Fight or Flight. Britain, France, and their Roads from Empire* (Oxford University Press, 2014), 193–200.

49  Tronchon, *L'Insurrection malgache*, 70–3; Jean Fremigacci, 'La vérité sur la grande révolte de Madagascar', *Histoire*, 318 (2007), 37–43.

50  James McDougall, *A History of Algeria* (Cambridge University Press, 2017), 185–8.

51  IEP, Centre d'Histoire, Témoignages sur la Guerre d'Algérie'. Interview with Claude Bourdet, 5 Apr. 1979, 12; McDougall, *History of Algeria*.

52  Alphonse Juin, *Le Maghreb en feu* (Paris: Plon, 1957), 65–86; Alphonse Juin, *Mémoires II* (Paris: Fayard, 1960), 135–209.

53  Juin, *Le Maghreb*, 22–86; Juin, *Mémoires II*, 146–54.

54  Charles-André Julien, *Et la Tunisie devint indépendant, 1951–1957* (Paris: Éditions Jeune Afrique, 1985), 24.

55  Julien, *Et la Tunisie devint indépendant*, 35; Fenner Brockway, *African Journeys* (London: Victor Gollancz, 1955), 198.

56  Vo Nguyen Giap, *Dien Bien Phu* (Hanoi: Foreign Language Publishing House, 1964), 166–7.

57  Marcel Bigeard, *Pour une Parcelle de gloire* (Paris: Plon, 1975), 188, 197.

58  *Le Procès Raoul Salan. Compte-rendu sténographique* (Paris: Albin Michel, 1962), 76.

59  Pierre Mendès-France, speech of 17 June 1954 in *Oeuvres complètes III. Gouverner c'est choisir* (Paris: Gallimard, 1986), 57.

60  Mendès-France, speech of 22–23 July 1954 in *Oeuvres complètes III*, 153–5.

61  Mendès France, speech of 12 Nov. 1954 in *Oeuvres complètes III*, 455.

62  Quoted by Felix Kloss, *Churchill's Last Stand. The Struggle to Unite Europe* (London and New York: I. B. Tauris, 2018), 128.

63  Cited by Geoffrey Warner, 'The Labour Government and the Unity of Western Europe', in Ritchie Ovendale (ed.), *The Foreign Policy of the British Labour Government, 1945–1951* (Leicester University Press, 1984), 71; Anne Deighton, 'Entente Néo-Coloniale? Ernest Bevin and the Proposal for an Anglo-French Third World Power, 1945–1949', *Diplomacy and Statecraft*, 17/4 (2006), 835–52.

64  Maurice Vaïsse, 'Le général de Gaulle et la défense de l'Europe, 1947–1958', *Matériaux pour l'histoire de notre temps*, 29 (1992), 5–8; Charles de Gaulle, *Mémoires de Guerre I. L'Appel* (Paris: Plon, 1954), 1.

65  Robert Gildea, *France since 1945* (Oxford University Press, 2002), 18; John W. Young, *Cold War Europe, 1945–1991. A Political History* (London and New York: Arnold, 1996), 43–52.

66  Benjamin Grob-Fitzgibbon, *Continental Drift. Britain and Europe from the End of Empire to the Rise of Euroscepticism* (Cambridge University Press, 2016), 204–22.

67  Abel Thomas, *Comment Israël fut sauvé. Les secrets de l'expédition de Suez* (Paris: Albin Michel, 1978), 166–76, 186–228; Keith Kyle, *Suez. Britain's End of Empire in the Middle East* (London and New York: I. B. Tauris, 2003), 315–29; Avi Shlaim, 'The Protocol of Sèvres: Anatomy of a War Plot', *International Affairs*, 73/3 (1997), 509–30.

68  Gamal Abdel Nasser, *Philosophy of Revolution* (Buffalo, NY: Economica Books, 1959), 59–78.

69  Richard Wright, *The Color Curtain. A Report on the Bandung Conference* (London: Dobson, 1956), 120.

70  Joseph Ortiz, *Mes Combats. Carnets de Route, 1954–1962* (Paris: Éditions de la Presse, 1964), 20.

71  Miles Kahler, *Decolonization in Britain and France. The Domestic Consequences of International Relations* (Princeton University Press, 1984), 197–9.

72  Patrick Rotman and Bertrand Tavernier, *La Guerre sans nom. Les appelés d'Algérie, 1954–1962* (Paris: Seuil, 1992), 24, 44–5.

73  Maurice Vaïsse, 'France and the Suez Crisis', in William Roger Louis and Roger Owen (eds.), *Suez 1956. The Crisis and its Consequences* (Oxford: Clarendon Press, 1989), 137; Thomas, *Comment Israël fut sauvé*, 78.

74  Thomas, *Fight or Flight*, 270–1.

75  Kyle, *Suez*, 161; Vaïsse, 'France and the Suez Crisis', 137.

76  Marc Ferro, *Suez. Naissance d'un tiers-monde* (Brussels: Complexe, 1982), 55–7.

77  Sue Onslow, *Backbench Debate within the Conservative Party and its Influence on British Foreign Policy, 1948–1957* (Basingstoke: Macmillan, 1997), 110–21; Kahler, *Decolonization*, 137–40.

78  Tony Shaw, *Eden, Suez and the Mass Media. Propaganda and Persuasion during the Suez Crisis* (London and New York: I. B. Tauris, 1996), 57.

79  Thomas, *Comment Israël fut sauvé*, 87.

80  Kyle, *Suez*, 405.

81  *Hansard. Parliamentary Debates. Commons*, 31 Oct. 1956, 1454.

82  *Hansard. Parliamentary Debates. Commons*, 1 Nov. 1956, 1699–1700, 1715; Tony Benn, *Years of Hope. Diaries, Letters and Papers, 1940–1962* (London: Hutchinson, 1994), 198.

83  *Hansard. Parliamentary Debates. Commons*, 3 Nov. 1956, 1858, 1908.

84  Kyle, *Suez*, 439–41.

85  Kyle, *Suez*, 456–7.

86  William Roger Louis, 'Public Enemy Number One: The British Empire in the Dock, 1957–71', in Lynn (ed.), *The British Empire in the 1950s*, 191.

87 *Journal Officiel de la République Française. Débats parlementaires. Assemblée nationale*, 19 Dec. 1956, 6165. Speech of Florimond Bonte.

88 *Assemblée nationale*, 20 Dec. 1956, 6175.

89 Thomas, *Fight or Flight*, 184.

90 Mark Mazower, *Governing the World. The History of an Idea* (London: Allen Lane, 2012), 263.

91 Denis Healey, *The Time of My Life* (London: Michael Joseph, 1989), 172.

92 Robert Marjolin, *Architect of European Unity. Memoirs, 1911–1986* (London: Weidenfeld & Nicolson, 1989), 297; David Hannay, *Britain's Quest for a Role. A Diplomatic Memoir from Europe to the UN* (London and New York: I. B. Tauris, 2013), 278–9.

93 Raoul Salan, *Mémoires. Fin d'un empire III: Algérie française* (Paris: Presses de la Cité, 1972), 148.

94 Jacques Massu, *La Vraie bataille d'Alger* (Paris: Plon, 1971), 111–12.

95 Bigeard, *Pour une Parcelle de gloire*, 229–30.

96 Interview with Jean-Marie Burguière, conducted by Robert Gildea, Larzac, 21 May 2008.

97 Jacques Pâris de la Bollardière, *Bataille d'Alger, bataille de l'homme* (Paris and Bruges: Desclée De Brouwer, 1972), 84, 98; Massu, *La Vraie bataille d'Alger*, 225–7.

98 Germaine Tillion, *Les Ennemis complémentaires* (Paris: Éditions de Minuit, 1960), 151–2; Pierre Vidal-Naquet, 'La Justice et la patrie: Une Française au secours de l'Algérie', *Esprit*, 261 (2000), 144–6.

99 Pierre-Henri Simon, *Contre la torture* (Paris: Seuil, 1957), 83–4, 88.

100 Laurent Schwartz, *A Mathematician Grappling with his century* (Berlin: Birkhausen Verlag, 2001), 328–41; Pierre Vidal-Naquet, *L'Affaire Audin* (Paris: Éditions de Minuit, 1958); Pierre Vidal-Naquet, *Mémoires. Le Trouble et la Lumière, 1955–1998* (Paris: Seuil/La Découverte, 1998), 60–3.

101 Salan, *Mémoires. Fin d'un empire III*, 285.

102 Raymond Dronne, *La Révolution d'Alger* (Paris: Éditions de l'Empire, 1958), 21.

103 Frantz Fanon, *L'an V de la revolution algérienne* (Paris: Maspéro, 1959), ch. 1, 'L'Algérie se dévoile', 15–16, 21–2, my translation; Frantz Fanon, *Studies in a Dying Colonialism* (New York: Monthly Review Press, 1965), 'Algeria Unveiled', 35–67.

104 *Hansard. Parliamentary Debates. Commons*, 16 June 1959.

105 *Hansard. Parliamentary Debates. Commons*, 27 July 1959, 221. See also Castle, *Fighting all the Way*, 288.

106 Malcolm Muggeridge, 'Appointment with Sir Roy Welensky', Granada Television, 1 Apr. 1961 (London: Voice and Vision, 1961), 6–7.

107 Harold Macmillan, *Riding the Storm, 1956–1959* (London: Macmillan, 1971), 733–5.

108 Ian Cobain, *The History Thieves. Secrets, Lies and the Shaping of a Modern Nation* (London: Portobello Books, 2016), 104–13, 122–32.

# 4 Neo-Colonialism, New Global Empire

1 Irwin M. Wall, *France, the United States and the Algerian War* (Berkeley, CA: University of California Press, 2001), 100, 120–30.

2 Saul Dubow, 'Macmillan, Verwoerd and the 1960 "Wind of Change" Speech', in L. J. Butler and Sarah Stockwell (eds.), *The Wind of Change. Harold Macmillan and British Decolonization* (Basingstoke: Palgrave Macmillan, 2013), 20–47.

3 Mark Mazower, *Governing the World. The History of an Idea* (London: Allen Lane, 2012), 258–63; Glenda Sluga, *Internationalism in the Age of Nationalism* (Philadelphia, PA: University of Pennsylvania Press, 2013), 116–23.

4 Kwame Nkrumah, *Neo-Colonialism. The Last Stage of Imperialism* (London: Nelson, 1965).

5 Julian Jackson, *A Certain Idea of France. The Life of Charles de Gaulle* (London: Allen Lane, 2018), ch. 19.

6 James McDougall, *A History of Algeria*, 217–27.

7 Wall, *France, the United States and the Algerian War*, 100, 120–30.

8 Jean-Marie Le Pen, *Les Français d'abord* (Paris: Éditions Carrère-Michel Lafon, 1984), 50.

9 Pierre Lagaillarde, 'On a triché avec l'honneur': *Texte intégral de l'interrogatoire et de la plaidoirie des audiences des 15 et 16 novembre 1960 du procès des 'Barricades'* (Paris: La Table Ronde, 1961).

10 Rémi Kauffer, *OAS. Histoire de la guerre franco-française* (Paris: Seuil, 2002).

11 Francine Dessaigne, *Journal d'une mère de famille pied-noir* (Paris: L'esprit nouveau, 1972), 85, 91. Entries for 22, 25, 28 Sept. and 2 Oct. 1962.

12 Jean Monneret, *Une Ténébreuse Affaire. La fusillade du 26 mars 1962 à Alger* (Paris: l'Harmattan, 2009).

13 Dessaigne, *Journal*, 184. Entry for 19 Apr. 1962.

14 Hadj Saloum Diakite, *Sékou Touré face au Général de Gaulle* (Dakar-Ponty: Éditions feu de brousse, 2007), 66.

15 Philippe Gaillard and Jacques Foccart, *Foccart parle. Entretiens avec Philippe Gaillard I* (Paris: Fayard/Jeune Afrique, 1995).

16 Jean-Marie Soutou, *Un Diplomate engagé. Mémoires 1939–1979* (Paris: Éditions de Fallois, 2011), 345.

17 John Chipman, *French Power in Africa* (Oxford: Blackwell, 1989), 233; Frédéric Turpin, *Jacques Foccart. Dans l'Ombre du pouvoir* (Paris: CNRS Éditions, 2015), 185–206; Jackson, *A Certain Idea of France*, 610–15.

18 Thomas Deltombe, Manuel Domergue, and Jacob Tatsita, *La Guerre du Cameroun. L'invention de la Françafrique* (Paris: La Découverte, 2016); François-Xavier Verschave, *La Françafrique. Le plus long scandale de la République* (Paris: Stock, 1998), 91–108.

19 Dubow, 'Macmillan, Verwoerd and the 1960 "Wind of Change" Speech', 32.

20 Tom Lodge, *Sharpeville. An Apartheid Massacre and its Consequences* (Oxford University Press, 2011).

21 Christabel Gurney, '"A Great Cause": The Origins of the Anti-Apartheid Movement, June 1959–March 1960', *Journal of Southern African Studies*, 26/1 (2000), 123–44; Håkan Thörn, *Anti-Apartheid and the Emergence of a Global Civil Society* (Basingstoke: Palgrave Macmillan, 2006).

22 Stuart Ward, *Australia and the British Embrace. The Demise of the Imperial Ideal* (Melbourne University Press, 2001), 147, 150.

23 Dubow, *Apartheid*, 99.

24 Dubow, *Apartheid*, 112.

25 Nadine Gordimer, foreword to Cosmas Desmond, *The Discarded People. An Account of African Resettlement* (Breamfontein, Transvaal: The Christian Institute of South Africa, 1970).

26 Dubow, *Apartheid*, 87–94, 132–41.

27 Charles H. Feinstein, *An Economic History of South Africa. Conquest, Discrimination and Development* (Cambridge University Press, 2005), 203–21.

28 Anthony Sampson, *Black and Gold. Tycoons, Revolutionaries and Apartheid* (London: Hodder & Stoughton, 1987), 90–6.

29 Thörn, *Anti-Apartheid*.

30 Sampson, *Black and Gold*, 99–102.

31 Roy Welensky, 'The Federation and Nyasaland: Speech', 8 Nov. 1961, Salisbury (Salisbury: Publications Department, Federal Public Relations Division, 1962), 1, 6.

32 Miles Kahler, *Decolonzation in Britain and France. The Domestic Consequences of International Relations* (Princeton University Press, 1984), 328.

33 Roy Welensky, *Welensky's 4000 Days. The Life and Death of the Federation of Rhodesia and Nyasaland* (London: Collins, 1964), 324.

34 Bill Schwarz, *Memories of Empire. The White Man's World* (Oxford University Press, 2011), 418.

35 Cecil King, *The Cecil King Diary, 1965–1970* (London: Jonathan Cape, 1972), 45. Entry of 8 Dec. 1964. Cited by Ben Pimlott, *Harold Wilson* (London: HarperCollins, 1992), 373.

36 Pimlott, *Harold Wilson*, 371.

37 Faan Martin, *James and the Duck. Tales of the Rhodesian Bush War, 1964–1980. The Memoirs of a Part-Time Trooper* (Milton Keynes: Author House, 2007), xiv–xv.

38 David Caute, *Under the Skin. The Death of White Rhodesia* (London: Allen Lane, 1983), 90.

39 Bernadette Devlin, *The Price of my Soul* (London: André Deutsch and Pan, 1969), 54.

40 Michael Dewar, *The British Army in Northern Ireland* (London: Arms and Armour Press, 1985), 27–8.

41 Tariq Ali, *The Coming British Revolution* (London: Jonathan Cape, 1972), 229.

42 Speech in Belfast, 2 June 1972, cited in Paul Corthorn, 'Enoch Powell: Ulster Unionism and the British Nation', *Journal of British Studies*, 51/4 (2012), 970.

43 Thomas G. Mitchell, *Native vs. Settler. Ethnic Conflict in Israel/Palestine, Northern Ireland and South Africa* (Westport, CT: Greenwood, 2000), 155–7.

44 Harold Wilson, *The Labour Government, 1964–1970. A Personal Record* (London: Weidenfeld & Nicolson, 1971), 445.

45 Alun Chalfont, *The Shadow of my Hand* (London: Weidenfeld & Nicolson, 2000), 144–5; see also Wilson, *Labour Government*, 445.

46 David Reynolds, *Britannia Overruled. British Power and World Power in the Twentieth Century* (London and New York: Longman, 1991), 261.

47 François Mitterand, *Réflexions sur la politique extérieure de la France* (Paris: Fayard, 1988), 317.

48 See above, p. 64–5.

49 Jean-Pierre Cot, *A l'Épreuve du pouvoir. Le tiers-mondisme, pourquoi faire?* (Paris: Seuil, 1984), 12–86.

50 Ezequiel Mercau, 'The War of the British Worlds: The Anglo-Argentines and the Falklands', *Journal of British Studies*, 55/1 (2016), 145–68.

51 Hansard. Parliamentary Debates. Commons, 3 Apr. 1982, 633–4, 641; D. George Boyce, *The Falklands War* (Basingstoke: Palgrave Macmillan, 2005), 46, 59.

52 Mark Connelly, *We Can Take It! Britain and the Memory of the Second World War* (Harlow: Pearson Longman, 2004), 273–7.

53 James Aulich, 'Introduction' and 'Wildlife in the South Atlantic: Graphic Satire, Patriotism and the Fourth Estate', in James Aulich (ed.), *Framing the Falklands War. Nationhood, Culture and Identity* (Milton Keynes: Open University Press, 1992), 1–12, 84–116.

54 www.margaretthatcher.org/document/105032.

55 Boyce, *The Falklands War*, 172, 183; Ian McEwan, *The Ploughman's Lunch* (London: Methuen, 1985), V, 30.

56 Cot, *A l'Épreuve*, 12.

57 Gilles Gaetner, *L'Argent facile. Dictionnaire de la corruption en France* (Paris: Stock, 1992), 278.

58 Robert Aldrich and John Connell, 'Remnants of Empire: France's Overseas Departments and Territories', in Aldrich and Connell (eds.), *France in World Politics* (London: Routledge, 1989), 155–69; *Le Monde*, 6 and 7 May 1988.

59 Robert Gildea, *The Past in French History* (New Haven, CT and London: Yale University Press, 1994), 60; Stephen Laurence Kaplan, *Farewell, Revolution. The Historians' Feud, France, 1789/1989* (Ithaca, NY and London: Cornell University Press, 1995), 302–30.

60 Richard Kohl (ed.), *Globalisation, Poverty and Inequality* (Paris: OECD, 2003), 83–4; Giuliano Garavini, *After Empires. European Integration, Decolonization, and the Challenge from the Global South, 1957–1986* (Oxford University Press, 2012), 2–3, 242–3.

61 Edwin Williamson, *The Penguin History of Latin America* (London: Penguin, 1992), 480.

62 Sarah Babb, *Behind the Development Banks. Washington Politics, World Poverty and the Wealth of Nations* (University of Chicago Press, 2009), 127–35; Ray Kiely, *The Clash of Globalisations. Neo-Liberalism, the Third Way and Anti-Globalisation* (Leiden: Brill, 2005), 63–78; Jürgen Osterhammel and Niels P. Petersson, *Globalization. A Short History* (Princeton University Press, 2005), 122–8; Ngaire Woods, *The Globalizers. The IMF, the World Bank and their Borrowers* (Ithaca, NY and London: Cornell University Press, 2006), 38–68; Garavini, *After Empires*, 208–51.

63 Kohl (ed.), *Globalization, Poverty and Inequality*, 46–67; Alex MacGillivray, *A Brief History of Globalization* (London: Robinson, 2006), 177–80.

64 Kiely, *Clash of Globalisations*, 205–8; Nick Higgins, 'Lessons from the Indigenous: Zapatista Poetics and a Cultural Humanism for the Twenty-First Century', in Catherine Eschle and Bice Maiguashca (eds.), *Critical Theories, International Relations and the Anti-Globalisation Movement. The Politics of Global Resistance* (London: Routledge, 2005), 86–100.

# 5 Colonising in Reverse and Colonialist Backlash

1 Louise Bennett, *Jamaica Labrish* (Jamaica: Sangster's Bookstores, 1966), 179–80. 'Gwine' means 'going'.

2 Anna Marie Smith, *The New Right Discourse on Race and Sexuality. Britain, 1968–1990* (Cambridge University Press, 1994), 146.

3 Enda Delaney, *The Irish in Post-War Britain* (Oxford University Press, 2007), 17.

4 Stephen Castles and Godula Kosack, *Immigrant Workers and Class Structure in Western Europe* (London: Oxford University Press and Institute of Race Relations, 1973), 29–30; D. Kay and R. Miles, *Refugees or Migrant Workers? European Volunteer Workers in Britain 1946–1951* (London: Routledge, 1992).

5 Richard Cavendish, 'Arrival of the SS Empire Windrush', *History Today*, 48/6 (1998).

6 *Manchester Guardian*, 2 Sept. 1952, and *Daily Telegraph*, 26 Aug. 1958, cited by Wendy Webster, *Englishness and Empire, 1939–1965* (Oxford University Press, 2005), 165.

7 Stuart Hall with Bill Schwarz, *Familiar Stranger. A Life between Two Islands* (London: Allen Lane, 2017), 190–1.

8 Hall with Schwarz, *Familiar Stranger*, 192.

9 Randall Hansen, *Citizenship and Immigration in Post-War Britain: the Institutional Origins of a Multicultural Nation* (Oxford University Press, 2000), 35–61.

10 Claire Alexander, Joya Chatterji and Annu Jalais, *The Bengal Diaspora. Rethinking Muslim Migration* (London and New York: Routledge, 2015), 57–73, 228.

11 John Rex and Sally Tomlinson, *Colonial Immigrants in a British City* (London: Routledge & Kegan Paul, 1979), 74–7.
12 Alexander et al., *Bengal Diaspora*, 106–17, 226–7.
13 Simon Jenkins and Victoria Randall, *Here to Live. A Study of Race Relations in an English Town* (London: Runneymde Trust, 1971), 10–11, 28, 77.
14 Jenkins and Randall, *Here to Live*, 12.
15 Jenkins and Randall, *Here to Live*, 17–19.
16 Klim McPherson and Julia Gaitskell, *Immigrants and Employment: Two Case Studies in East London and in Croydon* (London: Institute of Race Relations, 1969), 24–6.
17 McPherson and Gaitskell, *Immigrants and Employment*, 53, 70.
18 David Steel, *No Entry. The Background and Implications of the Commonwealth Immigrations Act, 1968* (London: Hurst & Co, 1969), 26–7, 35–6.
19 *Daily Telegraph*, 7 Aug. 1967, cited by Steel, *No Entry*, 132.
20 Paul Foot, *Immigration and Race in British Politics* (London: Penguin, 1965), 26–35, 50–4.
21 Anthony Barnett, *The Lure of Greatness. England's Brexit and America's Trump* (London: Unbound, 2017), 122–3.
22 Cited by John Rutherford, *Forever England. Reflections on Masculinity and Empire* (London: Lawrence & Wishart, 1997), 124–5; John Wood, *A Nation Not Afraid. The Thinking of Enoch Powell* (London: Batsford, 1965), 24–9.
23 Cited by Camilla Schofield, *Enoch Powell and the Making of Postcolonial Britain* (Cambridge University Press, 2013), 218.
24 Enoch Powell, *Freedom and Reality*, ed. John Wood (London: Batsford, 1969), 217–18.
25 Cited by Schofield, *Enoch Powell*, 243.
26 Cited by Schofield, *Enoch Powell*, 227.
27 Dipak Nandy, 'Introductory Note' in Augustine John, *Race in the Inner City. A Report from Handsworth, Birmingham* (London: Runneymede Trust, 1972), 7.
28 Derek Humphrey and Augustine John, *Because They're Black* (London: Penguin, 1970), 48–9.
29 Humphrey and John, *Because They're Black*, 52.
30 Humphrey and John, *Because They're Black*, 51; Trevor Huddleston, *Local Ministry in Urban and Industrial Areas* (London and Oxford: Mowbrays, 1972), 172.
31 Alain Girard and Jean Stoetzel, *Français et immigrés I. L'attitude française* (Paris: PUF, 1953), 18.
32 Castles and Kosack, *Immigrant Workers*, 32–3.
33 Alain Girard and Jean Stoetzel, *Français et immigrés II. Nouveaux documents* (Paris: PUF, 1954), 19–20.
34 Girard and Stoetzel, *Français et immigrés I*, 133–6.
35 Girard and Stoetzel, *Français et immigrés II*, 106–7.
36 Pascal Blanchard, Sandrine Lemaire and Nicolas Bancel (eds.), *Culture coloniale en France. De la Révolution française à nos jours* (Paris: CNRS/Autrement, 2008), 463.
37 See above, p. 102.
38 Tom Charbit, *Les Harkis* (Paris: La Découverte, 2006).
39 Emmanuelle Comtat, *Les Pieds-noirs et politique. Quarante ans après le retour* (Paris: Presses de la Fondation Nationale des Sciences Politiques, 2009), 78–139; Benjamin Stora with Alexis Jenni, *Les Mémoires dangereuses, suivi d'une nouvelle édition de Transfert d'une mémoire* (Paris: Albin Michel, 2016), 83.
40 Benjamin Stora, *La Dernière Génération d'Octobre* (Paris: Stock, 2003).
41 Interview with Jean-Pierre Le Dantec, recorded by Robert Gildea, Paris, 24 Apr. 2007, cited in Robert Gildea, James Mark and Niek Pas, 'European Radicals and the "Third World": Imagined Solidarities and Radical Networks, 1958–1973', *Cultural*

*and Social History*, 8/4 (2011), 455. See also Christophe Bourseiller, *Les Maoistes* (Paris: Plon, 2007) 110–14; Richard Wolin, *The Wind from the East. French Intellectuals, the Cultural Revolution and the Legacy of the 1960s* (Princeton University Press, 2010), 109–41.

42 John Gerassi (ed.), *Venceremos. The Speeches and Writings of Ernesto Che Guevara* (London: Weidenfeld & Nicolson, 1968), 420–2.

43 Robert Gildea, James Mark and Annette Warring (eds.), *Europe's 1968. Voices of Revolt* (Oxford University Press, 2013), 111.

44 Gildea et al. (eds.), *Europe's 1968*, 120. See also Alain Geismar, Serge July and Erlyne Morane, *Vers la Guerre civile* (Paris: Éditions et publications premières, 1969) and Alain Geismar, *Pourquoi nous combattons* (Paris: Maspéro, 1970).

45 Génériques. Fonds Bouziri. 1. Comités Palestine, 'Bilan des Comités de Soutien à la Révolution Palestinien dans la région parisienne', Nov. 1970 (9pp.).

46 Bibliothèque de Documentation Internationale Contemporaine [BDIC] FΔ Rés 576/ 5/9/2, 'Bilan de la Campagne Djellali' (13 pp.); Génériques. Fonds Bouziri. 1. Comités Palestine, 'Où en sont les comités Palestine depuis la champagne anti-racists sur Djellali' (10pp.).

47 *Sans Frontière*, 12, 22 Apr. 1980, 16.

48 BDIC FΔ 576/5/8, *Secours Rouge* no. 2, Feb. 1972.

49 Génériques. Fonds Bouziri 3, 'Pamphlet of Comité des residents du foyer Sonacotra, avenue Romain Rolland, Saint-Denis', 13 Sept. 1975.

50 F. Cornu, 'L'ordre regne à Grasse', *Le Monde 25–26 Juin 1973*, cited by Yvan Gastaut, 'La Flambe raciste de 1973 en France', *Revue européenne de migrations internationales*, 9/2 (1993), 63.

51 Jean Raspail, *Le Camp des Saints* [1973] (Paris: Robert Laffont, 2011).

52 G. Domenach, *Le Meridional*, 26 Aug. 1973, cited by Gastaut, 'La Flambe raciste de 1973 en France', 65; Daniel A. Gordon, *Immigrants and Intellectuals. May '68 and the Rise of Anti-Racism in France* (Pontypool: Merlin Press, 2012), 145–6.

53 See above, p. 100.

54 *Le Monde*, 18 Dec. 1973, cited by Gastaut, 'La Flambe raciste de 1973 en France', 67. See also Neil MacMaster, *Colonial Migrants and Racism. Algerians in France, 1900–1962* (Basingstoke: Macmillan, 1997), 212–13.

55 Georges Tapinos, 'Pour une introduction au débat contemporain', in Yves Lequin (ed.), *La Mosaïque France. Histoire des Étrangers et de l'Immigration* (Paris: Larousse, 1988), 429–36.

56 John Belchem, *Before the Windrush. Race Relations in 20th-Century Liverpool* (Liverpool University Press, 2014), 217.

57 Jean-Marc Terrasse, *Génération beur* (Paris: Plon, 1989), 85.

58 John, *Race in the Inner City*, 19.

59 Timeri Murari, *The New Savages* (London: Macmillan, 1975).

60 Leslie George Scarman, *The Brixton Disorders, 10–12 April 1981. Report of an Inquiry* (London: HMSO, 1986), 10.

61 Azouz Begag, *Le Gone de Chaâba* (Paris: Seuil, 1986), 224.

62 Terrasse, *Génération beur*, 133–5.

63 Toumi Djaïdja, *La Marche pour l'égalité. Une histoire dans l'histoire* (Paris: L'aube, 2013), 18, 24–7.

64 Werner Glinga, *Legacy of Empire. A Journey through British Society* (Manchester University Press, 1986), 122.

65 Linton Kwesi Johnson, *Selected Poems* (London: Penguin, 2006), 40.

66 P. J. Waller, 'The Riots in Toxteth, Liverpool: A Survey', *Journal of Ethnic and Migration Studies*, 9/3 (1981), 344–53; Martin Kettle and Lucy Hodges, *Uprising! Police, the People and the Riots in Britain's Cities* (London: Pan, 1982).

67 Scarman, *The Brixton Disorders*, 68, 73.

68 Glinga, *Legacy of Empire*, 140.

69 www.margaretthatcher.org/document/104989.

70 Salman Rushdie, 'The New Empire within Britain' [1982], in *Imaginary Homelands. Essays and Criticism 1981–1991* (London: Granta/Viking, 1991), 131.

71 *Education for All. The Report of the Committee of Inquiry into the Education of Children from Ethnic Minority Groups* (London: HMSO, 1985), 769. www.educationengland.org.uk/documents/swann/swann1985.html

72 Devla Murphy, *Tales from Two Cities. Travel of Another Sort* (London: John Murray, 1987), 103–42.

73 Djaïdja, *La Marche pour l'égalité*, 29, 43–54.

74 Robert Gildea and Andrew Tompkins, 'The Transnational in the Local: The Larzac Plateau as a Site of Transnational Activism since 1970', *Journal of Contemporary History*, 50/3 (2015), 581–605.

75 Djaïdja, *La Marche pour l'égalité*, 64–97.

76 Robert Gildea, *France since 1945* (Oxford University Press, 2002), 168–9.

77 Jean-Marie Le Pen, *Les Français d'abord* (Paris: Éditions Carrère-Michel Lafon, 1984), 239.

78 Le Pen, *Les Français d'abord*, 99–102.

79 James Shields, *The Extreme Right in France. From Pétain to Le Pen* (London: Routledge, 2007), 193–6.

80 Pierre Favier and Michel Martin-Roland, *La Décennie Mitterrand 2. Les Épreuves* (Paris: Seuil, 1991), 581.

81 Alain Griotteray, *Les Immigrés. Le choc* (Paris: Plon, 1984), 127–8, 145.

82 Olivier Milza, *Les Français devant l'immigration* (Brussels: Complexe, 1988), 179.

83 Commission de la Nationalité, *Être Français, aujourd'hui et demain. Rapport de la Commission de la nationalité, 22 juin 1987–7 janvier 1988, présenté par Marceau Long* (2 vols., Paris: Commission de la nationalité, 1988), I, 357, 502–3.

# 6 Europe: In or Out?

1 Macmillan to Menzies, 8 Feb. 1962, cited by Stuart Ward, *Australia and the British Embrace. The Demise of the Imperial Ideal* (Melbourne University Press, 2001), 152.

2 See above, pp. 85–6.

3 Giuliano Garavini, *After Empires. European Integration, Decolonization, and the Challenge from the Global South, 1857–1986* (Oxford University Press, 2012), 47–9.

4 Benjamin Grob-Fitzgibbon, *Continental Drift. Britain and Europe from the End of Empire to the Rise of Euroscepticism* (Cambridge University Press, 2016), 265–6.

5 Grob-Fitzgibbon, *Continental Drift*, 80.

6 Alain Peyrefitte, *C'était de Gaulle II* (Paris: Fayard, 1997), 84–6.

7 Piers Ludlow, *Dealing with Britain. The Six and the First UK Application to the EEC* (Cambridge University Press, 1997), 198.

8 Harold Macmillan, *At the End of the Day, 1961–1963* (London: Macmillan, 1973), 366.

9 Ludlow, *Dealing with Britain*, 207–8.

10 Piers Ludlow, *The European Community and the Crises of the 1960s. Negotiating the Gaullist Challenge* (London and New York: Routledge, 2006), 138.

11 Georges Pompidou, *Entretiens et Discours, 1968–1973* (Paris: Plon, 1975), II, 127.

12 Grob-Fitzgibbon, *Continental Drift*, 361.
13 Quoted by Camilla Schofield, *Enoch Powell and the Making of Postcolonial Britain* (Cambridge University Press, 2013), 300.
14 *The Sun*, 10 Mar. 1975, quoted by Robert Saunders, *Yes to Europe! The 1975 Referendum and Seventies Britain* (Cambridge University Press, 2018), 263.
15 Speech at Sidcup, 4 June 1975, quoted by Saunders, *Yes to Europe!*, 240.
16 *The Sun*, 7 June 1975, quoted by Saunders, *Yes to Europe!*, 364.
17 Grob-Fitzgibbon, *Continental Drift*, 398.
18 *Le Monde*, 25 Sept. 1984.
19 Jacques Delors with Jean-Louis Arnaud, *Mémoires* (Paris: Plon, 2004), 41.
20 Jacques Delors and Clisthène, *La France par l'Europe* (Paris: Grasset, 1988), 263.
21 François Mitterrand, *Réflexions sur la politique extérieure de la France* (Paris: Fayard, 1986), 104.
22 Charles Grant, *Delors. Inside the House that Jack Built* (London: Nicholas Brealey, 1994), 66–75.
23 Grant, *Delors*, 79–119.
24 *Sunday Express*, 3 Jan. 1988, quoted in Grob-Fitzgibbon, *Continental Drift*, 438.
25 Margaret Thatcher, *The Downing Street Years* (London: HarperCollins, 1993), 742.
26 www.margaretthatcher.org/document/107332.
27 Grob-Fitzgibbon, *Continental Drift*, 441.
28 Thatcher, *Downing Street Years*, 750.
29 Thatcher, *Downing Street Years*, 753.
30 *Le Monde*, 28 July 1989.
31 *Le Monde*, 10–11 Dec. 1989.
32 *The Independent*, 13 July 1990, cited by Grob-Fitzgibbon, *Continental Drift*, 286.
33 *The Spectator*, 14 July 1990, p. 8; Grob-Fitzgibbon, *Continental Drift*, 287.
34 Grant, *Delors*, 136–7.
35 www.margaretthatcher.org/document/108234.
36 Geoffrey Howe, *Conflict of Loyalty* (London: Macmillan, 1994), 697–700.
37 Howe, *Conflict of Loyalty*, 538.
38 *Journal Officiel, Débats parlementaires. Assemblée Nationale*, 5 May 1992, 840.
39 *Le Monde*, 2 May 1992; Jean-Pierre Chevènement (ed.), *La République, l'Europe et l'Universel. Colloque, Belfort, 21–22 septembre 1991* (Belfort: IRED, 1993), 255; Jean-Pierre Chevènement, *France-Allemagne. Parlons franc* (Paris: Plon, 1996), 37.
40 *Journal Officiel, Débats parlementaires. Assemblée Nationale*, 5 May 1992, 869.
41 Michel Debré, *Combattre Toujours, 1969–1993. Mémoires V* (Paris: Albin Michel, 1994), 175–6, 221.
42 *Le Monde*, 5 Sept. 1992.
43 *Le Monde*, 4 Sept. 1992.
44 *Le Monde*, 16 Sept. 1992.
45 *Le Monde*, 20–21 Sept. 1992.
46 *Le Monde*, 22 Sept. 1992.
47 Alain Duhamel, *Les Peurs françaises* (Paris: Gallimard, 1993), 50–72; Robert Gildea, 'Eternal France: Crisis and National Self-Perception in France, 1870–2005', in Susana Carvalho and François Gemenne (eds.), *Nations and their Histories: Constructions and Representations* (Basingstoke: Palgrave Macmillan, 2009), 147–8.
48 Norman Tebitt, *Unfinished Business* (London: Weidenfeld & Nicolson, 1991), 36, 69.

49 Andrew Gimson, *Boris. The Rise of Boris Johnson* (London: Simon & Schuster, 2012), 104.
50 William Cash, *Europe. The Crunch* (London: Duckworth, 1992), 16.
51 William Cash, *Against a Federal Europe. The Battle for Britain* (London: Duckworth, 1991), 9.
52 Mark Daniel, *Cranks and Gadflies. The Story of UKIP* (London: Timewell Press, 2005), 9-12, 28, 49.

# 7 Islamism and the Retreat to Monocultural Nationalism

1 Peter Mandaville, *Global Political Islam* (New York: Routledge, 2007); Saïd Amir Arjomand, 'Islamic Resurgence and its Aftermath', in R. W. Hefner (ed.), *The New Cambridge History of Islam VI. Muslims and Modernity: Culture and Society since 1800* (Cambridge University Press, 2010), 173-97.
2 John Esposito, *The Iranian Revolution. Its Global Impact* (Miami: Florida International University Press, 1990).
3 Iman Khomeini, *Islam and the Revolution. Writings and Declarations of Imam Khomeini* (Berkeley, CA: Mizan Press, 1981), 305.
4 Karen Armstrong, *Holy War. The Crusades and their Impact on Today's World* (London: Macmillan, 1988), 254.
5 Geoffrey Aronson, *Israel, Palestinians and the Intifada. Creating Facts on the West Bank* (London: Kegan Paul, 1990), 324-31.
6 Olivier Roy, *Globalized Islam. The Search for a New Ummah* (New York: Columbia University Press, 2004), 297-9.
7 Jason Burke, *Al-Qaeda. The True Story of Radical Islam* (London: Penguin, 2007), 44-58.
8 Gilles Kepel, *Terreur dans l'Hexagone* (Paris: Gallimard, 2015), 54-6.
9 George F. Will, 'The End of Our Holiday from History', *The Washington Post*, 12 Sept. 2012. This was taken up by Jonathan Freedland in 'The 1990s: A Holiday from History', BBC, 27 Apr. 2017, www.bbc.co.uk/programmes/b08n1hnh.
10 Andrew Hurrell, On Global Order. *Power, Values and the Constitution of International Solidarity* (Oxford University Press, 2007), 59-63, 145-61.
11 *The Atlantic*, Sept. 1990.
12 Samuel P. Huntington, 'The Clash of Civilizations?' *Foreign Affairs*, 72/3 (1993), 22-49; Samuel P. Huntington, *The Clash of Civilizations and the Remaking of World Order* (New York: Simon & Schuster, 1996).
13 Derek Gregory, *The Colonial Present* (Oxford: Blackwell, 2004), 151-9.
14 Mark Connelly, *We Can Take It! Britain and the Memory of the Second World War* (Harlow: Pearson Longman, 2004), 270.
15 Jacques Attali, *Verbatim III. 1988-1991* (Paris: Fayard, 1995), 702.
16 Gregory, *The Colonial Present*, 161-2.
17 Jean-Pierre Chevènement, *Une Certaine Idée de la France* (Paris: Albin Michel, 1991), 101.
18 Gregory, *The Colonial Present*, 168.
19 Chalmers Johnson, *Blowback. The Costs and Consequences of the American Empire* (London: Little, Brown, 2000), 9.
20 James McDougall, *A History of Algeria* (Cambridge University Press, 2017), 283-303.
21 *Middle East Quarterly*, Sept. 1994, cited by Lotfi Ben Rejeb, 'United States Policy towards Tunisia: What New Engagement after an Expendable "Friendship"?', in

Nouri Gana (ed.), *The Making of the Tunisian Revolution. Contexts, Architects, Prospects* (Edinburgh University Press, 2013), 91-2.

22 McDougall, *History of Algeria*, 306-17.

23 See above, p. 139.

24 Malise Ruthven, *A Satanic Affair. Salman Rusdie and the Wrath of Islam* (London: Hogarth Press, 1990); Chris Allen, *Islamophobia* (Farnham: Ashgate, 2010), 41-3.

25 *The Daily Mail*, 19 Jan. 1989; *The Independent*, 16 Mar. 1989.

26 *The Guardian*, 27 Feb. 1989, cited in Michael M. J. Fischer and Mehdi Abedi, *Debating Muslims. Cultural Dialogues in Postmodernity and Tradition* (Madison, WI: University of Wisconsin Press, 1990), 390; Shabbir Akhtar, *Be Careful with Muhammed! The Salman Rushdie Affair* (London: Bellow Publishing, 1989), 33-49.

27 Akhtar, *Be Careful with Muhammed!*, 43-5.

28 *Demos*, 11 (1997), quoted by Runnymede Trust, *Islamophobia. A Challenge for Us All.* Report of the Runnymede Trust Commission on British Muslims and Islamophobia (London: Runneymede Trust, 1997), 28.

29 http://articles.latimes.com/1990-04-19/news/mn-2009_1_conservative-party.

30 Tariq Modood, 'The Cricket Test: A Note to Mr Tebbit', *New Life*, 4 May 1990, in Tariq Modood, *Not Easy Being British* (Stoke-on-Trent: Runneymede Trust and Trentham Books, 1992), 23-4.

31 *The Spectator*, 19 Oct. 1991, 7.

32 www.independent.co.uk/arts-entertainment/at-the-gates-of-f-ortress-britain-1328604.html.

33 Melanie Griffiths, 'Who is Who Now? Truth, Trust and Identification in the British Asylum and Immigration Detention System', DPhil thesis, School of Anthropology and Museum Ethnography, Oxford (2014), 97-9.

34 Salman Rushdie, *The Satanic Verses* (London: Vintage Books, 1998), 343, 439.

35 *Q News*, 3/8 (20-27 May 1994).

36 Hanif Kureishi, *The Black Album* (London: Faber, 1995), 106-7.

37 Philip Lewis, *Islamic Britain. Religion, Politics and Identity among British Muslims* (London and New York: I. B. Tauris, 1994), 173-5.

38 Humayan Ansari, *The Infidel Within. Muslims in Britain since 1800* (London: Hurst & Co, 2004), 220.

39 www.pushstuff.co.uk/mmfeatures/fundamental090592.html, partly quoted in Lewis, *Islamic Britain*, 180.

40 Moazzam Begg, *Enemy Combatant. The Terrifying True Story of a Briton in Guantanamo* (London: Pocket Books, 2007), 8-92.

41 Gilles Kepel, *Les Banlieus d'Islam. Naissance d'une religion en France* (Paris: Seuil, 1987), 97, 192, 267.

42 Joan Wallach Scott, *The Politics of the Veil* (Princeton University Press, 2007), 22.

43 *Le Monde*, 6 and 7 Oct. 1989.

44 www.ina.fr/video/CAB89044653.

45 Christian Jelen, *Ils feront de bons Français* (Paris: Robert Laffont, 1991), 141.

46 *Le Monde*, 26 Oct. 1989.

47 *Le Nouvel Observateur*, 2 Nov. 1989; www.laicite.fr/voile-profs-ne-capitulons-pas/; Emile Chabal, *A Divided Republic. Nation, State and Citizenship in Contemporary France* (Cambridge University Press, 2015), 63.

48 Frantz Fanon, *L'an V de la revolution algérienne* (Paris: Maspéro, 1959), ch. 1, 'L'Algérie se dévoile', 15-16, 22-5; translated as 'Algeria Unveiled', in Frantz Fanon, *Studies in a Dying Colonialism* (New York: Monthly Review Press, 1965), 44-5. See above, p. 93.

49 *Le Monde*, 18 Mar. 1992.

50 Michèle Tribalat, 'Une estimation des populations d'origine étrangère en France en 2011', *Espace, Populations, Sociétés*, 1–2 (2015), 1–2.

51 Benjamin Stora, *La Gangrène et l'oubli. La mémoire de la guerre d'Algérie* (Paris: La Découverte, 1991), 289, 320.

52 Jim House and Neil MacMaster, *Paris 1961. Algerians, State Terror, and Memory* (Oxford University Press, 2006), 262–96.

53 Jean-Luc Einaudi, *La Bataille de Paris, 17 octobre 1961* (Paris: Seuil, 1991).

54 The signatories included former Second World War resisters Germaine Tillion and Jean-Pierre Vernant, and former opponents of the Algerian War or their widows: Josette Audin, Henri Alleg, Simone de Bollardière, Laurent Schwartz and Pierre Vidal Naquet.

55 Inathèque Paris, Simone de Bollardière, interviewed by Stephane Paoli, France Inter, 25 June 2001.

56 Inathèque Paris, 'Torture en Algerie, Ces aveux qui dértangent', France 3, 27 June 2001. See also his memoir: Paul Aussaresses, *Pour la France. Services speciaux 1942–1954* (Monaco and Paris: Éditions du Rocher, 2001).

57 *Liberation*, 23 Jan. 2002.

58 John R. Bowen, *Why the French Don't Like Headscarves. Islam, the State, and Public Space* (Princeton University Press, 2007), 90.

59 Emmanuelle Comtat, *Les Pieds-noirs et politique. Quarante ans après le retour* (Paris: Presses de la Fondation Nationale des Sciences Politiques, 2009), 249–55.

60 Pascal Perrineau, 'La dynamique du vote Le Pen. Le poids du "Gaucho-Lépenisme"', in Pascal Perrineau and Colette Ysmal (eds.), *Le Vote de crise. L'élection présidentielle de 1995* (Paris: Figaro/ FNSP, 1995), 244–60; Pascal Perrineau, *Le Symptôme Le Pen. Radiographie des electeurs du Front National* (Paris: Fayard, 1997), 135–44; Nonna Mayer, *Ces Français qui votent Le Pen* (Paris: Flammarion, 1999), 86–97, 113–4, 147, 223–33; Christophe Cambadélis and Éric Osmond, *La France blafarde. Une histoire politique de l'extrême droite* (Paris: Plon, 1998), 429–33.

61 Joan Gross, David McMurray and Ted Swedenburg, 'Raï, Rap and Ramadan Nights: Franco-Maghribi Cultural Identities', *Middle East Report*, 178 (1992), 11–16.

62 Alain Boyer, *L'Islam en France* (Paris: PUF, 1998), 321–5; Alain Boyer, 'Aux origines du mouvement des jeunes Musulmans: l'Union des Jeunes de France', in Ahmed Boubeker and Abdellaji Hajjat (eds.), *Histoire politique des immigrations postcoloniales. France, 1920–2008* (Paris: Éditions Amsterdam, 2008), 217–24.

63 Thomas Deltombe and Mathieu Rigouste, 'L'ennemi intérieur: la construction médiatique de la figure de l'Arabe', in Pascal Blanchard, Nicolas Bancel and Sandrine Lemaire (eds.), *La Fracture coloniale. La société française au prisme de l'héritage colonial* (Paris: La Découverte, 2005), 196–7.

64 *Le Monde*, 23 Aug. 1997.

65 *Le Temps*, 13 July 1998, cited in *Le Monde*, 18 July 1998.

66 *Le Monde*, 21 July 1998.

67 Stuart Hall with Bill Schwarz, *Familiar Stranger. A Life between Two Islands* (London: Allen Lane, 2017), 196–7.

68 Yasmin Alibai Brown, *Who Do We Think We Are?* (London: Allen Lane, 2000), 117, 121, 155–6.

69 Janet Bujra and Jenny Pearce, *The 2001 Bradford Riot and Beyond* (Skipton: Vertical Editions, 2011), 20–51.

70 Bujra and Pearce, *The 2001 Bradford Riot*, 164.

## 8 Hubris and Nemesis: Iraq, the Colonial Fracture and Global Economic Crisis

1 Jason Burke, *Al-Qaeda. The True Story of Radical Islam* (London: Penguin, 2007), 234–46.
2 Dominic Streatfield, *A History of the World since 9/11* (London: Atlantic Books, 2011), 3.
3 www.mtholyoke.edu/acad/intrel/bush/wspeech.htm.
4 David Harvey, *The New Imperialism* (Oxford University Press, 2003), 190–2; Derek Gregory, *The Colonial Present* (Oxford: Blackwell, 2004), 48–51.
5 Arabinda Acharya, *Ten Years after 9/11. Rethinking the Jihadist Threat* (Abingdon: Routledge, 2013), 17.
6 Jason W. Davidson, *America's Allies and War. Kosovo, Afghanistan and Iraq* (New York, Palgrave Macmillan, 2011), 106.
7 David Barsamian and Edward Said, *Culture and Resistance. Conversations with Edward Said* (London: Pluto Press, 2003), 140–1.
8 Gregory, *The Colonial Present*, 112–14, 130–3.
9 James A. Beckford, Dandle Joly and Farhad Khroskhavar, *Muslims in Prison. Challenge and Change in Britain and France* (Basingstoke: Palgeave Macmillan, 2005), 218.
10 Farhad Khroskhavar, *Inside Jihadism. Understanding Jihhadist Movements Worldwide* (Boulder, CO: Paradigm Publishers, 2009), 201.
11 Streatfield, *A History of the World since 9/11*, 183.
12 Stanley Hoffmann with Frédéric Bozo, *Gulliver Unbound. America's Imperial Temptation and the War in Iraq* (Lanham, MD: Rowman & Littlefield, 2004), 42.
13 Max Boot, 'The Case for American Empire', *The Weekly Standard*, 15 Oct. 2001.
14 www.nytimes.corM2002/07/28/magazineination-building-lite.html?pagewanted=all.
15 www.nytimes.com/2003/01/05/magazine/the-american-empire-the-burden.html?pagewanted=all.
16 See the documentary *The House of War* by Robert Young Pelton and Paul Yule.
17 See above, p. 180.
18 *The Report of the Iraq Inquiry: Report of a Committee of Privy Counsellors* (12 vols., London: Dandy Booksellers, 2016), I: 450.
19 *Report of the Iraq Inquiry*, II: 188.
20 Philip H. Gordon and Jeremy Shapiro, *Allies at War. America, Europe and the Crisis Over Iraq* (New York: McGraw-Hill, 2004), 127–8.
21 https://fr.wikisource.org/wiki/Discours_prononc%C3%A9_%C3%A0_l%27ONU_lors_de_la_crise_irakienne_-_14_f%C3%A9vrier_2003.
22 Gordon and Shapiro, *Allies at War*, 151.
23 Stefaan Walgrave and Dieter Rucht (eds.), *The World Says No to War. Demonstrations against the War on Iraq* (Minneapolis, MN: University of Minnesota Press, 2010), 1–19.
24 *Hansard. Parliamentary Debates. Commons*, 17 Mar. 2003, cols. 726–7; Robin Cook, *The Point of Departure* (London: Simon & Schuster, 2003), 243–4, 360–5.
25 Tony Blair, *A Journey* (London: Hutchinson, 2010), 434.
26 Nicholas Bayne, *Staying Togeher. The G8 Summit Confronts the 21st Century* (Aldershot: Ashgate, 2005), 92–3.
27 www.theguardian.com/politics/2001/oct/02/labourconference.labour6.
28 José Bové, *La Révolte d'un Paysan. Entretiens avec Paul Ariès et Christian Terras* (Villeurbanne: Éd. Golias, 2000), 75–87; José Bové and François Dufour, *The World is Not for Sale. Farmers against Junk Food* (London and New York: Verso, 2002).

29 William Fisher and Thomas Ponniah (eds.), *Another World is Possible. Popular Alternatives to Globalization at the World Social Forum* (Nova Scotia: Fernwood, 2003), 354–7; Jackie Smith, Marina Karides, Marc Becker and others, *Global Democracy and the World Social Forums* (Boulder, CO and London: Paradigm Publishers, 2015).

30 Michael Hardt and Antonio Negri, *Empire* (Cambridge, MA: Harvard University Press, 2000), xi–xii.

31 Michael Hardt and Antonio Negri, *Multitude. War and Democracy in the Age of Empire* (London: Penguin Books, 2006), 215.

32 Les Roberts, Riyadh Lafta, Richard Garfield, Jamal Khudhairi and Gilbert Burnham, 'Mortality Before and After the Invasion of Iraq: Cluster Sample Survey', *The Lancet*, 363/9448 (2004), 1857–64.

33 *Report of the Iraq Inquiry*, II: 72–4.

34 *Report of the Iraq Inquiry*, II: 154.

35 *Report of the Iraq Inquiry*, III: 212, 215.

36 *Report of the Iraq Inquiry*, VI: 451.

37 Robert J. C. Young, *Postcolonialism. A Very Short Introduction* (Oxford University Press, 2003), 44.

38 Tariq Ali, 'Re-colonizing Iraq', *New Left Review*, 21 (2003).

39 Jonathan Raban, 'The Greatest Gulf', *The Guardian*, 19 Apr. 2003.

40 *The Independent*, 17 Apr. 2003, cited in Gregory, *The Colonial Present*, 213.

41 Euan Ferguson, *The Observer*, 8 June 2003; Phil Reeves, *The Independent*, 27 Apr. 2003, cited by Gregory, *The Colonial Present*, 225.

42 *Report of the Iraq Inquiry*, III: 213.

43 Assessment by Joint Intelligence Committee, 3 Sept. 2003, *Report of the Iraq Inquiry*, VII: 257.

44 Gregory, *The Colonial Present*, 232–6.

45 *The New Yorker*, 10 May 2004.

46 Randall Robinson, *An Unbroken Agony. Haiti, from Revolution to the Kidnapping of a President* (New York: Basic Books, 2007), 159–222; Alex Dupuy, *The Prophet and the Power. Jean-Bertrand Aristide, the International Community and Haiti* (Lanham, MD: Rowman & Littlefield, 2007), 173–5.

47 Denis Lacorne, 'Anti-Americanism and Americanophobia: A French Perspective', in Tony Judt and Denis Lacorne (eds.), *With Us or Against Us. Studies in Global Anti-Americanism* (New York: Palgrave Macmillan, 2005), 39.

48 See note 9.

49 Milan Mai, 7/7. *The London Bombings, Islam and the Iraq War* (London: Pluto Press, 2006), 155.

50 Beckford et al., *Muslims in Prison*, 69, 84, 278.

51 Beckford et al., *Muslims in Prison*, 225.

52 Gilles Kepel, *Terreur dans l'Hexagone* (Paris: Gallimard, 2015), 60–1.

53 Paola Mattei and Andrew S. Aguilar, *Secular Institutions, Islam, and Education Policy. France and the U.S. in Comparative Perspective* (London: Palgrave Macmillan, 2016), 95–101.

54 www.legifrance.gouv.fr/affichTexte.do?cidTexte=JORFTEXT000000444898.

55 Houria Bouteldja and Sadri Khiari, *Nous sommes les Indigènes de la République* (Paris: Éditions Amsterdam, 2012), 27.

56 Bouteldja and Khiari, *Nous sommes les Indigènes*, 19–22.

57 Nicolas Bancel, Pascal Blanchard and Sandrine Lemaire, 'Les enseignements de l'étude conduite à Toulouse sur la mémoire coloniale', in Pascal Blanchard, Nicolas

Bancel and Sandrine Lemaire (eds.), *La Fracture coloniale. La société française au prisme de l'héritage colonial* (Paris: La Découverte, 2005), 247–54.

58 Ted Cantle, *Community Cohesion. A New Framework for Race and Diversity* (Basingstoke: Palgrave Macmillan, 2005), 11.

59 Niall Ferguson, *Empire. How Britain Made the Modern World* (London: Allen Lane, 2003), xii–xxv.

60 Niall Ferguson, *Colossus. The Rise and Fall of the American Empire* (London: Allen Lane, 2004).

61 James C. Bennett, *The Anglosphere Challenge. Why the English-Speaking Nations Will Lead the Way in the Twenty-First Century* (Lanham, MD: Rowman & Littlefield, 2004), 3–7, 79–81, 287; Michael Kenny and Nick Pearce, *Shadows of Empire. The Anglosphere in British Politics* (Cambridge: Polity Press, 2018), 128–9.

62 Andrew Roberts, *A History of the English-Speaking Peoples since 1900* (London: Weidenfeld & Nicolson, 2006), xi, 2, 635–6, 647–8.

63 Paul Gilroy, *After Empire. Melancholia or Convivial Culture?* (Abingdon: Routledge, 2004), 102.

64 Caroline Elkins, *Britain's Gulag. The Brutal End of Empire in Kenya* (London: Pimlico, 2005), xi–xiv.

65 David Anderson, *Histories of the Hanged. Britain's Dirty War in Kenya and the End of the Empire* (London: Weidenfeld & Nicolson, 2005), 4–8.

66 Mai, 7/7, 25–50, 81–4; Khosrokhavar, *Inside Jihadism*, 221–3; Faisal Devji, *The Terrorist in Search of Humanity. Militant Islam and Global Politics* (London: Hurst, 2008).

67 Mai, 7/7, 131; Frank Ledwige, *Investment in Blood. The Real Cost of Britain's Afghan War* (New Haven, CT and London: Yale University Press, 2013), 202–3.

68 Mai, 7/7, 149.

69 Ian Cobain, *Cruel Britannia. A Secret History of Torture* (London: Portobello Books, 2012), 246.

70 http://vigile.quebec/The-Duty-to-Integrate-Shared.

71 Sayeeda Warsi, *The Enemy Within. A Tale of Muslim Britain* (London: Allen Lane, 2017), 41.

72 Tyler Stovall, 'Diversity and Difference in Postcolonial France', in Charles Forsdick and David Murphy (eds.), *Postcolonial Thought in the French-Speaking World* (Liverpool University Press, 2009), 259–68.

73 Didier Fassin, *Enforcing Order. An Ethnography of Urban Policing* (Cambridge: Polity Press, 2013), 37–8, 98–9.

74 Kepel, *Terreur dans l'Hexagone*, 35–47.

75 John R. Bowen, *Can Islam be French? Pluralism and Pragmatism in a Secular State* (Princeton University Press, 2010), 42.

76 Michel Kokoreff, 'The Political Dimension of the 2005 Riots', in David Waddington, Fabien Jobard and Mike King (eds.), *Rioting in the UK and France. A Comparative Perspective* (Cullompton: Willan, 2009), 148.

77 Kepel, *Terreur dans l'Hexagone*, 40. HLM are council-built high-rise flats.

78 Kepel, *Terreur dans l'Hexagone*, 48–55.

79 *Le Monde*, 13 May 2005.

80 *Le Monde*, 7 May 2005.

81 *Le Monde*, 17 May 2015.

82 *Le Monde*, 31 May 2005.

83 Blair, *A Journey*, 526.

84 Anthony Barnett, *The Lure of Greatness. England's Brexit and America's Trump* (London: Unbound, 2017), 266–7.

85 Christian Marazzi, 'The Violence of Financial Capitalism', in Andrea Fumagalli and Sandro Mezzadra (eds.), *Crisis in the Global Economy. Financial Markets, Social Struggles and New Political Scenarios* (Los Angeles, CA: Semiotext(e), 2010), 17–59; Joseph Stiglitz, 'The Financial Crisis of 2007–8 and Its Macroeconomic Consequences', in Stephen Griffiths-Jones, José Antonio Ocampo and Joseph Stiglitz (eds.), *Time for a Visible Hand. Lessons from the 2008 World Financial Crisis* (Oxford University Press, 2010), 19–49; Engelbert Stockhammer, 'Neoliberalism, Income Distribution and the Causes of the Crisis', in Philip Arestis, Rugiéro Sobreira and José Luis Oreiro (eds.), *The Financial Crisis. Origins and Implications* (Basingstoke: Palgrave Macmillan, 2011), 234–58; P. W. Preston, *England after the Great Recession. Tracking the Political and Cultural Consequences of the Crisis* (Basingstoke: Palgrave Macmillan, 2012).

86 Karim Astrid Siegmann, 'The Crisis in South Asia: From Jobless Growth to Jobless Slump', and Astha Kapoor, 'Diamonds are for Never: The Economic Crisis and the Diamond Industry in India', both in Peter A. G. van Bergeijk, Arjan de Haan and Rolph van der Hoeven (eds.), *The Financial Crisis and Developing Countries. A Global Multidisciplinary Perspective* (Cheltenham: Edward Elgar, 2011), chs. 13 and 14.

87 Anatole Kaletsky, *Capitalism 4.0. The Birth of a New Economy* (London: Bloomsbury, 2010).

88 Matt Myers, *Student Revolt. Voices of the Austerity Generation* (London: Left Book Club and Pluto Press, 2017).

89 David Graeber, *The Democracy Project. A History, A Crisis, A Movement* (London: Allen Lane, 2013), 13–63.

90 Graeber, *Democracy Project*, 63–4.

# 9 The Empire Strikes Back

1 Adam Roberts (ed.), *Civil Resistance in the Arab Spring. Triumph and Disasters* (Oxford University Press, 2016).

2 www.nytimes.com/2009/06/04/us/politics/04obama.text.html.

3 Lotfi Ben Rejeb, 'United States Policy towards Tunisia', in Nouri Gana (ed.), *The Making of the Tunisian Revolution. Contexts, Architects, Prospects* (Edinburgh University Press, 2013), 81.

4 Tom Chesshyre, *A Tourist in the Arab Spring* (London: Bradt, 2013), 142; Bernard-Henri Lévy, *La Guerre sans l'aimer. Journal d'un écrivain au coeur du printemps libyen* (Paris: Grasset, 2011).

5 http://politiques-publiques.com/martinique/cesaire-au-pantheon-le-discours-de-n-sarkozy/.

6 www.theguardian.com/politics/2012/jul/28/olympics-opening-ceremony-multicultural-crap-tory-mp.

7 Nouri Gana, 'Introduction', in Gana (ed.), *The Making of the Tunisian Revolution*, 23–5; Michael J. Willis, 'Revolt for Dignity: Tunisia's Revolution and Civil Resistance', in Roberts (ed.), *Civil Resistance in the Arab Spring*, 48–51.

8 M. Cherif Bassiouni, 'Egypt's Unfinished Revolution', in Roberts (ed.), *Civil Resistance in the Arab Spring*, 64–70.

9 George Joffé, 'Civil Resistance in Libya during the Arab Spring', in Roberts (ed.), *Civil Resistance in the Arab Spring*, 133–40; Olivier Guitta, 'Libya: A Failed State', in Olivier Guitta, Emily Dyer, Robin Simcox, Hannah Stuart and Ripert Sutton (eds.), *The Arab Spring. An Assessment Three Years On* (London: Henry Jackson Society, 2014), 55–67.

10 Raymond Hinnebusch, Omar Imady and Tina Zintl, 'Civil Resistance in the Syrian Uprising: From Peaceful Protest to Sectarian Civil War' and Adam Roberts, 'Civil Resistance and the Fate of the Arab Spring', both in Roberts (ed.), *Civil Resistance in the Arab Spring*, 233–47, 292–312.

11 Nicolas Hénin, *Jihad Academy. The Rise of Islamic State* (New Delhi: Bloomsbury, 2015), 18–20, 74–5.

12 Gilles Kepel, *Terreur dans l'Hexagone* (Paris: Gallimard, 2015), 114–15, 121–2, 201–6.

13 Kepel, *Terreur dans l'Hexagone*, 117–18, 122–5, 130, 162; Abdelghani Merah with Mohammed Sifaoui, *Mon Frère ce terroriste. Un homme dénonce l'islamisme* (Paris: Calmann-Lévy, 2012), 2–11, 61–92, 131–99; Eric Pelletier and Jean-Marie Pontaut, *Affaire Merah. L'Enquête* (Paris: Michel Lafon, 2012), 151–215.

14 Kepel, *Terreur dans l'Hexagone*, 159–61.

15 www.gov.uk/government/speeches/pms-speech-at-munich-security-conference.

16 www.ifsecglobal.com/home-office-theresa-may-launches-new-prevent-counter-terrorism-strategy/.

17 Daniel Briggs (ed.), *The English Riots of 2011. A Summer of Discontent* (Hook: Waterside Press, 2012).

18 *Daily Mail*, 11 Aug. 2011.

19 Sayeeda Warsi, *The Enemy Within. A Tale of Muslim Britain* (London: Allen Lane, 2017), 207.

20 Greg Philo, Emma Brunt and Paul Donald, *Bad News for Refugees* (London: Pluto Press, 2013), 3–8.

21 www.ein.org.uk/news/home-secretary-announce-massive-shake-immigration-law.

22 Stuart Hall with Bill Schwarz, *Familiar Stranger. A Life between Two Islands* (London: Allen Lane, 2017), 211.

23 www.gov.uk/government/news/british-values-article-by-david-cameron.

24 Warsi, *The Enemy Within*, 47–9.

25 www.gov.uk/government/speeches/extremism-pm-speech.

26 www.thefader.com/2015/08/27/british-values-zine-kieran-yates-interview. See also Kieran Yates, 'On Going Home', in Nikesh Shukla (ed.), *The Good Immigrant* (London: Unbound, 2016), 109–10.

27 http://conservative-speeches.sayit.mysociety.org/speech/601441.

28 www.gov.uk/government/uploads/system/uploads/attachment_data/file/239075/SECONDARY_national_curriculum_-_History.pdf.

29 www.dailymail.co.uk/news/article-2061809/David-Starkey-row-British-history.html.

30 Hall with Schwarz, *Familiar Stranger*, 197, 199, 211.

31 www.banglastories.org/.

32 Claire Alexander, Joya Chatterji and Debbie Weekes-Bernard, *Making British Histories. Diversity and the National Curriculum* (London: Runnymede Trust, 2012), 3–14.

33 Claire Alexander, Joya Chatterji and Debbie Weekes-Bernard, *History Lessons: Teaching Diversity in and through the History National Curriculum* (London: Runnymede Trust, 2014), 12.

34 Jean Raspail, 'Big Other', preface to *Le Camp des Saints* (Paris: Laffont, 2011), 25–38.

35 www.liberation.fr/france/2015/09/16/le-livre-de-chevet-de-marine-le-pen-decrit-une-apocalypse-migratoire_1383026; www.huffingtonpost.co.uk/entry/steve-bannon-camp-of-the-saints-immigration_us_58b75206e4b0284854b3dc03.

36 www.generation-identitaire.com/

37 Renaud Camus, *Le Grand Remplacement* (Neuilly-sur-Seine: D. Reinharc, 2011).
38 www.youtube.com/watch?v=5xqHOBBOOOE.
39 www.education.gouv.fr/cid60317/discours-du-president-de-la-republique-en-hom
   mage-a-jules-ferry.html.
40 www.education.gouv.fr/cid73734/au-bo-du-12-septembre-2013-charte-de-la-lai
   cite-a-l-ecole-apprentissage-et-actions-educatives.html.
41 J.-P. Babelon, I. Backrouche, V. Duclert and A. James-Sarazin, *Quel Musée d'histoire
   pour la France?* (Paris: Armand Colin, 2011).
42 Paola Mattei and Andrew S. Aguilar, *Secular Institutions, Islam and Education
   Policy. France and the U.S. in Comparative Perspective* (London: Palgrave
   Macmillan, 2016), 7.
43 Isabel Hollis, 'Algeria in Paris: Fifty Years On', in Emile Chabal (ed.), *France since
   1970. History, Politics and Memory in an Age of Uncertainty* (London: Bloomsbury,
   2015), 135.
44 Quoted by Patrick Cockburn, *The Age of Jihad. Islamic State and the Great War for
   the Middle East* (London: Verso, 2016), 293.
45 See above, p. 196.
46 Kepel, *Terreur dans l'Hexagone*, 267–70.
47 *Nous sommes Charlie. 60 écrivains unis pour la Liberté d'Expression* (Paris:
   Librairie Générale Française, 2015), 107–8.
48 *Le Monde*, 13 Jan. 2015, 3.
49 *Le Monde*, 14 Jan. 2015, 3.
50 www.bbc.co.uk/programmes/b06p7b7l, *Start the Week*, France special, 16 Nov.
   2015.
51 Youssouf Sylla, 26 Jan. 2015, in Dominique Buffier and Pascal Galinier (eds.),
   *Les Lecteurs du Monde. Qui est vraiment Charlie? Ces 21 jours qui ébranlèrent
   les lecteurs du Monde* (Paris: Le Monde/Éditions François Bourin, 2015), 147–8.
52 Edgar Morin and Patrick Singaïny, *Avant, pendant, après le 11 janvier. Pour une
   nouvelle écriture collective de notre roman nationale* (Paris: Éditions de l'Aube,
   2015), 37.
53 Morin and Singaïny, *Avant, pendant, après le 11 janvier*, 27.
54 www.lefigaro.fr/actualite-france/2016/01/25/01016-20160125ARTFIG00243-le-
   francais-salim-benghalem-serait-le-cerveau-des-attentats-du-13-novembre.php.
55 BBC Radio 4, 'The French Culture War', 10 Nov. 2016.
56 *Le Monde*, 17 Nov. 2015.
57 BBC Radio 4, *Today Programme*, 15 June 2015.
58 *The Sun*, 17 Apr. 2015.
59 BBC Radio 4, *Today Programme*, 4 Sept. 2015.
60 www.publications.parliament.uk/pa/cm201516/cmhansrd/cm151202/debtext/
   151202-0001.htm, columns 332, 344, 403–4, 406.
61 https://blogs.spectator.co.uk/2013/09/nigel-farages-speech-full-text-and-audio/.
62 www.frontnational.com/videos/udt-2013-toutes-les-interviews/.
63 Chris Gifford, *The Making of Eurosceptic Britain. Identity and Economy in a Post-
   Imperial State* (Farnham: Ashgate, 2014), 159–63.
64 Roger Liddle, *The European Dilemma. Britain and the Drama of European
   Integration* (London and New York: I. B. Tauris, 2014), 215–19.
65 BBC Radio 4, *Today Programme*, 23 Mar. 2015.
66 BBC Radio 4, *Today Programme*, 8 June 2016.
67 Quoted by Anthony Barnett, *The Lure of Greatness. England's Brexit and America's
   Trump* (London: Unbound, 2017), 134.
68 Richard Lesmoir-Gordon to the author, 5 Apr. 2017.

69  www.ibtimes.co.uk/eu-referendum-boris-johnson-warns-risks-leaving-eu-will-be-exaggerated-uk-better-off-out-1545161.

70  *Daily Telegraph*, 25 Aug. 2013, www.telegraph.co.uk/news/politics/10265619/The-Aussies-are-just-like-us-so-lets-stop-kicking-them-out.html;Ben Wellings and Helen Baxendale, 'Euroscepticism and the Anglosphere: Traditions and Dilemmas in Contemporary English Nationalism', *JCMS: Journal of Common Market Studies*, 53 (2014), 1–17.

71  www.conservativehome.com/platform/2016/02/david-davis-britain-would-be-better-off-out-of-the-eu-and-heres-why.html. Cited by Michael Kenny and Nick Pearce, *Shadows of Empire. The Anglosphere in British Politics* (Cambridge: Polity Press, 2018), 153.

72  https://yougov.co.uk/news/2014/07/26/britain-proud-its-empire/.

73  www.shashitharoor.in/speeches-details.php?id=335.

74  Barnett, *The Lure of Greatness*, 101.

75  Geoffrey Evans and Anand Menon, *Brexit and British Politics* (Cambridge: Polity Press, 2017), 76–88.

76  *The Sun*, 25 June 2016.

77  www.irr.org.uk/app/uploads/2016/11/Racial-violence-and-the-Brexit-state-final.pdf.

# 10 Fantasy, Anguish and Working Through

1   www.gov.uk/government/speeches/statement-from-the-new-prime-minister-theresa-may.

2   www.independent.co.uk/news/uk/home-news/full-text-theresa-may-brexit-speech-global-britain-eu-european-union-latest-a7531361.html.

3   BBC Radio 4, *Today Programme*, 29 Mar. 2017.

4   *The Guardian*, 22 Mar. 2017; *The Observer*, 26 Mar. 2017.

5   *The Guardian*, 24 and 25 Mar. 2017.

6   *The Guardian*, 27 May 2017.

7   www.theguardian.com/uk-news/2017/may/23/manchester-attack-police-investigate-katie-hopkins-final-solution-tweet.

8   *The Guardian*, 20 June 2017; www.theguardian.com/uk-news/2018/feb/02/finsbury-park-attack-darren-osborne-jailed.

9   *The Observer*, 18 June 2018.

10  *The Guardian*, 5 June 2017.

11  www.independent.co.uk/news/world/middle-east/mosul-latest-news-amnesty-international-civilian-deaths.

12  BBC Radio 4, *Today Programme*, 12 July 2017.

13  www.thetimes.co.uk/article/ministers-aim-to-build-empire-2-0-with-african-commonwealth-after-brexit-v9bs6f6z9; Philip Murphy, *The Empire's New Clothes. The Myth of the Commonwealth* (Oxford University Press, 2018), 216–17.

14  *The Observer*, 2 July 2017.

15  Shashi Tharoor, *Inglorious Empire. What the British Did to India* (London: Hurst & Co, 2017), xxvii.

16  *The Observer*, 19 Mar. 2017.

17  *The Guardian*, 30 Sept. 2017.

18  www.independent.co.uk/news/uk/politics/gibraltar-michael-howard-got-to-war-with-spain-falklands-brexit-hilarious-never-going-to-happen.

19  Nicholas Macpherson, 'Radical Joe Sets a Bad Example', *The Financial Times*, 25 May 2017.

20  www.bbc.co.uk/news/uk-politics-37950198.
21  *The Guardian*, 7 Nov. 2017.
22  www.independent.co.uk/news/uk/politics/alan-miilburn-resigns-letter-read-in-full-statement-latest-theresa-may-social-mobility-tsar-a8089026.html.
23  *The Guardian*, 30 Dec. 2017.
24  *The Daily Telegraph*, 16 Sept. 2017.
25  Murphy, *The Empire's New Clothes*, 231.
26  www.dailymail.co.uk/wires/afp/article-5576623/Not-cricket-Australia-hit-reset-Commonwealth-Games.html.
27  *The Guardian*, 13 Apr. 2018.
28  *The Daily Mirror*, 17 Apr. 2018.
29  *The Guardian*, 20 Apr. 2018.
30  *The Guardian*, 28 Apr. 2018.
31  *The Daily Mirror*, 17 Apr. 2018.
32  *L'Obs*, 30 June–6 July 2016, 47.
33  *L'Obs*, 30 June–6 July 2016, 54–5.
34  *Le Monde*, 9 May 2017.
35  *Le Monde*, 5 May 2017.
36  *Le Monde*, 28 Sept. 2017.
37  Emmanuel Macron, *Révolution. C'est notre combat* (Paris: XO Éditions, 2016), 221–40.
38  Michael Broers, *Europe under Napoleon, 1799–1815* (London: Arnold, 1996).
39  www.elysee.fr/conferences-de-presse/article/conference-de-presse-avec-la-chanceliere-de-la-republique-federale-d-allemagne-angela-merkel/.
40  www.lemonde.fr/election-presidentielle-2017/article/2017/02/16/pour-macron-la-colonisation-fut-un-crime-contre-l-humanite_5080621_4854003.html.
41  www.vousnousils.fr/2017/04/07/lemission-politique-emmanuel-macron-repond-a-une-prof-sur-la-colonisation-602229.
42  indigenes-republique.fr/entretien-avec-houria-bouteldja-macron-est-un-stratege-de-la-contre-revolution/.
43  www.lemonde.fr/afrique/article/2017/11/29/le-discours-de-ouagadougou-d-emmanuel-macron_5222245_3212.html.
44  Robert Gildea, *France since 1945* (Oxford University Press, 2002), 272–8.
45  www.elysee.fr/declarations/article/transcription-du-discours-du-president-de-la-republique-a-l-institut-de-france-pour-la-strategie-sur-la-langue-francaise/.
46  www.lemonde.fr/proche-orient/article/2017/12/10/macron-exhorte-netanyahou-a-des-gestes-courageux-envers-les-palestiniens_5227562_3218.html.
47  *Le Monde*, 26 Apr. 2018.
48  www.youtube.com/watch?v=2Ot8ykOBluw.

# BIBLIOGRAPHY

## Archives

Archives Nationales, Paris
Bibliothèque de Documentation Internationale Contemporaine, Nanterre
British National Archives, Kew
Institut d'Études politiques, Centre d'Histoire, Paris

## Newspapers and magazines

- *The Atlantic*
- *The Daily Mail*
- *The Daily Telegraph*
- *Le Figaro*
- *The Guardian*
- *The Independent*
- *Liberation*
- *Los Angeles Times*
- *Le Monde*
- *The New York Times*
- *The New Yorker*
- *Le Nouvel Observateur*
- *The Observer*
- *Q News*
- *Sans Frontière*
- *The Spectator*

- *The Sun*
- *Tribune*
- *Venceremos*
- *The Washington Post*
- *The Weekly Standard*

## Reports and Official Documents

Commission de la Nationalité, *Être Français, aujourd'hui et demain. Rapport de la Commission de la nationalité, 22 juin 1987–7 janvier 1988, présenté par Marceau Long* (2 vols., Paris: Commission de la nationalité, 1988)

La Conférence Africaine Française, Brazzaville (30 janvier–8 février 1944) (Paris: Ministère des colonies, 1945)

*Education for All. The Report of the Committee of Inquiry into the Education of Children from Ethnic Minority Groups* [Swann report] (London: HMSO, 1985) www.educationengland.org.uk/documents/swann/swann1985.html

*Hansard. Parliamentary Debates. Commons*

*Journal Officiel de la République Française. Débats de l'Assemblée Consultative provisoire*

*Journal Officiel de la République Française. Débats de l'Assemblée Nationale Constituante*

*Journal Officiel de la République Française. Débats parlementaires. Assemblée nationale*

*Le Procès Raoul Salan. Compte-rendu sténographique* (Paris: Albin Michel, 1962)

*The Report of the Iraq Inquiry: Report of a Committee of Privy Counsellors* (12 vols., London: Dandy Booksellers, 2016)

Scarman, Leslie George, *The Brixton Disorders, 10–12 April 1981. Report of an Inquiry* (London: HMSO, 1986)

## Books, Journal Articles, and Essays

Abbas, Ferhat, *Guerre et Révolution d'Algérie* (Paris: Julliard, 1962)

Acharya, Arabinda, *Ten Years after 9/11. Rethinking the Jihadist Threat* (Abingdon: Routledge, 2013)

Ageron, Charles-Robert, 'L'Exposition Coloniale de 1931: Mythe républicain ou mythe impériale?', in Pierre Nora (ed.), *Les Lieux de Mémoire I. La République* (Paris: Gallimard, 1984)

Ageron, Charles-Robert, 'La survivance d'un mythe: La puissance par l'Empire colonial, 1944–1947', in René Girault and Robert Frank (eds.), *La Puissance française en question, 1945–1949* (Paris: Publications de la Sorbonne, 1988)

Akhtar, Shabbir, *Be Careful with Muhammed! The Salman Rushdie Affair* (London: Bellow Publishing, 1989)

Aldrich, Robert and Connell, John, 'Remnants of Empire: France's Overseas Departments and Territories', in Aldrich and Connell (eds.), *France in World Politics* (London, Routledge, 1989)

Alexander, Claire, Chatterji, Joya, and Jalais, Annu, *The Bengal Diaspora. Rethinking Muslim Migration* (London and New York: Routledge, 2015)

Alexander, Claire, Chatterji, Joya, and Weekes-Bernard, Debbie, *History Lessons. Teaching Diversity in and through the History National Curriculum* (London: Runnymede Trust, 2014)

Alexander, Claire, Chatterji, Joya, and Weekes-Bernard, Debbie, *Making British Histories. Diversity and the National Curriculum* (London: Runnymede Trust, 2012)

Ali, Tariq, *The Coming British Revolution* (London: Jonathan Cape, 1972)

Ali, Tariq, 'Re-colonizing Iraq', *New Left Review*, 21 (2003)

Allen, Chris, *Islamophobia* (Farnham: Ashgate, 2010)

Anderson, David, *Histories of the Hanged. Britain's Dirty War in Kenya and the End of the Empire* (London: Weidenfeld & Nicolson, 2005)

Andress, David, *Cultural Dementia. How the West has Lost its History and Risks Losing Everything Else* (London: Apollo, 2018)

Ansari, Humayun, 'Attitudes to Jihad, Martyrdom and Terrorism among British Muslims', in Tahir Abbas (ed.), *Muslim Britain. Communities Under Pressure* (London: Zed Books, 2005)

Ansari, Humayun, *The Infidel Within. Muslims in Britain since 1800* (London: Hurst & Co, 2004)

Appleyard, Reg, *The Ten Pound Immigrants* (London: Boxtree, 1988)

Arjomand, Saïd Amir, 'Islamic Resurgence and its Aftermath', in R. W. Hefner (ed.), *The New Cambridge History of Islam VI. Muslims and Modernity: Culture and Society since 1800* (Cambridge University Press, 2010)

Armstrong, Karen, *Holy War. The Crusades and their Impact on Today's World* (London: Macmillan, 1988)

Aronson, Geoffrey, *Israel, Palestinians and the Intifada. Creating Facts on the West Bank* (London: Kegan Paul, 1990)

Ashcroft, Bill, Griffiths, Gareth, and Tiffin, Helen, *The Empire Writes Back. Theory and Practice in Post-Colonial Literature* (London and New York: Routledge, 1989)

Attali, Jacques, *Verbatim III. 1988–1991* (Paris: Fayard, 1995)

Aulich, James (ed.), *Framing the Falklands War. Nationhood, Culture and Identity* (Milton Keynes: Open University Press, 1992)

Aussaresses, Paul, *Pour la France. Services spéciaux 1942–1954* (Monaco and Paris: Éditions du Rocher, 2001)

Austin, Dennis, *Britain and South Africa* (Oxford University Press, 1966)

Babb, Sarah, *Behind the Development Banks. Washington Politics, World Poverty and the Wealth of Nations* (University of Chicago Press, 2009)

Babelon, J.-P., Backrouche, I., Duclert, V., and James-Sarazin, A., *Quel Musée d'histoire pour la France?* (Paris: Armand Colin, 2011)

Bailkin, Jordanna, *The Afterlife of Empire* (Berkeley, CA: University of California Press, 2012)

Bancel, Nicolas, Blanchard, Pascal, and Lemaire, Sandrine, 'Les enseignements de l'étude conduite à Toulouse sur la mémoire coloniale', in Pascal Blanchard, Nicolas Bancel and Sandrine Lemaire (eds.), *La Fracture coloniale. La société française au prisme de l'héritage colonial* (Paris: La Découverte, 2005), 247–54.

Barnett, Anthony, *The Lure of Greatness. England's Brexit and America's Trump* (London: Unbound, 2017)

Barr, James, *A Line in the Sand. Britain, France and the Struggle that Shaped the Middle East* (London: Simon & Schuster, 2011)

Barsamian, David and Said, Edward, *Culture and Resistance. Conversations with Edward Said* (London: Pluto Press, 2003)

Bassiouni, M. Cherif, 'Egypt's Unfinished Revolution', in Adam Roberts (ed.), *Civil Resistance in the Arab Spring. Triumph and Disasters* (Oxford University Press, 2016)

Bates, Darrell, *The Fashoda Incident of 1898. Encounter on the Nile* (Oxford University Press, 1984)

Baumgart, Winfried, *Imperialism. The Idea and Reality of British and French Colonial Expansion, 1880–1914* (Oxford University Press, 1982)

Bayly, C. A., *The Birth of the Modern World, 1780–1914. Global Connections and Comparisons, 1780–1914* (Oxford: Blackwell, 2004)

Bayly, C. A., *Imperial Meridian. The British Empire and the World, 1780–1830* (London: Longman, 1989)

Bayly, C. A., *Indian Society and the Making of the British Empire* (Cambridge University Press, 1988)

Bayly, C. A. and Harper, Tim, *Forgotten Armies. Britain's Asian Empire and the War with Japan* (London: Penguin, 2005)

Bayne, Nicholas, *Staying Together. The G8 Summit Confronts the 21st Century* (Aldershot: Ashgate, 2005)

Beaumont, Joan, *Broken Nation: Australians in the Great War* (Sydney: Allen & Unwin, 2013)

Beckford, James A., Joly, Dandle, and Khosrokhavar, Farhad, *Muslims in Prison. Challenge and Change in Britain and France* (Basingstoke: Palgrave Macmillan, 2005)

Begag, Azouz, *Le Gone du Chaâba* (Paris: Seuil, 1986)

Begg, Moazzam, *Enemy Combatant. The Terrifying True Story of a Briton in Guantanamo* (London: Pocket Books, 2007)

Belchem, John, *Before the Windrush. Race Relations in 20th-Century Liverpool* (Liverpool University Press, 2014)

Benn, Tony, *Years of Hope. Diaries, Letters and Papers, 1940–1962* (London: Hutchinson, 1994)

Bennett, James C., *The Anglosphere Challenge. Why the English-Speaking Nations Will Lead the Way in the Twenty-First Century* (Lanham, MD, Rowman & Littlefield, 2004)

Bennett, Louise, *Jamaica Labrish* (Jamaica: Sangster's Bookstores, 1966)

Berbeijk, Peter A. G. van, Haan, Arjan de, and Hoeven, Rolph van de (eds.), *The Financial Crisis and Developing Countries. A Global Multidisciplinary Perspective* (Cheltenham: Edward Elgar, 2011)

Bigeard, Marcel, *Pour une Parcelle de gloire* (Paris: Plon, 1975)

Bills, Scott L., *Empire and Cold War. The Roots of US–Third World Antagonism, 1945–47* (London: Macmillan, 1990)

Blair, Tony, *A Journey* (London: Hutchinson, 2010)

Blanchard, Pascal, Bancel, Nicolas and Lemaire, Sandrine (eds.), *La Fracture coloniale. La société française au prisme de l'héritage colonial* (Paris: La Découverte, 2005)

Blanchard, Pascal and Chatelier, Armelle (eds.), *Images et colonies, 1880–1962. Nature, discours et influence de l'iconographie coloniale liée à la propagande coloniale et à la représentation des africains et de l'Afrique en France, de 1920 aux indépendances* (Paris: Association Connaissance de l'histoire de l'Afrique contemporaine/Syros, 1994)

Blanchard, Pascal, Lemaire, Sandrine, and Bancel, Nicolas (eds.), *Culture coloniale en France. De la Révolution française à nos jours* (Paris: CNRS/Autrement, 2008)

Bollardière, Jacques Pâris de la, *Bataille d'Alger, bataille de l'homme* (Paris and Bruges: Desclée De Brouwer, 1972)

Bouchène, Abderrahmane, Peyroulou, Jean-Pierre, Tengour, Ounassa, and Thénault, Sylvie, *Histoire de l'Algérie à la période coloniale* (Paris: La Découverte, 2012)

Bourseiller, Christophe, *Les Maoistes* (Paris: Plon, 2007)

Bouteldja, Houria and Khiari, Sadri, *Nous sommes les Indigènes de la République* (Paris: Éditions Amsterdam, 2012)

Bové, José, *La Révolte d'un paysan. Entretiens avec Paul Ariès et Christian Terras* (Villeurbanne: Éd. Golias, 2000)

Bové, José and Dufour, François, *The World is Not for Sale. Farmers against Junk Food* (London and New York: Verso, 2002)

Bowen, John R., *Can Islam be French? Pluralism and Pragmatism in a Secularist State* (Princeton University Press, 2010)

Bowen, John R., *Why the French Don't Like Headscarves. Islam, the State, and Public Space* (Princeton University Press, 2007)

Boyce, D. George, *The Falklands War* (Basingstoke: Palgrave Macmillan, 2005)

Boyer, Alain, 'Aux origines du mouvement des jeunes Musulmans: l'Union des Jeunes de France', in Ahmed Boubeker and Abdellali Hajjat (eds.), *Histoire politique des immigrations postcoloniales. France, 1920–2008* (Paris: Éditions Amsterdam, 2008)

Boyer, Alain, *L'Islam en France* (Paris: PUF, 1998)

Branche, Raphaëlle, *La torture et l'armée pendant la guerre d'Algérie, 1954–1962* (Paris: Gallimard, 2001)

Briggs, Daniel (ed.), *The English Riots of 2011. A Summer of Discontent* (Hook: Waterside Press, 2012)

Brocheux, Pierre, *Ho Chi Minh. A Biography* (Cambridge University Press, 2007)

Brocheux, Pierre and Hémery, David, *Indochina. An Amibguous Colonization, 1858–1954* (Berkeley, CA: University of California Press, 2009)

Brockway, Fenner, *African Journeys* (London: Victor Gollancz, 1955)

Brockway, Fenner, *Towards Tomorrow* (London: Hart-Davis, 1977)

Brockway, Fenner, *Why Mau Mau? An Analysis and a Remedy* (London: Congress of Peoples Against Imperialism, 1953)

Broers, Michael, *Europe under Napoleon, 1799–1815* (London: Arnold, 1996)

Brower, Benjamin Claude, *A Desert Named Peace. The Violence of France's Empire in the Algerian Sahara, 1844–1902* (New York: Columbia University Press, 2009)

Brown, Judith, *Modern India. The Origins of an Asian Democracy* (Oxford University Press, 1985)

Brown, Roger Glenn, *Fashoda Reconsidered. The Impact of Domestic Politics on French Policy in Africa, 1893–98* (Baltimore, MD: Johns Hopkins University Press, 1969)

Brown, Yasmin Alibai, *Who Do We Think We Are?* (London: Allen Lane, 2000)

Buchanan, Andrew, *American Grand Strategy in the Mediterranean during World War II* (Cambridge University Press, 2014)

Buettner, Elizabeth, *Europe after Empire. Decolonization, Society and Culture* (Cambridge University Press, 2016)

Buffier, Dominique and Galinier, Pascal (eds.), *Les Lecteurs du Monde. Qui est vraiment Charlie? Ces 21 jours qui ébranlèrent les lecteurs du Monde* (Paris: Le Monde/Éditions François Bourin, 2015)

Bujra, Janet and Pearce, Jenny, *The 2001 Bradford Riot and Beyond* (Skipton: Vertical Editions, 2011)

Bullock, Alan, *Ernest Bevin. A Biography* (London: Politico's, 2002)

Burke, Jason, *Al-Qaeda. The True Story of Radical Islam* (London: Penguin, 2007)

Cain, P. J., and Hopkins, A. G., *British Imperialism, 1688–2000* (Harlow: Longman, 2002)

Cambadélis, Christophe and Osmond, Éric, *La France blafarde. Une histoire politique de l'extrême droite* (Paris: Plon, 1998)

Camus, Renaud, *Le Grand Remplacement* (Neuilly-sur-Seine: D. Reinharc, 2011)

Cantle, Ted, *Community Cohesion. A New Framework for Race and Diversity* (Basingstoke: Palgrave Macmillan, 2005)

Cash, William, *Against a Federal Europe. The Battle for Britain* (London: Duckworth, 1991)

Cash, William, *Europe. The Crunch* (London: Duckworth, 1992)

Castle, Barbara, *Fighting all the Way* (London: Macmillan, 1993)

Castles, Stephen and Kosack, Godula, *Immigrant Workers and Class Structure in Western Europe* (London: Oxford University Press and Institute of Race Relations, 1973)

Caute, David, *Under the Skin. The Death of White Rhodesia* (London: Allen Lane, 1983)

Cavendish, Richard, 'Arrival of the SS Empire Windrush', *History Today*, 48/6 (1998)

Chabal, Emile, *A Divided Republic. Nation, State and Citizenship in Contemporary France* (Cambridge University Press, 2015)

Chalfont, Alun, *The Shadow of my Hand* (London: Weidenfeld & Nicolson, 2000)

Charbit, Tom, *Les Harkis* (Paris: La Découverte, 2006)

Chatterji, Joya, *Bengal Divided. Hindu Communalism and Partition, 1933–1947* (Cambridge University Press, 1994)

Chatterji, Joya, *The Spoils of Partition. Bengal and India, 1947–1967* (Cambridge University Press, 2007)

Chaudri, K. N., 'The East India Company in the 17th and 18th Centuries: A Pre-Modern Multinational Organisation', in Leonard Blussé and Femme Gaastra (eds.), *Companies and Trade. Essay on Overseas Trading Companies in the Ancien Regime* (Leiden University Press, 1981)

Chesshyre, Tom, *A Tourist in the Arab Spring* (London: Bradt, 2013)

Chevènement, Jean-Pierre (ed.), *La République, l'Europe et l'Universel. Colloque, Belfort, 21–22 septembre 1991* (Belfort: IRED, 1993)

Chevènement, Jean-Pierre, *France-Allemagne. Parlons franc* (Paris: Plon, 1996)

Chevènement, Jean-Pierre, *Une Certaine Idée de la France* (Paris: Albin Michel, 1991)

Chipman, John, *French Power in Africa* (Oxford: Blackwell, 1989)

Churchill, Winston, *The Second World War IV. The Hinge of Fate* (London: Cassell, 1951)

Clarke, Peter, *The Cripps Version. The Life of Sir Stafford Cripps, 1889–1952* (London: Allen Lane, 2002)

Clayton, Anthony, *France, Soldiers and Africa* (London: Brassey's Defence Publishers, 1988)

Cobain, Ian, *Cruel Britannia. A Secret History of Torture* (London: Portobello Books, 2012)

Cobain, Ian, *The History Thieves. Secrets, Lies and the Shaping of a Modern Nation* (London: Portobello Books, 2016)

Cockburn, Patrick, *The Age of Jihad. Islamic State and the Great War for the Middle East* (London: Verso, 2016)

Cohen, Michael J., *Palestine: Retreat from the Mandate. The Making of British Policy, 1936–1945* (London: Paul Elek, 1978)

Cohen, Michael J., 'The Zionist Perspective', in William Roger Louis and Robert Stokely (eds.), *The End of the Palestine Mandate* (London and New York: I. B. Tauris, 1986)

Cohn, Bernard S., 'Rethinking Authority in Victorian India', in Eric Hobsbawm and Terence Ranger (eds.), *The Invention of Tradition* (Cambridge University Press, 1983)

Comtat, Emmanuelle, *Les Pieds-noirs et politique. Quarante ans après le retour* (Paris: Presses de la Fondation Nationale des Sciences Politiques, 2009)

Conklin, Alice, *A Mission to Civilize. The Republican Idea of Empire in France and West Africa, 1895–1930* (Stanford University Press, 1997)

Connelly, Mark, *We Can Take It! Britain and the Memory of the Second World War* (Harlow: Pearson Longman, 2004)

Cook, Robin, *The Point of Departure* (London: Simon & Schuster, 2003)

Cooper, Frederick and Stoler, Ann Laura, 'Between Metropole and Colony: Rethinking a Research Agenda', in Cooper and Stoler (eds.), *Tensions of Empire. Colonial Cultures in a Bourgeois World* (Berkeley, CA: University of California Press, 1997)

Corthorn, Paul, 'Enoch Powell: Ulster Unionism and the British Nation', *Journal of British Studies*, 51/4 (2012)

Cot, Jean-Pierre, *A l'Épreuve du pouvoir. Le tiers-mondisme, pourquoi faire?* (Paris: Seuil, 1984)

Crémieux-Brilhac, Jean-Louis, *La France libre. De l'appel du 18 juin à la Libération* (Paris: Gallimard, 1996)

Curzon, George Nathaniel, *Lord Curzon in India. Being a Selection of his Speeches as Viceroy and Governor-General of India, 1898–1905*, ed. Thomas Raleigh (London: Macmillan, 1906)

Daniel, Mark, *Cranks and Gadflies. The Story of UKIP* (London: Timewell Press, 2005)

Darwin, John, *The Empire Project. The Rise and Fall of the British World-System, 1830–1970* (Cambridge University Press, 2009)

Darwin, John, 'Memory of Empire in Britain', in Dieter Rothermund (ed.), *Memories of Post-Imperial Nations. The Aftermath of Decolonisation, 1945–2013* (Cambridge University Press, 2015)

Darwin, John, 'Was There a Fourth British Empire?' in Martyn Lynn (ed.), *The British Empire in the 1950s. Retreat or Revival?* (Basingstoke: Palgrave Macmillan, 2006)

Davidson, Jason W., *America's Allies and War. Kosovo, Afghanistan and Iraq* (New York: Palgrave Macmillan, 2011)

De Gaulle, Charles, *Discours et messages II 1946–1958* (Paris: Plon, 1970)

De Gaulle, Charles, *Lettres, Notes et Carnets. Juin 1940–Juillet 1941* (Paris: Plon, 1981)

De Gaulle, Charles, *Mémoires de Guerre I. L'Appel* (Paris: Plon, 1954)

De Gaulle, Charles, *Mémoires de Guerre III. Le Salut, 1944–1946* (Paris: Plon, 1959)

Debré, Michel, *Combattre Toujours, 1969–1993. Mémoires V* (Paris: Albin Michel, 1994)

Deighton, Anne, 'Entente Néo-Coloniale? Ernest Bevin and the Proposal for an Anglo-French Third World Power, 1945–1949', *Diplomacy and Statecraft*, 17/4 (2006)

Delaney, Enda, *The Irish in Post-War Britain* (Oxford University Press, 2007)

Delors, Jacques with Arnaud, Jean-Louis, *Mémoires* (Paris: Plon, 2004)

Delors, Jacques and Clisthène, *La France par l'Europe* (Paris: Grasset, 1988)

Deltombe, Thomas, Domergue, Manuel, and Tatsitsa, Jacob, *La Guerre du Cameroun. L'invention de la Françafrique, 1948–1971* (Paris: La Découverte, 2016)

Deltombe, Thomas and Rigouste, Mathieu, 'L'ennemi intérieur: la construction médiatique de la figure de l'Arabe', in Pascal Blanchard, Nicolas Bancel and Sandrine Lemaire (eds.), *La Fracture coloniale. La société française au prisme de l'héritage colonial* (Paris: La Découverte, 2005)

Demaison, André, *Faidherbe* (Paris: Plon, 1932)

Desmond, Cosmas, *The Discarded People. An Account of African Resettlement* (Breamfontein, Transvaal: The Christian Institute of South Africa, 1970)

Dessaigne, Francine, *Journal d'une mère de famille pied-noir* (Paris: L'esprit nouveau, 1972)

Devji, Faisal, *The Terrorist in Search of Humanity. Militant Islam and Global Politics* (London: Hurst, 2008)

Devlin, Bernadette, *The Price of my Soul* (London: André Deutsch and Pan, 1969)

Dewar, Michael, *The British Army in Northern Ireland* (London: Arms and Armour Press, 1985)

Diakite, Hadj Saloum, *Sékou Touré face au Général de Gaulle* (Dakar-Ponty: Éditions feu de brousse, 2007)

Dickason, Olive Patricia with Mcnab, David T., *Canada's First Nations. A History of Founding Peoples from the Earliest Times* (Oxford University Press, 2009)

Djaïdja, Toumi, *La Marche pour l'égalité. Une histoire dans l'histoire* (Paris: L'aube, 2013)

Draper, Nicholas, *The Price of Emancipation. Slave-Ownership, Compensation and British Society at the End of Slavery* (Cambridge University Press, 2010)

Drayton, Richard, 'Where Does the World Historian Write From? Objectivity, Moral Conscience and the Past and Present of Imperialism', *Journal of Contemporary History*, 46/3 (2011)

Dronne, Raymond, *La Révolution d'Alger* (Paris: Éditions de l'Empire, 1958)

Du Bois, W. E. B., *Color and Democracy. Colonies and Peace* (New York: Harcourt, Brace & Co, 1945)

Du Bois, W. E. B., *Dark Water. Voices from within the Veil* (London and New York: Verso, 2016)

Dubow, Saul, *Apartheid, 1948–1994* (Oxford University Press, 2014)

Dubow, Saul, 'Macmillan, Verwoerd and the 1960 "Wind of Change" Speech', in L. J. Butler and Sarah Stockwell (eds.), *The Wind of Change. Harold Macmillan and British Decolonization* (Basingstoke: Palgrave Macmillan, 2013)

Duder, C. J. D., 'The Settler Response to the Indian Crisis of 1923 in Kenya: Brigadier-General Philip Wheatley and "Direct Action"', *Journal of Imperial and Commonwealth History*, 17/3 (1988–9)

Duffy, Michael, *Soldiers, Sugar and Sea Power. The British Expeditions to the West Indies and the War against Revolutionary France* (Oxford: Clarendon Press, 1987)

Duhamel, Alain, *Les Peurs françaises* (Paris: Gallimard, 1993)

Duncanson, Dennis, *Government and Revolution in Vietnam* (Oxford University Press, 1968)

Dupuy, Alex, *The Prophet and the Power. Jean-Bertrand Aristide, the International Community, and Haiti* (Lanham, MD, Rowman & Littlefield, 2007)

Echenberg, Myron, *Colonial Conscripts. The Tirailleurs sénégalais in French West Africa, 1857–1962* (Portsmouth, NH and London: Heinemann, 1991)

Einaudi, Jean-Luc, *La Bataille de Paris, 17 octobre 1961* (Paris: Seuil, 1991)

Eldrige, Claire, '"Le symbole de l'Afrique perdue": Carnoux-en-Provence and the *pied-noir* Community', in Kate Marsh and Nicola Frith (eds.), *France's Lost Empires. Fragmentation, Loss and la fracture coloniale* (Lanham, MD, Rowman & Littlefield, 2011)

Elkins, Caroline, *Britain's Gulag. The Brutal End of Empire in Kenya* (London: Pimlico, 2005)

English, Joe, 'Empire Day in Britain, 1904–1958', *Historical Journal*, 49/1 (2006)

Esposito, John, *The Iranian Revolution. Its Global Impact* (Miami: Florida International University Press, 1990)

Evans, Geoffrey and Menon, Anand, *Brexit and British Politics* (Cambridge: Polity Press, 2017)

Fanon, Frantz, *L'An V de la révolution algérienne* (Paris: François Maspéro, 1959)

Fanon, Frantz, *Studies in a Dying Colonialism* (New York: Monthly Review Press, 1965)

Fargettas, Julien, 'La révolte des tirailleurs sénégalais de Tiaroye', *Vingtième Siècle*, 92 (2006)

Fassin, Didier, *Enforcing Order. An Ethnography of Urban Policing* (Cambridge: Polity Press, 2013)

Favier, Pierre and Martin-Roland, Michel, *La Décennie Mitterrand 2. Les Épreuves* (Paris: Seuil, 1991)

Feinstein, Charles H., *An Economic History of South Africa. Conquest, Discrimination and Development* (Cambridge University Press, 2005)

Ferguson, Niall, *Colossus. The Rise and Fall of the American Empire* (London: Allen Lane, 2004)

Ferguson, Niall, *Empire. How Britain Made the Modern World* (London: Allen Lane, 2003)

Ferro, Marc, *Pétain* (Paris: Fayard, 1987)

Ferro, Marc, *Suez. Naissance d'un tiers-monde* (Brussels: Complexe, 1982)

Ferry, Jules, *Discours et Opinions V. Discours sur la politique extérieure et coloniale* (Paris: Armand Colin, 1897)

Fischer, Michael M. J. and Abedi, Mehdi, *Debating Muslims. Cultural Dialogues in Postmodernity and Tradition* (Madison, WI: University of Wisconsin Press, 1990)

Fisher, William and Ponniah, Thomas (eds.), *Another World is Possible. Popular Alternatives to Globalization at the World Social Forum* (Nova Scotia: Fernwood, 2003)

Fitzpatrick, J. P., *The Transvaal from Within* (London: Heinemann, 1899)

Foot, Michael, *Aneurin Bevan. A Biography I. 1887–1945* (London: MacGibbon & Lee, 1962)

Foot, Paul, *Immigration and Race in British Politics* (London: Penguin, 1965)

Frémeaux, Jacques, 'Les Contingents impériaux au cours de la guerre', *Histoire, économie et société*, 23/2 (2004)

Fremigacci, Jean, 'La vérité sur la grande révolte de Madagascar', *Histoire*, 318 (2007)

Freud, Sigmund, 'Remembering, Repeating and Working-Through (Further Recommendations on the Technique of Psycho-Analysis II)', in *The Standard Edition of the Complete Psychological Works of Sigmund Freud XII (1911–1913)* (London: Hogarth Press and the Institute of Psycho-Analysis, 1914)

Gaetner, Gilles, *L'Argent facile. Dictionnaire de la corruption en France* (Paris: Stock, 1992)

Gaillard, Philippe and Foccart, Jacques, *Foccart parle. Entretiens avec Philippe Gaillard I* (Paris: Fayard/Jeune Afrique, 1995)

Gallagher, Jack and Robinson, Ronald, 'The Imperialism of Free Trade', *Economic History Review*, 6/1 (1953)

Gallagher, John, *The Decline, Revival and Fall of the British Empire* (Cambridge University Press, 1982)

Galliéni, Joseph, *Galliéni Pacificateur. Écrits coloniaux de Galliéni*, eds. Hubert Deschamps and Paul Chauvet (Paris: PUF, 1949)

Galliéni, Joseph, *Voyage au Soudan Français* (Paris: Hachette, 1885)

Gana, Nouri (ed.), *The Making of the Tunisian Revolution. Contexts, Architects, Prospects* (Edinburgh University Press, 2013)

Ganiage, Jean, 'France, England and the Tunisian Affair', in Prosser Gifford and William Roger Louis (eds.), *France and Britain in Africa. Imperial Rivalry and Colonial Rule* (New Haven, CT and London: Yale University Press, 1971)

Garavini, Giuliano, *After Empires. European Integration, Decolonization, and the Challenge from the Global South, 1957–1986* (Oxford University Press, 2012)

Gastaut, Yvan, 'La Flambe raciste de 1973 en France', *Revue européenne de migrations internationales*, 9/2 (1993)

Geismar, Alain, *Pourquoi nous combattons* (Paris: Maspéro, 1970)

Geismar, Alain, July, Serge, and Morane, Erlyne, *Vers la Guerre civile* (Paris: Éditions et publications premières, 1969)

Geiss, Imanuel, *The Pan-African Movement* (London: Methuen, 1974)

Gerassi, John (ed.), *Venceremos. The Speeches and Writings of Ernesto Che Guevara* (London: Weidenfeld & Nicolson, 1968)

Giap, Vo Nguyen, *Dien Bien Phu* (Hanoi: Foreign Language Publishing House, 1964)

Gifford, Chris, *The Making of Eurosceptic Britain. Identity and Economy in a Post-Imperial State* (Farnham: Ashgate, 2014)

Gifford, Prosser and Louis, William Roger (eds.), *France and Britain in Africa. Imperial Rivalry and Colonial Rule* (New Haven, CT and London: Yale University Press, 1971)

Gilbert, Martin, *Winston S. Churchill, Volume 6: Finest Hour, 1939–1941; Volume 7: Road to Victory, 1941–1945* (London: Heinemann, 1966–88)

Gildea, Robert, 'Eternal France: Crisis and National Self-Perception in France, 1870–2005', in Susana Carvalho and François Gemenne (eds.), *Nations and their Histories: Constructions and Representations* (Basingstoke: Palgrave Macmillan, 2009)

Gildea, Robert, *France since 1945* (Oxford University Press, 2002)

Gildea, Robert, 'Myth, Memory and Policy in France since 1945', in Jan-Werner Müller (ed.), *Memory and Power in Postwar Europe* (Cambridge University Press, 2002)

Gildea, Robert, *The Past in French History* (New Haven, CT and London: Yale University Press, 1994)

Gildea, Robert, Mark, James, and Pas, Niek, 'European Radicals and the "Third World": Imagined Solidarities and Radical Networks, 1958–1973', *Cultural and Social History*, 8/4 (2011)

Gildea, Robert, Mark, James, and Warring, Annette (eds.), *Europe's 1968. Voices of Revolt* (Oxford University Press, 2013)

Gildea, Robert and Tompkins, Andrew, 'The Transnational in the Local: The Larzac Plateau as a Site of Transnational Activism since 1970', *Journal of Contemporary History*, 50/3 (2015)

Gillard, David, *The Struggle for Asia, 1828–1914* (London: Methuen, 1977)

Gilroy, Paul, *After Empire. Melancholia or Convivial Culture?* (Abingdon: Routledge, 2004)

Gimson, Andrew, *Boris. The Rise of Boris Johnson* (London: Simon & Schuster, 2012)

Girard, Alain and Stoetzel, Jean, *Français et immigrés I. L'attitude française* (Paris: PUF, 1953)

Girard, Alain and Stoetzel, Jean, *Français et immigrés II. Nouveaux documents* (Paris: PUF, 1954)

Glinga, Werner, *Legacy of Empire. A Journey through British Society* (Manchester University Press, 1986)

Gopal, Sarvepalli and Iyengar, Uma (eds.), *The Essential Writings of Jawaharlal Nehru II* (Oxford University Press, 2003)

Gordon, Daniel A., *Immigrants and Intellectuals. May '68 and the Rise of Anti-Racism in France* (Pontypool: Merlin Press, 2012)

Gordon, Philip H. and Shapiro, Jeremy, *Allies at War. America, Europe and the Crisis Over Iraq* (New York: McGraw-Hill, 2004)

Graeber, David, *The Democracy Project. A History, A Crisis, A Movement* (London: Allen Lane, 2013)

Grant, Charles, *Delors. Inside the House that Jack Built* (London: Nicholas Brealey, 1994)

Greenough, Paul R., *Prosperity and Misery in Modern Bengal. The Famine of 1943–1944* (Oxford University Press, 1982)

Gregory, Derek, *The Colonial Present* (Oxford: Blackwell, 2004)

Griotteray, Alain, *Les Immigrés. Le choc* (Paris: Plon, 1984)

Grob-Fitzgibbon, Benjamin, *Continental Drift. Britain and Europe from the End of Empire to the Rise of Euroscepticism* (Cambridge University Press, 2016)

Gross, Joan, McMurray, David, and Swedenburg, Ted, 'Raï, Rap and Ramadan Nights: Franco-Maghribi Cultural Identities', *Middle East Report*, 178 (1992)

Guitta, Olivier, 'Libya: A Failed State' in Guitta, Emily Dyer, Robin Simcox, Hannah Stuart and Ripert Sutton (eds.), *The Arab Spring. An Assessment Three Years On* (London: Henry Jackson Society, 2014)

Gurney, Christabel, '"A Great Cause": The Origins of the Anti-Apartheid Movement, June 1959–March 1960', *Journal of Southern African Studies*, 26/1 (2000)

Hale, Stephen, *Anticolonialism in British Politics. The Left and the End of Empire, 1918–1964* (Oxford: Clarendon Press, 1993)

Hall, Catherine, 'Doing Reparatory History: Bringing "Race" and Slavery Home', *Race & Class*, 60/1 (2018).

Hall, Catherine, Draper, Nicholas, McClelland, Keith, Donington, Katie, and Lang, Rachel, *Legacies of British Slave-Ownership. Colonial Slavery and the Formation of Victorian Britain* (Cambridge University Press, 2014)

Hall, Catherine and Rose, Sonya O. (eds.), *At Home with the Empire. Metropolitan Culture and the Imperial World* (Cambridge University Press, 2006)

Hall, Stuart with Schwarz, Bill, *Familiar Stranger. A Life between Two Islands* (London: Allen Lane, 2017)

Halperin, Sandra and Palan, Ronen (eds.), *Legacies of Empire. Imperial Roots of the Contemporary Global Order* (Cambridge University Press, 2015)

Hammerton, A. James and Thomson, Alistair, *Ten Pound Poms. Australia's Invisible Migrants* (Manchester University Press, 2005)

Hannay, David, *Britain's Quest for a Role. A Diplomatic Memoir from Europe to the UN* (London and New York: I. B. Tauris, 2013)

Hansen, Randall, *Citizenship and Immigration in Post-War Britain. The Institutional Origins of a Multicultural Nation* (Oxford University Press, 2000)

Hansen, Randall, 'The Politics of Citizenship in 1940s Britain: The British Nationality Act', *Twentieth Century British History*, 10/1 (1999)

Hardt, Michael and Negri, Antonio, *Empire* (Cambridge, MA: Harvard University Press, 2000)

Hardt, Michael and Negri, Antonio, *Multitude. War and Democracy in the Age of Empire* (London: Penguin, 2006)

Harper, Marjory and Constantine, Stephen, *Migration and Empire* (Oxford University Press, 2010)

Harvey, David, *The New Imperialism* (Oxford University Press, 2003)

Headrick, Rita, 'African Soldiers in World War II', *Armed Forces and Society*, 4/3 (1978)

Healey, Denis, *The Time of My Life* (London: Michael Joseph, 1989)

Hénin, Nicolas, *Jihad Academy. The Rise of Islamic State* (New Delhi: Bloomsbury, 2015)

Higgins, Nick, 'Lessons from the Indigenous: Zapatista Poetics and a Cultural Humanism for the Twenty-First Century', in Catherine Eschle and Bice Maiguashca (eds.), *Critical Theories, International Relations and the Anti-Globalisation Movement. The Politics of Global Resistance* (London: Routledge, 2005)

Hinnebusch, Raymond, Imady, Omar, and Zintl, Tina, 'Civil Resistance in the Syrian Uprising: From Peaceful Protest to Sectarian Civil War' in Adam Roberts (ed.), *Civil Resistance in the Arab Spring. Triumph and Disasters* (Oxford University Press, 2016)

Hirsch, Afua, *Brit(ish). On Race, Identity and Belonging* (London: Jonathan Cape, 2018)

Hoffmann, Stanley with Bozo, Frédéric, *Gulliver Unbound. America's Imperial Temptation and the War in Iraq* (Lanham, MD: Rowman & Littlefield, 2004)

Hoisington, William A., *Lyautey and the Conquest of Morocco* (Basingstoke: Macmillan, 1995)

Hollis, Isabel, 'Algeria in Paris: Fifty Years On', in Emile Chabal (ed.), *France since 1970. History, Politics and Memory in an Age of Uncertainty* (London: Bloomsbury, 2015)

Hopkins, A. G., 'Rethinking Decolonization', *Past & Present*, 200/1 (2008)

House, Jim and MacMaster, Neil, *Paris 1961. Algerians, State Terror, and Memory* (Oxford University Press, 2006)

Howe, Geoffrey, *Conflict of Loyalty* (London: Macmillan, 1994)

Huddleston, Trevor, *Local Ministry in Urban and Industrial Areas* (London and Oxford: Mowbrays, 1972)

Humphrey, Derek and John, Augustine, *Because They're Black* (London: Penguin, 1970)

Huntington, Samuel P., 'The Clash of Civilizations?' *Foreign Affairs*, 72/3 (1993)

Huntington, Samuel P., *The Clash of Civilizations and the Remaking of World Order* (New York: Simon & Schuster, 1996)

Hurrell, Andrew, *On Global Order. Power, Values, and the Constitution of International Solidarity* (Oxford University Press, 2007)

Isoart, Paul, 'Les Aspects politiques, constitutionnels et administratifs des recommendations', in Institut Charles de Gaulle/IHTP, *Brazzaville, janvier–février 1944. Aux sources de la decolonisation* (Paris: Plon, 1988)

Jackson, Ashley, *Distant Drums. The Role of Colonies in British Imperial Warfare* (Brighton: Sussex Academic Press, 2010)

Jackson, Julian, *A Certain Idea of France. The Life of Charles de Gaulle* (London: Allen Lane, 2018)

Jalal, Ayesha, *Partisans of Allah. Jihad in South Asia* (Cambridge, MA: Harvard University Press, 2008)

James, C. L. R., *The Black Jacobins. Toussaint Louverture and the San Domingo Revolution* (London: Secker & Warburg, 1938)

Jelen, Christian, *Ils feront de bons Français* (Paris: Robert Laffont, 1991)

Jenkins, Simon and Randall, Victoria, *Here to Live. A Study of Race Relations in an English Town* (London: Runnymede Trust, 1971)

Jennings, Eric, 'Angleterre, que veux-tu à Madagascar, terre française? La propagande vichyste, l'opinion publique et l'affaire anglaise sur Madagascar 1942', *Guerres mondiales et conflits contemporains*, 246 (2012)

Jennings, Eric, *La France Libre fut africaine* (Paris: Perrin, 2014)

Joffé, George, 'Civil Resistance in Libya during the Arab Spring', in Adam Roberts (ed.), *Civil Resistance in the Arab Spring. Triumph and Disasters* (Oxford University Press, 2016)

John, Augustine, *Race in the Inner City. A Report from Handsworth, Birmingham* (London: Runnymede Trust, 1972)

Johnson, Chalmers, *Blowback. The Costs and Consequences of the American Empire* (London: Little, Brown, 2000)

Johnson, Linton Kwesi, *Selected Poems* (London: Penguin, 2006)

Juin, Alphonse, *Le Maghreb en feu* (Paris: Plon, 1957)

Juin, Alphonse, *Mémoires II* (Paris: Fayard, 1960)

Julien, Charles-André, *Et la Tunisie devint indépendant, 1951–1957* (Paris: Éditions Jeune Afrique, 1985)

Julien, Charles-André and Ageron, Charles-Robert, *Histoire de l'Algérie contemporaine* (2 vols., Paris: PUF, 1964, 1979)

Kahler, Miles, *Decolonization in Britain and France. The Domestic Consequences of International Relations* (Princeton University Press, 1984)

Kaletsky, Anatole, *Capitalism 4.0. The Birth of a New Economy* (London: Bloomsbury, 2010)

Kaplan, Stephen Laurence, *Farewell, Revolution. The Historians' Feud, France, 1789/1989* (Ithaca, NY and London: Cornell University Press, 1995)

Kapoor, Astha, 'Diamonds are for Never: The Economic Crisis and the Diamond Industry in India', in Peter A. G. van Bergeijk, Arjan de Haan and Rolph van der Hoeven (eds.), *The Financial Crisis and Developing Countries. A Global Multidisciplinary Perspective* (Cheltenham: Edward Elgar, 2011)

Kauffer, Rémi, *OAS. Histoire de la guerre franco-française* (Paris: Seuil, 2002)

Kay, D. and Miles, R., *Refugees or Migrant Workers? European Volunteer Workers in Britain 1946–1951* (London: Routledge, 1992)

Kennedy, Dane, *Islands of White. Settler Society and Culture in Kenya and Southern Rhodesia, 1890–1939* (Durham, NC: Duke University Press, 1987)

Kenny, Michael and Pearce, Nick, *Shadows of Empire. The Anglosphere in British Politics* (Cambridge: Polity Press, 2018)

Kepel, Gilles, *Les Banlieues d'Islam. Naissance d'une religion en France* (Paris: Seuil, 1987)

Kepel, Gilles, *Terreur dans l'Hexagone* (Paris: Gallimard, 2015)

Kettle, Martin and Hodges, Lucy, *Uprising! Police, the People and the Riots in Britain's Cities* (London: Pan, 1982)

Khomeini, Imam, *Islam and the Revolution. Writings and Declarations of Imam Khomeini* (Berkeley, CA: Mizan Press, 1981)

Khosrokhavar, Farhad, *Inside Jihadism. Understanding Jihhadi Movements Worldwide* (Boulder, CO: Paradigm Publishers, 2009)

Kiely, Ray, *The Clash of Globalisations. Neo-Liberalism, the Third Way and Anti-Globalisation* (Leiden: Brill, 2005)

King, Cecil, *The Cecil King Diary, 1965–1970* (London: Jonathan Cape, 1972)

Kirby, M. W., *The Decline of British Economic Power since 1870* (London: George Allen & Unwin, 1981)

Kloss, Felix, *Churchill's Last Stand. The Struggle to Unite Europe* (London and New York: I. B. Tauris, 2018)

Kohl, Richard (ed.), *Globalisation, Poverty and Inequality* (Paris: OECD, 2003)

Kokoreff, Michel, 'The Political Dimension of the 2005 Riots', in David Waddington, Fabien Jobard and Mike King (eds.), *Rioting in the UK and France. A Comparative Perspective* (Cullompton: Willan, 2009)

Kureishi, Hanif, *The Black Album* (London: Faber, 1995)

Kyle, Keith, *Suez. Britain's End of Empire in the Middle East* (London and New York: I. B. Tauris, 2003)

Lacorne, Denis, 'Anti-Americanism and Americanophobia: A French Perspective', in Tony Judt and Denis Lacorne (eds.), *With Us or Against Us. Studies in Global Anti-Americanism* (New York: Palgrave Macmillan, 2005)

Lagaillarde, Pierre, *'On a triché avec l'honneur'. Texte intégral de l'interrogatoire et de la plaidoirie des audiences des 15 et 16 novembre 1960 du procès des 'Barricades'* (Paris: La Table Ronde, 1961)

Lake, Marilyn and Reynolds, Henry, *Drawing the Global Colour Line* (Cambridge University Press, 2008)

Langer, William and Gleason, S. Everet, *The Undeclared War, 1940–1941* (New York: Harper & Brothers, 1953)

Lattre de Tassigny, Jean de, *Ne Pas Subir. Écrits, 1914–1952* (Paris: Plon, 1984)

Le Gac, Julie, *Vaincre sans gloire. Le corps expéditionnaire français en Italie, novembre 1942–juillet 1944* (Paris: Les Belles Lettres, 2013)

Le Pen, Jean-Marie, *Les Français d'abord* (Paris: Éditions Carrère-Michel Lafon, 1984)

Leca, Dominique, *La Rupture de 1940* (Paris: Fayard, 1978)

Ledwige, Frank, *Investment in Blood. The Real Cost of Britain's Afghan War* (New Haven, CT and London: Yale University Press, 2013)

Lee, Hermione, *Virginia Woolf* (London: Chatto & Windus, 1996)

Lemon, Anthony, '"Rhodes Must Fall": The Dangers of Re-writing History', *The Round Table*, 105/2 (2016)

Lesseps, Ferdinand de, *Souvenirs de quarante ans* (2 vols., Paris: Nouvelle Revue, 1887)

Lévy, Bernard-Henri, *La Guerre sans l'aimer. Journal d'un écrivain au cœur du printemps libyen* (Paris: Grasset, 2011)

Lewis, Philip, *Islamic Britain. Religion, Politics and Identity among British Muslims* (London and New York: I. B. Tauris, 1994)

Liddle, Roger, *The European Dilemma. Britain and the Drama of European Integration* (London and New York: I. B. Tauris, 2014)

Lodge, Tom, *Sharpeville. An Apartheid Massacre and its Consequences* (Oxford University Press, 2011)

Lorcin, Patricia, *Algeria and France, 1800–2000. Identity, Memory, Nostalgia* (Syracuse, NY: Syracuse University Press, 2006)

Louis, William Roger, 'British Imperialism and the End of the Palestine Mandate', in William Roger Louis and Robert Stokely (eds.), *The End of the Palestine Mandate* (London and New York: I. B. Tauris, 1986)

Louis, William Roger, *Imperialism at Bay, 1941–1945. The United States and the Decolonization of the British Empire* (Oxford: Clarendon Press, 1979)

Louis, William Roger, 'Public Enemy Number One: The British Empire in the Dock at the United Nations, 1957–71', in Martin Lynn (ed.), *The British Empire in the 1950s. Retreat or Revival?* (Basingstoke: Palgrave Macmillan, 2006)

Louis, William Roger and Robinson, Ronald, 'The Imperialism of Decolonization', *Journal of Imperial and Commonwealth History*, 22/3 (1994)

Louis, William Roger and Stookey, Robert Wilson (eds.), *The End of the Palestine Mandate* (London and New York: I. B. Tauris, 1986)

Low, D. A. and Lonsdale, John, 'East Africa: Towards the New Order, 1945–1963', in Low (ed.), *Eclipse of Empire* (Cambridge University Press, 1991)

Ludlow, Piers, *Dealing with Britain. The Six and the First UK Application to the EEC* (Cambridge University Press, 1997)

Ludlow, Piers, *The European Community and the Crises of the 1960s. Negotiating the Gaullist Challenge* (London and New York: Routledge, 2006)

Luizard, Pierre-Jean, *La Formation de l'Iraq contemporain* (Paris: CNRS, 1991)

Lyautey, Pierre, *L'Empire colonial français* (Paris: Les Éditions de la France, 1931)

MacGillivray, Alex, *A Brief History of Globalization* (London: Robinson, 2006)

Mackenzie, John, *Propaganda and Politics. The Manipulation of British Public Opinion, 1880–1960* (Manchester University Press, 1984)

MacMaster, Neil, *Colonial Migrants and Racism. Algerians in France, 1900–1962* (Basingstoke: Macmillan, 1997)

Macmillan, Harold, *At the End of the Day, 1961–1963* (London: Macmillan, 1973)

Macmillan, Harold, *Riding the Storm, 1956–1959* (London: Macmillan, 1971)

Macmillan, Margaret, *Peacemakers. The Paris Peace Conference of 1919 and its Attempt to End the War* (London: John Murray, 2001)

Macron, Emmanuel, *Révolution. C'est notre combat* (Paris: XO Éditions, 2016)

Madjarian, Grégoire, *La Question coloniale et la politique du Parti Communiste Français, 1944–1947* (Paris: Maspéro, 1977)

Mai, Milan, *7/7. The London Bombings, Islam and the Iraq War* (London: Pluto Press, 2006)

Mandaville, Peter, *Global Political Islam* (New York: Routledge, 2007)

Manela, Erez, *Wilsonian Moment. Self-Determination and the International Origins of Anticolonial Nationalism* (Oxford University Press, 2007)

Manjari, Sri, *Through War and Famine. Bengal 1939–45* (New Delhi: Orient Black Swan, 2009)

Marazzi, Christian, 'The Violence of Financial Capitalism', in Andrea Fumagalli and Sandro Mezzadra (eds.), *Crisis in the Global Economy. Financial Markets, Social Struggles and New Political Scenarios* (Los Angeles, CA: Semiotext(e), 2010)

Marjolin, Robert, *Architect of European Unity. Memoirs, 1911–1986* (London: Weidenfeld & Nicolson, 1989)

Marshall, P. J., *Bengal. The British Colonial Bridgehead, 1740–1828* (Cambridge University Press, 1987)

Martin, Faan, *James and the Duck. Tales of the Rhodesian Bush War, 1964–1980. The Memoirs of a Part-Time Trooper* (Milton Keynes: Author House, 2007)

Massu, Jacques, *La Vraie bataille d'Alger* (Paris: J. Tallandier, 1971)

Mathias, Peter, *The First Industrial Nation. An Economic History of Britain, 1700–1914* (London: Methuen, 1969)

Mattei, Paola and Aguilar, Andrew S., *Secular Institutions, Islam and Education Policy. France and the U.S. in Comparative Perspective* (London: Palgrave Macmillan, 2016)

Mayer, Nonna, *Ces Français qui votent Le Pen* (Paris: Flammarion, 1999)

Mazower, Mark, *Governing the World. The History of an Idea* (London: Allen Lane, 2012)

Mbembe, Achille, *On the Postcolony* (Berkeley, CA: University of California Press, 2001)

Mbembe, Achille, 'La République et l'impensé de la "race"', in Pascal Blanchard, Nicolas Bancel and Sandrine Lemaire (eds.), *La Fracture coloniale. La société française au prisme de l'héritage colonial* (Paris: La Découverte, 2005)

McCullin, Don, *Unreasonable Behaviour* (London: Vintage, 1992)

McDougall, James, *A History of Algeria* (Cambridge University Press, 2017)

McEwan, Ian, *The Ploughman's Lunch* (London: Methuen, 1985)

McNeill, J. R., *Mosquito Empires. Ecology and War in the Greater Caribbean, 1620–1914* (Cambridge University Press, 2010)

McPherson, Klim and Gaitskell, Julia, *Immigrants and Employment. Two Case Studies in East London and in Croydon* (London: Institute of Race Relations, 1969)

Mendès-France, Pierre, *Oeuvres complètes III. Gouverner c'est choisir* (Paris: Gallimard, 1986)

Merah, Abdelghani with Sifaoui, Mohamed, *Mon Frère ce terroriste. Un homme dénonce l'islamisme* (Paris: Calmann-Lévy, 2012)

Mercau, Ezequiel, 'The War of the British Worlds: The Anglo-Argentines and the Falklands', *Journal of British Studies*, 55/1 (2016)

Merle, Robert, *Ahmed Ben Bella* (Paris: Gallimard, 1965)

Meyer, Jean, Tarrade, Jean, Rey-Goldzeigeur, Annie, and Thobie, Jacques (eds.), *Histoire de la France coloniale I. Des origines à 1914* (Paris: Armand Colin, 1991)

Michel, Marc, *Galliéni* (Paris: Fayard, 1989)

Milza, Olivier, *Les Français devant l'immigration* (Brussels: Complexe, 1988)

Minh, Ho Chi, *Selected Works, vol. 3* (Hanoi: Foreign Language Publishing House, 1960–2)

Miot, Claire, 'Le retrait des tirailleurs sénégalais de la Première Armée française en 1944', *Vingtième Siècle*, 125 (2015)

Mitchell, Thomas G., *Native vs. Settler. Ethnic Conflict in Israel/ Palestine, Northern Ireland and South Africa* (Westport, CT: Greenwood, 2000)

Mitter, Rana, *A Bitter Revolution. China's Struggle with the Modern World* (Oxford University Press, 2004)

Mitter, Rana, *China's War with Japan, 1937–1945. The Struggle for Survival* (London: Allen Lane, 2013)

Mitterrand, François, *Réflexions sur la politique extérieure de la France* (Paris: Fayard, 1986)

Modood, Tariq, *Not Easy Being British* (Stoke-on-Trent: Runnymede Trust and Trentham Books, 1992)

Moggridge, Donald, *Maynard Keynes. An Economist's Biography* (London and New York: Routledge, 1992)

Monneret, Jean, *Une Ténébreuse Affaire. La fusillade du 26 mars 1962 à Alger* (Paris: l'Harmattan, 2009)

Moore, R. J., *Escape from Empire. The Attlee Government and the Indian Problem* (Oxford: Clarendon Press, 1983)

Morin, Edgar and Singaïny, Patrick, *Avant, pendant, après le 11 janvier. Pour une nouvelle écriture collective de notre roman nationale* (Paris: Éditions de l'Aube, 2015)

Morris, Benny, 'Revisiting the Palestinian Exodus of 1948', in Eugene Rogan and Avi Shlaim (eds.), *The War for Palestine* (Cambridge University Press, 2007)

Mountbatten, Louis, *Reflections on the Transfer of Power and Jawaharlal Nehru* (Cambridge University Press, 1968)

Moussa, Nedjib Sidi, *La Fabrique du Musulmam* (Paris: Éditions Libertalia, 2017)

Muggeridge, Malcolm, 'Appointment with Sir Roy Welensky', Granada Television, 1 April 1961 (London: Voice and Vision, 1961)

Murari, Timeri, *The New Savages* (London: Macmillan, 1975)

Murphy, Devla, *Tales from Two Cities. Travel of Another Sort* (London: John Murray, 1987)

Murphy, Philip, *The Empire's New Clothes. The Myth of the Commonwealth* (Oxford University Press, 2018)

Murphy, Robert D., *Diplomat among Warriors* (New York: Doubleday, 1964)

Myers, Matt, *Student Revolt. Voices of the Austerity Generation* (London: Left Book Club and Pluto Press, 2017)

Nasser, Gamal Abdel, *Philosophy of Revolution* (Buffalo, NY: Economica Books, 1959)

Newsinger, John, 'Why Rhodes Must Fall', *Race & Class*, 58/2 (2016)

Nicholas, Siân, '"Brushing up your Empire": Dominion and Colonial Propaganda on the BBC's Home Services, 1939–45', *Journal of Imperial and Commonwealth History*, 31/2 (2003)

Nicolaïdis, Kalypso, Sèbe, Berny, and Maas, Gabrielle (eds.), *Memory, Identity and Colonial Legacies* (London and New York: I. B. Tauris, 2015)

Nkrumah, Kwame, *Autobiography* (Edinburgh: Nelson, 1959)

Nkrumah, Kwame, *Neo-Colonialism. The Last Stage of Imperialism* (London: Nelson, 1965)

*Nous sommes Charlie. 60 écrivains unis pour la Liberté d'Expression* (Paris: Librairie Générale Française, 2015)

Olusoga, David, *The World's War. Forgotten Soldiers of Empire* (London: Head of Zeus, 2014)

Onslow, Sue, *Backbench Debate within the Conservative Party and its Influence on British Foreign Policy, 1948–1957* (Basingstoke: Macmillan, 1997)

Ortiz, Joseph, *Mes Combats. Carnets de Route, 1954–1962* (Paris: Éditions de la Presse, 1964)

Osterhammel, Jürgen and Petersson, Niels P., *Globalization. A Short History* (Princeton University Press, 2005)

Ovendale, Ritchie, *Britain, the United States and the End of the Palestine Mandate, 1942–1948* (London: Royal Historical Society, 1989)

Padmore, George, *Gold Coast Revolution* (London: Dobson, 1953)

Pappé, Ilan, *The Making of the Arab–Israeli Conflict, 1947–51* (London and New York: I. B. Tauris, 1992)

Parsons, Timothy, *The African Rank-and-File. Social Implications of Colonial Military Service in the King's African Rifles, 1902–1964* (Portsmouth, NH: Heinemann, 1999)

Patti, Archimedes, *Why Vietnam? Prelude to the American Albatross* (Berkeley, CA: University of California Press, 1980)

Pedersen, Susan, 'Empires, States and the League of Nations', in Glenda Sluga and Patricia Clavin (eds.), *Internationalisms. A Twentieth-Century History* (Cambridge University Press, 2017)

Pedersen, Susan, *The Guardians. The League of Nations and the Crisis of Empire* (Oxford University Press, 2015)

Pelletier, Eric and Pontaut, Jean-Marie, *Affaire Merah. L'Enquête* (Paris: Michel Lafon, 2012)

Perrineau, Pascal, 'La dynamique du vote Le Pen. Le poids du "Gaucho-Lépenisme"', in Perrineau and Colette Ysmal (eds.), *Le Vote de Crise. L'Élection présidentielle de 1995* (Paris: Figaro/ FNSP, 1995)

Perrineau, Pascal, *Le Symptôme Le Pen. Radiographie des electeurs du Front National* (Paris: Fayard, 1997)

Peyrefitte, Alain, *C'était de Gaulle II* (Paris: Fayard, 1997)

Phillips, Barnaby, *Another Man's War. The Story of a Burma Boy in Britain's Forgotten African Army* (London: One World, 2014)

Philo, Greg, Briant, Emma, and Donald, Pauline, *Bad News for Refugees* (London: Pluto Press, 2013)

Pimlott, Ben, *Harold Wilson* (London: HarperCollins, 1992)

Pompidou, Georges, *Entretiens et discours, 1968–1973* (Paris: Plon, 1975)

Ponteil, Félix, *La Mediterranée et les puissances depuis l'ouverture jusqu'à la nationalisation du Canal de Suez* (Paris: Payot, 1964)

Powell, Enoch, *Freedom and Reality*, ed. John Wood (London: Batsford, 1969)

Preston, P. W., *England after the Great Recession. Tracking the Political and Cultural Consequences of the Crisis* (Basingstoke: Palgrave Macmillan, 2012)

Prévost-Paradol, A., *La France nouvelle* (Paris: Michel Lévy, 1868)

Prochaska, David, *Making Algeria French. Colonialism in Bône, 1870–1920* (Cambridge University Press, 1990)

Provence, Michael, *The Great Syrian Revolt and the Rise of Arab Nationalism* (Austin, TX: University of Texas Press, 2005)

Ramm, Agatha, 'Great Britain and France in Egypt', in Prosser Gifford and William Roger Louis (eds.), *France and Britain in Africa. Imperial Rivalry and Colonial Rule* (New Haven, CT and London: Yale University Press, 1971)

Raspail, Jean, *Le Camp des Saints* (Paris: Robert Laffont, 2011)

Rejeb, Lotfi Ben, 'United States Policy towards Tunisia: What New Engagement after an Expendable "Friendship"?', in Nouri Gana (ed.), *The Making of the Tunisian Revolution. Contexts, Architects, Prospects* (Edinburgh University Press, 2013)

Rex, John and Tomlinson, Sally, *Colonial Immigrants in a British City* (London: Routledge & Kegan Paul, 1979)

Reynolds, David, *Britannia Overruled. British Power and World Power in the Twentieth Century* (London and New York: Longman, 1991)

Roberts, Adam (ed.), *Civil Resistance in the Arab Spring. Triumph and Disasters* (Oxford University Press, 2016)

Roberts, Adam, 'Civil Resistance and the Fate of the Arab Spring', in Roberts (ed.), *Civil Resistance in the Arab Spring. Triumph and Disasters* (Oxford University Press, 2016)

Roberts, Andrew, *A History of the English-Speaking Peoples since 1900* (London: Weidenfeld & Nicolson, 2006)

Roberts, Les, Lafta, Riyadh, Garfield, Richard, Khudhairi, Jamal, and Burnham, Gilbert, 'Mortality Before and After the Invasion of Iraq: Cluster Sample Survey', *The Lancet*, 363/9448 (2004)

Robinson, Randall, *An Unbroken Agony. Haiti, from Revolution to the Kidnapping of a President* (New York: Basic Books, 2007)

Robinson, Ronald and Gallagher, John, with Denny, Alice, *Africa and the Victorians. The Official Mind of Imperialism* (London: Macmillan, 1967)

Rotman, Patrick and Tavernier, Bertrand, *La Guerre sans nom. Les appelés d'Algérie, 1954–1962* (Paris: Seuil, 1992)

Roy, Olivier, *Globalized Islam. The Search for a New Ummah* (New York: Columbia University Press, 2004)

Runnymede Trust, *Islamophobia. A Challenge for Us All*. Report of the Runnymede Trust Commission on British Muslims and Islamophobia (London: Runnymede Trust, 1997)

Rushdie, Salman, *Imaginary Homelands. Essays and Criticism 1981–1991* (London: Granta/Viking, 1991)

Rushdie, Salman, *The Satanic Verses* (London: Vintage Books, 1998)

Rutherford, John, *Forever England. Reflections on Masculinity and Empire* (London: Lawrence & Wishart, 1997)

Ruthven, Malise, *A Satanic Affair. Salman Rushdie and the Wrath of Islam* (London: Hogarth Press, 1990)

Ryan, Lyndal, *The Aboriginal Tasmanians* (St Lucia and London: University of Queensland Press, 1981)

Saint-Arnaud, Armand-Jacques Leroy de, *Lettres II* (Paris: Michel Lévy, 1855)

Saito, Fred and Hayashida, Tatsuo, 'To Delhi! To Delhi! 1943–1945', in Sisir K. Bose (ed.), *A Beacon across Asia. A Biography of Subhas Chandra Bose* (New Delhi: Orient Longman, 1973)

Salan, Raoul, *Mémoires. Fin d'un empire I: Le sens d'un engagement* (Paris: Presses de la Cité, 1970)

Salan, Raoul, *Mémoires. Fin d'un empire III: Algérie française* (Paris: Presses de la Cité, 1972)

Sampson, Anthony, *Black and Gold. Tycoons, Revolutionaries and Apartheid* (London: Hodder & Stoughton, 1987)

Sarraut, Albert, *La Mise en Valeur des Colonies Françaises* (Paris: Payot, 1923)

Saunders, Robert, *Yes to Europe! The 1975 Referendum and Seventies Britain* (Cambridge University Press, 2018)

Schofield, Camilla, *Enoch Powell and the Making of Postcolonial Britain* (Cambridge University Press, 2013)

Schwartz, Laurent, *A Mathematician Grappling with his Century* (Berlin: Birkhausen Verlag, 2001)

Schwarz, Bill, *Memories of Empire. The White Man's World* (Oxford University Press, 2011)

Scott, Joan Wallach, *The Politics of the Veil* (Princeton University Press, 2007)

Sédar Senghor, Léopold, *Oeuvre poétique* (Paris: Points, 2006)

Seeley, J. R., *The Expansion of England. Two Courses of Lectures* (London: Macmillan, 1885)

Sen, Amartya, *Poverty and Famines. An Essay on Entitlement and Deprivation* (Oxford: Clarendon Press, 1981)

Sessions, Jennifer, *By Sword and Plough. France and the Conquest of Algeria* (Ithaca, NY and London: Cornell University Press, 2011)

Shaw, Tony, *Eden, Suez and the Mass Media. Propaganda and Persuasion during the Suez Crisis* (London and New York: I. B. Tauris, 1996)

Shepard, Todd, *The Invention of Decolonization. The Algerian War and the Remaking of France* (Ithaca, NY and London: Cornell University Press, 2006)

Shepard, Todd, 'Thinking between Metropole and Colony: The French Republic, "Exceptional Promotion" and the "Integration" of Algerians, 1955–1962', in Martin Thomas (ed.), *The French Colonial Mind I. Mental*

*Maps of Empire and Colonial Encounters* (Lincoln, NE: University of Nebraska Press, 2011)

Shields, James, *The Extreme Right in France. From Pétain to Le Pen* (London: Routledge, 2007)

Shlaim, Avi, 'The Protocol of Sèvres: Anatomy of a War Plot', *International Affairs*, 73/3 (1997)

Siegmann, Karim Astrid, 'The Crisis in South Asia: From Jobless Growth to Jobless Slump', in Peter A. G. van Bergeijk, Arjan de Haan and Rolph van der Hoeven (eds.), *The Financial Crisis and Developing Countries. A Global Multidisciplinary Perspective* (Cheltenham: Edward Elgar, 2011)

Simon, Pierre-Henri, *Contre la Torture* (Paris: Seuil, 1957)

Sluga, Glenda, *Internationalism in the Age of Nationalism* (Philadelphia, PA: University of Pennsylvania Press, 2001)

Sluglett, Peter, *Britain in Iraq. Contriving King and Country* (London and New York: I. B. Tauris, 2017)

Smith, Adam, *The Wealth of Nations* (London: Dent, 1977)

Smith, Anna Marie, *The New Right Discourse on Race and Sexuality. Britain, 1968–1990* (Cambridge University Press, 1994)

Smith, Jackie, Karides, Marina, Becker, Marc, and others, *Global Democracy and the World Social Forums* (Boulder, CO and London: Paradigm Publishers, 2015)

Smuts, J. C., *Africa and Some World Problems* (Oxford: Clarendon Press, 1930)

Smuts, J. C., *Thoughts on the New World* (London: Empire Parliamentary Association, 1943)

Soutou, Jean-Marie, *Un Diplomate engagé. Mémoires 1939–1979* (Paris: Éditions de Fallois, 2011)

Spence, Jonathan, *In Search of Modern China* (New York and London: Norton, 1999)

Spivak, Gayatri Chakravorty, 'Can the Subaltern Speak?', in Cary Nelson and Lawrence Grossberg (eds.), *Marxism and the Interpretation of Culture* (Urbana, IL: University of Illinois Press, 1988)

Steel, David, *No Entry. The Background and Implications of the Commonwealth Immigrations Act, 1968* (London: Hurst & Co, 1969)

Stein, Leonard, *The Balfour Declaration* (London: Valentine Mitchell, 1961)

Stephen, Daniel, *The Empire of Progress. West Africans, Indians and Britons at the British Empire Exhibition, 1924–25* (New York: Palgrave Macmillan, 2013)

Stiglitz, Joseph, 'The Financial Crisis of 2007–8 and Its Macroeconomic Consequences', in Stephen Griffiths-Jones, José Antonio Ocampo and Joseph Stiglitz (eds.), *Time for a Visible Hand. Lessons from the 2008 World Financial Crisis* (Oxford University Press, 2010)

Stockhammer, Engelbert, 'Neoliberalism, Income Distribution and the Causes of the Crisis', in Philip Arestis, Rugiéro Sobreira and José Luis Oreiro (eds.), *The Financial Crisis. Origins and Implications* (Basingstoke: Palgrave Macmillan, 2011)

Stora, Benjamin, *La Dernière Génération d'Octobre* (Paris: Stock, 2003)

Stora, Benjamin, *La Gangrène et l'oubli. La mémoire de la guerre d'Algérie* (Paris: La Découverte, 1991)

Stora, Benjamin and Harbi, Mohammed (eds.), *La Guerre d'Algérie, 1954–2004, la fin de l'amnésie* (Paris: Robert Laffont, 2004)

Stora, Benjamin with Jenni, Alexis, *Les Mémoires dangereuses, suivi d'une nouvelle édition de Transfert d'une mémoire* (Paris: Albin Michel, 2016)

Stovall, Tyler, 'Diversity and Difference in Postcolonial France', in Charles Forsdick and David Murphy (eds.), *Postcolonial Thought in the French-Speaking World* (Liverpool University Press, 2009)

Streatfield, Dominic, *A History of the World since 9/11* (London: Atlantic Books, 2011)

Taithe, Bernard, *The Killer Trail. A Colonial Scandal in the Heart of Africa* (Oxford University Press, 2009)

Talbot, Ian and Singh, Gurharpal, *The Partition of India* (Cambridge University Press, 2009)

Tapinos, Georges, 'Pour une introduction au débat contemporain', in Yves Lequin (ed.), *La Mosaïque France. Histoire des étrangers et de l'immigration* (Paris: Larousse, 1988)

Tebbit, Norman, *Unfinished Business* (London: Weidenfeld & Nicolson, 1991)

Terrasse, Jean-Marc, *Génération beur* (Paris: Plon, 1989)

Teveth, Shabtai, *Ben Gurion. The Burning Ground, 1886–1948* (London: Robert Hale, 1987)

Tharoor, Shashi, *Inglorious Empire. What the British Did to India* (London: Hurst & Co, 2017)

Thatcher, Margaret, *The Downing Street Years* (London: HarperCollins, 1993)

Thobie, Jacques, Meyer, Jean, Tarrade, Jean, and Rey-Goldzeiger, Anne, *Histoire de la France coloniale II. 1914–1990* (Paris: Armand Colin, 1990)

Thomas, Abel, *Comment Israël fut sauvé. Les secrets de l'expédition de Suez* (Paris: Albin Michel, 1978)

Thomas, Martin, *Fight or Flight. Britain, France, and their Roads from Empire* (Oxford University Press, 2014)

Thomas, Martin (ed.), *The French Colonial Mind I. Mental Maps of Empire and Colonial Encounters* (Lincoln, NE: University of Nebraska Press, 2011)

Thomas, Martin, *The French Empire between the Wars. Imperialism, Politics and Society* (Manchester University Press, 2005)

Thomas, Martin, 'Imperial Backwater or Strategic Outpost? The British Takeover of Vichy Madagascar, 1942', *Historical Journal*, 39/4 (1996)

Thompson, Andrew, *The Empire Strikes Back? The Impact of Imperialism on Britain from the Mid-Nineteenth Century* (Harlow: Pearson Longman, 2005)

Thompson, Leonard, *A History of South Africa* (New Haven, CT and London: Yale University Press, 1990)

Thörn, Håkan, *Anti-Apartheid and the Emergence of a Global Civil Society* (Basingstoke: Palgrave Macmillan, 2006)

Tillion, Germaine, *Les Ennemis complémentaires* (Paris: Éditions de Minuit, 1960)

Trevor-Roper, Hugh, 'The Rise of Christian Europe', *The Listener*, 70/1809, 28 November 1963

Trevor-Roper, Hugh, *The Rise of Christian Europe* (London: Thames & Hudson, 1965)

Tribalat, Michèle, 'Une estimation des populations d'origine étrangère en France en 2011', *Espace, populations, sociétés*, 1–2 (2015)

Tronchon, Jacques, *L'Insurrection malgache de 1947* (Paris: Maspéro, 1974)

Tsuzuki, Chushichi, *The Pursuit of Power in Modern Japan, 1825–1995* (Oxford University Press, 2000)

Turpin, Frédéric, *Jacques Foccart. Dans l'Ombre du pouvoir* (Paris: CNRS Éditions, 2015)

Vaïsse, Maurice, 'France and the Suez Crisis', in William Roger Louis and Roger Owen (eds.), *Suez 1956. The Crisis and its Consequences* (Oxford: Clarendon Press, 1989)

Vaïsse, Maurice, 'Le général de Gaulle et la défense de l'Europe, 1947–1958', *Matériaux pour l'histoire de notre temps*, 29 (1992)

Verney, Sébastien, *L'Indochine sous Vichy. Entre révolution nationale, collaboration et identités nationales, 1940–1945* (Paris: Riveneuve, 2012)

Verschave, François-Xavier, *La Françafrique. Le plus long scandale de la République* (Paris: Stock, 1998)

Vidal-Naquet, Pierre, *L'Affaire Audin* (Paris: Éditions de Minuit, 1958)

Vidal-Naquet, Pierre, 'La Justice et la patrie: Une Française au secours de l'Algérie', *Esprit*, 261 (2000)

Vidal-Naquet, Pierre, *Mémoires. Le Trouble et la lumière, 1955–1998* (Paris: Seuil/La Découverte, 1998)

Wakefield, Edward Gibbon, *The Collected Works of Edward Gibbon Wakefield*, ed. M. F. Lloyd Pritchard (Glasgow and London: Collins, 1968)

Walgrave, Stefaan and Rucht, Dieter (eds.), *The World Says No to War. Demonstrations Against the War on Iraq* (Minneapolis, MN: University of Minnesota Press, 2010)

Wall, Irwin M., *France, the United States and the Algerian War* (Berkeley, CA: University of California Press, 2001)

Waller, P. J., 'The Riots in Toxteth, Liverpool: A Survey', *Journal of Ethnic and Migration Studies*, 9/3 (1981)

Ward, Stuart, *Australia and the British Embrace. The Demise of the Imperial Ideal* (Melbourne University Press, 2001)

Warner, Geoffrey, 'The Labour Government and the Unity of Western Europe', in Ritchie Ovendale (ed.), *The Foreign Policy of the British Labour Government, 1945–1951* (Leicester University Press, 1984)

Warsi, Sayeeda, *The Enemy Within. A Tale of Muslim Britain* (London: Allen Lane, 2017)

Weber, Henry, *La Compagnie Française des Indes, 1604–1875* (Paris: Arthur Rousseau, 1904)

Webster, Wendy, *Englishness and Empire, 1939–1965* (Oxford University Press, 2005)

Welensky, Roy, 'The Federation and Nyasaland: Speech', 8 Nov. 1961, Salisbury (Salisbury: Publications Department, Federal Public Relations Division, 1962)

Welensky, Roy, *Welensky's 4000 Days. The Life and Death of the Federation of Rhodesia and Nyasaland* (London: Collins, 1964)

Wellings, Ben and Baxendale, Helen, 'Euroscepticism and the Anglosphere: Traditions and Dilemmas in Contemporary English Nationalism', *Journal of Common Market Studies*, 53 (2014)

Williamson, Edwin, *The Penguin History of Latin America* (London: Penguin, 1992)

Willis, Michael J., 'Revolt for Dignity: Tunisia's Revolution and Civil Resistance', in Adam Roberts (ed.), *Civil Resistance in the Arab Spring. Triumph and Disasters* (Oxford University Press, 2016)

Wilson, Harold, *The Labour Government, 1964–1970. A Personal Record* (London: Weidenfeld & Nicolson, 1971)

Wolfe, Patrick, 'Settler Colonialism and the Elimination of the Native', *Journal of Genocide Research*, 8/4 (2006)

Wolin, Richard, *The Wind from the East. French Intellectuals, the Cultural Revolution and the Legacy of the 1960s* (Princeton University Press, 2010)

Wood, John, *A Nation Not Afraid. The Thinking of Enoch Powell* (London: Batsford, 1965)

Woods, Ngaire, *The Globalizers. The IMF, the World Bank and their Borrowers* (Ithaca, NY and London: Cornell University Press, 2006)

Woolf, Virginia, *The Captain's Death Bed and Other Essays* (London: Hogarth Press, 1950)

Wright, Richard, *Black Power* (New York: Harper, 1954)

Wright, Richard, *The Color Curtain. A Report on the Bandung Conference* (London: Dobson, 1956)

Yates, Kieran, 'On Going Home', in Nikesh Shukla (ed.), *The Good Immigrant* (London: Unbound, 2016)

Young, John W., *Cold War Europe, 1945–1991. A Political History* (London and New York: Arnold, 1996)

Young, Robert J. C., *Postcolonialism. A Very Short Introduction* (Oxford University Press, 2003)

## Unpublished Material

Griffiths, Melanie, 'Who is Who Now? Truth, Trust and Identification in the British Asylum and Immigration Detention System', DPhil thesis, School of Anthropology and Museum Ethnography, Oxford (2014)

Ofrath, Avner, 'Demarcating the *cité française*: Exclusion and Inclusion in Colonial Algeria under the Third Republic', DPhil thesis, Oxford (2017)

## Audio-Visual Sources

Fraser, Nick, 'The French Culture War', BBC Radio 4, 10 November 2016

Freedland, Jonathan, 'The 1990s: A Holiday from History', BBC Radio 4, 27 April 2017

*The House of War* (dir. Paul Yule, prod. Robert Young Pelton, United States, 2005)

Inathèque Paris, 'Torture en Algerie, Ces aveux qui dérangent', France 3, 27 June 2001

Marr, Andrew, 'Start the Week. France Special', BBC Radio 4, 16 November 2015

'Today Programme', BBC Radio 4, 2015–16

## Online

www.banglastories.org/
www.conservativehome.com
www.conservative-speeches.sayit.mysociety.org
www.education.gouv.fr
www.ein.org.uk
www.frontnational.com
www.generation-identitaire.com/
www.gov.uk/government/news
www.gov.uk/government/speeches
www.huffingtonpost.co.uk
www.ibtimes.co.uk/
www.ifsecglobal.com
www.ina.fr
www.irr.org.uk

www.laicite.fr/
www.legifrance.gouv.fr/
www.lematin.ma
www.margaretthatcher.org
www.mtholyoke.edu
www.politiques-publiques.com
www.publications.parliament.uk
www.shashitharoor.in
www.thefader.com
www.vigile.quebec
www.winstonchurchill.org
www.yougov.co.uk
www.youtube.com

# INDEX